www.wadsworth.com

www.wadsworth.com is the World Wide Web site for Thomson Wadsworth and is your direct source to dozens of online resources.

At *www.wadsworth.com* you can find out about supplements, demonstration software, and student resources. You can also send email to many of our authors and preview new publications and exciting new technologies.

www.wadsworth.com
Changing the way the world learns®

Readings in Presidential Politics

GEORGE C. EDWARDS III

Editor

Texas A&M University

THOMSON

™

WADSWORTH

Australia • Canada • Mexico • Singapore • Spain
United Kingdom • United States

THOMSON

WADSWORTH

Publisher: Clark Baxter
Executive Editor: David Tatom
Senior Development Editor: Stacey Sims
Assistant Editor: Rebecca Green
Editorial Assistant: Cheryl Lee
Technology Project Manager: Michelle Vardeman
Senior Marketing Manager: Janise Fry
Marketing Assistant: Teresa Jessen
Senior Project Manager, Editorial Production: Kimberly Adams
Executive Art Director: Maria Epes
Print Buyer: Karen Hunt

Permissions Editor: Kiely Sisk
Production Service: Buuji
Copy Editor: Kristina Rose McComas
Illustrator: International Typesetting and Composition
Cover Designer: StarText
Cover Image: Dwight D. Eisenhower. Photo by John Dominis/Time Life
Cover Printer: Webcom
Compositor: International Typesetting and Composition
Printer: Webcom

For more information about our products, contact us at:
Thomson Learning Academic Resource Center
1-800-423-0563

For permission to use material from this text or product, submit a request online at
http://www.thomsonrights.com.
Any additional questions about permissions can be submitted by email to
thomsonrights@thomson.com.

Library of Congress Control Number: 2005921832

ISBN 0-495-00670-X

Thomson Higher Education
10 Davis Drive
Belmont, CA 94002-3098
USA

Asia (including India)
Thomson Learning
5 Shenton Way
#01-01 UIC Building
Singapore 068808

Australia/New Zealand
Thomson Learning Australia
102 Dodds Street
Southbank, Victoria 3006
Australia

Canada
Thomson Nelson
1120 Birchmount Road
Toronto, Ontario M1K 5G4
Canada

UK/Europe/Middle East/Africa
Thomson Learning
High Holborn House
50–51 Bedford Row
London WC1R 4LR
United Kingdom

Latin America
Thomson Learning
Seneca, 53
Colonia Polanco
11560 Mexico
D.F. Mexico

Spain (including Portugal)
Thomson Paraninfo
Calle Magallanes, 25
28015 Madrid, Spain

Brief Contents

Contents

II The Context of the Presidency   67

V The President and the Government 261

⚜
Preface

The course on the presidency is a mainstay of undergraduate education. Typically professors assign their students a core textbook like *Presidential Leadership*. Most instructors agree that students need—and deserve—more. Most importantly, we need to expose students to the best thinkers on the presidency, and we need to let these scholars flex their intellectual muscles to make arguments about key dimensions of presidential politics.

To meet these needs, I have asked some of the best scholars studying the presidency to write essays that make a point. Over the years, I have found that presenting students with thoughtful arguments engages their interest. Students, like their instructors, quickly recognize that the principal reason for studying presidential politics is to understand why it matters that we govern as we do. What students may otherwise see as "dry" subjects become interesting when they understand that what they are learning makes a difference. Even introductory students feel comfortable asking, "So what?"

It is not enough to arouse students' interest, however. To be useful as teaching tools, chapters must be accessible to students and enjoyable to read. We believe that a principal reason for the success of *Presidential Politics* is its high level of readability. In addition, to be most useful, essays must encourage classroom discussion. I am confident that instructors will find the chapters in this volume do exactly that because each essay offers a provocative answer to a central question of presidential politics.

We begin with presidential selection. William Mayer addresses a key question regarding campaigns and governing when he asks whether presidential candidates keep their campaign promises. He finds that they sometimes do not and then explains why this occurs. George Edwards focuses on America's unique mechanism for electing the president, the electoral college. He argues that it violates core principles of democratic governance and that the arguments made on its behalf are based on faulty premises. Instructors should have little difficulty encouraging class discussion on these essays.

The next section of the reader examines three central aspects of the context in which the president functions. Gary Jacobson investigates what is perhaps the dominant feature of contemporary politics: partisan polarization. He traces the roots of this polarization to electoral politics and shows why presidents are likely to have a difficult time obtaining support in Congress. William Howell then offers a perspective that challenges Richard Neustadt's dominant paradigm of presidential politics: that presidential power is the power to persuade. Howell shows the many ways in which presidents exercise power *without* persuasion. Finally, Stephen Wayne raises the issue of the importance of the president's personality, as opposed to the roles and institutional trappings of the presidency. He argues that George W. Bush's personality helps explain his decisions regarding the two wars the United States fought in his first term in office. Once again, these chapters will be a useful catalyst for class discussion.

The president's relations with the public are at the core of the modern presidency. Presidents feel that public support is critical to their success. James Pfiffner asks, "Do presidents lie?" His answer is that they often do, with consequences for their ability to govern. Contemporary presidents have typically adopted "going public" as their core governing strategy. George Edwards focuses on the use of the "bully pulpit" and finds that—contrary to the conventional wisdom—this strategy usually fails. These aspects of the public presidency are visible to students, and they can use these chapters to develop their own views on presidential politics.

Similarly, understanding the relationship between the White House and the press is central to understanding the presidency. Martin Wattenberg examines the changing presidential media environment, especially the declining audience for presidential speeches and for political news in general. Because of these changes, presidents now face a significantly more difficult task in getting messages through to the entire public, with young adults being less and less likely to follow presidential actions. Jeffrey Cohen describes four trends of the contemporary news environment that somewhat insulate the president from the impact of the news. However, these same trends impede the president's ability to lead the mass public, forcing presidents to mobilize select constituencies. In the process, presidents reinforce polarized politics and alienate the broad middle from American politics. Students are likely to grasp these provocative points readily, which will encourage further reflection about their consequences.

President spends much of their time dealing with the various branches of government. They know that working with Congress is critical to their legacies because the assent of the legislature is necessary for most of the president's important policy initiatives. The White House often finds itself lacking the legislature's support, however. Barbara Sinclair focuses on one of the most prominent features of contemporary American politics: gridlock in Congress. She explains the basis of this gridlock and the prospects for overcoming it. Louis Fisher addresses one of the great questions of the American constitutional system: the appropriate role of Congress in national security policy. He concludes, contrary to the view of most presidents, that the framers intended Congress to have a central role in making foreign policy and that the country benefits when Congress plays such a role.

Moving to the bureaucracy, George Edwards asks whether it is necessary for the White House to make a trade-off between loyalty to the president and managerial competence in appointing men and women to run executive agencies. He argues—contrary to the conventional wisdom—the trade-off is not necessary. There are few issues of more significance to a president's legacy—and of more interest to organized groups—than nominating judges to the federal courts. Sheldon Goldman examines the crisis in judicial nominations and explains the largely invisible process of selecting judges, as well as the highly charged partisanship surrounding the Senate's consideration of the president's nominees. Each of the essays on interbranch relationships goes well beyond any text, and each presents a basis for informed class discussion.

I hope you find the chapters in this volume as useful as I have and that your students benefit from them as you help them to understand the politics of the presidency.

George C. Edwards III
College Station, Texas

PART I

Presidential Selection

1

⚜

Why Presidents Break Promises

WILLIAM G. MAYER[1]
Northeastern University

Presidential campaigns, virtually everyone agrees, are supposed to be about issues: about how well the U.S. government is currently performing and, even more importantly, what it should do in the next four years. And at least on the surface, all recent presidential candidates have tried to live up to this standard. Gone forever are the days when it was thought undignified for a presidential nominee to actively solicit votes, when almost all candidates therefore stayed at home during the fall campaign and rarely said much about what they would do if elected. No presidential candidate in the last 50 years has gotten through the campaign without making a long string of promises, of varying degrees of specificity, about what he will do if elected.

The more significant question today is whether any of this talk is meaningful. Though few observers seriously doubt that contemporary presidential candidates make lots of promises, voters, journalists, and political activists are often quite skeptical about whether the winning candidate will live up to those promises once the election is over. Public opinion polls, in particular, indicate that the American public is highly ambivalent about presidential campaign promises. The CBS News/*New York Times* polling consortium, for example, has periodically asked its respondents whether various presidential candidates or newly elected presidents would "try to keep" all, most, some, or hardly any of their campaign promises. As shown in Table 1–1, the public seems to be split approximately in half: On average, 48 percent said that these presidential candidates would keep "all" or "most" of their promises, versus 49 percent who believed that only "some" or "hardly any" of their promises would be redeemed.

The first set of questions in Table 1–1 measures public perceptions of a president's *intentions*. But Americans also recognize that, where presidents are

1. I would like to thank Gerald Pomper, Lois Timms Ferrara, Stephen Nathanson, and Paul Weithman for their help in the preparation of this article.

Table 1–1 Public Attitudes about the Likelihood that Presidents Will Keep Their Promises

CBS/*NYT*: "How many of his campaign promises do you think _____ will try to keep—all of them, most of them, some of them, or hardly any of them?"

Date	All	Most	Some	Hardly Any	Don't Know
"Ronald Reagan"					
Jan. 1981	20	42	31	5	2
"Bill Clinton"					
Jan. 1993	7	36	46	11	*
Feb. 1993	15	40	35	7	3
March 1993	15	40	35	7	3
"Al Gore"					
Sept. 2000	8	38	40	9	5
Nov. 2000	9	32	40	14	5
"George W. Bush"					
Sept. 2000	8	36	42	11	3
Nov. 2000	9	36	38	14	3
Jan. 2001	10	38	42	8	2
April 2001	11	33	39	15	3
Average	**11**	**37**	**39**	**10**	**3**

CBS/NYT: "How many of his campaign promises do you think _____ will be able to keep—all of them, most of them, some of them, or hardly any of them?"

Date	All	Most	Some	Hardly Any	Don't Know
"Ronald Reagan"					
Jan. 1981	2	24	58	13	3
"Bill Clinton"					
Feb. 1993	2	16	56	23	3
"George W. Bush"					
April 2001	1	18	57	21	3
Average	**2**	**19**	**57**	**19**	**3**

concerned, there is a substantial gap between intention and accomplishment. The CBS/*New York Times* pollsters have also asked their samples about how many campaign promises presidents would be "able to keep" and found the public considerably more skeptical (see Table 1–1). Only about 20 percent, on average, thought that the presidents could deliver on "all" or "most" of their promises, versus 57 percent who said that only "some" promises would actually be fulfilled and 19 percent who said "hardly any" would be kept.

Do the ambivalence and skepticism shown in Table 1–1 have any basis in fact? The purpose of this chapter is to take another look at the issue of presidential promise keeping. I begin by presenting a brief reexamination of a small number of studies that have been conducted about whether and to what extent presidents live up to the promises they make during their campaigns. Though most of these studies conclude that presidents at least *attempt* to deliver on most of their promises, the bulk of this article looks at a subject that has not received much attention from presidency scholars: why some promises are *not* kept.

PRESIDENTIAL PROMISE KEEPING: A REVIEW OF THE LITERATURE

Public skepticism about the value of presidential promises was once widely shared by political scientists. In one of the most influential political science books written in the 1950s, David Truman summed up the then-conventional view of national party platforms: "The platform is generally regarded as a document that says little, binds no one, and is forgotten by politicians as quickly as possible after it is adopted."[2] Yet it was not until the late 1960s that anyone attempted to put this proposition to a serious test.

The first and still probably the best empirical study of campaign promise keeping was published by Gerald Pomper in 1968, though he has several times updated his original findings.[3] Pomper began by analyzing the 12 previous major-party national platforms on a sentence-by-sentence basis. A substantial part of the typical platform consisted, not surprisingly, of general rhetoric and evaluations of past party performance. But every platform also included a sizable number of specific promises and commitments—sufficiently specific that one could meaningfully ask if these promises were fulfilled or ignored during the next four years.

In evaluating platform fulfillment, Pomper distinguished six possible ways that the parties could respond to their promises:

1. Full action: "The passage of a law (or section of a law) directly related to the platform provision."

2. Executive action: Executive orders or other presidential actions "which directly accomplish commitments."

---

2. David B. Truman, *The Governmental Process: Political Interests and Public Opinion* (New York: Knopf, 1951), 282–83.

3. See Gerald M. Pomper, *Elections in America: Control and Influence in Democratic Politics* (New York: Dodd, Mead, 1968), chap. 8. For results from 1968–1976, see Gerald M. Pomper with Susan S. Lederman, *Elections in America: Control and Influence in Democratic Politics,* 2nd ed. (New York: Longman, 1980), chap. 8. For 1992–2000 data, see Pomper, "Parliamentary Government in the United States?" in John C. Green and Rick Farmer, eds., *The State of the Parties: The Changing Role of Contemporary American Parties,* 4th ed. (Lanham, MD: Rowman & Littlefield, 2003), 273–74.

3. Negative fulfillment: Many promises pledge "*not* to act, to maintain the status quo." Where the party is true to its promise, this too is considered adequate performance.

4. Similar action: "Pledges may not be directly fulfilled, but similar actions may be taken by either Congress or the executive branch."

5. Defeated: "An attempt [is] made to accomplish the goal, but it is defeated." For example, the president proposes an appropriate bill, but Congress is unwilling to pass it.

6. No action: "The pledge is ignored or, in rare instances, completely opposite action is taken."[4]

Pomper's detailed results for the party that won the presidency are shown in Table 1–2.

The figures published in the original edition of Pomper's book, covering the years between 1944 and 1964, tell a remarkably optimistic story. Platform pledges, he concluded, "are indeed redeemed." If we leave aside the clearly anomalous results of 1944, about 64 percent of all platform promises were kept (categories 1, 2, and 3 in Table 1–2), and another 14 percent were partially fulfilled. Where promises were not kept, moreover, the chief culprit seemed to be the separation of powers. In 16 percent of the cases, some attempt was made by either the president or Congress to fulfill the platform, but the two branches were unable to reach agreement on a final bill. *Only about 6 percent of all promises were broken, in the sense that the platform was ignored or a contradictory action was taken.*

Though this conclusion continues to be echoed by those who cite Pomper,[5] the data he compiled for the second edition of his book and for two later articles actually tell a considerably darker story. Between 1968 and 2000, the rate at which parties delivered fully on their platform promises declined quite dramatically—from 64 percent to 36 percent, though another 31 percent were partially fulfilled. Broken promises also became substantially more common, rising from 6 percent to 27 percent. In recent years, it appears, about a third of all platform promises have been fulfilled, another third have been partially fulfilled, and the final third have been ignored.

Another landmark study of campaign promise keeping was published by Jeff Fishel in 1985. Unlike Pomper, who looked at the national party platforms, Fishel focused on the positions and promises made by the presidential candidates themselves, as revealed in their speeches and position papers.

---

4. For further details, see Pomper, *Elections in America*, 182–85.

5. See, for example, Thomas E. Patterson, *Out of Order* (New York: Random House, 1994), 11.

Table 1–2 Gerald Pomper's Data on the Fulfillment of National Party Platforms (in percentages)

	1944 Democrat	1948 Democrat	1952 Republican	1956 Republican	1960 Democrat	1964 Democrat
Full action	11	48	45	42	46	54
Executive action	0	4	8	4	14	10
Negative fulfillment	0	7	11	18	5	5
Similar action	45	6	16	19	16	14
Defeated	33	27	10	13	14	16
No action	11	8	10	4	5	1
Total fulfilled[1]	11	59	64	64	65	69
Partially fulfilled[2]	45	6	16	19	16	14

	1968 Republican	1972 Republican	1976 Democrat	1992 Democrat	1996 Democrat	2000 Republican
Full action	23	26	20	13	8	17
Executive action	11	11	11	8	12	9
Negative fulfillment	3	9	7	9	6	11
Similar action	28	29	23	40	44	22
Defeated	7	4	5	11	3	8
No action	28	22	34	19	27	33
Total fulfilled[1]	37	46	38	30	26	37
Partially fulfilled[2]	28	29	23	40	44	22

	1948–1964 Average	1968–1992 Average
Full action	47	18
Executive action	8	10
Negative fulfillment	9	8
Similar action	14	31
Defeated	16	6
No action	6	27
Total fulfilled[1]	64	36
Partially fulfilled[2]	14	31

1. Sum of "full action," "executive action," and "negative fulfillment" categories

2. Similar action

SOURCE: All 1944–1976 data taken from Gerald M. Pomper with Susan S. Lederman, *Elections in America: Control and Influence in Democratic Politics* (New York: Longman, 1980), Table 8.1, pp. 162–63. All 1992–2000 data taken from Gerald M. Pomper, "Parliamentary Government in the United States: A New Regime for a New Century?" in John C. Green and Rick Farmer, eds., *The State of the Parties: The Changing Role of Contemporary American Parties,* 4th ed. (Lanham, MD: Rowman & Littlefield, 2003), pp. 273–74.

Also unlike Pomper, Fishel focused on how the *proposals* presidents made while in office matched up with their campaign promises.

Fishel's results, based on the presidential campaigns of 1960, 1964, 1968, 1976, and 1980, are shown in Table 1–3. On average, about 38 percent of campaign promises resulted in a presidential proposal that was "fully comparable"— where the proposal "met the requirements of the pledge in a complete and comprehensive manner." Another 23 percent of promises led to proposals that were "partially comparable"—not meeting "the full requirements of the pledge but still contain[ing] large and similar components." At the other end of the spectrum, 11 percent of promises produced no discernible presidential response, and in 5 percent of the cases the president actually did the reverse of what he had promised. Fishel also distinguished two intermediate cases: 8 percent of campaign promises resulted only in what he called "token action"; another 8 percent were met by "mixed action"—a presidential proposal that "simultaneously met some requirements of the pledge, but went in opposite directions on other parts."[6]

As noted earlier, the numbers discussed in the previous paragraph deal only with presidential *proposals*. To make Fishel's figures more comparable with Pomper's, we need to determine how many of these proposals actually get translated into law or some other sort of authoritative action. Table 1–3 provides three useful pieces of information that bear on this last question. First, about 70 percent of presidential promises required congressional action; only about 30 percent, in other words, could be implemented by executive action alone. Second, where congressional action was required, presidents submitted legislation in only about 60 percent of the cases. Finally, 74 percent of these presidentially endorsed bills were passed by both houses of Congress. Once again, the separation of powers emerges as a major obstacle to promise fulfillment.

One final set of figures on presidential promise keeping, compiled by Michael Krukones, is often grouped with the work of Pomper and Fishel. Like Fishel, Krukones examined the promises made by the presidential candidates themselves rather than their parties, but unlike Fishel, Krukones based his list on contemporary press coverage. This method undoubtedly misses a substantial number of promises that would have been picked up by Fishel's more encyclopedic procedure but has the advantage of focusing on major promises and those of which the typical voter would more likely be aware.

When compared to Pomper and Fishel, Krukones seems remarkably generous in the standards he uses to evaluate whether or not presidents keep their promises. Where Pomper and Fishel both explicitly recognize that

---

6. For specific definitions of these categories and some useful examples, see Jeff
   Fishel, *Presidents and Promises: From Campaign Pledge to Presidential Performance*
   (Washington, DC: CQ Press, 1985), 37–38.

Table 1–3 Jeff Fishel's Data on Presidential Promise Keeping (in percentages)

	Kennedy (1961–1963)	Johnson (1965–1968)	Nixon (1969–1972)	Carter (1977–1980)	Reagan (1981–1984)	Average
Fully comparable	36	41	34	45	35	38
Partially comparable	31	22	26	20	18	23
Token action	6	8	5	11	9	8
Contradictory action	5	4	2	8	7	5
No action	6	5	27	10	9	11
Mixed action	12	13	4	2	11	8
Indeterminate	4	8	3	4	11	6
Percent of promises requiring congressional action	68	63	75	85	65	71
Percent where legislation was actually submitted	61	70	56	56	64	61
Percent in which this legislation passed	81	89	61	71	68	74
(No. of promises)	(133)	(63)	(153)	(186)	(108)	

SOURCE: Jeff Fishel, *President and Promises: From Campaign Pledge to Presidential Performance* (Washington, DC: Congressional Quarterly Press, 1985), Tables 2-3, p. 39; and 2-4, p. 42.

Table 1–4 Michael Krukones's Data on Presidential Promise Keeping (in percentages)

President/Year	Promises Fulfilled	Good Faith Effort Made	(No. of Promises)
Truman, 1948	67	27	(15)
Eisenhower, 1952	77	3	(31)
Eisenhower, 1956	71	0	(31)
Kennedy, 1960	82	12	(34)
Johnson, 1964	88	0	(24)
Nixon, 1968	74	6	(34)
Carter, 1976	59	22	(51)
Average	74	10	

SOURCE: Michael G. Krukones, *Promises and Performance: Presidential Campaigns as Policy Predictors* (Lanham, MD: University Press of America, 1984), Table 5, p. 124.

promises can be fulfilled to varying degrees, Krukones considers a promise fulfilled if the president took any "positive action in carrying out his campaign pledges and ... some results were put into effect." During the 1976 campaign, for example, Jimmy Carter promised to reorganize the entire federal executive branch, cutting the number of government agencies from 1,900 to 200. Though Carter came nowhere close to achieving this objective, Krukones gives Carter credit for fulfilling this pledge on the grounds that Congress passed his "proposed revision of the civil service system, along with additional [unspecified] government reorganization plans."

These caveats stated, Krukones's results are shown in Table 1–4. On average, he found, the presidents who served between 1948 and 1980 kept 74 percent of their reported promises.[7] In another 10 percent of the cases, the president made what Krukones felt was a "good-faith effort" to fulfill his promises but was unable to get Congress to go along with him.

Taken together, Pomper, Fishel, and Krukones's work suggests three principal conclusions. First, contrary to popular mythology and the reflexive cynicism of the press, presidents do make a reasonable effort to redeem *most* of their promises. Second, where presidents are unable to deliver on their promises, one of the chief culprits is undoubtedly the separation of powers. A great deal of what presidents promise to do during the campaign requires congressional

---

7. Krukones actually compiled data for every presidential election between 1912 and 1976. I do not include the 1912–1944 results in Table 1–3 partly to make this table more comparable with Pomper and Fishel's results, partly because, according to Krukones, presidential candidates made substantially fewer promises during this period.

approval, and in a substantial number of cases, Congress is unwilling to comply with the president's wishes.

Finally, there are a substantial number of promises that presidential candidates do *not* fulfill—not because of congressional opposition but because they themselves decide to ignore or contravene what they said during the campaign. Both Fishel and Krukones found that about 16 percent of candidate promises went unredeemed. Between 1968 and 1992, Pomper's data show that 27 percent of platform commitments resulted in no action.

WHY PROMISES GET BROKEN

If broken promises are not the norm in recent presidential campaigns, then, they do occur sufficiently often that they cannot simply be dismissed as rare or exceptional. Moreover, even if the number of broken promises does not loom very large in the sort of counting procedure employed by Pomper, Fishel, and Krukones, broken promises have sometimes involved matters of enormous political and policy significance. No American political history of the last 50 years would be complete that neglected to mention the consequences that ensued from three major presidential campaign promises that were *not* kept:

1. Lyndon Johnson's promise during the 1964 campaign that he would not pursue a wider war in Vietnam

2. George H. W. Bush's promise during the 1988 campaign that he would never increase taxes

3. Bill Clinton's promise in 1992 that he would at least cut taxes for the middle class and certainly would not increase them

Why were these promises broken? In none of these cases is there evidence that the president underwent a fundamental change in his basic philosophy of government. None of these presidents, that is to say, experienced an Arthur Vandenberg-like moment, where he suddenly came to realize that a policy he had been pushing vigorously for much of his political career was wrong or no longer viable. Instead, each of these promises was broken *because the presidential candidate greatly underestimated the difficulty of achieving one of his major goals.* That put him in the position of either (1) keeping his promise but thereby compromising several other important objectives, or (2) breaking the promise. In at least two of these cases, in fact, the president was faced with a conflict between two different campaign promises. Inevitably, one of them had to be broken.

Johnson and Vietnam

Lyndon Johnson's handling of the Vietnam war issue during the 1964 campaign provides a particularly good example of the basic problem.[8] As of mid-1964, Johnson's basic policy stance in Vietnam, which he set forth in at least half a dozen major campaign speeches, had two principal pillars. As the president explained in a speech before the American Bar Association:

> For 10 years our response to these attacks has followed a consistent pattern. First, that the South Vietnamese have the basic responsibility for the defense of their own freedom. Second, we would engage our strength and our resources to whatever extent needed to help others repel aggression.[9]

The South Vietnamese, in other words, would do most of the real fighting; the United States would help, but only in certain limited ways. In a speech delivered at a party held to celebrate his 56th birthday, Johnson was more specific about the American role; it was "to furnish advice, give counsel, express good judgment, give them trained counselors, and help them with equipment."[10] In yet another speech, Johnson quoted with approval a statement President Eisenhower had made to the president of Vietnam in 1954: "We want to help you help yourselves, and we will provide you advice and military assistance to preserve your country and keep the Communists from enveloping it *if you will help yourselves.*"[11]

Throughout the 1964 campaign, Johnson repeatedly described his Vietnam policy as a moderate, middle position between the extremes of escalation and withdrawal:

---

8. The best single account of Johnson's decision to escalate the war in Vietnam in 1964–1965 is Brian VanDeMark, *Into the Quagmire: Lyndon Johnson and the Escalation of the Vietnam War* (New York: Oxford University Press, 1991). The following account draws heavily on VanDeMark, as well as on George C. Herring, *America's Longest War: The United States and Vietnam, 1950–1975,* 3rd ed. (New York: McGraw-Hill, 1996), chap. 4; Lyndon Baines Johnson, *The Vantage Point: Perspectives of the Presidency 1963–1969* (New York: Holt, Rinehart and Winston, 1971), chap. 6; and Robert Dallek, *Flawed Giant: Lyndon Johnson and His Times, 1961–1973* (New York: Oxford University Press, 1998), chap. 5.

9. Remarks in New York City before the American Bar Association, August 12, 1964, *Public Papers of the Presidents: Lyndon B. Johnson, 1963–64,* Book II (Washington, DC: U.S. Government Printing Office), 953.

10. Remarks at a Barbecue in Stonewall, Texas, August 29, 1964, *Public Papers,* Book II, 1022.

11. Remarks in Louisville, Ky., at a breakfast for Indiana and Kentucky State Party Leaders, October 9, 1964, *Public Papers,* Book II, 1267 (emphasis added). The statement seems to have been a paraphrase of Eisenhower's general policy, rather than a direct quote.

> Some say that we should withdraw from South Viet-Nam, that we have lost almost 200 lives there in the last 4 years, and we should come home. But the United States cannot and must not and will not turn aside and allow the freedom of a brave people to be handed over to Communist tyranny. This alternative is strategically unwise, we think, and it is morally unthinkable.
>
> Some others are eager to enlarge the conflict. They call upon us to supply American boys to do the job that Asian boys should do. They ask us to take reckless action which might risk the lives of millions and engulf much of Asia and certainly threaten the peace of the entire world.[12]

Johnson's own policy was to stay, but in a limited role. As he told an audience in Eufala, Oklahoma, "We are not about to start another war and we're not about to run away from where we are."[13]

In Johnson's defense, then, he clearly did indicate that he had no intention of withdrawing or even of reducing the American presence in Vietnam. Yet he also made clear, in speech after speech, his unwillingness to escalate the war.

> We don't want our American boys to do the fighting for Asian boys.
>
> We are trying as best we can not to enlarge that war, not to get the United States tied down in a land war in Asia . . .
>
> We have tried very carefully to restrain ourselves and not to enlarge the war.
>
> We are not about to send American boys 9 or 10,000 miles away from home to do what Asian boys ought to be doing for themselves.[14]

There is, it is important to say, nothing illogical or incoherent about such a policy. Indeed, as Johnson also pointed out in a number of speeches, this was the same policy that had been pursued by Presidents Eisenhower and Kennedy for the previous 10 years. Yet as 1964 and 1965 progressed, it soon became clear that the military and political situation in South Vietnam was starting to "deteriorate" (that word is used over and over again in contemporary reports)[15] at a very rapid pace. The troubles on the political front actually began in the final days of John Kennedy's presidency, when Kennedy tacitly encouraged (or at least declined to prevent) the assassination of South

---

12. Remarks before the American Bar Association, *Public Papers,* Book II, 953.

13. Remarks in Oklahoma at the Dedication of the Eufala Dam, September 25, 1964, *Public Papers,* Book II, 1127.

14. Remarks in Memorial Hall, Akron University, October 21, 1964, *Public Papers,* Book II, 1391.

15. For some examples, see VanDeMark, *Into the Quagmire,* 48, 52, 65, 87, 95, and 103.

Vietnamese Premier Ngo Dinh Diem on November 1, 1963. Though Diem's regime had been marked by numerous problems, he had at least managed to bring some measure of political stability to a highly fractionalized country. As one U.S. official later remarked, "I doubt that anyone appreciated the magnitude of the centrifugal political forces which had been kept under control by his [Diem's] iron rule."[16] With Diem gone, South Vietnam went through a numbing succession of coups and countercoups over the next year and a half.

With most of the nation's military and political leadership engaged in fighting each other, South Vietnam's military effort also began to collapse. The Vietcong, moving to exploit the government's disarray, stepped up its military offensive and quickly secured control over large sections of the countryside. Meanwhile, the South Vietnamese army was plagued by desertion and poor morale; the pacification program was also in severe decline.

The bottom line, by early 1965, was that it was no longer possible to preserve the independence of South Vietnam *and* still maintain a limited role for the American military there. Johnson's advisors included both advocates and opponents of escalating the war, but both sides agreed that the old Eisenhower–Kennedy policy was no longer tenable. As Maxwell Taylor, the U.S. ambassador to Vietnam, reported to Johnson in January 1965, "We are presently on a losing track and must risk a change. . . . To take no positive action now is to accept defeat in the fairly near future."[17]

Contrary to the impression that has been conveyed by some early histories of this crucial decision period (particularly the reporting of the *Pentagon Papers*), Johnson had not decided in favor of escalation before the 1964 election nor was it a decision that he took lightly. To the contrary, the historical record indicates quite clearly that Johnson agonized over the matter for months, desperately hoping to avoid any extensive foreign commitment that might undermine his beloved Great Society program but always reluctantly concluding that the costs of inaction or withdrawal were greater than the costs of escalation. By February 1965, the United States had initiated a sustained bombing campaign against North Vietnam; shortly thereafter, troop levels began to increase, and in July, the President committed the country to what he himself called "major combat in Vietnam."[18]

One final point is worth underscoring: Though Johnson is often criticized for breaking his promise not to escalate the war in Vietnam, he had also, as indicated earlier, promised not to withdraw from that country. Given the realities of the Vietnam situation in early 1965, one of these promises had to be broken.

---

16. Maxwell Taylor, as quoted in VanDeMark, *Into the Quagmire,* 15.

17. As quoted in Johnson, *Vantage Point,* 122.

18. See Johnson, *Vantage Point,* 153.

Bush and "No New Taxes"

If Lyndon Johnson's decision to escalate the Vietnam war seems in many ways like a Greek tragedy, the saga of how George H. W. Bush broke his celebrated "no new taxes" campaign promise more nearly resembles a farce.[19]

That Bush should have felt impelled to make the promise at all is an interesting case study in political one-upsmanship. In 1984, Walter Mondale had explicitly promised to increase taxes during his acceptance speech at the Democratic convention, thereby leaving Ronald Reagan free to adopt a position that, while generally opposed to tax increases, nevertheless allowed for some flexibility on the issue. After specifically noting that "a President of the United States should never say never," Reagan declared, "For him [Mondale], raising taxes is a first resort. For me, it is a last resort."[20] In 1988, however, Michael Dukakis adopted the same position that Reagan had embraced in 1984, promising to increase taxes only as a "last resort." Hence, Bush's campaign handlers came to feel that, in order to distinguish Bush from his Democratic opponent, the vice president had to take a firmer line. The result was one of the most categorical, uncompromising campaign promises in American history. As finally delivered, it read:

> My opponent won't rule out raising taxes. But I will. And the Congress will push me to raise taxes, and I'll say no, and they'll push, and I'll say no, and they'll push again. And I'll say to them: Read my lips. No new taxes.[21]

What is most distressing, in retrospect, is how little serious forethought or commitment seems to have gone into the formulation of this promise, at least on the part of the candidate. By all accounts, the person who first decided to have Bush assume such a dogmatic position was not the vice president himself or one of his top political or policy advisors, but his speechwriter, Peggy Noonan. Noonan was a first-rate wordsmith, who had written some of

---

19. My account of the "no new taxes" promise and how Bush broke it draws on Bob Woodward, "Making Choices: Bush's Economic Record," *Washington Post,* October 4–7, 1992; Richard Darman, *Who's in Control? Polar Politics and the Sensible Center* (New York: Simon & Schuster, 1996), chaps. 10–13; Jack W. Germond and Jules Witcover, *Mad as Hell: Revolt at the Ballot Box, 1992* (New York: Warner Books, 1993), chap. 2; John Robert Greene, *The Presidency of George Bush* (Lawrence: University Press of Kansas, 2000), chaps. 3 and 6; and Peggy Noonan, *What I Saw at the Revolution* (New York: Random House, 1990), chap. 17; as well as the contemporary coverage in the *New York Times* and *Congressional Quarterly.*

20. Both quotations are taken from the *New York Times,* August 13, 1984, A1, A16.

21. For the full text of the speech, see *Congressional Quarterly Weekly Report,* August 20, 1988, 2353–56.

Reagan's best speeches, but she apparently did not know Bush very well when she first began working on his acceptance speech. For her part, Noonan claims that it was Jack Kemp who planted the idea in her mind: "Kemp told me, [h]it hard on taxes, Bush will be pressured to raise them as soon as he's elected, and he has to make clear he won't budge."[22]

Noonan's wording did a fine job of summarizing Kemp's thinking on the issue, but it was never a good fit with Bush. In 1984, in the immediate aftermath of Mondale's acceptance speech, Bush was, if anything, even more insistent than Reagan that it was irresponsible to rule out any possibility of raising taxes. "Any president would keep options open," he stated at the time. "Conditions can dramatically change one way or the other."[23] In 1986 and 1987, Bush had generally resisted signing a formal anti-tax pledge put out by a conservative group called Americans for Tax Reform, saying that it was "too gimmicky and bad policy." Throughout the spring and early summer of 1988, Bush similarly claimed that he was "hardline" against tax increases but declined to rule them out entirely.[24]

Moreover, even the most superficial look at the circumstances that would confront the new president in 1989 would have plainly indicated that "no new taxes" would be a difficult promise to keep. The size of the federal deficit had come down a bit from its peak level in 1986 but was still quite substantial: $150 billion in 1987, an estimated $144 billion in 1988. And unlike Reagan, who could at least say that he *wanted* to make significant cuts in federal domestic spending (even if Congress wouldn't go along with him), Bush had a considerably more positive view about the role of government. Indeed, Bush had actually promised to *increase* spending in a number of domestic areas, including education, the environment, enforcement of anti-drug laws, and aid for the homeless.[25] As for defense spending, Bush, as *Congressional Quarterly* noted during the 1988 campaign, "continues to support every Pentagon spending program on the table."[26]

So how did Bush hope to deal with the federal deficit? Though Bush had never been terribly specific in discussing the issue during the 1988 campaign, he had endorsed a general approach to the problem known as a "flexible freeze." During periods of economic growth, the argument behind this proposal noted, federal revenues grew significantly faster than the rate of inflation.

---

22. Noonan, *What I Saw*, 307.

23. Bush's words are quoted in the *New York Times,* August 13, 1984, A16.

24. For Bush's position on taxes prior to his speech at the Republican convention, see Woodward, "Making Choices," October 4, 1992; and Germond and Witcover, *Mad as Hell,* 22–24.

25. See *Congressional Quarterly Weekly Report,* November 26, 1988, 3381.

26. *Congressional Quarterly Weekly Report,* October 22, 1988, 3043.

Hence, if federal spending on all programs was allowed to grow no faster than the inflation rate—that is, if it were "frozen" in real terms—revenues would increase faster than spending and the country would gradually "grow its way" out of the deficit.

Contrary to what contemporary news reports sometimes suggested, the flexible freeze proposal was not simply wishful thinking or campaign gimmickry; it had been endorsed by a number of top-flight economists. But it did rest on a number of assumptions that made it a far from certain way to reduce the deficit. First, it assumed the economy would continue to grow at a reasonable pace, even though there were already signs that the economic boom of the mid-1980s was starting to slow down. Second, while holding spending on some types of federal programs to the rate of inflation was not particularly problematic, the freeze concept was much less well-suited to other areas, especially entitlements. Social Security, in particular, would almost certainly grow faster than inflation, since the number of recipients was steadily increasing and the size of the payments each individual received was indexed to inflation. The Bush campaign effectively acknowledged this point, since it specifically excluded Social Security from the freeze. Interest payments on the national debt were similarly problematic. Since the federal government was legally obligated to make these payments, the savings from the freeze were closely tied to the level of interest rates.

Third, the flexible freeze idea assumed that the government would not suddenly be required to shoulder any major new fiscal burdens. In fact, however, though it hadn't received much attention at that point, Bush and his advisors surely knew that the federal government might have to spend a substantial amount of money bailing out the savings and loan system, expenditures that the government was legally committed to as a result of federal deposit guarantee provisions. Finally, the flexible freeze—or any other major deficit-reduction program Bush proposed—would require the cooperation and consent of Congress. Unlike Reagan, however, who had a Republican majority in the Senate in 1981 and at least a working majority in the House, Bush confronted a situation in which both the Senate and the House were firmly in Democratic hands. Many Democrats were unfavorably disposed toward the freeze concept, since they believed that domestic spending in many areas needed to grow a good deal faster than the rate of inflation.

If the freeze didn't work or did not work fast enough, there was one other way to deal with the deficit: just put up with it. This was, after all, the "solution" that had effectively been adopted during most of the 1980s. With a Republican president unwilling to agree to large new tax increases and a Democratic Congress that refused to make major cuts in domestic spending, the path of least resistance was simply to tolerate large budget deficits. But by the late 1980s, this posture had become considerably more problematic, for at least two reasons. First, Alan Greenspan, who had been appointed chairman of the Federal Reserve Board in 1987, had made it clear that he was concerned about the size of the deficit and that until it was brought down, he would pursue a tight monetary policy that was likely to slow down the rate of economic growth and perhaps even push the country into a recession. Whatever the economic merits of Greenspan's stance, it undoubtedly had the effect of making inaction on the deficit significantly more costly. Second, in late 1985, Congress had adopted the Gramm-Rudman-Hollings anti-deficit law, which set progressively lower targets for the deficit over the next six years and further specified that, if these targets were not met, automatic cuts would be made in both defense and domestic spending—cuts that both Republicans and Democrats were anxious to avoid.[27] The Gramm-Rudman-Hollings strictures could be altered or set aside—this had already occurred in 1987— but again, this would require congressional approval.

Given the economic and political conditions and Bush's own political credo, then, the prospects for avoiding a tax increase between 1989 and 1993 were not very bright. Yet, with one exception, there is little evidence that Bush or anyone in his campaign was much troubled by this problem. When Noonan finished the first draft of the acceptance speech, it was reviewed by a small number of other top campaign officials, including Richard Darman, who hoped to become budget director if Bush won the election. According to Bob Woodward, Darman immediately called the "read my lips" promise "stupid and irresponsible" and tried to have the entire section deleted.[28] But each time a new draft was created, Noonan would put back in the offending passage, which she liked because it was "definite. It's not subject to misinterpretation. It means, I mean this."[29] Bush's political managers, particularly media strategist Roger Ailes and pollster Robert Teeter, also liked "read my lips" because it would make a good sound bite and help Bush overcome his "wimp image." Darman apparently hoped that the line would be vetoed by James Baker, Bush's longtime friend and political confidant who had recently become his campaign manager—but Baker declined to intervene. Since Darman did not know Bush very well at that point, he finally decided not to press the issue.

Notably absent from most of these discussions was Bush himself, who seems to have provided Noonan with certain broad ideas and suggestions but otherwise left the speech largely in her hands. In one meeting where the speech was being reviewed, Bush reportedly expressed some misgivings about

---

27. For a good summary of the Gramm-Rudman-Hollings law as it existed in 1989 (it had had to be rewritten in 1987, when parts of the first bill were declared unconstitutional), see *Congressional Quarterly Weekly Report,* September 26, 1987, 2309–11.

28. Woodward, "Making Choices," October 4, 1992.

29. Noonan, *What I Saw,* 307.

the "no new taxes" line. At a second meeting, after Darman raised only mild objections, Bush ended the uncertainty: "Read my lips" would be included in the acceptance speech.[30]

In the end, the "no new taxes" pledge was broken in a quite predictable fashion. Indeed, there is evidence that, within months after the new administration took office, top officials were already trying to figure out how to increase taxes in the least politically damaging way.[31] Bush did manage to avoid breaking his promise in 1989, partly because the Gramm-Rudman targets were not particularly demanding that year, partly because a number of top Democrats decided not to press the issue in the new president's first year in office. By early 1990, however, with the economy sliding into recession and the prospect of huge automatic spending cuts looming, the White House was under enormous pressure to put together a truly substantial deficit reduction package. For that, they needed a *lot* of Democratic votes, particularly in the House, and before the Democrats were willing to begin serious negotiations, they demanded that Bush abandon his insistence that new taxes could not be part of the deal. On May 7, Bush agreed, somewhat ambiguously, that he would impose "no preconditions" on the budget discussions.[32] When White House Chief of Staff John Sununu told reporters that this only meant that the Democrats were free to propose tax increases, even though the president would reject them, the Democrats demanded that Bush go a step further and issue a statement specifically indicating that tax increases were a necessary part of any deficit reduction package. On June 26, Bush finally bit the bullet and released the following statement:

> It is clear to me that both the size of the deficit problem and the need for a package that can be enacted require all of the following: entitlement and mandatory program reform, tax revenue increases, growth incentives, discretionary spending reductions, orderly reductions in defense expenditures and budget process reform, to assure that any bipartisan agreement is enforceable and that the deficit problem is brought under responsible control. The bipartisan leadership agrees with me on these points. The budget negotiations will resume promptly with a view toward reaching substantive agreement as quickly as possible.[33]

In short, "no new taxes" was history. Four and a half months later, Bush signed into law a comprehensive deficit reduction package that, among other provisions, increased federal taxes by $146.3 billion over the next five years.

---

30. See Woodward, "Making Choices," October 4, 1992.

31. See Woodward, "Making Choices," October 4, 1992.

32. *New York Times,* May 8, 1990, A1.

33. As quoted in the *New York Times,* June 27, 1990, A1.

Clinton and the Middle-Class Tax Cut

Democrats and liberals made great sport of Bush's irresponsible 1988 campaign promise and his subsequent attempts to squirm out of it, but in 1992 their presidential nominee advanced a budget plan that was, in its own way, equally problematic.[34] Like Ronald Reagan in 1980, Bill Clinton put forward a very ambitious economic program. He also set forth that program with unusual specificity, at least by campaign standards, eventually publishing a 232-page book on the subject, called *Putting People First*.

In that book—and in all of the major speeches he gave after late June—Clinton clearly committed himself to three major economic promises:

1. *Increased spending on "investment" programs.* Though it is easy to forget in light of subsequent events, the centerpiece of the Clinton program was the claim that the United States needed to greatly increase the amount of money directed at investment as opposed to consumption spending. In part, this meant that Clinton favored a variety of targeted tax cuts that were specifically designed to encourage private investment. But Clinton also called for large increases in public investment, via spending on infrastructure, community development, education, and job training. The specific amounts the Clinton campaign said it would spend on these "new investments" are listed as the first two items in Table 1–5. Across the four years of what would be Clinton's first term in office (1993–96), the combination of targeted tax cuts and new spending was estimated to cost $197 billion.

2. *Cutting taxes for the middle class.* Though Clinton's promise in this area was somewhat more cautious than the one he had made during the primaries, his basic intention was unmistakable: "We will lower the tax burden on middle-class Americans by asking the very wealthy to pay their fair share. Middle-class taxpayers will have a choice between a children's tax credit or a significant reduction in their income tax rate."[35] Though the campaign did not put a specific price tag on these middle-class tax cuts, these cuts plus an increase

---

34. My account of the 1992 Clinton economic plan draws on Bill Clinton and Al Gore, *Putting People First: How We Can All Change America* (New York: Times Books, 1992); Elizabeth Drew, *On the Edge: The Clinton Presidency* (New York: Simon and Schuster, 1994); Bob Woodward, *The Agenda: Inside the Clinton White House* (New York: Simon and Schuster, 1994); Rich Lowry, *Legacy: Paying the Price for the Clinton Years* (Washington, DC: Regnery, 2003), chap. 3; and contemporary coverage in the *New York Times* and *Congressional Quarterly*.

35. Clinton and Gore, *Putting People First,* 15.

Table 1–5 Basic Outline of the 1992 Clinton Economic Plan

	FOUR-YEAR				
	1993	1994	1995	1996	Total
"New Investments" (new spending and tax cuts)					
Infrastructure, community development, incentives for private investment	28.3	34.6	35.4	35.4	133.7
Education and worker retraining	10.1	14.2	17.3	21.7	63.3
Middle-class tax cut and earned income tax credit	3.5	5.5	6.5	7.0	22.5
TOTAL	41.9	54.3	59.2	64.1	219.5
"New Savings" (spending cuts and tax increases)					
Increased taxes on upper-income individuals	19.8	22.7	23.9	25.3	91.7
Increased taxes on U.S. and foreign corporations	11.3	14.4	15.3	17.3	58.3
Spending cuts	26.1	32.4	36.8	45.0	140.3
Entitlement reform	0.6	1.0	1.0	1.8	4.4
TOTAL	57.8	70.5	77.0	89.4	294.7
Deficit Projections					
Current deficit[1]	323.0	268.0	212.0	193.0	
Clinton-Gore plan: moderate growth	295.7	243.0	174.0	141.0	
Clinton-Gore plan: strong growth	282.6	207.0	125.5	75.8	

SOURCE: Adapted from Bill Clinton and Al Gore, *Putting People First: How We Can All Change America* (New York: Times Books, 1992), esp. pp. 27–31.

in the Earned Income Tax Credit, which was directed at the working poor, were estimated to cost $22.5 billion over four years.

3. *Reduce the federal deficit.* Though Clinton did not promise to eliminate the deficit, as some of his rivals had, he did promise to "cut the deficit in half within four years and assure that it continues to fall each year after that."[36]

How did Clinton propose to pay for all this? His book sets forth—again, quite specifically—two major mechanisms. First, he did recommend a sizable list of tax increases. But—and this is the key point—the taxes were all directed

---

36. Clinton and Gore, *Putting People First*, 7.

at wealthy Americans and corporations, especially foreign corporations; the working and middle classes would go untouched. Specifically, Clinton said that he would increase the income tax rate on those earning more than $200,000 and impose a further surtax on millionaires. He also hoped to raise a lot of money by "preventing tax avoidance by foreign corporations." In all, the Clinton campaign maintained, these tax increases would yield $150 billion in additional revenue over the 1993–96 period.

The Clinton economic program also proposed a substantial series of spending cuts, beginning with the defense budget but extending into a variety of other areas as well. Along with a rather small change in one entitlement program (Medicare), the spending cuts were said to save the federal government a total of $144.7 billion during the first term of a Clinton presidency.

Unfortunately for the Democrats, it did not work out anything like as promised, a fact that became clear as soon as the new administration took office. In February 1993, Clinton submitted an economic plan to Congress that included far less new investment spending than his campaign plan had promised and reneged entirely on the middle-class tax cut. In fact, Clinton ended up proposing *increased* taxes for all Americans, in the form of a broad-based energy tax.

Why didn't Clinton deliver on his 1992 campaign promise of a middle-class tax cut? The short answer is that while the Clinton economic plan seemed to be very specific and precise in its proposals, the numbers it put forward just were not reliable, particularly when it came to estimating the effects of tax increases and spending cuts. On issue after issue, the Clinton campaign overestimated the amount of money it could free up for new investments, deficit reduction, and middle-class tax cuts.

Consider a few examples:

■   Of all the tax increases proposed in the Clinton campaign manifesto, surely none was an easier political sell than the promise that the new administration would "prevent tax avoidance by foreign corporations." Here, it seemed, was a way to increase revenues without asking a single American voter to shoulder a larger tax burden. In fact, as *Congressional Quarterly* noted at the time, a recent House Ways and Means Committee report had "identified a significant amount of tax evasion by foreign corporations" that did business in the United States. But the Ways and Means analysis also suggested that the new revenues that could be raised by closing such loopholes "would be much smaller than those claimed by Clinton."[37] Where the Clinton campaign plan said it could raise an additional $45 billion over four years by preventing foreign tax avoidance, the plan finally submitted

37. *Congressional Quarterly Weekly Report,* June 27, 1992, 1900.

to Congress estimated that a series of changes in the tax laws applying to foreign and multinational businesses would yield just $8.6 billion over six years.[38]

- For several decades, Democrats had ridiculed Republican candidates who claimed that they could substantially reduce federal spending just by better "management," without any reduction in the quality or quantity of government services. Yet the 1992 Clinton economic plan made several promises of exactly the same type. Clinton claimed, for example, that he could save $22 billion over four years through "cuts in administrative waste," simply by "requir[ing] federal managers and workers to achieve 3 percent across-the-board administrative savings in every federal agency."[39] The Clinton plan similarly asserted that it could save $15.3 billion over four years by eliminating "100,000 unnecessary positions in the bureaucracy."[40] Who these employees were and how Clinton knew they were truly "unnecessary" was, of course, not made clear.

- In a similar fashion, the Clinton plan claimed that it could save $17.1 billion through "management reform" in the Resolution Trust Corporation (RTC), the agency that had been set up to close down failed savings and loans and sell off their assets. Though the RTC was widely attacked for its management practices, actually getting the agency to perform better was easier said than done. It was, moreover, not clear that many of the proposed "reforms" would save money. For example, Democratic members of Congress had sometimes criticized the RTC for not doing enough business with women and minority contractors.[41] While working with a more diverse pool of contractors might have helped achieve a number of other goals, any attempt to have the RTC seek out minority purchasers and comply with extensive new affirmative action requirements almost certainly would have *increased* the agency's administrative expenses. In the end, so far as I can determine, the economic plan that Clinton submitted to Congress in early 1993 did not claim *any* savings from RTC management reform.

- The Clinton plan also claimed it could save $9.8 billion over four years by using the "line item veto to cut pork-barrel projects." A long line of presidents, notably including both Reagan and Bush, had asked

---

38. For details, see *Congressional Quarterly Weekly Report,* February 20, 1993, 363.

39. Clinton and Gore, *Putting People First,* 25.

40. Clinton and Gore, *Putting People First,* 25.

41. See, for example, *Congressional Quarterly Weekly Report,* March 20, 1993, 659–60.

Congress to grant them this power (it would require a constitutional amendment) so that they could eliminate pork-barrel spending that is often tacked on to otherwise necessary legislation. But as Clinton surely knew, there was almost no chance that Congress would actually grant this power to the president in 1993, no matter what party he belonged to.

Perhaps the most optimistic element in the entire Clinton plan, however, was its approach to the federal deficit. As the figures in Table 1–5 indicate, even if the Clinton numbers are taken at face value, the "new savings" barely pay for the "new investments." In 1996, for example, Clinton claimed that his proposed spending cuts and tax increases would yield $89.4 billion in additional revenue—but $64.1 billion of that money was allocated to new spending and tax cuts. Only $25.3 billion, in other words, was left over for deficit reduction.

So how did the Clinton plan intend to deal with the deficit? Though it wasn't widely noted at the time, Clinton's deficit-reduction strategy was actually the same one that George H. W. Bush had hoped to use in 1988: letting economic growth do most of the work. Said one Clinton advisor at the time, "The way to decrease the deficit is not to increase it by taxing and spending, but to *grow our way out of it*."[42] Or, as an analysis in the *Washington Post* noted,

> Some economists wonder, however, whether Clinton's program represents a type of Democratic supply-side theory. Whereas Republican supply-siders believed that lower tax rates would spur growth rapid enough to catch up with big budget deficits, Clinton's economic program suggests that new government spending can spur faster economic growth while the economy grows its way through much of the deficit problem.[43]

The specific deficit projections released by the Clinton campaign are shown in the bottom third of Table 1–5. The most noteworthy aspect of these figures is how much reliance they placed on the deficit reduction program that the Bush administration had enacted two years earlier: Between 1993 and 1996, the deficit was already projected to go down by $130 billion. To quote the *Washington Post* again, "Most of the decline in the budget deficit promised by Clinton would come about without any new policies."[44] If the Clinton plan produced "moderate growth" during these years, the deficit would decline by another $52 billion. "Strong growth" would cut the deficit by $65.2 billion more.

---

42. Derek Shearer, as quoted in *Congressional Quarterly Weekly Report*, June 27, 1992, 1901 (emphasis added).

43. *Washington Post*, October 11, 1992, A34.

44. *Washington Post*, October 11, 1992, A34.

The deficit projections Clinton relied on when developing his economic manifesto had been published by the Congressional Budget Office (CBO) in early 1992. As 1992 progressed, however, and the U.S. economy failed to show much improvement, both the CBO and the Office of Management and Budget (OMB) substantially increased their estimates of future deficits. By early January, 1993, OMB was forecasting a 1996 deficit of $266 billion—more than $85 billion higher than it had estimated just one year earlier.[45] Yet both the Clinton and Bush campaigns essentially ignored the new, updated estimates during the general election—the former because it would have completely upset their carefully worked-out economic strategy, the latter because it would have raised questions about their own economic management.

Once the election was over and the new administration was preparing to take office, however, the new deficit projections became impossible to ignore any longer. In December 1992, Clinton held a highly publicized "economic summit" meeting, where the central message, reiterated by speaker after speaker, concerned the need to get after the deficit more aggressively. The result was that the Clinton economic program of early 1993 (1) included far smaller spending increases than the campaign manifesto had promised and (2) replaced the promised middle-class tax cut with a broad-based energy tax that was estimated to cost the average American family between $100 and $150 a year.

CAN WE DO BETTER?

Is there some way that we can, if not eliminate these sorts of broken promises, at least make them less likely? There are three actors to whom one might look for relief—the candidates, the media, and the voters—and to cut to the bottom line, none of the three seems likely to change the fundamental dynamics of presidential campaign promises.

Candidates

For presidential candidates who wish to avoid breaking their promises, the preceding analysis suggests an obvious remedy: Be more pessimistic in the assumptions you make about the anticipated outcomes of your programs and policy choices. Do not propose budgets that assume unrealistically high rates of growth or that large savings can be achieved by simple and politically acceptable changes in the way government operates. Do not assume that foreign

---

45. Compare *Congressional Quarterly Weekly Report*, February 1, 1992, 226; and
     January 9, 1993, 72.

military interventions will work out according to the best-case scenario. Do not underestimate the costs of new regulations designed to protect workers or the environment. Unfortunately, if this sort of advice is easy to give, it is very difficult for the candidates to accept. For the simple fact is that candidates generally have a strong incentive to do precisely the opposite: to underestimate costs and to overestimate the ease with which their goals can be accomplished.

Imagine an election in which the candidates are frequently asked about their plans for achieving two major goals—low-cost energy and a clean environment. Voters, let us assume, want both and haven't spent a lot of time reading detailed analyses about energy or environmental policy options. The last thing most candidates would want in this sort of situation is to admit that they are willing to do significant damage to a goal or value the public cares about. Any candidate who openly declares that "Energy costs will go up if I'm elected president" or "I'm willing to harm the environment" knows that he will see that line endlessly quoted in his opponent's speeches and advertisements. To be sure, many voters may *suspect* that the candidate's policies will have such a result—or can be convinced of that by the other candidate. But it is one thing to suspect that a candidate's policies will have negative effects—and quite another to have those effects confirmed by the candidate himself. For those candidates who actually want to win the election, then, it is far easier—indeed, almost irresistible—to insist that they can achieve both goals at once: low-cost energy *and* a clean environment, deficit reduction *and* lower taxes, an independent South Vietnam *without* escalation.

What needs to be stressed here, in fairness to the candidates, is that whether and to what extent two policy goals conflict is usually not something that can be decided on abstract or theoretical grounds. It is, rather, an empirical question—and the evidence that can be brought to bear on that question is frequently ambiguous or uncertain or can be interpreted in multiple ways. To stick with the example of energy and the environment, while most serious policy analysts would surely insist that there is at least some conflict between these two values—in the sense that concern for the environment does impose some restriction on our energy choices—there is ample room for disagreement about how stark the tradeoff is and how much it is implicated in any particular policy choice. Some regulations may significantly improve the environment with only modest effects on energy prices; some new energy sources can be exploited with relatively little cost to the environment. Experts disagree about the safety of nuclear power, the dangers of drilling in the Arctic National Wildlife Refuge, or the likelihood that various types of "renewable energy" will ever be cost effective.

Against that background, most presidential candidates find it all too easy to convince themselves that their favorite programs will work without substantial costs or conflict with other important objectives. And both the right and left have produced a small army of policy "experts" who will assure them that is, in fact, the case. The presidential selection process also probably contributes to this mentality: Given the remarkable amount of time and effort needed to win a contemporary presidential nomination, the doubters and the ambivalent are usually weeded out. Most nominees are likely to be people with an extraordinary faith in their own ability to make government work better, even where many others have failed.

The Media

Given the incentives that candidates clearly have to oversell their programs, many commentators have argued it is the media's responsibility to help make the candidates more honest. Reporters must press candidates to explain more fully how they can balance the budget without raising taxes or to specify what particular programs they will cut. Candidates must be compelled to clarify their priorities: Yes, you would *like* to have both cheap energy and a clean environment—but which is more important? If a conflict occurs, which goal or value will give way? What if things don't work out as planned?

As a general rule, reporters should ask tough questions—but it is naive to think that even the most aggressive questioning will force candidates to abandon their unrealistic promises. Like the old maxim that claims you can lead a horse to water but you can't make him drink, of presidential candidates it may be said that you can ask them any question you want, but you can't force them to give sensible answers. When asked if we can balance the budget without raising taxes or cutting valuable programs, many candidates will insist that we can—no matter what the reporter or some ill-defined set of experts believes. Asked what they would do if things don't work out as planned, most candidates would probably insist that things *will* work out—as long as they are elected president.

A wonderful example of this predicament occurred at the very beginning of the third presidential debate in 1992. Moderator Jim Lehrer opened with a pointed question directed at then-Governor Clinton:

> You are promising to create jobs, reduce the deficit, reform the health-care system, rebuild the infrastructure, guarantee college education for everyone who is qualified, among many other things, all with financial pain only for the very rich. Some people are having trouble apparently believing that is possible. Should they have that concern?

Clinton's response was direct and unflinching:

> No. There are many people who believe that the only way we can get this country turned around is to tax the middle class more and punish them more, but the truth is that middle-class Americans are basically

the only group of Americans who've been taxed more in the 1980s and during the last 12 years, even though their incomes have gone down. . . .

I believe we can increase investment and reduce the deficit at the same time if we not only ask Americans and foreign corporations to pay their share, we also provide over $100 billion in tax relief, in terms of incentives for new plants, new small businesses, new technologies, new housing, and for middle-class families. . . . This will work.

Several minutes later, Lehrer pressed Clinton again:

Governor, the word "pain"—one of the other leadership things that's put on you is that you don't speak of pain, that you speak of all things—nobody's going to really have to suffer under your plan. You've heard what Mr. Perot has said. He's said it's got—to do the things that you want to do, you can't do it just taking the money from the rich. That's what the president says as well. How do you respond to that? They said the numbers don't add up.

But Clinton refused to give an inch:

I disagree with both of them. . . . I don't think the answer is to slow the economy down more, drive unemployment up more and undermine the health of the private sector. The answer is to invest and grow this economy. That's what works in other countries, and that's what'll work here.

It is hard to know how Lehrer could have done more—yet, in the end, all his efforts were unavailing. Asked if he could really accomplish all his goals without raising taxes on the middle class, Clinton simply said that he could. End of story.

The Voters

There is a pronounced tendency, when discussing the shortcomings of American election campaigns, to portray the voters as the pure and innocent victims in the whole process. Seeking only to do right by their country, they are foiled by an evil cabal of politicians and reporters. My own attitude, by contrast, is closer to that of a political consultant who told one of my classes, "The voters are no picnic either, you know."

Voters could demand more realistic answers from the candidates; they could reject those who promise to solve difficult and intractable problems without imposing pain on anyone. But the overwhelming evidence is that they do not. There is, for example, not the slightest indication that Walter Mondale was rewarded for having the courage and honesty to tell the voters that if elected, he would raise their taxes to balance the budget. Paul Tsongas, who advocated the kind of strong anti-deficit medicine that Clinton avoided, did win a few primaries in 1992—but in the end, it was the Arkansas governor who won the Democratic nomination and then the White House.

In democracies, it is often said, voters get the candidates they deserve. As long as the voters prefer simple and painless "solutions," candidates will advocate those sorts of policies, get elected—and then break their promises.

2

✣

The Flawed Foundations
of the Electoral College

GEORGE C. EDWARDS III
Texas A&M University

Political equality lies at the core of democratic theory. It is difficult to imagine a definition of democracy that does not include equality in voting as a central standard for a democratic process. Robert Dahl, the leading democratic theorist, includes equality in voting as a central standard for a democratic process: "Every member must have an equal and effective opportunity to vote, and all votes must be counted as equal."[1]

Because political equality is central to democratic government, we must evaluate any mechanism for selecting the president against it. A popular misconception is that electoral votes are simple aggregates of popular votes. In reality, the electoral vote regularly deviates from the popular will as expressed in the popular vote—sometimes merely in curious ways, usually strengthening the electoral edge of the popular vote leader, but at times in such a way as to deny the presidency to the popular preference.

The percentage of electoral votes received by a candidate nationwide rarely coincides with the candidate's percentage of the popular vote because of several factors, the most important of which is the winner-take-all (or unit-vote) system.[2] All states except Maine and Nebraska have a winner-take-all system in which they award *all* their electoral votes to the candidate who finishes first in that state. The winner-take-all system takes the electoral votes allocated to a state based on its population and awards them all to the plurality winner of the state. *In effect, the system gives the votes of the people who voted against the winner to the winner.*

---

1. Robert A. Dahl, *On Democracy* (New Haven, CT: Yale University Press, 2000), 37. See Also Robert A. Dahl, *Democracy And Its Critics* (New Haven, CT: Yale University Press, 1989), 110.

2. See George C. Edwards III, *Why The Electoral College Is Bad For America* (New Haven, CT: Yale University Press, 2004), Chap. 2.

The operation of the winner-take-all system effectively disenfranchises voters who support losing candidates in each state. In the 2000 presidential election, nearly 3 million people voted for Al Gore for president in Florida. Because George W. Bush won 537 more votes than Gore, however, he received *all* of Florida's electoral votes. A candidate thus can win some states by very narrow margins, lose other states by large margins (as Bush did in California and New York in 2000), and so win the electoral vote while losing the popular vote. The votes for candidates who do not finish first in a state play no role in the outcome of the election, since they are not aggregated across states.

In a multiple-candidate contest (as in 1992, 1996, and 2000), the winner-take-all system may suppress the votes of the majority as well as the minority. In the presidential election of 1996, less than a majority of votes decided the blocs of electoral votes of 26 states. In 2000, pluralities rather than majorities determined the allocation of electoral votes in 9 states, including Florida and Ohio.[3] In each case, a minority of voters determined how *all* of their state's electoral votes would be cast. One net result of these distorting factors is that there is typically a substantial disparity in almost all elections between the national popular vote a candidate receives and that candidate's percentage of the electoral vote. In 1876, 1888, 1960,[4] and 2000, the candidate who finished second in the popular vote won the election.

The electoral college violates political equality. It is not a neutral counting device. Instead, it favors some citizens over others, depending solely upon the state in which voters cast their votes for president. The contemporary electoral college is not just an archaic mechanism for counting the votes; it is an institution that aggregates popular votes in an inherently unequal manner.

What good reason is there to continue such a voting system in an advanced democratic nation in which the ideal of popular choice is the most deeply ingrained of governmental principles?

DEFENDING INTERESTS

One of the core justifications for the electoral college, and its violations of political equality, is that it is necessary to protect important interests that would be overlooked or harmed under a system of direct election of the president. Advocates argue that allocating electoral votes by states and states casting their votes as units ensures that presidential candidates will be attentive to

---

3. U.S. Department of Commerce, *Statistical Abstract of the United States, 2003* (Washington, DC: U.S. Government Printing Office, 2004), p. 254.

4. See Edwards, *Why the Electoral College Is Bad for America,* pp. 48–51, for a discussion of the 1960 election.

and protective of state-based interests, especially the interests of states with small populations. Some supporters of the electoral college go further and argue that the electoral college forces candidates to pay greater attention to the interests of racial minorities. Most supporters of the electoral college also maintain that it is an essential bulwark of federalism and that electing the president directly would undermine the entire federal system.

On their face, such claims seem far-fetched. It is no secret, for example, that candidates allocate proportionately more campaign stops and advertisements to competitive and large states.[5] Because these justifications for the electoral college are so common, however, we must investigate them more systematically. (It is illuminating—and frustrating—that advocates of the electoral college virtually never offer systematic evidence to support their claims.) How much additional protection do states—especially small states—require? Does the electoral college give minorities special influence in the selection of the president? Do presidential candidates appeal directly to state interests and give disproportionate attention to small states in their campaigns? Finally, is the electoral college an essential element in our federal system?

DO STATE INTERESTS REQUIRE PROTECTION?

The argument that one of the major advantages of the electoral college is that it forces candidates to be more attentive to and protective of state-based interests, especially the interests of states with small populations,[6] is based on the premises that (1) states have interests as states, (2) that these interests

---

5. Raymond Tatalovich, "Electoral Votes and Presidential Campaign Trails, 1932–1976," *American Politics Quarterly* 7 (October 1979): 489–497; Scott C. James and Brian L. Lawson, "The Political Economy of Voting Rights Enforcement in America's Gilded Age: Electoral College Competition, Partisan Commitment, and the Federal Election Law," *American Political Science Review* 93 (March 1999): 115–131; Daron R. Shaw, "The Methods behind the Madness: Presidential Electoral College Strategies, 1988–1996," *Journal of Politics* 61 (November 1999): 893–913.

6. For examples of these assertions, see Judith A. Best, *The Choice of the People? Debating the Electoral College* (Lanham, MD: Rowman and Littlefield, 1996), chap. 3; Curtis Gans, "Electoral College Reform: How to Keep, But Improve, the Current System," *Congressional Digest* (January 2001): 12; James R. Stoner, Jr., "Federalism, the States, and the Electoral College," in Gary L. Gregg, ed., *Securing Democracy: Why We Have an Electoral College* (Wilmington, DE: ISI Books, 2001), 52; Paul A. Rahe, "Moderating the Political Impulse," in Gregg, ed., *Securing Democracy,* 68; Michael M. Uhlman, "Creating Constitutional Majorities: The Electoral College after 2000," in Gregg, ed., *Securing Democracy,* 105–106.

require protection, and (3) that interests in states with smaller populations both require and deserve special protection from federal laws.

State Interests

The view that the electoral college protects state interests is based, first, on the assumption that states embody coherent, unified interests and communities. However, they do not. Even the smallest state has substantial diversity within it. There is not just one point of view within a state. That is why Alaska may have a Democratic governor and Republican senators, why "conservative" states like Montana and North and South Dakota can vote for Republican presidential candidates and then send liberal Democrats to the U.S. Senate. As historian Jack Rakove put it, "States have no interest, as states, in the election of the president; only citizens do." He adds:

> The winner-take-all rule might make sense if states really embodied coherent, unified interests and communities, but of course they do not. What does Chicago share with Galena, except that they both are in Illinois; Palo Alto with Lodi in California; Northern Virginia with Madison's home in Orange County; or Hamilton, N.Y., with Alexander Hamilton's old haunts in lower Manhattan?[7]

Madison, recognizing the diversity within states, was opposed to aggregating the presidential vote by state (as in the unit rule) and hoped that, at the least, votes could be counted by districts within states. Disaggregating the vote and allowing districts within different states to support the same candidate would help encourage cohesiveness within the country and counter the centrifugal tendencies of regionalism.[8] Moreover, Madison did not want candidates to make appeals to special interests. As he proclaimed at the Constitutional Convention, "Local considerations must give way to the general interest [even on slavery]. As an individual from the S[outhern] States, he was willing to make the sacrifice."[9]

Judith Best, perhaps the most diligent defender of the electoral college, recognizes the heterogeneity within states but nevertheless argues that citizens within states share a common interest—the managing of the resources of a community—that includes roads, parks, schools, local taxes, and the like. True enough. She also argues that these interests are as or more important than the

---

7. Jack Rakove, "The Accidental Electors," *New York Times,* December 19, 2000, A35.

8. James Madison to George Hay, August 23, 1823. Gaillard Hunt, ed., *The Writings of James Madison,* Vol. 9 (New York: G. P. Putnam's Sons, 1900–1910), 47–55.

9. Max Farrand, ed., *The Records of the Federal Convention of 1787,* rev. ed., Vol. II (New Haven, CT: Yale University Press, 1966), 111.

characteristics they share with people in other states, like race, gender, religion, and ethnicity.[10] Many women, blacks, Hispanics, farmers, and members of other groups will be surprised to hear that the local roads and parks are more important to their lives than their fundamental position in the economic and social structure of the country.

Equally important, Best makes a series of either logically or empirically incorrect statements about the relation between community interests and the election of the president. First, she confuses local communities with states. Her examples are largely local, not state, issues, and there is a wide variance in the policies of local governments within states. Second, she argues that the president must be responsive to state interests to win and that candidates must "build [the] broadest possible coalitions of local interests" to win.[11] Simply no evidence exists to support such assertions, and Best provides none whatsoever. We have already seen that "state interest" is a dubious concept. Best cannot offer a single example of such an interest.

Do presidents focus on local interests in building their electoral coalitions? They do not. As I will show, candidates ignore most of the country in their campaigns, and they do not focus on local interests where they do campaign. Similarly, nowhere in the vast literature on voting in presidential elections has anyone found that voters choose candidates on the basis of their stands on state and local issues. Indeed, candidates avoid such issues because they do not want to be seen in the rest of the country as pandering to special interests. In addition, once elected, the president has little to do with the issues that Best raises as examples of the shared interests of members of communities. There is no reason, and certainly no imperative, to campaign on these issues.

The Need for Protection

As every student of American politics knows, the Constitution places many constraints on the acts a simple majority can make. Minorities have fundamental rights to organize, communicate, and participate in the political process. The Senate greatly overrepresents small states, and the extraconstitutional filibuster is a powerful tool for thwarting majorities in the upper chamber. Moreover, simple majorities cannot overcome minority opposition by changing the Constitution.

The system thus already contains many powerful checks on simple majorities. Do some minority rights or interests require additional protection from national majorities? If so, are these minorities concentrated in certain geographic areas? (Because it allocates electoral votes on the basis of geography,

---

10. Best, *Choice of the People,* 37.

11. Best, *Choice of the People,* 35.

the electoral college only protects geographically concentrated interests.) Is there a justification for interests in certain geographical locations—small states—to receive additional protections (in the form of extra representation in the electoral system), and more than those of citizens in other states?[12]

Two of the most important authors of the Constitution, James Wilson and James Madison, understood well the diversity of state interests and the protections of minorities embodied in the Constitution. They saw little need to confer additional power to small states through the electoral college. "Can we forget for whom we are forming a government?" Wilson asked. "Is it for *men*, or for the imaginary beings called *States*?"[13] Madison was equally dubious, proclaiming that experience had shown no danger of state interests being harmed[14] and that "the President is to act for the *people* not for *States*."[15]

Congress is designed to be responsive to constituency interests. The president, as Madison points out, is to take a broader view. When advocates of the electoral college express concern that direct election of the president would suppress local interests in favor of the broader national interest,[16] or declare approvingly that the electoral college will force George W. Bush to placate the interests of states he carried narrowly in 2000,[17] they are supporting a presidency responsive to parochial interests in a system that is already prone to gridlock and that offers minority interests extraordinary access to policymakers and opportunities to thwart policies they oppose.

It is illuminating that supporters of the electoral college virtually never specify geographically concentrated rights or interests in need of special protection through the electoral system. They certainly have not developed a general principle to justify additional protections for certain interests. Nevertheless, we can do our own analysis of the distribution of interests in the United States.

The Interests of Small States

Do states with small populations, those that receive special consideration in the electoral college, have common interests to protect? In the Constitutional Convention, Madison pointed out that it was not necessary to protect small

---

12. See Robert A. Dahl, *How Democratic Is the American Constitution?* (New Haven, CT: Yale University Press, 2001), 50–53, 84.

13. Max Farrand, ed., *The Records of the Federal Convention of 1787,* rev. ed., Vol. I (New Haven, CT: Yale University Press, 1966), 483.

14. Farrand, ed., *Records of the Federal Convention of 1787,* Vol. I, 447–449.

15. Farrand, ed., *Records of the Federal Convention of 1787,* Vol. II, 403.

16. James R. Stoner, Jr., "Federalism, the States, and the Electoral College," 52. Stoner, somewhat contradictorily, also agrees that campaigns for national office ought to focus on national issues and feature candidates of national stature.

17 Uhlman, "Creating Constitutional Majorities," 109.

states from large ones because the large ones—Virginia, Massachusetts, and Pennsylvania—were divided by economic interests, religion, and other circumstances. Their size was not a common interest. Indeed, rivalry was more likely than coalition.[18] States were thus not divided into different interests by their size but by other circumstances. Madison was prescient. The great battles of American history—in Congress or in presidential elections—have been over ideology and economic interests, not on a basis of small states against large states.

A brief look at the 17 states with the fewest electoral votes (three, four, or five) shows that this group is quite diverse.[19] Maine, Vermont, New Hampshire, and Rhode Island are in New England; Delaware and West Virginia are in the Middle Atlantic region; North and South Dakota, Montana, and Nebraska are in the Great Plains; New Mexico is in the Southwest; and Nevada, Wyoming, Utah, and Idaho are in the Rocky Mountain region. Alaska and Hawaii are in their own, very different regions.

Some of these states have high average levels of income and education, whereas others have considerably lower levels. Some of the states are quite liberal and others are very conservative, and their policies and levels of taxation reflect these differences. Several of these states and Washington, DC, are primarily urban, whereas many others are rural. They represent a great diversity of core economic interests, including agriculture, mining, gambling, chemicals, tourism, and energy. Even the agricultural interests are quite diverse, ranging from grain and dairy products to hogs and sheep. In sum, small states do not share common interests. It is not surprising that their representatives do not vote as a bloc in Congress and that their citizens do not vote as a bloc for president.

Even if small states share little in common, are there some interests that occur only in states with small populations? Not many. The first interest that may come to mind is agriculture, with visions of rural farmers in small states. But most farmers live in states with large populations, such as California, Texas, Florida, and Illinois. Low-population states on the Great Plains may have a larger percentage of their population working in agriculture, but there are actually more farmers in states with large populations. The market value of the agricultural production of California, Texas, Florida, and Illinois exceeds that of all 17 of the smallest states combined.[20]

---

18. Farrand, ed., *Records of the Federal Convention of 1787,* Vol. I, 447–449.

19. I have omitted Washington, DC, from this analysis because it is limited to the number of electoral votes of the least populous state and is not over-represented in the electoral college.

20. U.S. Bureau of the Census, *1997 Census of Agriculture,* Vol. 1, chap. 2, Table 1. (This census occurs every five years.)

Agriculture is a widespread enterprise in the United States and does not lack for champions. In addition, it is Congress that has taken the lead in providing benefits, principally in the form of subsidies, for agriculture. Rather than competing to give farmers more benefits, presidents of both parties have attempted to restrain congressional spending on agriculture. The electoral college has not turned presidents into champions of rural America.

It is difficult to identify interests that are centered in a few small states. Even if we could, however, the question remains whether these few interests out of the literally thousands of economic interests in the United States deserve special protection. I know of no principle that would support such a view. Why should those who produce wheat and hogs have more say in electing the president than those who produce vegetables, citrus, and beef? Is not the disproportionate Senate representation of states in which wheat and hogs are produced enough to protect these interests? There is simply no evidence that interests like these deserve or require additional protection from the electoral system.

THE INTERESTS OF AFRICAN AMERICANS AND OTHER MINORITIES

An argument on behalf of the electoral college that arose in the 1960s, and is still articulated today, is that it gives an advantage to African Americans.[21] The reasoning is that minorities are concentrated in large, politically competitive states and thus could determine which candidate wins those states and perhaps the election. As a result of their power, minorities could force candidates to bargain for their votes by promising to advance their interests.

This argument is actually built on a tower of faulty premises. First, African Americans are not concentrated in large states. The greatest concentration of blacks, for example, is in the Deep South states of Louisiana, Mississippi, Alabama, Georgia, South Carolina, North Carolina, and Virginia, where they compose from 20 to 37 percent of the population.

---

21. See, for example, Best, *Choice of the People,* 24; Judith A. Best, "Should the Current Electoral College System Be Preserved," *Congressional Digest* (January 2001): 22; Rahe, "Moderating the Political Impulse," 63; Alexander M. Bickel, "Wait a Minute!", *New Republic* (May 10, 1969): 11–13; "Prepared Statement of Curtis Gans on Behalf of Americans for Democratic Action," *The Electoral College and Direct Election: Hearings before the Subcommittee on the Constitution of the Committee on the Judiciary, Supplement, United States Senate,* July 20, 22, 28, and August 2, 1977, 95th Congress, 1st session, 398; Wallace S. Sayre and Judith H. Parris, *Voting for President: The Electoral College and the American Political System* (Washington, DC: Brookings Institution, 1970), 72–73.

They make up 28 percent of the population of Maryland. In contrast, blacks make up only 7 percent of Californians, 12 percent of Texans, 18 percent of New Yorkers, 16 percent of those living in Florida, 15 percent in Illinois, and 10 percent of Pennsylvanians.[22] It is also the case that African Americans are not concentrated in small states that benefit from the allocation of a minimum of three votes for each state.[23]

Second, the large states are not necessarily competitive ones. In the elections of 2000 and 2004, for example, the three largest states—California, Texas, and New York—were not competitive in the presidential election and, as I show later in this chapter, the candidates largely ignored them. There was not much chance for bargaining for policies favorable to minorities.

The electoral college provides no more advantage for blacks in the southern states, where they compose substantial percentages of the population. Almost all African Americans in these states vote for Democratic presidential candidates, but in a competitive election nationally, these states are likely to go Republican. The electoral college thus prevents the votes of blacks in these states from contributing to the national totals of the Democratic candidate.

Third, African Americans are not "swing" voters. They are the most loyal component of the Democratic electoral coalition. How would any leader persuade blacks (or any other group) to break radically from their traditional political loyalties and shift their votes rapidly to another candidate? It is not a sensible proposition.

Few politicians miss the point, and few Republican presidential candidates under the electoral college have been willing to compete aggressively for African American votes. For example, what did Nixon, Ford, or Reagan offer? Republicans often attempt to inject race into presidential politics[24] but not to appeal for black votes. From opposition to the Civil Rights Act in 1964 to the Willie Horton ads in 1992, some campaigns have employed code words and careful manipulation of racial imagery to appeal to racially conservative white voters. The shift of southern conservative whites from the Republican to the Democratic party is partially the result of such appeals and also encourages their persistence.

---

22. U. S. Bureau of the Census, *Statistical Abstract of the United States* (Washington, DC: US Government Printing Office, 2003), 25.

23. Robert L. Lineberry, Darren Davis, Robert Erikson, Richard Herrera, and Priscilla Southwell, "The Electoral College and Social Cleavages: Ethnicity, Class, and Geography," in Paul D. Schumaker and Burdett A. Loomis, eds., *Choosing a President* (New York: Chatham House, 2002), 168–169.

24. Edward G. Carmines and Robert Huckfeldt, "Party Politics in the Wake of the Voting Rights Act," in Bernard Grofman and Chandler Davidson, eds., *Controversies in Minority Voting: The Voting Rights Act in Perspective* (Washington, DC: Brookings Institution, 1992), 120–125.

Blacks are not in a position to swing either large states or medium-sized states to the candidate who offers them the most favorable policies. It is difficult to bargain when only one side is making offers. It is equally difficult to receive credit from winning candidates for being the decisive element in a successful coalition. Not only have African Americans been in few winning coalitions for president in the past four decades (there have been only three Democratic victories since 1964), but it is also difficult to determine the "decisive" element in any election.

In reality, neither party invests much time in appealing directly for black votes. Later in this chapter I analyze speeches of the presidential candidates in the 2000 election. The only speeches among this large group that focused on black interests were the addresses of both George W. Bush and Al Gore to the annual convention in July of the National Association for the Advancement of Colored People. Democratic candidates have to walk a fine line between preserving the bloc of black votes without alienating white voters. To demonstrate his independence of black interests in 1992, Bill Clinton made a point of publicly criticizing Sister Souljah, a black rap singer, at a meeting of Jesse Jackson's Rainbow Coalition shortly before the Democratic convention.

The electoral college thus *discourages* attention to the interests of African Americans because they are unlikely to shift the outcome in a state as a whole.[25] The winner-take-all system ensures that blacks have little or no voice in presidential elections in the South.[26] This lack of attention to African American interests as a result of the electoral college is nothing new. Research has found a positive and significant relationship between a state's competitiveness and voting rights enforcement activity in the late 19th century.[27]

Under direct election of the president in which all votes are valuable, black voters in the South and in the urban Northeast, for example, could coalesce their votes and become an effective national bloc. The votes of southern blacks, in particular, might for the first time be important in determining the election outcome. One reason that Judith Best, perhaps the best-known advocate of the electoral college, supports the status quo is precisely

25. See Larry M. Bartels, "Where the Ducks Are: Voting Power in a Party System," in John G. Geer, ed., *Politicians and Party Politics* (Baltimore, MD: Johns Hopkins University Press, 1998), 53, 57, 59, 63–68, on the lack of centrality of black voters.

26. For an argument that the electoral college seriously dilutes the votes of minorities, see Matthew M. Hoffman, "The Illegitimate President: Minority Vote Dilution and the Electoral College," *Yale Law Journal* 105, no. 4 (1996): 935–1021.

27. James and Lawson, "The Political Economy of Voting Rights Enforcement in America's Gilded Age."

because it inhibits what she calls "private minorities" from uniting votes across state lines.[28]

The evidence clearly shows, then, that the argument that the electoral college aids blacks is based on false premises. Although it may be possible to construct a principled argument that members of a disadvantaged race deserve more say in the election of the president than members of other races, such an argument is unlikely to win many adherents in the 21st century. It is difficult in a democracy to give people electoral weight based on the rightness of their cause.

Hispanics are now the largest minority group in the United States. Although they lack the history of discrimination that blacks have endured, they do represent something of an economic underclass. Hispanics are concentrated in few states and compose 34 percent of the population of Texas and California, 16 percent of New Yorkers, and 18 percent of Floridians. They also make up large percentages of smaller states like Arizona, New Mexico, Nevada, and Colorado.[29] Does the electoral college provide them special protections that they would lose in a system of direct election of the president?

Because Hispanics represent 13 percent of the population of the whole country, because they are a rapidly growing segment of the public, and because they less uniformly support one party than African Americans do, it is difficult to imagine a political party ignoring them. Certainly the Republican party has made great efforts to appeal to them in recent years. California, Texas, and New York are not reliably swing states, as we have seen. There seems little need to jerry-rig an electoral system to accord special protection to the interests of Hispanics.

Florida certainly has been a swing state, but only a particular subgroup of Hispanics—Cubans—has benefited, extracting promises from some presidential candidates of a stiff embargo on Cuba and loose interpretations of immigration rules for those escaping the island.

The electoral college provides the potential for *any* cohesive special interest concentrated in a large competitive state to exercise disproportionate power. Wall Street workers in New York, movie industry employees in California, and those earning a living in the energy business in Texas could, in theory, swing their states to one candidate or the other. Do we really want a system of electing the president that provides such potential to special interests? Should Cuban Americans set our foreign policy toward Cuba? Disproportionate power to any group is difficult to reconcile with political equality. Once again we can recall Madison's advice to subordinate local interests to the general interest.[30]

---

28. Best, *Choice of the People*, 36.

29. Bureau of the Census, *Statistical Abstract of the United States*, 26.

30. Farrand, ed., *Records of the Federal Convention of 1787*, Vol. II, 111.

ATTENTION TO STATE INTERESTS

As we have seen, a core justification for the electoral college and its violations of political equality is that allocating electoral votes by states forces candidates to pay attention to state-based interests in general and to the interests of small states in particular. In their enthusiasm for the electoral college, some advocates go further and claim that under the electoral college, "all states are 'battlegrounds'" in the presidential election[31] and that candidates "rarely" write off regions in the presidential campaign.[32]

Although defenders of the electoral college almost never specify just what interests the electoral college is protecting, they nevertheless argue that candidates would ignore these interests if the president were elected in a direct popular election. This argument is based on the premise, among others, that candidates do appeal directly to state interests and give disproportionate attention to small states.

Do presidential candidates in fact focus on state-level interests in their campaigns? Do they devote a larger percentage of their campaign efforts to small states than they would if there were direct election of the president? To answer these questions, I examine the speeches, campaign visits, and advertising of presidential candidates to see what candidates actually do and whether there is evidence that the electoral college forces candidates to be more attentive to small states. If candidates are not more oriented to small states and the interests within them than we would expect in a system of direct election, then we have reason to reject one of the principal justifications for the electoral college's violation of political equality.

Candidate Speeches

A prominent means by which a candidate can attend to the interests in a state is by addressing them in speeches to that state's voters. What do candidates actually say when they campaign in the various states? The presidential election of 2000 provides an excellent test of the hypothesis that the electoral college forces candidates to focus on state-based interests. Because the outcome in every single state was crucial to an electoral college victory in this extraordinarily close election, each candidate had the maximum incentive to appeal to state interests.

A team of researchers led by Shanto Iyengar at the Political Communications Lab at Stanford University compiled, read, and classified by broad topics the public speeches delivered by George W. Bush and Al Gore from June 1 until October 7, 2000. This period covers the bulk of the 2000 presidential

---

31. Uhlman, "Creating Constitutional Majorities," 106.

32. Rahe, "Moderating the Political Impulse," 63.

Table 2–1 Focus of Candidate Speeches, 2000

Focus of Speech State	AL GORE		GEORGE W. BUSH	
	Number of Speeches	Percentage of Speeches	Number of Speeches	Percentage of Speeches
Small state	1	2	0	0
Large state	1	2	7	18
National	49	96	33	82

SOURCE: *In Their Own Words: Sourcebook for the 2000 Presidential Election* © 2000 by The Board of Trustees of Leland Stanford Junior University and http://pcl.stanford.edu/

election. In some instances, the Stanford researchers coded two or three topics for the same speech.[33]

The candidates provided the speeches to Iyengar and his colleagues. The speeches do not necessarily represent a statistical sample, but they represent a much larger percentage of the total speeches than would a sample. Most importantly, they give us the best view of what candidates actually say on the stump.

My research assistants and I then coded the speeches by such issue areas as the economy, crime, and the environment to allow for finer delineations of the subject matter. We further coded each speech as focused on interests concentrated in an individual state or on a national constituency. For example, we coded a speech on salmon conservation as aimed at a local rather than a national constituency. Because we wanted to bias our results *against* a national focus, we were generous in our attributions of focus on state interests. Thus, when the candidates spoke about Social Security or Medicare prescription drug benefits in Florida, we coded the speech as aimed at an interest concentrated in a state—even though there is clearly a national constituency for Social Security, health care, and related issues of special interests to seniors.

The results are instructive (Table 2–1). Only 2 of the 51 speeches by Al Gore focused on interests concentrated in a state. One was in Tallahassee, Florida, and discussed a prescription drug plan for senior citizens. The other speech, and the only one in a small state (Iowa), discussed reform of the estate tax. Gore also gave a speech in Tennessee that focused on his upbringing there. He did not discuss issues, however, and made no appeal to interests concentrated in that state. Similarly, in a speech in Arkansas he focused on the importance of that state to the election outcome but did not address Arkansas-specific issues.

33. The results were published by Stanford University in a CD entitled *In Their Own Words: Sourcebook for the 2000 Presidential Election*. Five additional speeches obtained after the CD was made can be found at http://pcl.stanford.edu. The Stanford team edited out remarks at the beginning of some speeches, generally those thanking the organizers of the event.

George W. Bush delivered no speeches focused on the special interests of small states during this period. The closest he came was a speech in Monroe, Washington, on September 13, dealing with salmon recovery and environmental protection. Washington had 11 electoral votes in 2000, more than all but 14 states.

The other six state-oriented speeches Bush delivered were in Florida and focused on Social Security, health care for seniors, and cooperation and trade with Latin America. Florida is the fourth largest state, hardly one requiring special protection by the electoral college. In addition, it is highly likely that a candidate would address Social Security and health care for seniors under any mechanism for electing the president. These issues are simply too important to ignore, especially given the graying of the entire nation's population. Florida simply provided a symbolically useful venue for Bush's speeches.

Was the presidential election of 2000 unique in the focus of the candidates' speeches? Apparently not. The Annenberg School for Communication and the Annenberg Public Policy Center of the University of Pennsylvania collected transcripts of 102 speeches given by Bill Clinton and 71 speeches given by Robert Dole during the period of September 1 until election day in 1996.[34] Only two of Clinton's speeches and none of Dole's focused on issues that could be viewed as being of primarily local interest. On October 14, Clinton made a 600-word speech on firefighting to firefighters in New Mexico, emphasizing the importance of the issue to the West. This was in effect a brief bill-signing ceremony. The next day he made a 445-word speech that was almost completely symbolic to Native Americans in the same state. These two speeches together probably lasted about five minutes.

Whether or not advocates of the electoral college choose to recognize it, there are actually few interests concentrated within particular states. In addition, whatever state interests there may be, the candidates do not focus on them. They certainly do not devote attention to interests concentrated in small states. In other words, the fundamental justification of the electoral college—that it forces candidates to be attentive to particular state interests, especially those concentrated in small states—is based on a faulty premise.

Contributing to the lack of candidate pandering to state interests is the fact that they largely ignore many of the states.

Candidate Visits

The most direct means of appealing to voters is for candidates to visit their states and address them directly. Modern transportation has made it relatively easy for candidates to crisscross the nation in search of votes. Proponents of

---

34. *Annenberg/Pew Archive of Presidential Campaign Discourse* (CD-ROM) 2000.

the electoral college argue that one of its principal advantages is that it forces candidates to pay attention to small states that would otherwise be lost in a national electorate and to build a broad national coalition by appealing to voters in every region.

I have tabulated the visits of presidential and vice presidential candidates to each state during the presidential elections of 2000 and 2004 (Tables 2–2 and 2–3). In 2000, only one of the seven states with only three electoral votes had a visit from a presidential candidate in this election (a single visit to Delaware). (I have not included Washington, DC, the home of Al Gore, in any totals.)

Six states had four electoral votes, and they received a total of seven visits from presidential candidates of both parties—including vacation visits by George W. Bush to Maine. Four more states had five electoral votes, and two of them had no visits from presidential candidates. New Mexico and West Virginia, highly competitive states, were the exceptions. In sum, presidential candidates did not visit 11 of the 17 smallest states at all. One candidate only paid a visit to two other states.

Among the 11 states with 6, 7, or 8 electoral votes, Arkansas, Iowa, Oregon, and Kentucky were highly competitive, and presidential candidates paid them multiple visits. The candidates visited only one of the other seven states with 6, 7, or 8 electoral votes, however—a single visit to Arizona. Thus, 17 of the 28 smallest states had no visits from presidential candidates. Three others had a single visit from the candidate of only one party.

Vice presidential candidate visits tell a similar story. In 2000, these candidates visited the 10 smallest states a total of only 4 times. Eight of the 17 smallest states did not receive a visit from a single presidential or vice presidential candidate of either party.

In the 2004 general election, no presidential candidate visited any of the seven states with only three electoral votes, and the only visit from a vice-presidential candidate was that of Dick Cheney to his home state of Wyoming. Presidential candidates did not visit 12 of the 17 smallest states, and vice presidential candidates also did not visit 10 of these states.

Candidates also ignored the three states with six electoral votes except for a single vice-presidential candidate visit to Arkansas. Indeed, presidential candidates appeared at campaign events in only 9 of the 29 smallest states during the entire general election. In two of the nine states, only one candidate visited, making a single visit in each case. The presidential candidates also avoided 8 of the 15 states with 10–15 electoral votes.

On the other hand, the candidates lavished attention on the 13 competitive states of New Hampshire, West Virginia, New Mexico, Nevada, Iowa, Colorado, Minnesota, Wisconsin, Missouri, Michigan, Ohio, Pennsylvania, and Florida.

Table 2–2 Visits to States by Candidates in 2000 Presidential General Election*

State	Electoral Votes (2000)	CANDIDATE VISITS		Total Visits
		Presidential Candidates	Vice-Presidential Candidates	
Wyoming	3	0	1	1
Alaska	3	0	0	0
Vermont	3	0	3	3
Dist. of Columbia	3	5[1]	9	14
North Dakota	3	0	0	0
Delaware	3	1	1	2
South Dakota	3	0	0	0
Montana	3	0	0	0
Rhode Island	4	0	0	0
Idaho	4	0	2	2
Hawaii	4	0	0	0
New Hampshire	4	3	4	7
Nevada	4	1	4	5
Maine	4	3[2]	5	8
New Mexico	5	8	7	15
Nebraska	5	0	0	0
Utah	5	0	0	0
West Virginia	5	3	2	5
Arkansas	6	5	8	13
Kansas	6	0	0	0
Mississippi	7	0	1	1
Iowa	7	19	7	26
Oregon	7	7	8	15
Oklahoma	8	0	0	0
Connecticut	8	0	8[3]	8
Colorado	8	0	2	2
South Carolina	8	0	0	0
Arizona	8	1	0	1
Kentucky	8	3	9	12
Alabama	9	1	0	1
Louisiana	9	7	3	10
Minnesota	10	2	7	9
Maryland	10	3	1	4
Washington	11	9	9	18
Tennessee	11	14	10	24
Wisconsin	11	18	18	36
Missouri	11	17	14	31

(Continued)

Table 2–2 (*Continued*)

| | | CANDIDATE VISITS | | |
State	Electoral Votes (2000)	Presidential Candidates	Vice-Presidential Candidates	Total Visits
Indiana	12	2	2	4
Massachusetts	12	6	0	6
Virginia	13	0	0	0
Georgia	13	1	1	2
North Carolina	14	5	1	6
New Jersey	15	2	7	9
Michigan	18	31	12	43
Ohio	21	14	19	33
Illinois	22	20	16	36
Pennsylvania	23	22	20	42
Florida	25	26	35	61
Texas	32	3[4]	7	10
New York	33	7	9	16
California	54	31	13	44

*Beginning immediately after each party's national convention. Visits for the Bush–Cheney ticket cover August 4–November 6. Gore–Lieberman visits cover August 18–November 6.

Notes

1. The presidential candidate visits are for Al Gore, who lived in Washington.

2. Includes vacation time for George W. Bush.

3. Home of vice presidential candidate Joe Lieberman.

4. The presidential candidate visits are for George W. Bush, who lived in Texas.

SOURCE: Daron Shaw, "A Simple Game: Uncovering Campaign Effects in the 2000 Presidential Election" (manuscript, University of Texas at Austin, July 2003).

In addition to its failure to encourage candidate visits to small states, the electoral college also provides incentives to ignore many larger states. For example, in 2004, the total campaign visits to the highly populated states of California, Texas, New York, and Illinois for both presidential and vice-presidential candidates was two. This total includes a home-state rally for George Bush in Texas on the last night of the campaign.

It is clear that, contrary to the arguments of its proponents, the electoral college does *not* provide an incentive for candidates to be attentive to small states and take their cases directly to their citizens. Indeed, it is difficult to imagine how presidential candidates could be *less* attentive to small states.

What actually happens is that the electoral college distorts the political process by providing an incentive to visit *competitive* states, especially large competitive states. Thus, in 2004 the citizens of New Mexico and Iowa, with a total of 12 electoral votes, received as many visits as the other 30 of

Table 2–3 Visits to States by Candidates in 2004 Presidential General Election*

State	Electoral Votes (2004)	CANDIDATE VISITS		Total Visits
		Presidential Candidates	Vice-Presidential Candidates	
Wyoming	3	0	1	1
Dist. of Columbia	3	1	1	2
Vermont	3	0	0	0
Alaska	3	0	0	0
North Dakota	3	0	0	0
South Dakota	3	0	0	0
Delaware	3	0	0	0
Montana	3	0	0	0
Rhode Island	4	0	0	0
Hawaii	4	0	1	1
New Hampshire	4	7	4	11
Maine	4	1	3	4
Idaho	4	0	0	0
Nebraska	5	0	0	0
West Virginia	5	5	7	12
New Mexico	5	8	5	13
Nevada	5	5	5	10
Utah	5	0	0	0
Arkansas	6	0	1	1
Kansas	6	0	0	0
Mississippi	6	0	0	0
Iowa	7	19	23	42
Connecticut	7	0	0	0
Oregon	7	1	10	11
Oklahoma	7	0	0	0
South Carolina	8	0	1	1
Kentucky	8	0	1	1
Colorado	9	9	4	13
Alabama	9	0	0	0
Louisiana	9	0	0	0
Minnesota	10	9	11	20
Arizona	10	0	1	1
Maryland	10	0	0	0
Wisconsin	10	28	19	47
Missouri	11	7	3	10
Tennessee	11	0	0	0

(*Continued*)

Table 2–3 (*Continued*)

| State | Electoral Votes (2004) | CANDIDATE VISITS | | Total Visits |
		Presidential Candidates	Vice-Presidential Candidates	
Washington	11	0	0	0
Indiana	11	0	0	0
Massachusetts	12	0	0	0
Virginia	13	0	0	0
North Carolina	15	2	2	4
Georgia	15	0	0	0
New Jersey	15	1	3	4
Michigan	17	11	15	26
Ohio	20	40	33	73
Pennsylvania	21	22	14	36
Illinois	21	0	0	0
Florida	27	38	36	74
New York	31	1	0	1
Texas	34	1	0	1
California	55	0	0	0

*September 3-November 2, 2004.

the smallest 32 states in the union combined! They also received more visits than California, Texas, New York, Illinois, Michigan, and New Jersey combined.

Moreover, the candidates do not take their campaigns to voters of every region of the country. After carefully studying candidate visits in the 2000 presidential election, Michael Hagen, Richard Johnston, and Kathleen Hall Jamieson concluded that "the candidates made little effort to appear before the residents of the Great Plains, the Rockies, the Southwest (with the exception of New Mexico), and the Deep South." The candidates ignored even the big cities in these regions, among them Atlanta, Phoenix, Denver, Charlotte, Salt Lake City, and Birmingham.[35] The pattern was similar in 2004.

In the presidential election of 2000, one of the most competitive elections in history, the electoral college distorted the political system by providing incentives for candidates to campaign actively in only 17 "battleground" states and largely to ignore the other 33 states and Washington, DC. With few exceptions,

35. Hagen, Johnston, and Jamieson, "Effects of the 2000 Presidential Campaign," 3.

small states were not included among the battleground states. Indeed, the *National Journal* reported there were no presidential candidate visits at all to 14 states, all with 8 or fewer electoral votes, over the more than seven months from April 1 through November 7, 2000.[36] In 2004, the candidates actively campaigned in even fewer states in the general election.

Were 2000 and 2004 simply deviant elections? Relying on the Annenberg collection of presidential speeches discussed earlier, we find that in 1996, Bill Clinton visited only 5 of the 17 smallest states. In all, he did not visit 19 of the 50 states. Bob Dole visited only 3 of the 17 smallest states—and also ignored those with 6 or 7 electoral votes. In all, he visited only 21 of the 50 states.[37]

The most competitive election preceding 2000 was that of 1976, when President Gerald Ford faced Democratic challenger Jimmy Carter. Elsewhere, I have tabulated the number of candidate campaign stops for each state and the number of electoral votes those states had in that election.[38] The results are much like those in Table 2–2. The candidates ignored many states, especially small states. President Gerald Ford, locked in an extremely tight race with Jimmy Carter, visited only 4 of the 25 smallest states between September 15 and October 31. He visited none of the 19 smallest states during that period. Competitive states received the lion's share of candidate visits. All four candidates made a combined total of only 25 campaign stops in the 15 smallest states (those with 3 or 4 electoral votes). They made more campaign stops in *each* of the large states of Ohio (38), Illinois (37), Pennsylvania (27), New York (42), and California (43) than in the smallest 15 states put together. The candidates made another 35 campaign stops in Florida and Texas. Small and mid-size states that were exceptions to the general trend of campaign stops were either the homes of one of the candidates (Kansas, Minnesota, and Georgia) or highly competitive, such as New Mexico, Oregon, Iowa, and Missouri.[39]

Candidates' emphasis on campaigning in competitive states is not unusual. Daron Shaw identified similar patterns in the elections of 1988, 1992, and 1996.[40] Stanley Kelley found that in 1960, John F. Kennedy and Richard Nixon spent 74 percent of their campaign time in 24 competitive states.[41]

---

36. "How Would They Campaign?" *National Journal* (November 18, 2000): 3653.

37. *Annenberg/Pew Archive of Presidential Campaign Discourse.*

38. Edwards, *Why the Electoral College is Bad for America,* 108–109.

39. See also Larry M. Bartels, "Resource Allocation in a Presidential Campaign," *Journal of Politics* 47 (August 1985): 928–936.

40. Daron R. Shaw, "The Effect of TV Ads and Candidate Appearances on Statewide Presidential Votes, 1988–96," *American Political Science Review* 93 (June 1999): 359–360.

41. Stanley Kelley, Jr., "The Presidential Campaign," in Paul T. David, ed., *The Presidential Election and Transition 1960–1961* (Washington, DC: Brookings Institution, 1961), 70–72.

When we examine where candidates actually campaign in person, we thus can see that the premises that the electoral college forces candidates to take their cases to small states and to build coalitions in person from all regions of the country are simply false.[42] Candidates are not fools. They go where the electoral college makes them go, and it makes them go to competitive states, especially large competitive states. They ignore most small states; in fact, they ignore most of the country.

Candidate Advertising

Candidates most typically reach voters through television advertising. Technology makes it easy to place advertisements in any media market in the nation at short notice. Do candidates operating under the electoral college system compensate for their lack of visits by advertising in small or noncompetitive states?

In the hotly contested presidential election of 2000, advertising expenditures in each state closely resembled the number of candidate appearances in that state. Some voters were bombarded with television advertising; others saw none at all. Hagen, Johnston, and Jamieson found that Americans living west of Kansas City and east of Las Vegas, with the exception of those living in New Mexico, saw virtually no presidential campaign advertising, and Americans from Natchez to Richmond saw very little. The states receiving the most advertising were the large, competitive states of Florida, Pennsylvania, Michigan, and Ohio.[43]

I have tabulated data showing the large media markets and states in which the two major-party campaigns ran no or only a few ads during the general election period (beginning on August 17, 2000, the day after the Democratic National Convention).[44] The candidates and their parties ran no ads at all in 25

---

42. For work on elections before 1976, see Steven J. Brams and Morton D. Davis, "The 3/2's Rule in Presidential Campaigning," *American Political Science Review* 68 (March 1974): 113–134; Claude S. Colantoni, Terrence J. Levasque, and Peter C. Ordeshook, "Campaign Resource Allocation under the Electoral College," *American Political Science Review* 69 (March 1975): 141–154; Steven J. Brams and Morton D. Davis, "Comment on 'Campaign Resource Allocations under the Electoral College,'" *American Political Science Review* 69 (March 1975): 155–156.

43. Hagen, Johnston, and Jamieson, "Effects of the 2000 Presidential Campaign," pp. 1, 3–4.

44. The data were obtained from a joint project of the Brennan Center for Justice at New York University School of Law and Professor Kenneth Goldstein of the University of Wisconsin–Madison, and includes media tracking data from the Campaign Media Analysis Group in Washington, DC. The Brennan Center–Wisconsin project was sponsored by a grant from The Pew Charitable Trusts. The opinions expressed in this book article are those of the author and do not necessarily reflect the views of the Brennan Center, Professor Goldstein, or The Pew Charitable Trusts.

of the 75 largest media markets in the country (Table 2–4). In another 10, their advertising campaigns were purely symbolic, sometimes numbering in the single digits. (An ad counts as one if it is run one time. To provide perspective on the small number of ads in these 10 states, it is useful to note that the candidates ran 28,635 ads in Florida, 28,099 in Ohio, 24,282 in Michigan, 16,740 in Wisconsin, and 14,838 in West Virginia.)

The candidates thus ignored 35—nearly half—of the 75 largest media markets in the nation in their advertising in a hotly contested campaign! In doing so, they bypassed such major American cities as Phoenix, Denver, Indianapolis, Washington, Baltimore, New York City, Charlotte, Houston, and Dallas/Ft. Worth. The Gore campaign also bypassed Los Angeles, San Francisco, and San Diego.

In some states, the campaigns ran few or no ads (Table 2–4, third column). In most instances we can interpret these in a straightforward manner. However, some media markets cross state boundaries, and ads placed in a market centered in one state may spill over into the living rooms of citizens of another state. Iowa ads, for example, spilled over to Nebraska, South Dakota, and Illinois; Missouri ads spilled over into Kansas, Oklahoma, Illinois, Kentucky, and Tennessee.

Usually the spillover reached only a small percentage of the population. But there are some examples of citizens of a state having access to ads even though none were placed in a media market in that state. In New Jersey, which is sandwiched between two large media markets, New York and Philadelphia, most residents saw no ads at all. However, about 25 percent of the population in New Jersey was saturated with them as a result of ads placed in the Philadelphia media market aimed at winning competitive Pennsylvania.

In contrast, some media markets are credited with ads actually aimed at the citizens of another state. Some media markets centered outside competitive states provided the avenues into competitive states. Ads had to be run in the Boston and Vermont markets to reach New Hampshire—even though the candidates were not actively campaigning in those states. Candidates reached the Florida panhandle through Mobile, Alabama.[45]

We must interpret the data with care on little or no media advertising. Even so, the story of advertising in the 2000 presidential election is clear. People in a large percentage of the country saw little or no advertising on behalf of the presidential candidates, as the candidates essentially ignored 26 states and the

---

45. Hagen, Johnston, and Jamieson, "Effects of the 2000 Presidential Campaign," 6.

Table 2–4 States and Large Media Markets with Few or No Ads in the 2000 Presidential General Election

State	Major Media Market with Few or No Ads	States with Few or No Ads in Any Media Market*	Campaign Not Running Ads
Alabama	Birmingham-Anniston-Tuscaloosa		Bush and Gore
Alaska		entire state	Bush and Gore
Arizona	Phoenix	entire state	Bush and Gore
Arkansas			
California	Fresno-Visalia[1]	entire state	Gore
	Los Angeles		Gore
	Sacramento-Stockton-Modesto		Gore
	San Diego		Gore
	San Francisco-Oakland-San Jose		Gore
Colorado	Denver[2]	entire state	Bush and Gore
Connecticut	Hartford-New Haven[3]	entire state	Bush and Gore
Delaware			
District of Columbia	District of Columbia	entire district	Bush and Gore
Florida			
Georgia	Atlanta[4]		
Hawaii		entire state	Bush and Gore
Idaho		entire state	Bush and Gore
Illinois			
Indiana	Indianapolis	entire state	Bush and Gore
Iowa			
Kansas	Wichita-Hutchinson	entire state	Bush and Gore
Kentucky	Lexington		Gore
Louisiana			
Maine			
Maryland	Baltimore		Bush and Gore
Massachusetts			
Michigan			
Minnesota			
Mississippi		entire state	Bush and Gore
Missouri			
Montana		entire state	Bush and Gore
Nebraska	Omaha[5]	entire state	Bush and Gore

(Continued)

Table 2–4 (Continued)

State	Major Media Market with Few or No Ads	States with Few or No Ads in Any Media Market*	Campaign Not Running Ads
Nevada			
New Hampshire			
New Jersey		entire state	Bush and Gore
New Mexico			
New York	New York City	entire state	Bush and Gore
	Rochester		Bush and Gore
	Albany-Schenectady-Troy		Bush and Gore
	Buffalo		Bush and Gore
	Syracuse		Bush and Gore
North Carolina	Charlotte[6]	entire state	Bush and Gore
	Greensboro-High Point-Winston Salem[7]		Bush and Gore
	Raleigh-Durham[8]		Bush and Gore
North Dakota		entire state	Bush and Gore
Ohio			
Oklahoma	Oklahoma City[9]	entire state	Bush and Gore
	Tulsa		Bush and Gore
Oregon			
Pennsylvania		entire state	Bush and Gore
Rhode Island	Providence-New Bedford[10]	entire state	Bush and Gore
South Carolina	Greenville-Spartanburg-Asheville-Anderson	entire state	Bush and Gore
South Dakota		entire state	Bush and Gore
Tennessee			
Texas	Austin	entire state	Bush and Gore
	Dallas-Ft. Worth		Bush and Gore
	Houston		Bush and Gore
	San Antonio		Bush and Gore
Utah	Salt Lake City	entire state	Bush and Gore
Vermont		entire state[11]	Bush and Gore
Virginia	Norfolk-Portsmouth-Newport News	entire state	Bush and Gore
	Richmond-Petersburg		Bush and Gore
	Roanoke-Lynchburg		Bush and Gore

(Continued)

Table 2–4 (*Continued*)

State	Major Media Market with Few or No Ads	States with Few or No Ads in Any Media Market*	Campaign Not Running Ads
Washington			
West Virginia			
Wisconsin			
Wyoming		entire state	Bush and Gore

*Market centered in that state.

Notes

1. 1 Gore ad
2. 8 Gore ads
3. 230 Bush ads and 82 Gore ads
4. 217 Bush ads
5. 218 Bush ads and 148 Gore ads
6. 131 Bush ads
7. 196 Bush ads
8. 191 Bush ads
9. 5 Bush ads
10. 23 Gore ads
11. A very few ads were run, aimed at New Hampshire

SOURCE: Michael Hagen, Richard Johnston, and Kathleen Hall Jamieson, "Effects of the 2000 Presidential Campaign" (paper delivered at the Annual Meeting of the American Political Science Association, August 29-September 1, 2002); Daron Shaw, "A Simple Game: Uncovering Campaign Effects in the 2000 Presidential Election" (manuscript, University of Texas at Austin, July 2003); and Kenneth Goldstein, Michael Franz, and Travis Ridout, *Political Advertising in 2000* (Combined File [dataset], Department of Political Science, University of Wisconsin-Madison and Brennan Center for Justice at New York University, 2002).

District of Columbia. Although the data on advertising in the 2004 election is not yet available, there is little question that the pattern will be similar to that in 2000. Thus, just as in the case of candidate visits, we find that the premises that the electoral college forces candidates to take their cases to small states and to build coalitions from all regions of the country are erroneous. To win candidates' attention, states must be "in play" and have a significant number of electoral votes. As a result, the electoral college encourages campaigns largely to ignore most people in the nation.

The focus of advertising on competitive states is nothing new. Hubert Humphrey, the 1968 Democratic presidential candidate, told the Senate Judiciary Committee in 1977 that campaigns are directed disproportionately at large states: "We had to ignore large sections of the country." Douglas Bailey, who headed the advertising firm that handled Gerald Ford's 1976 campaign,

added, "Those areas that you are sure to win or lose, you ignore."[46] Daron
Shaw shows similar patterns for 1988, 1992, and 1996.[47]

In sum, the electoral college not only discourages candidates from paying
attention to small states, it also distorts the presidential campaign, causing candidates to ignore most of the country. In theory, candidates make their cases
to the people and citizens then choose for whom to vote. In reality, candidates
under the electoral college do *not* take their cases to the people.

Can the Media Compensate?

It is possible that the mass media could compensate for the absence of active
presidential campaigns in most states by providing in-depth coverage of the
candidates' issue stances. Yet this is not what occurs. Viewers who watched
one network news program during the 2000 general election for president saw
an average of 4.2 minutes of coverage of the exceedingly close election campaign each evening. They heard even less from the candidates. The average
length of a presidential candidate's sound bite in 2000 was 7.8 seconds. The
television reporters who covered the presidential candidates took three-fourths
(74 percent) of spoken airtime, whereas the candidates had a mere 12 percent
and other sources had 14 percent. On an average night, Al Gore and George
W. Bush spoke for less than 10 seconds on each network.[48]

To hear candidates deliver their messages in 2000, in fact, voters had to
bypass the network television newscasts and watch the TV talk shows.
George W. Bush was on-screen for 13 minutes during his appearance on the
Late Show with David Letterman on October 19, which exceeded his entire
speaking time on all three network news shows during that month. Similarly,
Al Gore received more speaking time on his *Letterman* appearance on

---

46. "Testimony of Hon. Hubert H. Humphrey, U.S. Senator from the State of
    Minnesota," *The Electoral College and Direct Election: Hearings before the
    Committee on the Judiciary, United States Senate,* January 27, February 1, 2, 7,
    and 10, 1977, 95th Congress, 1st session, 25, 35; "Testimony of Douglas
    Bailey," *The Electoral College and Direct Election: Hearings before the
    Subcommittee on the Constitution of the Committee on the Judiciary, Supplement,
    United States Senate,* July 20, 22, 28, and August 2, 1977, 95th Congress, 1st
    session, 267, 258–273; as well as the testimony at the same hearings by
    Sen. Robert Dole, "Testimony of Hon. Robert Dole, U.S. Senator from the
    State of Kansas," *The Electoral College and Direct Election: Hearings before the
    Subcommittee on the Constitution of the Committee on the Judiciary, Supplement,*
    30, who also stressed the campaign distortions created by the electoral col-
    lege. See also Bartels, "Resource Allocation in a Presidential Campaign."

47. Shaw, "The Effect of TV Ads and Candidate Appearances on Statewide
    Presidential Votes, 1988–96."

48. "Campaign 2000 Final: How TV News Covered the General Election
    Campaign," *Media Monitor* 14 (November/December 2000).

September 14 than he did during the entire month of September on the network evening newscasts.[49]

Superficiality, as well as brevity, characterizes media coverage of presidential election campaigns, especially on television. Reporting of issues is spotty, and the press usually reports substantive issues in terms of their impact on politics, not their merits. In 2000, issue coverage appeared in only one-third of election stories in major print and broadcast media, taking a back seat to stories focused on political strategies and the campaign horse race.[50] This coverage was typical. Major media outlets devote most of their attention to the campaign, as opposed to what the campaign is ostensibly about. Stories feature conflict, make brief points, are easily understood (often in either/or terms), and, especially on television, have film value.[51]

PRESERVING FEDERALISM

One of the most serious assertions in opposition to abolishing the electoral college and instituting direct popular election of the president is that doing so would undermine the federal nature of our government. Judith Best argues that direct popular election would "deform our Constitution" and would constitute a serious "implicit attack on the federal principle."[52] William C. Kimberling argues that national popular election "would strike at the very heart of the federal structure laid out in our Constitution and would lead to the nationalization of our central government—to the detriment of the States."[53]

---

49. "Campaign 2000 Final."

50. See Marjorie Randon Hershey, "The Campaign and the Media," in Gerald M. Pomper, ed., *The Election of 2000* (New York: Chatham House, 2001); Matthew R. Kerbel, "The Media: Old Frames in a Time of Transition," in Michael Nelson, ed., *The Elections of 2000* (Washington, DC: Congressional Quarterly Press, 2001).

51. George C. Edwards III, *The Public Presidency* (New York: St. Martin's, 1983), 149, and sources cited therein. See also Bruce Buchanan, *Electing a President* (Austin: University of Texas Press, 1991), chap. 4; Graber, *Mass Media and American Politics*, 210–211; Thomas E. Patterson, "The Press and Its Missed Assignment," in Michael Nelson, ed., *Elections of 1988* (Washington, DC: Congressional Quarterly Press, 1989); Thomas E. Patterson, *Out of Order* (New York: Knopf, 1993), chapters 2, 4; Matthew Robert Kerbel, *Edited for Television* (Boulder, CO: Westview, 1994), chapters 2, 4; Guido Stempel and John Windhauser, eds., *The Media in the 1984 and 1988 Presidential Campaigns* (Westport, CT: Greenwood Press, 1991); S. Robert Lichter and Richard E. Noyes, *Good Intentions Make Bad News*, 2nd ed. (Lanham, MD: Rowman and Littlefield, 1996), chapters 4, 8, postscript.

52. Best, *Choice of the People*, 55.

53. William C. Kimberling, "The Electoral College," on the Federal Election Commission website (www.fec.gov/pdf/eleccoll.pdf).

These defenders of the electoral college base their assertions[54] on the premise that the electoral college is a key underpinning of the federal system. It is unclear what federalism has to do with the presidency, the one part of the government that is designed to represent the nation as a whole rather than as an amalgam of states. Federalism is certainly an important component of the constitutional system, but is the electoral college system an example of the federative principle or essential to maintaining the federal system? Would direct election of the president have other deleterious effects on federalism?

A Federal Principle?

To begin, the founders did *not* design the electoral college on the federal principle. The electoral college does not enhance the power or sovereignty of the states. Moreover, the founders expected electors to exercise their discretion and cast individual votes (as they actually did in the early district system). They did not expect electors to vote as state blocks of electoral votes. There is no reference in the Constitutional Convention to the electoral college being an element of the federal system or important to the overall structure of the Constitution.

Similarly, the founders did not see the electoral college serving as a means of implementing the Connecticut Compromise. The two extra votes given to each state were not allocated on a federative principle. Instead, the extra votes were to serve as a corrective for large state power. The federative principle would have required that these extra electors be organized like the Senate as a separate body with a veto on popular representation.

The electoral college was not designed to protect state interests. If it were, the founders would have insisted that state legislatures choose electors, who would be agents of state officials. But they did not do so. Indeed, the electoral college was "an anti-states-rights device," designed to keep the election of the president away from state politicians.[55]

Essential for Federalism?

Even if the electoral college is not an aspect of federalism itself, is it essential for preserving federalism? We have already seen that the electoral college does not force presidential candidates to devote attention to states as states in general or small states in particular. Neither the existence nor the powers and responsibilities of state governments depend in any way on the existence of the electoral college. If it were abolished, states would have the same rights and duties they

---

54. For another example, see James R. Stoner, Jr., "Federalism, the States, and the Electoral College," in Gregg, ed., *Securing Democracy*, 51–52.

55. Martin Diamond, *The Electoral College and the American Idea of Democracy* (Washington, DC: American Enterprise Institute, 1977), 4.

have now. Federalism is deeply embodied in congressional elections, in which two senators represent each state just because it is a state and in which members of the House are elected from districts within states. Direct election of the president would not alter these aspects of the constitutional structure.

Would federalism be endangered by direct election of the president? Federalism is well protected by members of the House and Senate as well as by the legislatures and governors of the states. It is simply unthinkable that a constitutional amendment altering the federal structure could pass with the support of two-thirds of both houses of Congress and three-fourths of the states. There is virtually no aspect of the constitutional system more secure against fundamental change than federalism.

Representation in Congress and the constitutionally guaranteed rights of states are the core protections of federalism, not the system of electing the president. This makes it difficult to imagine how direct election of the president would undermine federalism. A leading expert on federalism, Neal Peirce, has said it best: "The vitality of federalism rests chiefly on the constitutionally mandated system of congressional representation and the will and capacity of state and local governments to address compelling problems, not on the hocus-pocus of an 18th-century vote count system."[56]

A Lesser Role for State Parties and Politicians?

Martin Diamond and others have raised a related issue, expressing concern that under a system of direct election of the president, state and local politicians would become less important in the election of the president because winning a city or state per se would be less important than under the electoral college. Candidates, he feared, would rely more on direct mail, media experts, and personal coteries in their campaigns. These new features of campaigning would in turn disengage the presidential campaign from both the party machinery and from the state parties and isolate the presidency from their moderating effect.[57]

Diamond and others base their apprehensions on the premise that presidential campaigns are now decentralized efforts, relying heavily on state and local politicians to deliver votes. It is highly questionable how many current state and local leaders can "deliver" votes. There certainly is no systematic

---

56. Twentieth Century Fund, *Winner Take All* (New York: Holmes and Meier, 1978), chap. 6.

57. Martin Diamond, *The Electoral College and the American Idea of Democracy* (Washington, DC: American Enterprise Institute, 1977), 21. See also Charles Fried, "Should the Current Electoral College System Be Preserved," *Congressional Digest* (January 2001): 30; Stoner, "Federalism, the States, and the Electoral College," in Gregg, ed. *Securing Democracy*, 46; Uhlman, "Creating Constitutional Majorities," in Gregg, ed., *Securing Democracy*, 107; Gans, "Electoral College Reform," 12; Sayre and Parris, *Voting for President*, 78–79.

evidence to support such an assertion. Moreover, even if a few leaders could deliver votes, why would we wish to encourage such a system?

In addition, it is clear that exactly what Diamond feared has occurred—*under the electoral college.* Presidential candidates run national campaigns managed from the center. They rely on direct mail and media experts, and they take control of the party machinery by placing their personal representatives in charge. Campaigns develop and coordinate advertising from a central point. They run ads designed to appeal to different parts of the country in those areas. The campaigns do this now, and there would be no difference under direct election of the president. More generally, the national organizations of parties have become stronger in relation to state parties. They are more effective in raising funds. They have made strides in nationalizing party programs, such as the Republicans' "Contract with America" in the 1990s.

It is not at all evident, however, that either the party machinery or state parties have moderating effects. Equally important, successful candidates, such as Bill Clinton, running as a New Democrat, and George W. Bush, running as a compassionate conservative, know that they can only win by taking moderate stances. It is the voters, not state parties, who enforce moderation.

There are many reasons for state party organizations to exist, such as electing thousands of state-level officials and all members of Congress. Filling these offices provides more than sufficient incentive for the maintenance of vigorous state parties. In addition, although presidential campaigns are candidate rather than party centered, state party organizations can provide invaluable aid. Interviews with national party professionals found that they saw the role of state parties becoming *stronger* under direct election of the president because of the vital function these organizations would play in maximizing voter registration and turnout.[58]

Other advocates of the electoral college express concern that direct election of the president would change the system of nominating the president, leading to a national primary and the elimination of the nominating conventions.[59] Yet these fears seem misplaced and, again, are based on faulty premises. Political parties, not states, determine how many delegates a state receives and acceptable means of selecting them. States choose whether to hold primaries or caucuses, and when to have them, to advantage themselves. It is not clear that the nation benefits from Iowa and New Hampshire's disproportionate say in culling presidential candidates, but direct election of the president would not change their ability to schedule delegate selection at their discretion.

---

58. Reported in Neal R. Peirce and Lawrence D. Longley, *The People's President*, rev. ed. (New Haven, CT: Yale University Press, 1981), 223.

59. See, for example, Michael M. Uhlman, "Creating Constitutional Majorities" Gregg, ed., *Securing Democracy*, 107.

In addition, no imperative of the electoral college encourages a particular form or date of nominating delegates. For most of U.S. history under the Constitution, states held few presidential primaries. Now, under the electoral college system, almost all states hold primaries, and they have moved toward "Super Tuesday"–style primaries in which states across the country hold primaries on the same day. The front-loading of delegate selection has moved states toward a version of a regional or national primary—*under the electoral college*. There is no reason to think that direct election of the president would accelerate such a trend.

The widespread use of state presidential primaries and of holding them in the winter or early spring of presidential election years has led to the emergence of a nominee long before the nominating conventions occur. Decisions about presidential nominees are not made at the conventions. National conventions do have other functions, however, such as rallying the faithful and providing an opportunity for a party to make its case to the public. These functions would be valuable under any system of electing the president and are certainly not dependent on the electoral college.

Greater National Control of the Electoral Process?

Occasionally, a defender of the electoral college laments the fact that direct election of the president would likely bring greater national control of the electoral process. Actually, however, this has already occurred. The Fifteenth, Eighteenth, Nineteenth, Twenty-third, Twenty-fourth, and Twenty-sixth Amendments to the Constitution expanded the electorate. Federal law effectively determines voter eligibility now, and in the wake of the debacle in counting votes in Florida in the presidential election of 2000, federal law provides rules for voter registration, voter access to the polls, counting votes, correcting voters' errors on their ballots, resolving challenges to a citizen's right to vote, and ensuring that voting systems have minimal rates of error. The federal government also provides aid to states to improve their voting machinery and registration lists.

Federal standards are here to stay—*under the electoral college*. Moreover, Americans and their elected representatives overwhelmingly support such legislation. The enormous disparity in ballot designs across the states and the large number of inconsistent and needlessly complex individual state ballot designs make a strong case for greater uniformity.[60] The Caltech/MIT Voting Technology Project concluded that between 4 and 6 million votes were lost in the 2000 election as a result of problems with ballots, voting equipment,

---

60. See Richard G. Niemi and Paul S. Herrnson, "Beyond the Butterfly: The Complexity of U.S. Ballots," *Perspectives on Politics* 1 (June 2003): 317–326.

and registration databases.[61] As President George W. Bush said when he signed the Help America Vote Act of 2002, "The administration of elections is primarily a state and local responsibility. The fairness of all elections, however, is a national priority."[62]

Why Not Elect Everyone by the Same Rules?

A common refrain from advocates of the electoral college goes something like this: "If you insist on majority—or at least plurality—rule, why don't you insist on abolishing the Senate, where seats are allocated to states rather than by population?" This is easily answered. The Senate is explicitly designed to represent states and the interests within them. The presidency is designed to do something quite different. The president is to rise above parochial interests and represent the nation as a whole, not just one part of it.

Perhaps the most compelling argument that the president should be elected by direct popular vote is based on the premise that the president and vice president are the only national officials who represent the people as a whole and that the candidate who wins the most votes best approximates the choice of the people. As the declaration in the Preamble to the Constitution says: "We the people . . ." The framers intentionally required that the Constitution be ratified by special conventions called in the separate states and not by the state legislatures. The import of their decision is that "the people" created the Constitution. It is not too far a stretch to argue that the choice of the people ought to determine the only national elective offices in the government.

Similarly, some defenders of the electoral college ask, "If you are so concerned about at least plurality rule in choosing the president, what about all the nonelected judges and other officials in government? Shouldn't we be electing them as well?" Of course not. It is not feasible to elect executive officials, no matter how we select the president. The issue is not electing additional officials. The issue is letting a plurality of voters select the president who nominates judges and executive officials.

WEAKENING STATE INTERESTS

It is difficult to see whose interests the electoral college protects. Rather than protecting the interests of states and minorities, the electoral college weakens incentives for voter participation in states that are safe for a candidate and similarly weakens the incentive for either the majority or minority party to

---

61. *Voting: What Is, What Could Be* (2003).

62. Remarks of President George W. Bush at signing ceremony for the Help America Vote Act of 2002, The White House, October 29, 2002.

attempt to persuade citizens to support them and to go to the polls. It does not make sense under the electoral college for candidates to allocate scarce resources to states they cannot win or, if they will win them, in which the size of their victory is irrelevant.

Candidates would be much more attentive to small states or minorities under direct election of the president than they are under the electoral college. (They could hardly be *less* attentive than they are under the electoral college.) Under direct election of the president, where votes are not aggregated by state, candidates would have incentives to appeal to all voters and not just those strategically located in swing states.[63] An extra citizen's vote in Massachusetts or Texas would count as much as one in Michigan or Florida.[64]

Presidential and vice-presidential candidate Bob Dole explained that under direct election of the president, candidates would have to pay more attention to areas within states that are now ignored because they are safe for one party or the other. Thus, under direct election of the president, "The voters in the majority of States would receive greater attention and the objective of federalism would be served better."[65]

Moreover, it is quite feasible for candidates to spread their attention more evenly across the country. Because the cost of advertising is mainly a function of market size, it does not cost more to reach 10,000 voters in Wyoming than it does to reach 10,000 voters in a neighborhood in Queens or Los Angeles. Actually, it may cost *less* to reach voters in smaller communities because larger markets tend to run out of inventory and the price of advertising is bid up. Politicians know this, even if advocates of the electoral college do not. That is why in the election of 2000 (within states) the candidates "devoted nearly as much advertising to Yakima as in Seattle, as much to Traverse City as to Flint, as much to Wausau as to Milwaukee."[66]

Direct election of the president would also provide the incentive for candidates to encourage all their supporters, no matter where they lived, to go to the polls, because under direct election, every vote counts. Conversely, under

---

63. See Eric R. A. N. Smithy and Peverill Squire, "Direct Election of the President and the Power of the States," *Western Political Quarterly* 40 (March 1987): 29–44.

64. Electoral college supporter James Stoner seems to recognize this but misses the point of how this would advance democracy in America. See Stoner, "Federalism, the States, and the Electoral College," in Gregg, ed., *Securing Democracy*, 46.

65. "Prepared Statement of Senator Bob Dole," *The Electoral College and Direct Election: Hearings before the Subcommittee on the Constitution of the Committee on the Judiciary, Supplement*, 40.

66. Hagen, Johnston, and Jamieson, "Effects of the 2000 Presidential Campaign," 3.

the electoral college, it does not matter how many votes a candidate receives in a state as long as the number is more than the opponent receives. The goal is to win states, not voters. As Douglas Bailey, the media manager of the 1976 Ford–Dole campaign, put it, "There is a vast population [outside urban areas], with every vote counting, that you cannot ignore in a direct election."[67]

It is possible, but by no means certain, that some candidates would find it more cost-effective to mobilize votes in urban areas or to visit urban areas where they would receive free television coverage before the largest audiences. Such actions would do nothing to undermine the argument against the electoral college, however. Small states cannot be worse off than they are now, as under the electoral college candidates rarely visit or campaign there. Direct election of the president cannot diminish a campaign effort that does not exist. Instead, direct election would provide *increased* incentives for candidates to campaign in most small states, as well as increased incentives to campaign in many large states. Direct election would disperse campaign efforts rather than deprive small states of them.

Direct election, unlike the electoral college, thus encourages citizen participation in elections and encourages candidates to take their campaigns to these citizens, enhancing our civic culture. Direct election would increase voter turnout and stimulate party-building efforts in the weaker party, especially in less competitive states. Counting all votes equally (and making all votes equally valuable to the candidate) would not only strengthen political equality but also provide candidates an incentive to clarify their stances rather than hedging them to persuade only the undecided in competitive states.

CONCLUSION

A core justification for the electoral college, and its violations of political equality, is that it is necessary to protect important interests that would be overlooked or harmed under a system of direct election of the president. Yet such claims are based on faulty premises. States—including states with small populations—do not embody coherent, unified interests and communities, and they have little need for protection. Even if they did, the electoral college does not provide it. Contrary to the claims of its supporters, candidates do not pay attention to small states. The electoral college actually distorts the campaign so that candidates ignore many large and most small states and devote most of their attention to competitive states.

---

67. Quoted in "Direct Popular Election of the President and Vice President of the United States," 124.

Similarly, African Americans do not benefit from the electoral college because they are not well positioned to determine the outcomes in states. As a result, the electoral college system actually discourages attention to their interests.

The electoral college is also not a bastion of federalism. It is not based on federative principles and is not essential for the continuance of a healthy federal system. Direct election of the president would not diminish the role of state and local parties and officials or the nominating conventions and national standards, for elections are already in place and not to be feared. As Bob Dole put it, direct election is "commonsense federalism."[68]

---

68. "Prepared Statement of Senator Bob Dole," *The Electoral College and Direct Election: Hearings before the Subcommittee on the Constitution of the Committee on the Judiciary, Supplement,* 39.

PART II

The Context
of the Presidency

3

꙰

Partisan Polarization
in Presidential Support

The Electoral Connection

GARY C. JACOBSON
University of California, San Diego

The Washington DC community responded to the terrorist attacks of September 11, 2001, on the World Trade Center and Pentagon with a remarkable display of bipartisan unity. The day's events provoked human responses that transcended party; conservative Republican Dick Armey was observed draping a consoling arm around Maxine Waters, among the House's most liberal Democrats. Republican and Democratic leaders found themselves getting acquainted in a new way as they shared an emergency bunker while waiting out the immediate threat of further attacks.[1] President George W. Bush, whose path to the White House had left many Democrats embittered and questioning the legitimacy of his presidency, received a thundering bipartisan ovation as he addressed a joint session of Congress on the crisis. In the days that followed, bipartisan consultation and cooperation flourished as Congress quickly complied with the president's requests for emergency legislation to deal with the consequences of the attack.[2]

The display of unity was all the more striking in its contrast to the political climate prevailing prior to the attack. By every measure, national politics had

---

1. Janet Hook, "Under the Shadow of War, Congress Declares a Truce," *Los Angeles Times*, September 22, 2001, p. A21.

2. Only a single member of Congress, Democratic Representative Barbara Lee of California, voted against the joint resolution passed on September 14 authorizing the president "to use all necessary and appropriate force against the nations, organizations, or people that he determines planned, authorized, committed, or aided the terrorist attacks on the United States that occurred September 11, 2001" (PL 107-46). A week later, the airline relief bill (PL 107-42) passed 356–54 in the House, 96–1 in the Senate. A broad anti-terrorism bill requested by the administration (PL 107-56) passed 357–66 in the House, 98–1 in the Senate during the last week of October.

become increasingly polarized along partisan and ideological lines over the decades between the Nixon and George W. Bush administrations. Indeed, partisan rancor in Washington had grown so familiar that it became a central target of Bush's 2000 campaign. Promising to be "a uniter, not a divider," Bush emphasized his status as a Washington outsider with "no stake in the bitter arguments of the last few years" who could "change the tone of Washington to one of civility and respect."[3] That hope, apparently dashed by a victory that came only after the fierce partisan struggle over Florida's electoral votes, revived with the bipartisan surge of support for Bush after September 11. Not for long, however; it quickly became clear that bipartisan consensus on administration measures to combat terrorism did not extend to measures dealing with the issues that had split the parties before the attacks. Although muted in tone, aggressive partisanship continued to shape congressional–presidential relations even as Democrats almost uniformly accepted the administration's leadership in the war on terrorism.

The swift reemergence of partisan conflict is not surprising, for sharp partisan divisions have become deeply embedded in national political life. The growth of party-line voting and the widening ideological gulf between the congressional parties have been thoroughly documented.[4] The growing polarization of the congressional parties is most clearly depicted in the Poole–Rosenthal DW-Nominate index, summarized in Figure 3–1. DW-Nominate scores are calculated from all nonunanimous roll-call votes cast by House and

---

3. Speech to Republican National Convention, August 3, 2000, accepting the nomination.

4. John H. Aldrich, *Why Parties? The Origin and Transformation of Party Politics in America* (Chicago: University of Chicago Press, 1995); David W. Rohde, *Parties and Leaders in the Postreform House* (Chicago: University of Chicago Press, 1991); Barbara Sinclair, "Hostile Partners: The President, Congress, and Lawmaking in the Partisan 1990s," in Jon R. Bond and Richard Fleisher, eds., *Polarized Politics: Congress and the President in a Partisan Era* (Washington, DC: Congressional Quarterly Press, 2000), pp. 134–53; Nolan M. McCarty, Keith T. Poole, and Howard Rosenthal, *Income Redistribution and the Realignment of American Politics* (Washington, DC: AEI Press, 1997); Keith T. Poole and Howard Rosenthal, *Congress: A Political-Economic History of Roll Call Voting* (New York: Oxford University Press, 1999); Richard Fleisher and Jon R. Bond, "Why Has Party Conflict among Elites Increased if the Electorate Is Dealigning?" (Paper presented at the Annual Meeting of the Midwest Political Science Association, Chicago, 1996); Richard Fleisher and Jon R. Bond, "Partisanship and the President's Quest for Votes on the Floor of Congress," in *Polarized Politics*, pp. 154–85; Melissa P. Collie and John Lyman Mason, "The Electoral Connection between Party and Constituency Reconsidered: Evidence from the U.S. House of Representatives, 1972–1994," in David W. Brady, John F. Cogan, and Morris P. Fiorina, eds., *Continuity and Change in House Elections* (Stanford, CA: Stanford University Press, 2000), pp. 211–34; and Gary C. Jacobson, "Party Polarization in National Politics: The Electoral Connection," in *Polarized Politics*, pp. 9–30.

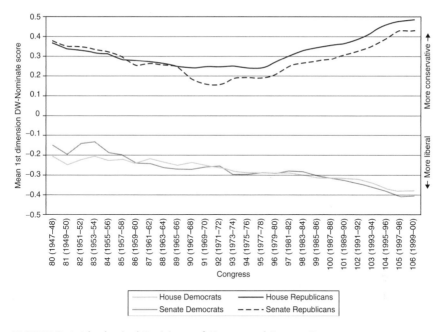

FIGURE 3–1 Ideological Positions of House and Senate Party Coalitions 80th to 106th Congresses.

Senate members; the score locates each member for each Congress on a liberal–conservative scale that ranges from -1.0 to 1.0; the higher the score, the more conservative the member.[5] On average, Democrats in both Houses became increasingly liberal over the last half of the 20th century (mainly through the gradual atrophy of their conservative southern wing). Republicans drifted left until the mid-1970s; since then, they have moved strongly to the right. By the 106th Congress, ideological divisions between parties in the House and Senate were widest for the entire time period depicted and, indeed, wider than at any time since before World War I.

A parallel and closely related trend has been the growing partisan disparity in congressional support for presidential initiatives and preferences, displayed in Figures 3–2 through 3–4. For this analysis, presidential support is measured as the percentage of votes for the president's position on conflictual roll calls, defined as those on which less than 80 percent of members in a chamber voted with the president.[6] Despite some noticeable differences,

---

5. For an explanation of their methodology, see Poole and Rosenthal (1999). I am obliged to Keith Poole for providing the data through the 106th Congress.

6. The data were compiled by George C. Edward III and are available at http://bush.tamu.edu/cps/cps/archivedata/index.html. For these charts, the annual scores are averaged for each Congress.

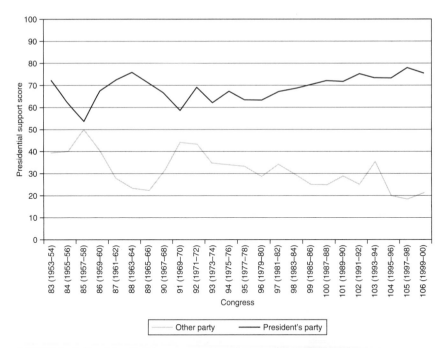

FIGURE 3–2 Presidential Support in the House of Representatives, 83rd to 106th Congresses.

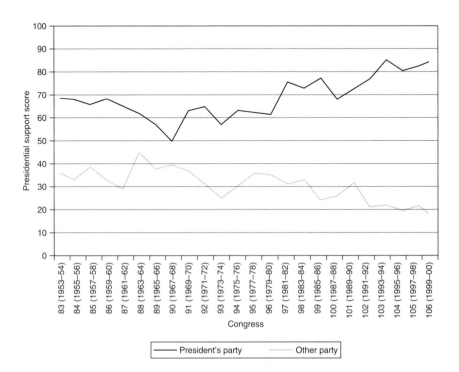

FIGURE 3–3 Presidential Support in the Senate, 83rd to 106th Congresses.

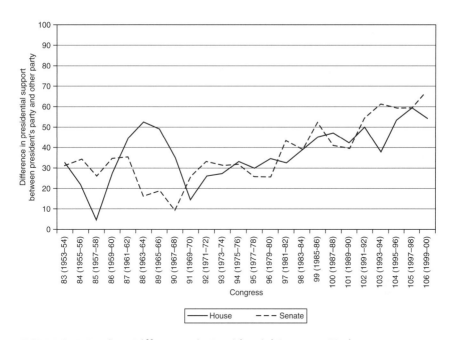

FIGURE 3–4 Partisan Differences in Presidential Support, 83rd to 106th Congresses.

Figures 3–2 (House) and 3–3 (Senate) reveal the same pattern of increasing partisan polarization in presidential support scores that we observe in DW-Nominate scores. The differences are clearest from Figure 3–4, which traces the partisan gap in average presidential support scores from the Eisenhower through the Clinton administrations. The House parties were somewhat more polarized on presidential initiatives than on ideology during the Kennedy and Johnson administrations, and the Senate parties were somewhat less polarized during Bill Clinton's first Congress. Still, the spreading partisan disparity in presidential support from the Nixon administration onward is unmistakable, and party differences were greater during the Clinton administration than in any other in the series. Figures 3–2 and 3–3 indicate that both the president's partisans and opposition partisans contributed to the trend, although on the House side, opposition partisans made the larger contribution.

Another graphic perspective on the trend is presented in Figures 3–5 and 3–6, which display the frequency distributions of House and Senate members' presidential support scores for selected administrations during the period of growing partisan polarization. During the first Nixon administration, presidential support scores of Republicans and Democrats in both houses overlapped extensively. Eight years later, during the first Reagan administration, the degree of overlap had diminished but was still notable. The parties in both houses had moved further apart on this dimension by the George H. W. Bush

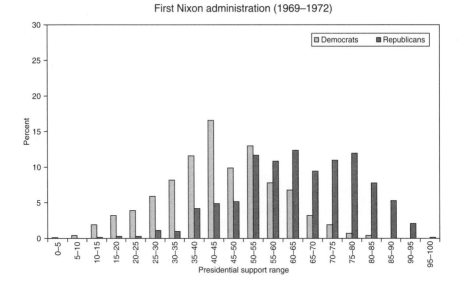

First Nixon administration (1969–1972)

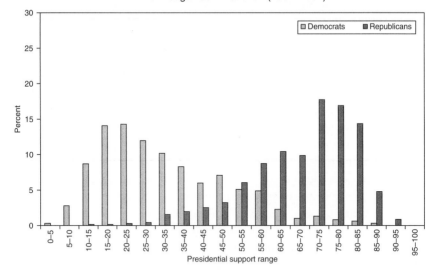

First Reagan administration (1981–1984)

FIGURE 3–5 House of Representatives.

administration. And during Clinton's second administration, polarization was nearly complete; only a handful of members had support scores overlapping those of the other party's members.

What is behind the growing partisan difference in support for the president's issue positions? Clearly, the trend is intimately linked to the increasing

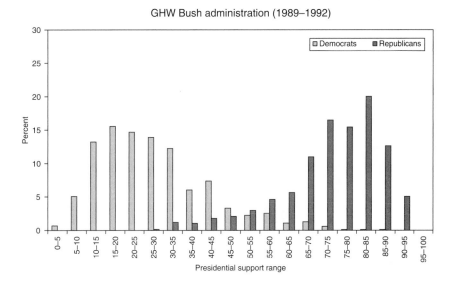

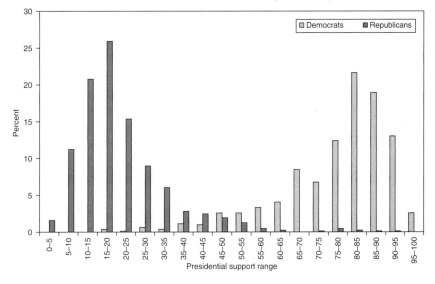

FIGURE 3–5 *Continued.*

ideological polarization of the congressional parties. Fleisher and Bond, for example, note that the near-disappearance of "cross-pressured" members—those whose DW-Nominate scores are closer to the other party's mean than to their own party's mean—has made it more difficult for presidents to win support from the opposition party and easier to win support from their

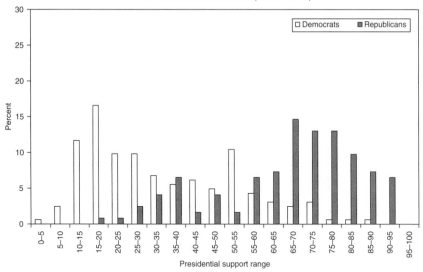

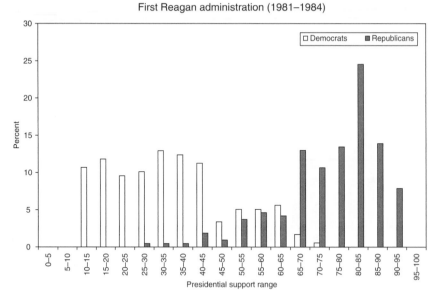

FIGURE 3–6 Senate.

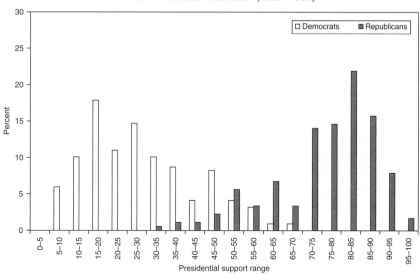

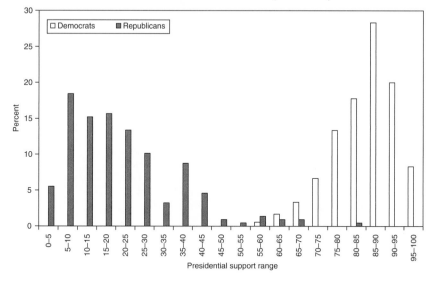

FIGURE 3–6 *Continued.*

own party.[7] Although the relationship between ideology and presidential support has not always taken the expected form,[8] since the 92nd Congress (1971–72), the correlation between the two measures has averaged .68 for House members of the president's party and .81 for members of the opposing party. The equivalent averages for the Senate from the 101st Congress (1989–1990) forward are .55 and .85.[9] Thus, whatever explains the parties' ideological polarization should also help to explain growing partisan differences in presidential support, and vice versa. That "vice versa" is crucial, for presidents and their agendas have been major contributors to the ideological polarization of the parties, both in Congress and in the electorate.

In previous work, I have sought to show that the widening ideological divide between the congressional parties is firmly rooted in electoral politics.[10] Contrary to arguments implying that elite and popular partisanship have been moving in opposite directions,[11] the electoral coalitions that members of Congress rely on to keep their jobs have, like the members themselves, also become more sharply divided by partisanship and ideology. In this article, I focus on the electoral and popular bases for the growing party disparities in presidential support scores. I find that electoral changes have reduced incentives for opposition party members to support the president, while making it politically more attractive for the president's own partisans to support his positions. The extent to which presidents and members of the opposition party in Congress share electoral constituencies has declined significantly, and the parties' respective electoral coalitions have become increasingly polarized in term of both ideology and presidential voting patterns.

---

7. "Partisanship and the President's Quest for Votes on the Floor of Congress," in *Polarized Politics*, pp. 154–85.

8. During the four congresses of the Eisenhower administration, conservatism was negatively correlated with presidential support among House members of both parties (the range was from −.37 to −.86 across congresses and parties). The sign was also "wrong" for both parties during Nixon's first Congress (the 91st, 1969–70); the more liberal the Republican or Democrat, the higher the support for Nixon's positions.

9. Information to match Senate data sets on presidential support and DW-Nominate scores is not available for senators prior to the 101st Congress; for this analysis, liberalism is correlated with support for Democratic presidents, conservatism is correlated with support for Republican presidents, so the expected sign is always positive.

10. Jacobson, "Party Polarization in National Politics"; Gary C. Jacobson, "The Electoral Basis of Partisan Polarization in Congress" (paper presented at the Annual Meeting of the American Political Science Association, Washington, DC, August 31–September 3, 2000).

11. Martin P. Wattenberg, *The Decline of American Political Parties*, Cambridge, MA: Harvard University Press, 1998); Everett C. Ladd, "The 1994 Congressional Elections: The Realignment Continues," *Political Science Quarterly* 111 (Spring 1995): 1–23; Daniel M. Shea, "The Passing of Realignment and the 'Base-Less' Party System," *American Politics Quarterly* 27 (January 1999): 33–57.

These changes have been consequential because presidential support scores among members of Congress vary with the president's electoral support in their constituencies, although the structure of the relationship varies across administrations, parties, and chambers. Presidential job approval data also show a widening gap in approval ratings of self-identified Republicans and Democrats, largely because of declining approval ratings from partisans of the opposition party. These trends have substantially reduced incentives for opposition members to support the president. Presidents have not been passive figures in this process, to be sure; rather, their own ideological positions have strongly influenced the level of support they have received from each congressional party. Presidents have in fact been instrumental in creating and sustaining national partisan and ideological divisions.

In the sections that follow, I present arguments and evidence for these claims. I then consider whether any of the extraordinary events the United States has experienced during the present Bush administration might have altered the political configurations promoting partisan conflict, and conclude that they have not.

PRESIDENTIAL SUPPORT IN CONGRESS: THE ELECTORAL CONNECTION

The extensive literature on the "electoral connection"[12] suggests a simple hypothesis regarding presidential support in Congress: Other things equal, the greater the support for the president among the voters that a member relies on to win and hold office, the more inclined the member will be to vote for the president's positions. In this formulation, members are expected to be sensitive mainly to what Fenno identifies as their "reelection constituency"[13] and that I will call their "electoral constituency,"[14] not to the entire constituency. Within the electoral constituency, support for the president can take several forms, including voting for the president, favoring the president's positions, sharing the president's party or ideology, and approving of the president's performance in office.

A companion hypothesis is that, in general, the more a member's electoral constituency overlaps with that of a president, the more supportive of the president voters in that constituency are likely to be. If this hypothesis is accurate, then partisan changes in support for presidents in Congress will

---

12. David R. Mayhew, *Congress: The Electoral Connection* (New Haven, CT: Yale University Press, 1974); and countless followers.

13. Richard F. Fenno, Jr., *Home Style: House Members in Their Districts* (Boston: Little, Brown, 1978).

14. I use this slightly different terminology because my analysis extends beyond congressional incumbents seeking reelection.

reflect changes in the extent to which members from each party share electoral constituencies with the president. More specifically, we would expect a decline in support for the president among opposition party members of congress to be associated with a decline in the overlap between the electoral constituencies of the president and the opposition party members. This is exactly what both survey and aggregate data indicate.

The Decline in Shared Constituencies: Survey Evidence

The American National Election Studies provide unambiguous evidence of growing partisan coherence in the electorate over the past 30 years.[15] The relationships among party identification, ideology, issue positions, and electoral choice have all become stronger. Voters' views of the parties and candidates have become increasingly differentiated and polarized. As a consequence, the electoral constituencies of Republicans and Democrats in Congress have become increasingly disparate.[16]

The trend toward increased partisan coherence has affected presidential and congressional voting alike, strengthening the connection between the two. As Figure 3–7 shows, the incidence of ticket splitting between presidential and congressional candidates has declined noticeably from its peak; in the two most recent elections it has fallen to levels last seen in the 1960s. Figure 3–8 reveals one source of the decline in ticket splitting: As the proportion of voters able to place themselves on the 7-point liberal-conservative scale has grown,[17] so has the extent to which vote choices in both presidential and congressional elections have been consistent with the respondent's ideological self-location.[18] In the two most recent elections, about 60 percent of votes in all three kinds of elections have been cast in line with ideology. Of the remainder, only about 15 percent were cast for the "wrong" candidate ideologically; the rest were cast by voters who placed themselves in the middle of the scale.

These changes have reduced the proportion of electoral constituents the president has shared with members of the opposition party in Congress and

---

15. The National Election Studies data analyzed in this paper are from Virginia Sapiro, Steven J. Rosenstone, and the National Election Studies, *American National Election Studies Cumulative Data File, 1948–2000* [Computer file], 11th ICPSR version (Ann Arbor: University of Michigan, Center for Political Studies [producer], 2002).

16. Jacobson, "Party Polarization in National Politics"; Jacobson, "The Electoral Basis of Partisan Polarization in Congress."

17. From 77 percent of voters in 1972 and a low of 70 percent in 1980 to 88 percent in 1996 and 2000.

18. Defined as respondents placing themselves right of center and voting for Republicans or respondents placing themselves left of center and voting for Democrats; respondents placing themselves at the center ("4" on the scale) are included in the denominator.

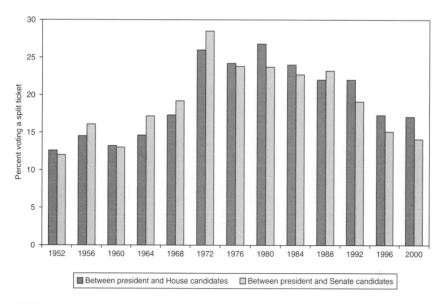

FIGURE 3–7 Ticket Splitting in National Elections, 1952–2000.

SOURCE: American National Election Studies.

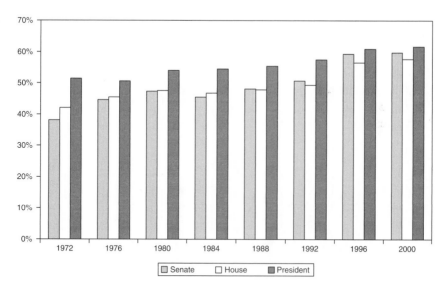

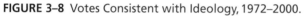

FIGURE 3–8 Votes Consistent with Ideology, 1972–2000.

SOURCE: American National Election Studies.

have increased the ideological differences between the two parties' respective electoral constituencies. Figures 3–9 and 3–10 show how the proportion of voters for opposition party's representatives and senators who also voted for the president has declined over the past three decades. For example, when Ronald Reagan took office in 1981, he faced a congress in which 34 percent

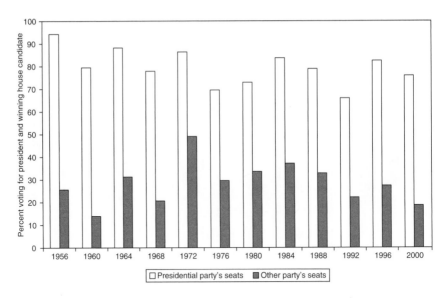

FIGURE 3–9 Shared Electoral Constituencies, U.S. Representative and President, 1956–2000.

SOURCE: American National Election Studies.

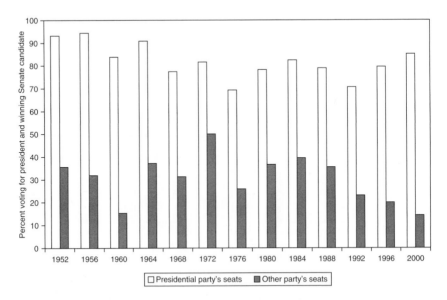

FIGURE 3–10 Shared Electoral Constituencies, U.S. Senator and President, 1952–2000.

SOURCE: American National Election Studies.

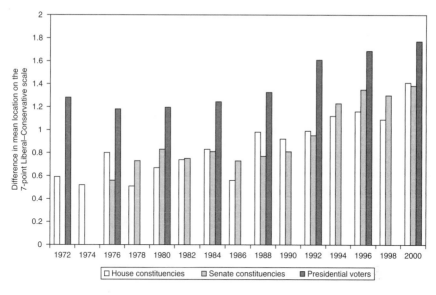

FIGURE 3–11 Differences in Ideological Self-Placement of Republican and Democratic Electoral Constituencies.

of House Democrats' voters and 37 percent of Senate Democrats' voters had also voted for him. When George W. Bush took office in 2001, he shared only 19 percent of House Democrats' voters and only 14 percent of Senate Democrats' voters. This represents the lowest proportion of overlapping electoral constituencies since 1960 and the second-lowest in the entire time series. The proportion of electoral constituents that presidents share with their own party's members has fluctuated but remains high, averaging nearly 80 percent in recent elections.

The electoral constituencies of the two parties have also become more dissimilar ideologically. The difference in average self-placement on the 7-point liberal–conservative scale between the congressional parties' electoral constituencies more than doubled over the period under observation (Figure 3–11).[19] The gap between Republican and Democratic presidential voters, larger to begin with, also increased noticeably.

As a consequence, the opposition party's congressional voters have located themselves and the president increasingly further apart on this scale. The data in Table 3–1 show that since the 1970s, voters electing congressional Democrats have placed Republican presidents farther to their right, and voters electing congressional Republicans have placed Democratic presidents farther to their left. Electoral constituents of the presidential party's members have

---

19. The scale takes the value of 1 for most liberal, 7 for most conservative, with 4 representing the middle of the road.

Table 3–1 Differences in Placement of President and Self on the 7-Point Liberal Conservative Scale by House and Senate Electoral Constituencies

	HOUSE		SENATE	
	Presidential Party's Electoral Constituents	Other Party's Electoral Constituents	Presidential Party's Electoral Constituents	Other Party's Electoral Constituents
Republican Presidents				
Nixon (1972)	−0.29	−1.17	−0.54	−0.78
Reagan (1980)	−0.59	−1.40	−0.38	−1.51
Reagan (1984)	−0.57	−1.39	−0.80	−1.07
GHW Bush (1988)	−0.36	−1.34	−0.70	−2.04
GW Bush (2000)	−0.48	−1.73	−0.03	−1.85
Democratic Presidents				
Carter (1976)	0.78	1.92	0.55	1.70
Clinton (1992)	0.59	2.17	0.43	1.83
Clinton (1996)	0.35	2.54	0.46	2.97

Note: Entries are derived from 7-point scales where 1 is most liberal and 7 is most conservative.

SOURCE: American National Election Studies.

seen themselves as somewhat more centrist than the president, but the gap is much more modest and shows no clear temporal trend.

Polarizing Electorates: Aggregate Evidence

Aggregate electoral data tell the same story. They confirm, first of all, the growing articulation of voting across federal offices. Figure 3–12 shows how the correlation between district-level presidential and House shares (here taken as the percent Democratic of the major party vote) shares has changed over the past half-century. The correlation of the district-level vote for the two offices was above .80 during the 1950s, fell to a low of .52 in 1972, then rose until it again surpassed .80 in 1996 and 2000. Figure 3–13 shows the comparable trend involving elections at the state level. The analysis here is more complicated because only two-thirds of the states hold elections in any presidential election year, and each subset of Senate contests coincides with the presidential election only once in 12 years. To get more complete cover-age, I have therefore computed the correlations for mid-term elections (using the presidential vote in the most recent past presidential election) as well as for each presidential election year. The three Senate "classes" are color coded to facilitate comparisons. Correlations were highest in the 1950s, but note that

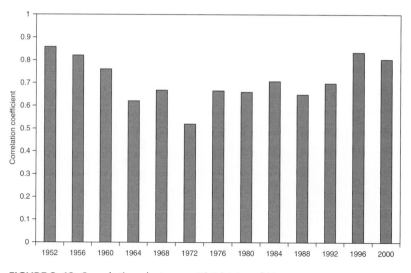

FIGURE 3–12 Correlations between District-Level House and Presidential Voting, 1952–2000.

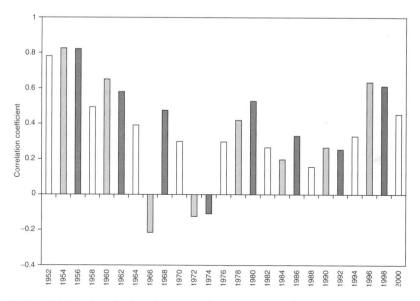

FIGURE 3–13 Correlations between Senate Vote and Most Recent Presidential Vote in the State.

those for the three most recent elections were higher for their respective classes than at any time since then.[20]

---

20. This remains true if analysis is confined to non-southern states, although dropping southern states does get rid of the negative relationships between presidential and Senate voting in 1966, 1972, and 1974.

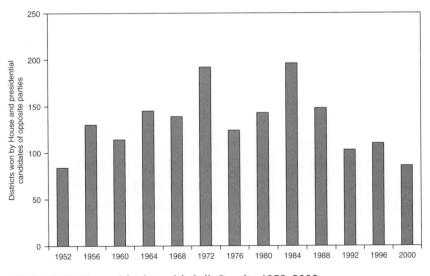

FIGURE 3–14 House Districts with Split Results, 1952–2000.

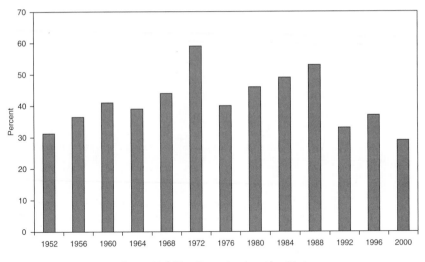

FIGURE 3–15 Senate Seats Held by Party Losing the State
in the Presidential Election, 1952–2000.

The greater articulation between presidential and congressional voting is
also evident in the diminished proportion of districts and states producing
split results—majorities for a presidential candidate of one party and for the
House or Senate candidate of the other. As Figure 3–14 shows, the proportion
of split House districts, which reached a peak of 45 percent in 1984, had fallen
to 20 percent in 2000, its lowest level since 1952. Outcomes also became
more consistent at the state level (Figure 3–15), with the proportion of Senate
seats held by the party losing the state in the presidential election, which stood

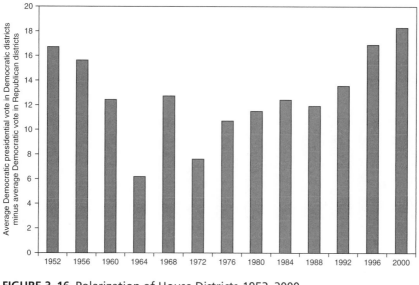

FIGURE 3–16 Polarization of House Districts, 1952–2000 (Presidential Vote).

as high as 59 percent in 1972, reaching its lowest level for the entire half–century (29 percent) in 2000. To be sure, close presidential elections such as that of 2000 are less likely to yield split outcomes, but note that state and district level outcomes showed more partisan consistency in 2000 than in any of the other close elections (1960, 1968, and 1976) in the series.

The increasing partisan articulation of aggregate voting across offices contributed to a widening disparity between the presidential voting patterns in Republican and Democratic districts and states (Figures 3–16 and 3–17). Back in 1972, for example, the vote for George McGovern was, on average, only 7.6 percentage points higher in House districts won by Democrats than in those won by Republicans; in 2000, the average vote for Al Gore was 18.3 percentage points higher in Democratic than in Republican districts. In terms of presidential voting, the parties' respective House district electorates were more polarized after 1996 and 2000 than after any other election during the period under review. By the same measure, Democratic and Republican Senate constituencies—whole states—were also more polarized after these two elections than after any since the 1950s.[21]

---

21. The presidential vote gap between the parties' Senate constituencies is smaller than for House districts in part because, with two senators each, some states have split delegations, netting out to zero. But the increase in electoral consistency has also produced a decrease in the proportion of split Senate delegations; at the high point in the 96th Congress (1979–80), 54 percent of the states' Senate delegations were split between the parties; by the 107th Congress (2001–2002), only 26 percent remained split, the lowest proportion since the 1950s.

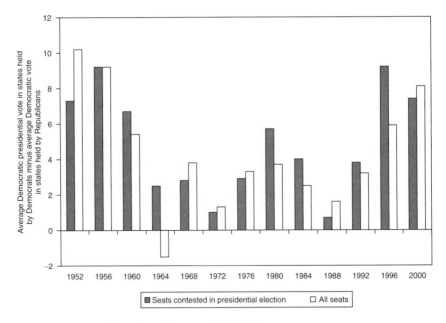

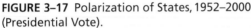

FIGURE 3–17 Polarization of States, 1952–2000
(Presidential Vote).

Constituency polarization is also evident in changes in the distribution of each party's House seats according to the presidential vote in the district. Figure 3–18 displays the distribution of seats held by each party after the 1972, 1980, 1988, and 1996 elections (the same set displayed earlier in Figure 3–5) across the range of presidential vote divisions (using 5 percentage-point intervals to define the categories and smoothing the lines connecting them). Notice how the overlap in these distributions has diminished across these four elections. Again, the evidence indicates that the two parties have represented increasingly divergent electoral coalitions and therefore have faced increasingly divergent incentives to support the president.[22]

CONSTITUENCY VOTING
AND PRESIDENTIAL SUPPORT

Aggregate electoral data, like the survey data presented earlier, leave no doubt that the proportion of electoral constituents a typical member of the opposition party in Congress shared with the president declined substantially during the same period that the opposition party's support for the

---

22. A similar pattern of change can be detected among Senate seats, although it is muted by the Senate's larger constituencies, smaller size, and overlapping six-year terms.

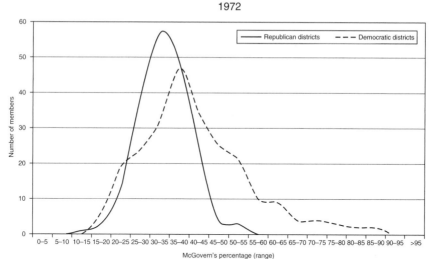

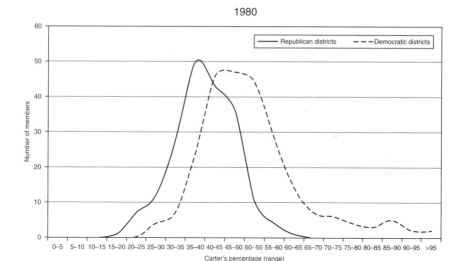

FIGURE 3–18 The Distribution of Republican and Democratic House Districts by Presidential Vote.

president on roll-call votes declined. If the connection between the two trends is more than coincidental, we should also observe that, for any particular president, other things equal, the higher his vote in a district or state, the greater his level of support from its representative or senator. With some interesting and informative exceptions, this is precisely what we do observe. Table 3–2 presents the results of the regression of presidential support scores on the state- or district-level presidential vote for each party's delegation in each administration since Eisenhower's first. For this analysis, the dependent

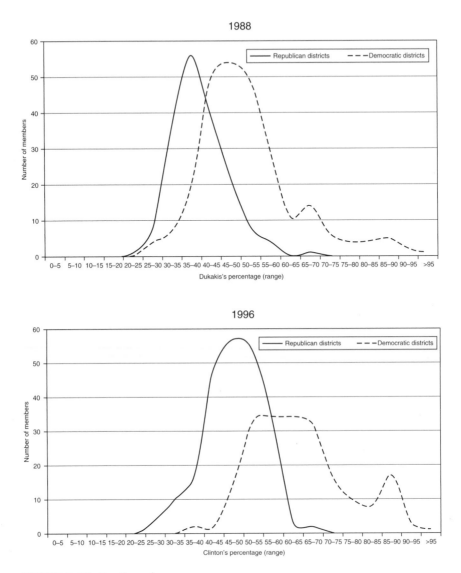

FIGURE 3–18 *Continued.*

variable is the support score for each member in each session of the two congresses in each administration; the independent variable is the share of votes won by the president in the state or district in the election that installed the administration.[23]

---

23. This means that the number of cases analyzed is approximately four times the average size of the party delegation in the chamber during the administration; House data from congresses after midterm elections that had been preceded by extensive redistricting and for which the presidential vote was not recalculated for the new districts (1962 and 1966) are omitted.

Table 3–2 Coefficients from Regression of Presidential Support Scores on the State- or District-Level Presidential Vote

Administration	PRESIDENT'S PARTY			OPPOSITION PARTY		
	Coefficient	Standard Error	R^2	Coefficient	Standard Error	R^2
Senate						
Eisenhower I	−1.05**	.21	.11	.31*	.13	.03
Eisenhower II	−.13	.28	.00	.12	.11	.01
Kennedy-Johnson	−1.15**	.25	.08	1.31**	.36	.09
Johnson	.70**	.07	.25	1.24**	.16	.31
Nixon I	.84**	.18	.11	−.32*	.16	.02
Nixon II	1.66**	.21	.29	1.42**	.12	.37
Carter	−.00	.15	.00	1.66**	.21	.14
Reagan I	.22*	.10	.02	.26	.16	.00
Reagan II	1.16**	.17	.19	1.55**	.22	.20
GHW Bush	1.13**	.15	.27	1.24**	.17	.19
Clinton I	.50**	.09	.13	1.06**	.14	.23
Clinton II	.19*	.09	.02	.92**	.12	.23
House						
Eisenhower I	−.50**	.10	.03	.22**	.05	.03
Eisenhower II	−.21	.11	.01	.27**	.05	.03
Kennedy-Johnson[a]	.37**	.10	.03	1.12**	.14	.17
Johnson[a]	1.21**	.06	.40	.93**	.09	.28
Nixon I	.19*	.08	.01	.22**	.04	.03
Nixon II	.54**	.03	.26	.65**	.08	.10
Carter	.46**	.07	.07	.18**	.04	.02
Reagan I	.50**	.06	.08	.33**	.04	.06
Reagan II	1.10**	.07	.26	.57**	.03	.25
GHW Bush	.91**	.06	.23	.62**	.06	.28
Clinton I	.29**	.03	.08	.40**	.06	.05
Clinton II	.57**	.04	.22	.64**	.05	.18

[a]Data are from the first Congress of the administration only; the presidential vote was not available for the second Congress because of redistricting.

*$p < .05$.

**$p < .001$.

For most administrations, the president's share of votes in a member's constituency has a positive and statistically significant effect on his or her level of support for the president's position on roll-call votes. From Nixon's first administration onward, the average coefficient for the president's party's delegation is .71 in the Senate, .57 in the House; for the opposition party's delegation, it is .97 in the Senate, .45 in the House. Roughly speaking, then, a one percentage-point difference in the presidential vote in a constituency is associated with a one-half to one percentage-point difference in its member's presidential support score. There is, however, considerable variation across administrations, parties, and chambers in the size of the coefficient and the share of variance explained by the presidential vote (see the R^2s [in Table 3–2]). In the first Nixon administration, party differences were relatively small, and in the Senate, Democrats from states where Nixon ran more strongly actually supported him less frequently. In the other cases, presidential support is estimated to increase by between 6 and 40 percentage points as the presidential vote increases from its lowest to highest value. The results of this analysis thus suggest that the growing divergence in the distribution of presidential vote shares in states and districts held by opposing congressional parties contributed to partisan polarization in presidential support scores. But the results also make it clear that this is only part of the explanation, for the gap between the parties' support scores increases independently of changes in constituency voting patterns.

THE IMPACT
OF THE PRESIDENT'S POSITION

The anomalies in the regression results (negative or zero coefficients) are also informative, for they suggest that the president's own ideological position has something to do with the support he receives from the two party coalitions. Eisenhower got less support from House and Senate Republicans the larger his share of the vote in their constituencies. The relationship between roll-call ideology (measured by DW-Nominate scores) and presidential support is also negative for House Republicans in these congresses (data for Senate comparisons are not available). Apparently, conservative Republicans, those representing the most solidly Republican districts, were more likely to reject Eisenhower's "modern Republicanism." Nixon also pursued relatively moderate domestic policies during his first administration, muting partisan differences.[24] The Kennedy–Johnson administration, in contrast, pursued a liberal agenda that put it at odds with conservative southern Democrats who represented states that, in 1960, still voted disproportionately Democratic in presidential elections.

More systematic evidence for the importance of the president's own ideological location in determining his level of partisan support is provided by the

---

24. Jon R. Bond and Richard Fleisher, *The President in the Legislative Arena* (Chicago: University of Chicago Press, 1990).

analyses reported in Tables 3–3 and 3–4.[25] Table 3–3 shows that, generally, the more moderate the president (for example, the closer the president's DW-Nominate score is to the center point, zero), the less ideologically distant the opposing party's senators and representatives.[26] The relationship is not perfect because, as we saw in Figure 3–1, the distance between the party delegations has widened substantially since the 1970s; hence, for example, Clinton was more moderate than Carter by this measure, but he was farther from the Republican House and Senate means. But the overall pattern makes the important, if obvious, point that the president's own ideological location, no less than that of the opposition party coalition, determines the width of the ideological gap between the president and the congressional parties.

The regression equations in Table 3–4 show how this gap affected presidential support in the House. Leaving out the Eisenhower administration, with its anomalous relationships between ideology and presidential support,[27] we find a robust relationship between ideological distance and presidential support. For comparison, the first equation in each pair displays the bivariate relationship between ideology and presidential support. The two are indeed related, as we would expect, and the coefficients indicate that ideology has a large substantive impact on presidential support.[28] The relationship is even stronger, however, when we take the president's own ideological position into account by including as an independent variable the gap between the DW-Nominate score of the House member and the president.[29] For representatives of the president's party, both ideology and ideological distance make a major difference in the level of presidential support. But for opposition party members, ideological distance has a much larger effect than ideology per se when both are in the equation. In every case, taking ideological distance into account significantly improves the equation's ability to predict presidential support, confirming that the president's own stance affects the level of support he

---

25. The president's first dimension DW-Nominate score was estimated by Poole and Rosenthal from his positions on legislation before Congress during his administration.

26. More moderate presidents also tend to be closer to their own party's congressional delegations.

27. Including the Eisenhower administration weakens the relevant relationships in the "Republican Administrations" set and produces smaller coefficients but does not change the substantive conclusions.

28. For example, the difference in predicted presidential support scores between members whose DW-Nominate scores are one standard deviation above and one standard deviation below the party mean ranges from 13.4 percentage points for Republicans during Republican administrations to 29.2 percentage points for Democrats during Democratic administrations.

29. The president's ideology entered by itself would produce identical substantive results, but the procedure I use here makes the results easier to interpret.

Table 3–3 Presidential and Congressional DW-Nominate Scores

	HOUSE				SENATE			
	President's DW-Nominate Score	Difference from Own Party's Mean	Difference from Other Party's Mean	% Closer to President Than to Own Party's Mean	President's DW-Nominate Score	Difference from Own Party's Mean	Difference from Other Party's Mean	% Closer to President Than to Own Party's Mean
Republicans								
Eisenhower	.267	-.032	.492	26.4		-.038	.459	26.4
Nixon	.280	.032	.543	17.5		.117	.551	15.9
Ford	.251	.012	.539	13.3		.060	.546	13.1
Reagan	.479	.148	.783	2.9		.215	.775	0.5
GHW Bush	.456	.083	.775	2.3		.145	.792	0.0
Democrats								
Kennedy	-.524	-.300	-.793	0.8		-.277	-.781	5.4
Johnson	-.412	-.169	-.656	3.9		-.142	-.625	11.4
Carter	-.470	-.188	-.725	1.3		-.185	-.665	7.6
Clinton	-.363	.003	-.827	0.2		.022	-.763	5.2

Table 3–4 DW-Nominate Scores and Presidential Support Scores, Kennedy through Clinton Administrations

	Republican Administrations				Democratic Administrations			
	Republicans		Democrats		Republicans		Democrats	
Constant	57.3**	67.0**	45.9**	63.0**	43.9**	67.1**	53.0**	69.1**
	(0.5)	(0.6)	(0.4)	(0.8)	(0.5)	(1.8)	(0.4)	(0.8)
DW-Nominate score	35.3**	26.0**	46.4**	4.7*	−51.2**	−8.2*	−62.3**	−36.2**
	(1.4)	(1.3)	(1.0)	(2.0)	(1.1)	(3.4)	(1.0)	(1.5)
Absolute difference from president's DW-Nominate score		−42.2**		−42.6**		−49.7**		−40.0**
		(1.9)		(1.8)		(3.7)		(1.9)
R^2	.27	.44	.49	.58	.54	.58	.60	.67
Number of cases	1701	1701	2461	2461	1785	1785	2352	2352

Note: The dependent variable is the member's presidential support score; standard errors are in parentheses.

*p <.05.

**p <.001.

receives from both parties. Thus, the ideological extremity of both the president and the congressional parties determines the extent of party polarization on presidential initiatives.

PRESIDENTIAL APPROVAL

Elections are not the only venue in which a representative or senator's constituents register their level of support for the president. Between elections, polls regularly ask voters whether they approve or disapprove of the way the president is handling his job and thus provide something of an ongoing referendum on the president. When these job approval ratings of partisan identifiers are viewed separately, yet another pattern of increasing partisan polarization emerges.[30] Figure 3–19 displays the average quarterly presidential job approval ratings offered by the president's and the opposition's partisans from 1953 through 2000.[31] The data carry vivid reminders of the varying fortunes of different administrations: Even Democrats liked Ike; the Vietnam War brought Johnson down; Nixon's approval plummeted as Watergate unfolded; Carter managed to alienate both parties; and Bush rode high through the Gulf War, then saw his support among Democrats collapse in the subsequent recession. Amid the shifting tides of fortune, however, is a discernable secular trend toward lower presidential approval by opposition party identifiers.[32] Only George H. W. Bush managed to buck the trend—until the fall of 1991—by keeping an unusual proportion of Democratic identifiers happy.

Figure 3–20 shows how this trend widened party differences in presidential job approval. From Eisenhower through Carter, the partisan approval gap never exceeded an average of 48 percentage points in any quarter or an average of 41 percentage points for any president. For Reagan, the average gap exceeded 50 percentage points in 26 of 32 quarters and stood at 52.9 points

---

30. Jon R. Bond and Richard Fleisher, "The Polls: Partisanship and Presidential Performance Evaluations," *Presidential Studies Quarterly* 21 (September 2001): 529–40; and Richard Fleisher and Jon R. Bond, "Increasing Partisan Polarization Among Ordinary Citizens," in Jeffrey Cohen, Richard Fleisher, and Paul Kantor, eds., *American Political Parties: Decline or Resurgence?* (Washington, DC Congressional Quarterly Press, 2001).

31. The data are from the Gallup Polls; data for 1953 through 1998 were kindly supplied by George C. Edwards III; later data were supplied by the Gallup Organization.

32. The trend is statistically significant, with the regression coefficient on time (measured in quarters) estimated at −.12 with a t-ratio of 7.9 and an adjusted R^2 of .25. The same analysis applied to the partisan gap shown in Figure 3–21 produces a regression coefficient of .11 with a t-ratio of 9.3 and an adjusted R^2 of .32. Thus, the gap has widened by an estimated 1.75 percentage points per four-year administration, or from 32 to 53 points over the entire period.

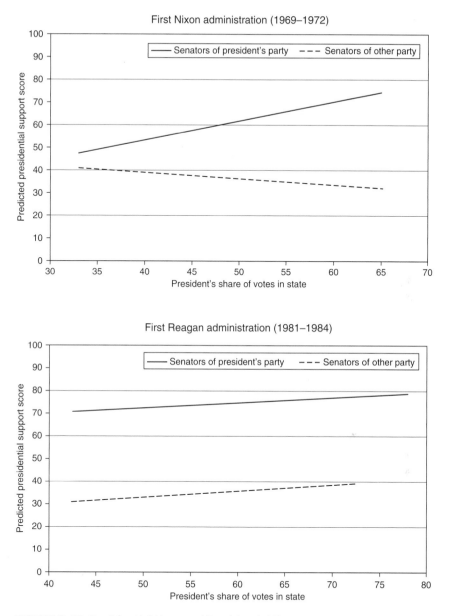

FIGURE 3–19 Presidential Vote and Presidential Support.

for his entire presidency. The average party difference in approval of Clinton's performance during his presidency was 55.1 percentage points; it was greater than 50 points in every quarter but two (when it was 49.5 points and 49.8 points); during five quarters, it exceeded 60 percentage points.

Although electoral logic would suggest that the incentive for a member to support the president would vary with the popular standing of the president,

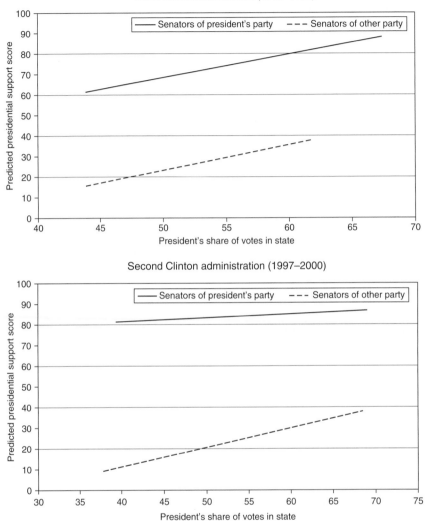

FIGURE 3–19 *Continued.*

particularly among people identifying with the member's party and therefore likely to be part of his or her electoral constituency, the literature leaves this connection in considerable doubt. The relationship between overall approval and presidential success in Congress has been subject to extensive research and debate, with the balance of research indicating, at best, a very modest relationship.[33] However, the main focus of this literature is on presidential success

---

33. George C. Edwards III, *At the Margins: Presidential Leadership of Congress* (New Haven, CT: Yale University Press, 1989); Douglas Rivers and Nancy Rose,

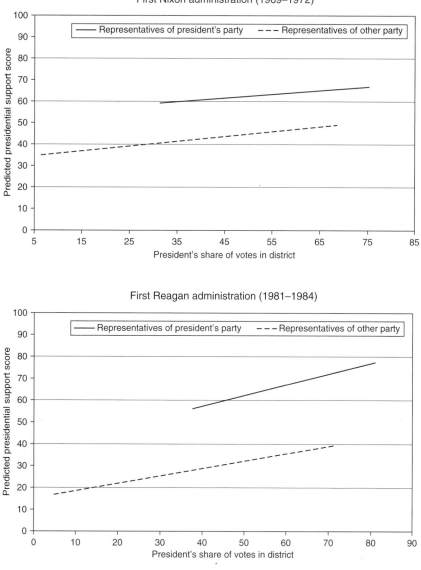

FIGURE 3–19 *Continued.*

"Passing the President's Program: Public Opinion and Presidential Influence in Congress," *American Journal of Political Science* 29 (May 1985):183–96; Bond and Fleisher, *The President in the Legislative Arena*; Charles W. Ostrom and Dennis M. Simon, "Promise and Performance: A Dynamic Model of Presidential Popularity," *American Political Science Review* 79 (June 1985): 334–58; Kenneth Collier and Terry Sullivan, "New Evidence Undercutting the Linkage of Approval with Presidential Support and Influence," *Journal of Politics* 57 (February 1995): 197–209.

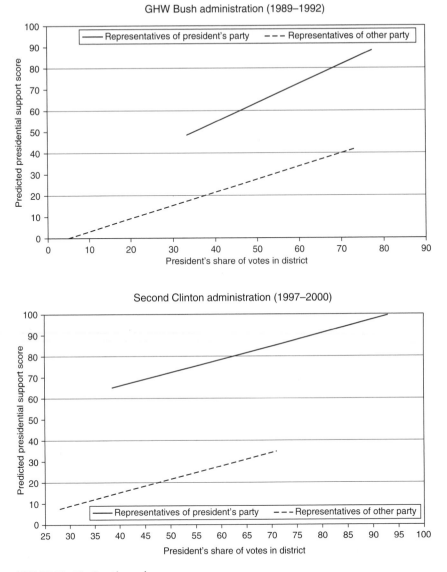

FIGURE 3–19 *Continued.*

rates rather than individual member's support scores, and researchers typically use a fine-grained (monthly) measure of presidential approval designed to pick up the effects of short-term changes, not the broader impact of sustained higher or lower approval levels.[34] Their analysis is thus not designed to assess the effects on presidential support of the broad secular trend toward wider

---

34. See, for example, Bond and Fleisher, *The President in the Legislative Arena.*

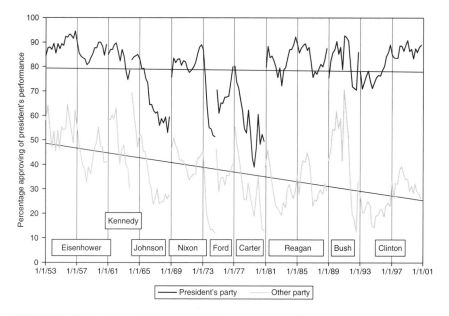

FIGURE 3–20 Presidential Approval, Eisenhower to Clinton (Quarterly Averages).

partisan disparity in presidential approval. More to the point is Edwards's coarse-grained analysis (based on yearly approval and success data) indicating that approval levels do affect presidential support, the more so when partisans (members and respondents) are analyzed separately.[35] If Edwards is right, then the widening partisan gap in presidential approval would help explain the widening partisan gap in presidential support scores.

Certainly we know that party differences in presidential approval and in House and Senate support scores have grown in rough parallel. Figure 3–21 maps all three trends (based on yearly averages) on the same scale, and their kinship is unmistakable. It is far from perfect, however. While the party difference in presidential approval is highly correlated with party difference in presidential support in the Senate (r = .75), it is not strongly related to party difference in presidential support in the House (r = .27), partly because of poor fit in the Kennedy–Johnson years (if analysis is confined to the Nixon administration forward, the correlation rises to .50).

Regression analysis also supports the idea that partisan approval levels affect presidential support, again with a stronger relationship in the Senate than in the House. Table 3–5 reports estimates of the regression of presidential support

35. George C. Edwards III, "Aligning Tests with Theory: Presidential Approval as a Source of Influence in Congress," *Congress and the Presidency* (Fall 1997): 113–30.

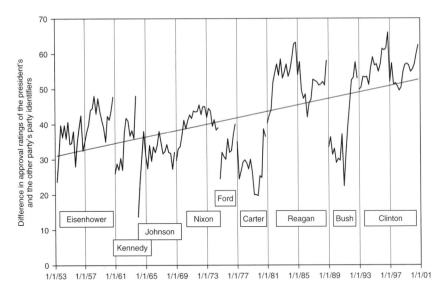

FIGURE 3–21 Partisan Differences in Presidential Approval, Eisenhower through Clinton (Quarterly Averages).

scores on presidential approval, controlling for presidential vote in the member's state or district, for each party in each chamber for each type of administration (Democratic or Republican).[36] As before, the presidential vote in the constituency has a strong effect on presidential support. So, however, does presidential approval (by the member's fellow partisans), except in the case of House Republicans, for whom one coefficient is small and the other displays the wrong sign.[37] These are, to be sure, underspecified models,[38] and the analysis ignores all of the important time series complications. Still, the results make it clear that the growing partisan disparity in presidential support in Congress is consistent with, rather than contrary to, partisan trends in public approval of the president. Again, party polarization in Congress appears to have a solid popular basis.

36. Presidential approval is the yearly average approval rating; to facilitate comparisons across administrations, the Democratic presidential vote is entered as the deviation from the mean Democratic vote in the relevant election year.

37. Edwards, "Aligning Tests with Theory," analyzing the support data aggregated by party and year ($N = 42$), and thus without the constituency vote variable, got virtually the same substantive results.

38. Although, adding DW-Nominate scores and difference from the president's DW-Nominate score as controls (in the House equations, where this can be done) does not alter the substantive conclusions.

Table 3–5 Presidential Approval, Constituency Presidential Vote, and Presidential Support, 1953–2000

	Constant	Presidential Approval by Member's Partisans	Adjusted Democratic Presidential Vote in Constituency	R^2	Number of Cases
House of Representatives					
Democrats, Democratic administrations	51.3***	.24***	.52***	.16	4352
	(1.4)	(.02)	(.02)		
Republicans, Republican administrations	59.9***	.05*	-.36***	.03	4945
	(2.1)	(.03)	(.04)		
Republicans, Democratic administrations	32.5***	-.08**	.66***	.13	3275
	(0.7)	(.02)	(.03)		
Democrats, Republican administrations	26.3***	.28***	-.41***	.11	6822
	(0.7)	(.02)	(.02)		
Senate					
Democrats, Democratic administrations	30.9***	.51***	.44***	.16	1133
	(2.9)	(.04)	(.07)		
Republicans, Republican administrations	43.3***	.31***	-.45***	.06	1259
	(4.6)	(.06)	(.07)		
Republicans, Democratic administrations	19.5***	.40***	1.23***	.23	839
	(1.7)	(.05)	(.09)		
Democrats, Republican administrations	23.7***	.26***	-.44***	.07	1442
	(1.4)	(.04)	(.06)		

Note: Standard errors are in parentheses.
*p <.05.
**p <.01.
***p <.001.

GEORGE W. BUSH

Implicit in George W. Bush's campaign pledge to end the partisan bickering in Washington was the idea that party conflict in national politics was largely an inside-the-beltway phenomenon having little resonance among ordinary Americans elsewhere. The evidence presented here suggests otherwise. Like other manifestations of greater congressional partisanship, the growth of party differences in presidential support rests on a firm electoral and popular foundation. Over the past three decades, presidents have shared progressively fewer constituents with senators and representatives of the opposing party. They have become more ideologically distant from these members' electoral constituents as well. The difference in presidential voting patterns between districts and states electing the parties' respective congressional delegations has widened substantially. And between elections, party differences in presidential job approval ratings have grown.

Nothing in the data from the 2000 elections even hints at any reversal of these trends; quite the contrary, they were almost uniformly extended (review Figures 3–7–3–17 and Table 3–1). Moreover, the aftermath in Florida that had politicians and activists of the two parties at each other's throats also split ordinary citizens sharply along party lines. Polls found huge differences between Bush and Gore supporters (that is, largely between Republicans and Democrats) on a variety of relevant questions. For example, among Bush voters, 92 percent thought Bush had won legitimately, and 92 percent approved of the Supreme Court's decision stopping the manual recount of ballots in Florida. Among Gore voters, 81 percent thought Bush was not the legitimate victor, and 80 percent disapproved of the Supreme Court's decision. Most Gore supporters (65 percent) thought the Court's decision was partisan, while most Bush supporters (84 percent) thought it was impartial. The two sides were also starkly divided over whom the Florida voters had intended to vote for and whether the Court's decision to stop the recount was fair.[39]

With such profound partisan disagreement over the legitimacy of his election, it is not surprising that Bush entered the White House with the widest partisan difference in approval ratings of any newly elected president since approval has been polled. In doing so, however, he merely extended a trend toward greater partisan polarization during the early-term "honeymoon" period that had begun during Reagan's first administration (Figure 3–22). By this indicator, the honeymoon was already largely a thing of the past.

---

39. Gary C. Jacobson, "A House Divided: The Clinton Legacy and the Congressional Elections of 2000," *Political Science Quarterly* 116 (Spring 2001): 5–28.

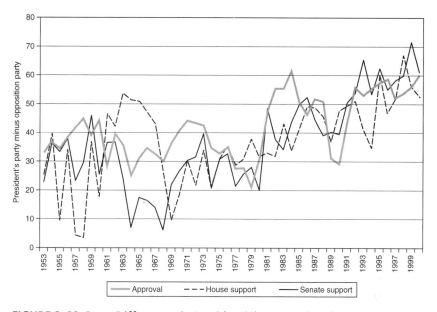

FIGURE 3–22 Party Differences in Presidential Approval and Support, 1953–2000.

There was little sign during the first eight months of Bush's administration that partisan conflict had subsided.[40] The administration's strategy of moderating its conservative proposals only far enough to peel off the moderate Democrats needed to win 60 votes in the Senate paid off in a victory on the $1.35 billion tax cut bill but was not designed to diminish partisan conflict.[41] Exceedingly narrow House and Senate majorities put a premium on party discipline. The dramatic political impact of Senator Jeffords's defection, which broke the tie and gave the Democrats a one-vote Senate majority, underlined the primacy of party.[42] The future portended a continuing partisan power struggle that only some decisive future election could end.

This, like almost every other assumption about the continuity of national political life, was thrown into question by the terrorist attacks of September 11.

---

40. Most of the public did not notice any diminution; when an ABC NEWS/*Washington Post* poll conducted April 12–22, 2001, asked, "Do you think Bush has reduced the political partisanship in Washington, or not?" 54 percent said no, 34 percent said yes, and 11 percent had no opinion.

41. Ordinary Democrats and Republicans were nearly 50 percentage points apart on the wisdom of Bush's tax cut proposals (CBS News Poll, April 4–5, 2001; Gallup Poll Release, March 9, 2001).

42. Citizens were, characteristically, sharply divided along party lines over Jeffords's switch; according to the CNN/*USA Today*/Gallup Poll of May 24, 2001, Democrats thought it would be good for the country (75% said good, 9%, bad), while Republicans thought it would be bad for the country, (75% said bad, 14% said good).

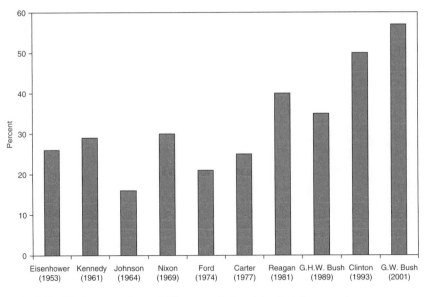

FIGURE 3–23 Average Party Difference in Presidential Approval During the First Quarter of a New Administration.

The bipartisan unity displayed by Congress in its response to Bush's call for action against terrorism was echoed in the public, as Americans of all political stripes rallied around the president. Bush's approval ratings shot up from the 50s to the highest levels ever recorded, topping 90 percent in some September and October polls. The largest change by far occurred among Democratic identifiers, as Figure 3–23 indicates. Approval of Bush among Democrats jumped by more than 50 percentage points, from an average of 30 percent in the period before September 11 to an average of 81 percent in the month following the attacks. Support also rose among Republicans (to 98 percent in polls taken through October), but it was already so high (89 percent) that the Republican contribution to the overall rise could be only modest.[43]

In this new context, the partisan gap in presidential approval, which, with an average of nearly 59 percentage points, had been well on its way to eclipsing the record set during the Clinton administration, plummeted to as low as 14 percentage points. But as Figure 3–24 shows, the gap began to widen again almost immediately, as Republican approval remained very high while Democratic approval began a steady decline, temporarily reversed only by reactions to the successful military phase of the Iraq war in April 2003 and the capture of Saddam Hussein in December 2003. By the

---

43. As usual, self-defined independents approximated the national figures, going from an average of 52 percent approving before September 11 to an average of 86 percent approving over the next month.

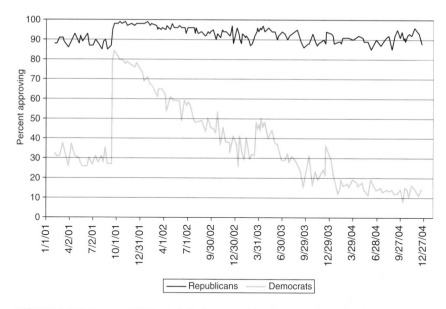

FIGURE 3–24 George W. Bush Job Approval Ratings During His First Term.

SOURCE: Gallup Polls.

final quarter of 2004, the gap had widened to an average of 79 percentage points, setting an all-time record of 83 points in one October Gallup Poll (94 percent of Republicans but only 11 percent of Democrats approving of Bush's performance).

Like Democrats in Congress, Democratic identifiers in the public responded to Bush's leadership in a bifurcated way. He initially got strong bipartisan approval for leadership in the war on terrorists, but this did not spill over into unrelated domestic matters, and it did not survive growing disillusion among Democrats over the Iraq war and the administration's justifications for it. With Democrats' approval of Bush's handling of domestic policy areas running 30 to 40 points lower than his handling of terrorism, congressional Democrats were free to continue to oppose Bush on matters that had divided the parties before September 11, such as energy policy, how to stimulate the economy, and what to do about HMOs. *Congressional Quarterly's* vote studies for 2001 reflect this circumstance; while the proportion of "party unity" votes[44] in the House and Senate was well below its mid-1990s peak, Democratic and Republican party unity scores on those party unity votes remained at or near their highest levels since *CQ* began keeping track in 1954 and stayed there through the remainder of Bush's first

---

44. CQ defines party unity votes as those floor votes in which a majority of one party votes against a majority of the other party

term.[45] Presidential support scores comparable to those analyzed in this paper are not yet available for the Bush administration, but, among Democrats, the difference between votes on proposals dealing directly with the terrorist threat and those dealing with the domestic agenda are likely to be dramatic.

CONCLUSION

The surge of national unity provoked by terrorist attacks on the United States in September 2001 set up something of a natural experiment testing the durability of the strong party divisions that had emerged over the previous three decades. The results so far suggest that polarized politics is indeed a durable component of national politics. This is not surprising, for, as I have tried to show in this paper and others, deep party divisions in Washington are firmly rooted in electoral politics and consistent with divisions in popular opinion. Elite and popular consensus supporting the president's war on terrorism was initially strong but narrowly focused; it did not spread to issues that split the parties before September 11, and congressional Democrats felt little pressure from electoral constituents to support Bush's positions on those issues. As Bush's support among ordinary Democrats deteriorated in the year following the invasion of Iraq, Democrats in Congress had even less reason to follow his lead. Meanwhile, congressional Republicans remained overwhelmingly loyal to the president, leaving Congress highly polarized once again.

If the analysis presented here is correct, the only force able to affect party differences in presidential support (on issues unrelated to the war on terrorism) in the short run is the president himself. More moderate presidents win greater support from the opposing party; Bush could presumably increase his support among Democrats by pursuing policies closer to those they prefer, as he did on his education package. But given his own ideological instincts and considering the resistance he would get from the highly disciplined, largely conservative Republican majorities in the House and Senate, Bush's second term will most likely resemble his first. The extraordinarily partisan and polarized race for the presidency left neither side in a mood to back down. Unless and until electoral constituents tell them otherwise, there will be little pressure on either party to bend.

---

45. For the House and Senate combined, Democrats had a party unity score of 85 percent for 2001, tying their highest ever (1993); the combined Republican score was 90 percent, surpassed only by 91 percent in 1995; 85 and 90 were the parties' respective average unity scores for the next three years as well (*Congressional Quarterly Weekly Report*, December 11, 2004, 2953).

4

⚜

Power without Persuasion

Rethinking Foundations
of Executive Influence

WILLIAM G. HOWELL
Harvard University[1]

Ours is a system of federated and separated powers, a government that by its very design frustrates passions and stymies change. For activists with a new idea and a sweeping policy agenda, the legislative process can be nothing short of maddening. As a practical matter, a few individuals—a key committee chair, two-fifths of the Senate, and, not least, the president himself—can block the enactment of laws. What with the proliferation of subcommittees, the weakening of parties, and the growing involvement of interest groups during the past 30 years, the chances of assembling and sustaining coalitions is further complicated. And if that were not enough, transaction costs and collective action problems further undermine possibilities for passing a wide assortment of laws. Politicians who set their sights on advancing new policy initiatives invariably have a harder time of it than those who take it upon themselves to protect the status quo.

That all politicians struggle, however, does not mean that all politicians struggle equally. Presidents, in particular, have an ace up their sleeves. Using a wide variety of mechanisms, presidents can unilaterally set public policy and thereby place upon others the onus of coordinating a response. Through executive orders, executive agreements, national security directives, proclamations, memos, and other kinds of unilateral directives, presidents can exert power and initiate change to an extent not possible in a strictly legislative setting. During eras defined by gridlock, presidents have deployed these policy devices with increasing frequency and effect—so much so, in fact, that they constitute a defining feature of the modern presidency itself.

---

1. I would like to thank Doug Kriner, David Lewis, Kenneth Mayer, and Paul Peterson for helpful feedback. As always, standard disclaimers apply.

This chapter speaks to the larger, more conceptual issues that these unilateral powers raise, exploring some of the ways in which they challenge the more traditional notions of bargaining and negotiating that have guided scholarly research on the American presidency for almost half a century. More specifically, this essay engages Richard Neustadt's central thesis that presidential power is synonymous with persuasion and that the ability of presidents to accomplish anything of consequence depends upon the goodwill and cooperation of other political actors located in others parts of the federal government. The White House, I suggest, is itself a vital center of activity, one where policies are not only devised but also issued. And precisely because the president can act unilaterally, he (someday she) can place other political actors in a defensive posture, scrambling to manufacture an effective response. Should they fail, then the president's orders stand, as a unilateral directive retains the weight of law until and unless somebody else overturns it. As such, the boundaries of unilateral powers depend less upon the inclination of other political actors in other branches of government to do the president's bidding and more upon their willingness and capacity to intervene and dismantle executive actions already taken.

From the outset, let me be absolutely clear about two matters. First, the president's unilateral powers are not boundless. If their directives are to endure, presidents must issue them only when opportunities permit, lest their actions provoke retaliation from either Congress or the courts. And second, persuasion and unilateral action are not mutually exclusive enterprises. When implementing their orders, or when trying to secure funding for unilaterally created agencies and programs, persuasion can be valuable. But the fact that unilateral powers have limits does not mean that they are inconsequential; and the fact that persuasion sometimes complements unilateral action does not mean that Neustadt identified all aspects of presidential power. Unilateral powers augment presidential power in material ways, enabling the Chief Executive to create policies that look markedly different from those that would emerge through the legislative process. And as presidents have deployed them with increasing regularity, it seems long overdue that we update our thinking about the foundations of executive power.

A FLURRY OF ACTIVITY

From the moment he took office, President George W. Bush began issuing executive orders, proclamations, and national security directives that dramatically reshaped the domestic and foreign policy landscapes. In the spring of 2001, he issued an executive order that instituted a ban on all federal project labor contracts, temporarily setting in flux Boston's $14 billion dollar "Big Dig" and dealing a major blow to labor unions. He later required federal contractors to post notices advising employees that they have a right to with-hold the portion of union dues used for political purposes. He created the White House Office of Faith-Based and Community Initiatives, which was charged with "identify[ing] and remov[ing] needless barriers that thwart the heroic work of faith-based groups."[2] He set new guidelines on federal funding of fetal tissue research. In order to block the release of presidential papers, he claimed the power for presidents and their kin to invoke executive privilege years after leaving office. By including salmon raised in fish hatcheries in counts for the Endangered Species Act, Bush managed to take numerous species of wild salmon off the list of endangered species and thereby lifted federal regu-lations that applied to the rivers and streams where they spawn. Without secur-ing a congressional authorization, Bush withdrew from the Kyoto Protocols, the International Criminal Court, and the Antiballistic Missile Treaty. And just as Truman used a 1950 national security directive to identify the doctrine of deterrence, which guided foreign policy during the Cold War, Bush issued a national security strategy endorsing the principle of preemptive war, which may guide foreign policy efforts to confront terrorism in the 21st century.

For Bush, scaling back environmental and industry regulations has been a major priority. "Stymied in [their] efforts to pass major domestic initiatives in Congress," a recent *New York Times* feature story revealed, "officials have turned to regulatory change."[3] Under Bush's watch, "Health rules, environmental reg-ulations, energy initiatives, worker-safety standards and product-safety disclo-sure policies have been modified in ways that often please business and industry leaders while dismaying interest groups representing consumers, workers, drivers, medical patients, the elderly and many others. And most of it was done through regulation, not law—lowering the profile of the actions. The admin-istration can write or revise regulations largely on its own, while Congress must pass laws. For that reason, most modern-day presidents have pursued much of their agendas through regulation." The Bush administration has issued rules that alter the amount of allowable diesel-engine exhaust, that extend the number of hours that truck drivers can remain on the road without resting, and that permit Forest Service managers to approve logging in federal forests without standard environmental reviews. These rule changes, moreover, represent but a fraction of the total.

Considerable activity has centered around the president's war on terrorism. In the aftermath of September 11, Bush created a series of agencies—the

---

2. For a thorough review of this particular executive order, as well as Bush's aggressive use of his unilateral powers more generally, see Anne Farris, Richard P. Nathan, and David J. Wright, "The Expanding Administrative Presidency: George W. Bush and the Faith-Based Initiative," (Washington, DC: The Roundtable on Religion and Social Policy, 2004).

3. David Brinkley, "Out of Spotlight, Bush Overhauls U.S. Regulations," *New York Times,* August 14, 2004, p. A1.

Office of Homeland Security, the Office of Global Communications, and the Commission on the Intelligence Capabilities of the United States Regarding Weapons of Mass Destruction—to collect and disseminate new intelligence while coordinating the activities of existing bureaus. He issued a national security directive lifting a ban (which Ford originally instituted via executive order 11905) on the CIA's ability to "engage in, or conspire to engage in, political assassination"—in this instance, the target being Osama bin Laden and his lieutenants within al Qaeda. He signed executive orders that froze all financial assets in U.S. banks that were linked to bin Laden and other terrorist networks. And perhaps most controversially, Bush signed an order allowing special military tribunals to try noncitizens suspected of plotting terrorist acts, committing terrorism, or harboring known terrorists.

The most visible of Bush's unilateral actions consisted of military strikes in Afghanistan and Iraq. Having secured congressional authorizations to respond to the mounting crises as he saw fit,[4] in the fall of 2001, Bush directed the Air Force to begin a bombing campaign against Taliban strongholds while Special Forces conducted stealth missions on the ground; and in the spring of 2003, he launched a massive air and ground war against Iraq, plunging the United States into the most protracted military conflict since the Vietnam War. And if recent reports are true, the president is using "findings and executive orders" to launch a wide range of covert military actions in the Middle East, just as he shifts numerous intelligence-gathering responsibilities from the CIA to the Pentagon.[5] Though not always packaged as traditional policy directives, these commands nonetheless instigate some of the most potent expressions of executive power. Within a year, Bush's orders resulted in the collapse of the Taliban and Baathist regimes; the flight of tens of thousands of refugees into Pakistan, Iran, and Turkey; the destruction of Afghanistan and Iraq's social and economic infrastructures; and the introduction of new governing regimes.

Bush hardly invented these powers. Nor was he the first president to utilize them with such frequency and consequence. During his tenure, Clinton "perfected the art of go-alone governing."[6] Though Republicans effectively

---

4. In many policy arenas, presidents find the authority they need to act unilaterally in some vague statute or broad delegation of power. And when doing so, it is difficult to make the case that the president is merely fulfilling the expressed wishes of Congress (more on this in a later note). In this instance, it is worth noting that Congress refused to formally declare war against Afghanistan or Iraq. Rather, it passed authorizations in the falls of 2001 and 2002 that gave the president broad discretion to use the military as he deemed appropriate in the nation's campaign against terrorism.

5. Seymour M. Hersh, "The Coming Wars: What the Pentagon Can Now Do in Secret," *The New Yorker*, January 24 & 31, 2004, pp. 40–47.

6. Francine Kiefer, "Clinton Perfects the Art of Go-Alone Governing," *Christian Science Monitor*, July 24, 1968, p. 3.

undermined his 1993 health care initiative, Clinton subsequently managed to issue directives that established a patient's bill of rights, reformed health care programs' appeals process, and set new penalties for companies that deny health coverage to the poor and people with preexisting medical conditions. During the summer of 1998, just days after the Senate abandoned major tobacco legislation, Clinton imposed smoking limits on buildings owned or leased by the executive branch and ordered agencies to monitor the smoking habits of teenagers, a move that helped generate data needed to prosecute the tobacco industry. While his efforts to enact gun-control legislation met mixed success, Clinton issued executive orders that banned numerous assault weapons and required trigger safety locks on new guns bought for federal law enforcement officials. Nor did this activity decline in the waning years of his administration. Instead, Clinton "engaged in a burst of activity at a point when other presidents might have coasted . . . Executive orders have flown off Clinton's desk, mandating government action on issues from mental health to food safety."[7] And during the final months of his presidency, Clinton turned literally millions of acres of land in Nevada, California, Utah, Hawaii, and Arizona into national monuments. Though Republicans in Congress condemned the president for "usurping the power of state legislatures and local officials" and vainly attempting to "salvage a presidential legacy," in the end they had little choice but to accept the executive orders as law.[8] Rather than wait on Congress, Clinton simply acted, daring his Republican opponents and the courts to try to overturn him. With a few notable exceptions,[9] neither did.

Nor are Clinton and George W. Bush unique in this regard. Throughout the 20th century, presidents have used their powers of unilateral action to intervene in a whole host of policy arenas. Examples abound: By creating the Fair Employment Practices Committee (and its subsequent incarnations) and desegregating the military in the 1940s and 1950s, presidents defined federal government involvement in civil rights decades before the 1964 and 1965 Civil Rights Acts; from the Peace Corps to the Environmental Protection

---

7. Sonya Ross, "Searching for a Way to Make History Forget Impeachment," December 20, 1999, posted on CNN.com.

8. Quotes in "Clinton's Lands Designation Refuels Efforts to Narrow Monuments Law," *Congressional Quarterly Weekly Report,* January 15, 2000, p. 86. In 1999, the House passed HR 1487 that would have restricted the president's authority to designate national parks, but the bill died in the Senate. William G. Howell, *Power without Persuasion: The Politics of Direct Presidential Action* (Princeton, NJ: Princeton University Press, 2003).

9. One of the more visible repudiations of an executive order issued by Clinton concerned the permanent replacement of striking workers. *Chamber of Commerce of the United States v. Reich* (DC Cir. 1996). For more discussion on the institutional constraints of presidential power, see a later section of the chapter.

Agency to the Bureau of Alcohol, Tobacco, and Firearms to the National
Security Agency to the Federal Emergency Management Agency, presidents
unilaterally have created some of the most important administrative agencies
in the modern era. With Reagan's executive order 12291 the most striking
example, presidents have issued a long string of directives aimed at improving
their oversight of the federal bureaucracy. Without any prior congressional
authorization of support, recent presidents have launched military strikes
against Grenada, Libya, Lebanon, Panama, Haiti, Bosnia, and Somalia. These,
moreover, are just a small sampling of the policies issued and actions taken via
executive orders, proclamations, reorganization plans, and other kinds of
directives.[10] As Peter Shane and Harold Bruff argue in their casebook on the
presidency, "Presidents [now] use executive orders to implement many of
their most important policy initiatives, basing them on any combination of
constitutional and statutory powers that is thought to be available."[11] A defining feature of presidential power during the modern era is a propensity and a
capacity to go it alone.

"PRESIDENTIAL POWER IS THE POWER TO PERSUADE"

What theoretical tools currently are available for understanding when presidents exercise their unilateral powers and what influence they glean from
doing so? For answers, scholars habitually turn to Richard Neustadt, who
continues to set the terms by which every student of American politics comes
to understand presidential power. His seminal book *Presidential Power*, originally published in 1960 and updated several times since, not only set an agenda
for research on the American presidency, it structured the ways scholars
thought about presidents as they operated in a highly fragmented system of
governance. It defined the parameters and scope of all subsequent debate and,
by Robert Shapiro, Martha Kumar, and Lawrence Jacobs's account, it "has
continued to be the most widely assigned and read book on the subject and
has been the cornerstone of far-reaching research on the presidency."[12] Nearly
a half century since its original publication and with over a million copies
sold, *Presidential Power* continues to be assigned in nearly every graduate and

---

10. See Philip Cooper, *By Order of the President: The Use and Abuse of Executive
    Direct Action* (Lawrence: University Press of Kansas, 2002), for many more.

11. Peter Shane and Harold Bruff, *The Law of Presidential Power* (Durham, NC:
    Carolina Academic Press, 1988), p. 88.

12. Robert Shapiro, Martha Kumar, and Lawrence Jacobs, eds., *Presidential
    Power: Forging the Presidency for the Twenty-First Century* (New York:
    Columbia University Press, 2004), pp. 1–2.

undergraduate course on the American presidency. It is quite simply, as George Edwards notes, "the most influential, and most admired, book on the American presidency."[13]

What, then, does this book say? When thinking about presidents since Franklin Delano Roosevelt, Neustadt argues, "weak remains the word with which to start."[14] Held captive by world events, by competing domestic interests and foreign policy pressures, by his party, his cabinet, the media, a fickle public, and partisan Congress, the modern president is more clerk than leader. To make matters worse, the president exercises little control over any of these matters—current events and the political actors who inhabit them regularly disregard his expressed wishes. As a result, the pursuit of the president's policy agenda is marked more by compromise than conviction, and his eventual success or failure (as determined by either the public at the next election or historians over time) ultimately depends upon the willingness of others to do things that he cannot possibly accomplish on his own.

To be sure, Neustadt effectively identified the basic dilemma facing all modern presidents: The public expects them to accomplish far more than their formal powers alone permit. This has been especially true since the New Deal, when the federal government took charge of the nation's economy, commerce, and the social welfare of its citizens. But now presidents must address almost every conceivable social and economic problem, from the proliferation of terrorist activities around the globe to the "assaults" on marriage posed by same-sex unions. Armed with little more than the powers to propose and veto legislation and recommend the appointment of bureaucrats and judges, however, modern presidents appear doomed to failure from the very beginning. As one recent treatise on presidential leadership puts it, "Modern presidents bask in the honors of the more formidable office that emerged from the New Deal, but they find themselves navigating a treacherous and lonely path, subject to a volatile political process that makes popular and enduring achievement unlikely."[15]

If a president is to enjoy any measure of success, Neustadt counsels, he must master the art of persuasion. Indeed, for Neustadt, power and persuasion are synonymous. As George Edwards notes in his moving tribute to the scholar and public servant, "perhaps the best known dictum regarding the

---

13. George Edwards, "Neustadt's Power Approach to the Presidency," in Robert Shapiro, Martha Kumar, and Lawrence Jacobs, eds., *Presidential Power, Forging the Presidency for the Twenty-First Century* (New York: Columbia University Press, 2000), p. 14.

14. Richard E. Neustadt, *Presidential Power and the Modern Presidents* (New York: Free Press, 1990), p. xix.

15. Marc Landy and Sidney Milkis, *Presidential Greatness* (Lawrence: University of Kansas Press, 2000), p. 197.

American presidency is that 'presidential power is the power to persuade.' This wonderfully felicitous phrase captures the essence of Neustadt's argument in *Presidential Power* and provided scholars with a new orientation to the study of the presidency."[16] The ability to persuade, to convince other political actors that his interests are their own, defines political power and is the key to presidential success. Power, under this formulation, is about bargaining and negotiating; about convincing other political actors that the president's interests are their own; about brokering deals and trading promises; and about cajoling legislators, bureaucrats, and justices to do his bidding. The president wields influence when he manages to enhance his bargaining stature and build governing coalitions—and the principal way to accomplish as much, Neustadt claims, is to draw upon the bag of experiences, skills, and qualities that the president brings to the office.[17]

Plainly, the image of presidents striking out on their own to conduct a war on terrorism or revamp civil rights policies or reconstruct the federal bureaucracy stands in stark relief to scholarly literatures that equate executive power with persuasion and, consequently, place presidents at the peripheries of the lawmaking process. Conducting a secretive war on terrorism, dismantling international treaties brokered by previous administrations, and performing end runs around some of the most important environmental laws enacted during the past half-century, George W. Bush has hardly capitulated to members of Congress nor has he stood idly by while committee chairs debated whether to introduce legislation on his behalf. Instead, in each instance he seized the initiative, he acted boldly (some would say irresponsibly, even unconstitutionally), and then he dared his political adversaries to counter. Having issued a directive, the challenge Bush faced was not so much to invigorate Congress's support as it was to neutralize its criticism. An inept and enervated opponent, rather than a cooperative and eager friend, typically contributes more to the president's powers of unilateral action.

The actions that Bush and his modern predecessors have taken by fiat do not fit easily within a theoretical framework of executive power that emphasizes frailty and dependence, and offers only persuasion as recourse. For at least two reasons, I suggest, the ability to act unilaterally is conceptually distinct from the array of powers presidents rely upon within a bargaining framework. First, when presidents act unilaterally, they stand at the front end

---

16. George Edwards, "In Memorium, Richard Neustadt," *PS* 37, no. 1 (2004): 126.

17. This last claim that power ultimately is personal, and that its evaluation requires notions of prestige and reputation, has been subject to considerable controversy. For one of the more trenchant critiques, see Terry Moe, "Presidents, Institutions, and Theory," in George Edwards, John Kessel, and Bert Rockman, eds., *Researching the Presidency: Vital Questions, New Approaches* (Pittsburgh, PA: University of Pittsburgh Press, 1993).

of the policymaking process and thereby place upon Congress and the courts the burden of revising a new political landscape.[18] If they choose not to retaliate, either by passing a law or ruling against the president, then the president's order stands. Only by taking (or credibly threatening to take) positive action can either adjoining institution limit the president's unilateral powers. Second, when the president acts unilaterally, he acts alone. Now, of course, he relies upon numerous advisors to formulate the policy, to devise ways of protecting it against congressional or judicial encroachment, and to oversee its implementation (more on this later). But in order to issue the actual policy, the president need not rally majorities, compromise with adversaries, or wait for some interest group to bring a case to court. The president, instead, can strike out on his own. By doing so, the modern president is in a unique position to lead, to break through the stasis that pervades the federal government, and to impose his will in more and more areas of governance.

The ability to move first and act alone, then, distinguishes unilateral actions from all other sources of influence. Indeed, the central precepts of Neustadt's argument are turned upside down, for unilateral action is the virtual antithesis of bargaining and persuading. Rather than leaning on individual members of Congress in quiet deliberations and then standing back and waiting for them to do things that suit White House interest, here presidents just act. Their power does not hinge upon their capacity to "convince [political actors] that what the White House wants of them is what they ought to do for their sake and for their authority."[19] To make policy, presidents need not secure the formal consent of Congress, the active support of bureaucrats, or the official approval of justices. Instead, presidents simply set public policy and dare others to counter. And as long as Congress lacks the votes (usually two-thirds of both chambers) to overturn him, the president can be confident that his policy will stand.

INSTITUTIONAL CONSTRAINTS ON PRESIDENTIAL POWER

Plainly, presidents cannot institute every aspect of their policy agenda by decree. The checks and balances that define our system of governance are alive, though not always well, when presidents contemplate unilateral action. Should the president proceed without statutory or constitutional authority, the courts stand to overturn his actions, just as Congress can amend them, cut

---

18. Terry Moe, "The Presidency and the Bureaucracy: The Presidential Advantage," in Michael Nelson, ed., *The Presidency and the Political System* (Washington, DC: Congressional Quarterly Press, 1999).

19. Neustadt, *Presidential Power and the Modern Presidents,* p. 30.

funding for their operations, or eliminate them outright.[20] Even in those moments when presidential power reaches its zenith—namely, during times of national crisis—judicial and congressional prerogatives may be asserted.[21] In 2004, as the nation braced itself for another domestic terrorist attack and images of car bombings and suicide missions filled the evening news, the courts extended new protections to citizens deemed enemy combatants by

---

20. Future presidents, too, can overturn the unilateral directives of their predecessors. Incoming presidents regularly relax, or altogether undo, the regulations and orders of past presidents; and in this respect, the influence a sitting president wields is limited by the anticipated actions of his forbearers. As Richard Waterman correctly notes, "subsequent presidents can and often do . . . reverse executive orders. Clinton reversed abortion policy established via executive order by the Reagan and G. H. W. Bush administrations. G. W. Bush reversed Clinton's orders on abortion . . . This is not a constraint if we think only within administrations, but for presidents who wish to leave a long-term political legacy, the fact that the next president may reverse their policies may force them, at least on occasion, to move to the legislative arena." Richard W. Waterman, "Unilateral Politics," *Public Administration Review* 64, no. 2 (2004). Many of Bush's actions overturned Clinton orders passed in the waning days (and, in some instances, hours) of the Democrat's administration. As soon as he took office, George W. Bush instructed the Government Printing Office to halt publication in the Federal Register of any new rules, "to ensure that the president's appointees have the opportunity to review any new or pending regulations." (Final regulations have the force of law once they are printed in the Federal Register.) The new administration then issued a 60-day stay on regulations that were published in the Register but had not yet taken effect. Shortly thereafter, Bush undid a number of Clinton environmental orders that extended federal protections to public lands, tightened restrictions on pollution runoff in rural areas, established new pollution-reporting requirements for manufacturers of lead compounds. In addition, Bush reinstituted the ban on federal funding for international agencies that provide abortion counseling, a ban that Clinton lifted eight years prior.

    It is not at all clear, though, that because of these dynamics we should downwardly adjust our assessments of presidential power. Two points deserve consideration, neither of which suggests that we do. First, from the perspective of any individual president, these tendencies may wash out. Just as future presidents may subsequently overturn or amend his actions, a sitting president is not forced to abide by every standing order that he inherits from past presidents. And second, the transfer and exchange of unilateral directives across administrations is not always as seamless as all this supposes. Often, presidents cannot alter orders set by their predecessors without paying a considerable political price, undermining the nation's credibility, or confronting serious, often insurmountable, legal obstacles. William Howell and Kenneth Mayer, "The Last 100 Days," *Presidential Studies Quarterly*, 2005.

21. William Howell and Jon Pevehouse, "Presidents, Congress, and the Use of Force," *International Organization* (2005); William Howell and Jon Pevehouse, *While Dangers Gather: Congressional Checks on Presidential War Powers* (forthcoming); James M. Lindsay, "Congress and the Use of Force in the Post-Cold War Era," in The Aspen Strategy Group, ed., *The United States and the Use of Force in the Post-Cold War Era* (Queenstown, MD: The Aspen Institute, 1995); James M. Lindsay, "Deference and Defiance: The Shifting Rhythms of Executive Legislative Relations in Foreign Policy," *Presidential Studies Quarterly* 33, no. 3 (2003).

the president,[22] as well as noncitizens held in protective custody abroad.[23] And while Congress, as of this writing, continues to authorize as much funding for the Iraq occupation as Bush requests, members have imposed increasing numbers of restrictions on how the money is to be spent and have articulated increasing numbers of objections to how the war is being conducted.

Though we occasionally witness adjoining branches of government rising up and striking down presidential orders, the deeper effects of judicial and congressional restraints remain hidden. George W. Bush might like to unilaterally institute a ban on same-sex marriages or to extend additional tax relief to citizens or to begin the process of privatizing aspects of social security accounts, but he lacks the constitutional and statutory basis for taking such actions and therefore prudently foregoes them.[24] And so it is with all presidents. Unilaterally, they do as much as they think they can get away with. But in those instances when a unilateral directive can be expected to spark some kind of congressional or judicial reprisal, presidents will proceed with caution; and knowing that their orders will promptly be overturned, presidents usually will not act at all.

Elsewhere, I survey the historical record on legislative and judicial efforts to amend and overturn executive orders issued by presidents.[25] On the whole, Congress has had a difficult time enacting laws that amend or overturn orders issued by presidents, though efforts to either codify in law or fund an executive order enjoy markedly higher success rates; and while judges and justices have appeared willing to strike down executive orders, the vast majority of these orders are never challenged, and for those that are, presidents win over 80 percent of the time. Providing an exhaustive account of these findings is beyond the reach of this chapter.[26] Instead, here I want to make two points about the

---

22. *Hamdi v. Rumsfeld* 03-6696, June 28, 2004; *Rumsfeld v. Padilla* 03-1027, June 28, 2004.

23. *Bush v. Gherebi* 03-1245, Ninth Circuit U.S. Court of Appeals, December 18, 2003. On June 30, 2004, the Supreme Court remanded the case back to the appellate level in light of the *Hamdi* and *Padilla* decisions.

24. But for a discussion on the difficulties of constraining the president through crafting carefully worded statutes, see Terry Moe and William Howell, "Unilateral Action and Presidential Power: A Theory," *Presidential Studies Quarterly* 29, no.4 (1999); Terry M. Moe and William G. Howell, "The Presidential Power of Unilateral Action," *Journal of Law, Economics and Organization* 29, no.4 (1999).

25. Howell, *Power without Persuasion: A Theory of Direct Presidential Action,* chaps. 5–6.

26. For longer treatment of Congress's capacity to check the president's unilateral powers, see ibid; Kenneth Mayer, *With the Stroke of a Pen: Executive Orders and Presidential Power* (Princeton, NJ: Princeton University Press, 2001); Moe, "The Presidency and the Bureaucracy: The Presidential Advantage"; Moe and Howell, "Unilateral Action and Presidential Power: A Theory"; Moe and Howell, "The Presidential Power of Unilateral Action."

institutional limitations on presidential power, the first of which involves bud-
getary politics and the second of which concerns the relationship between
strategic behavior and persuasion.

First, some programs and agencies that presidents create unilaterally require
funding. And when they do, Congress retains additional leverage to influence
them, as its members can attach any number of stipulations on how the president spends the appropriated moneys, limiting what the program, agency, or
commission does; whom it serves; what it reports; and how effectively it operates. Still, for at least three reasons, presidents manage to eke out a measure of
influence even when they must reengage Congress within a bargaining framework. First, and most obviously, not all bargaining frameworks are equivalent.
The appropriations process is considerably more streamlined and therefore
easier to navigate, than the legislative process; hence, presidents will enjoy a
higher rate of success when seeking funding for an existing program or agency
than when trying to establish one legislatively. Second, when attempting to
extract funding from Congress, the president does not always need to convince
majorities of the merits of a particular program or agency. Instead, due to the
complexities of budgets, presidents retain opportunities to shuffle funding
sources around and draw from discretionary accounts to fund them.[27] And
third, it is considerably easier to rally support for entities that are already up and
running. By unilaterally establishing a policy or program, presidents can often
shift in their favor the terms of the subsequent debate over funding.

Recall, by way of example, President George W. Bush's efforts in October
2003 to secure $87 billion in supplemental appropriation for an occupation
of Iraq that was proving to be much more expensive than originally anticipated. Because troops were already in the field and because the United States'
credibility in the region had already been wagered, the terms of the debate
had shifted to the president's advantage. A number of members who initially
opposed the military venture nonetheless saw fit to keep the military's coffers
full, as the world had been remade by a series of presidential orders, and a
prior status quo could no longer be recovered. Consider the reflections of
Senator Jon Corzine (D-NJ):

> There is no getting around the fact that our troops are in Iraq, and they
> must be supported. Similarly, we have to accept that, even if we should-
> n't have begun this conflict, it is now our Nation's responsibility, and it
> is in our Nation's interest, to ensure that Iraq is rebuilt and emerges as a
> modern democratic state in the context of its own culture. We simply
> can't walk away from Iraq. And it is imperative that we demonstrate to

---

27. Louis Fisher, *Presidential Spending Power* (Princeton, NJ: Princeton
University Press, 1975).

the Iraqi people, and the international community, that Americans across the political spectrum are committed to this cause, and will fully support the Iraqi people as they move toward a free Iraq. Reluctantly, after balancing these many considerations, I will cast my vote "aye."[28]

And so did a supermajority of members of the House and Senate. They did manage to place some restrictions on how the funding would be spent, and they refused to fund certain requests made by the administration. But in the end, members enacted a resolution that actually exceeded the president's request by roughly $500 million.

The second point concerning institutional constraints on presidential power is more foundational. That presidents anticipate congressional and judicial actions before issuing a unilateral directive does not mean that presidents are intent on persuading nor that the foundations of these executive powers revert back to a Neustadtian paradigm. Executive orders, proclamations, and their ilk cannot be simply added to the list of other powers (formal and informal) that presidents regularly employ in order to persuade. Within a bargaining framework, politics centrally involves consensus building—and presidential power is checked where consensus breaks down. In a unilateral policy-making framework, the president acts as an independent entrepreneur, advancing policies and implementing change where opportunities allow—and his power is checked by the deliberate efforts of Congress, the courts, and other interested parties (the public, interest groups, foreign nations) to either stop him a priori or undo his actions thereafter. The institutional constraints on presidential powers are real; indeed, they are the building blocks of any theory of unilateral action. But though there are important legal and political limits to such powers, and though presidents must exercise them with care, it is a mistake to conceive of them as a special case of persuasion.

THE EXERCISE OF POWERS
AND THE DEMONSTRATION OF INFLUENCE

Reflecting on changes in the modern presidency since the original publication of *Presidential Power,* Neustadt concluded in 1990 that the president "still shares most of his authority with others and is no more free than formerly to rule by sheer command. Persuasion in a sense akin to bargaining remains for major

---

28. Congressional Record, Emergency Supplemental Appropriations for Iraq and Afghanistan Security and Reconstruction Act, 2004 (Senate—October 17, 2003), p. S12809.

purposes the order of his day."[29] The facts suggest otherwise. Virtually every indicator suggests that modern presidents have deployed their unilateral powers with increasing frequency and effect.

From the very beginning, presidents have issued important unilateral directives, the Neutrality Proclamation, Louisiana Purchase, and Emancipation Proclamation being early highlights. But since the Supreme Court formally acknowledged the constitutionality of executive orders and agreements in the 1930s and 40s,[30] the practice has really taken hold. Almost all the trend lines point upward. During the first 150 years of the nation's history, treaties (foreign agreements that must be ratified by Congress) regularly outnumbered executive agreements (foreign agreements that automatically take effect); but during the last 50 years, presidents have signed roughly 10 executive agreements for every treaty submitted to Congress.[31] With rising frequency, presidents are issuing national security directives (policies that are not even released for public review) to institute aspects of their policy agenda.[32] Though the total number of executive orders has declined, the number of "significant" orders has increased by roughly an order of three.[33] Using executive orders, department orders, and reorganizations plans, presidents have unilaterally created a majority of the administrative agencies listed in the United States Government Manual.[34] These policy mechanisms, what is more, hardly exhaust the totality of options available to presidents, who regularly invent new mechanisms or redefine old ones in order to suit their own strategic interests.

That presidents are using their unilateral powers with rising frequency, of course, does not necessarily indicate that they are getting more of what they want. Neustadt fairly warns that one must distinguish the exercise of powers

29. Neustadt, *Presidential Power and the Modern Presidents,* p. 199.

30. See *United States v. Curtiss-Wright,* 299 U.S. 304 (1936); *United States v. Belmont,* 301 U.S. 324 (1937); and *United States v. Pink,* 315 U.S. 203 (1942). Glendon Schubert, *The Presidency in the Courts* (New York: Da Capo Press, 1973) contains a useful summary of these cases.

31. Lawrence Margolis, *Executive Agreements and Presidential Power in Foreign Policy* (New York: Praeger, 1986); Moe and Howell, "The Presidential Power of Unilateral Action."

32. Cooper, *By Order of the President: The Use and Abuse of Executive Direct Action;* Philip Cooper, "Power Tools for an Effective and Responsible Presidency," *Administration & Society* 29, no. 5 (1997).

33. Howell, *Power without Persuasion: A Theory of Direct Presidential Action,* p. 83. See also Kenneth Mayer and Kevin Price, "Unilateral Presidential Powers: Significant Executive Orders, 1949–99," *Presidential Studies Quarterly* 32, no. 2 (2002).

34. William Howell and David Lewis, "Agencies by Presidential Design," *Journal of Politics* 64, no. 4 (2002); David E. Lewis, *Presidents and the Politics of Agency Design* (Stanford, CA: Stanford University Press, 2003).

(plural) from the demonstration of power (singular),[35] for one hardly guarantees the other. As *powers,* Neustadt would surely concede that unilateral directives are an integral part of the president's arsenal. His skepticism lies in whether these powers yield *power,* and he outright rejects the notion that commands enable presidents to meaningfully address the awesome tide of responsibilities laid before their feet.[36] Just as it is difficult, if not impossible, to gauge the influence that other formal powers (for example, vetoes) afford presidents by assessing the frequency with which they are utilized,[37] so too is it difficult to measure the influence of unilateral directives by counting the sheer number issued. For if presidents are merely acting on behalf of other political actors and issuing orders that otherwise would be printed as laws, as much of the "congressional dominance" literature presumes,[38] then unilateral powers hardly augment executive power. To identify power, the president's actions must leave a unique imprint on the law and, ultimately, on the doings of government.[39]

When will presidents exercise their unilateral powers, and what influence do they gain from doing so? Under two circumstances,[40] presidents have strong incentives to issue unilateral policy directives; and in both, they create policies that differ markedly from those that other branches of government would produce were they left to their own devices. First, when Congress is poised to enact sweeping policy changes that the president opposes, the president occasionally can preempt the legislative process with more moderate policy shifts. Recall, by way of example, the weakling Office Safety and Health

---

35. Neustadt, *Presidential Power and the Modern Presidents.* See note on p. 7.

36. Ibid., pp. 10–28. More on this in a later note.

37. Charles Cameron and Nolan M. McCarty, "Models of Vetoes and Veto Bargaining," *Annual Review of Political Science* 7 (2004): 414.

38. See, for example, Roderick Kiewet and Mathew McCubbins, *The Logic of Delegation* (Chicago: University of Chicago Press, 1991). For critiques of this perspective, see Terry Moe, "An Assessment of the Positive Theory of 'Congressional Dominance,'" *Legislative Studies Quarterly* 12, no. 4 (1987); Moe, *The Presidency and the Bureaucracy: The Presidential Advantage;* Keith Whittington and Daniel Carpenter, "Executive Power in American Institutional Development," *Perspectives on Politics* 1, no. 3 (2004).

39. In a critique of this view, Matthew Dickinson insists that unilateral directives "must be evaluated in the context of their overall impact on [presidents'] bargaining power," Matthew Dickinson, "Agendas, Agencies and Unilateral action: New Insights on Presidential Power?" *Congress & the Presidency* 31 (Spring 2004). But this suggestion confuses power's means and ends. Presidents do not issue directives and commands in order to augment their bargaining stature. Rather, they do so in order to materially change the world around them. And to the extent that these unilateral powers accomplish as much, president are well advised to continue issuing them.

40. Derived formally in Howell, *Power without Persuasion: A Theory of Direct Presidential Action.*

Administration created under Nixon, the modest sanctions levied by Reagan against South Africa's Apartheid regime, and the narrow focus and minimal powers assigned to independent commissions investigating intelligence failures on Iraq and weapons proliferation. In each of these cases, Congress stood poised to create either a stronger agency or more robust public policy, and the president lacked the support to kill these initiatives with a veto. And so in each, executive influence was measured by the president's ability to unilaterally impose portions of the proposed legislation and thereby derail the support of moderates within Congress who were considering stronger and more sweeping policy change.

More often, presidents use their unilateral powers to shift status quo policies over which Congress remains gridlocked. And here, the signature of power is not an altered policy but the creation of one that otherwise would not exist at all. As Congress failed to deal in any substantive way with civil rights issues during the 1940s and 50s, the classification of information during much of the post-War era, or terrorism since September 11th, presidents have stepped in and unilaterally defined the government's involvement in these policy arenas.[41] As Joel Fleishman and Arthur Aufses recognize, "Congressional inertia, indifference, or quiescence may sometimes, at least as a practical matter, enable, if not invite, measures on independent presidential responsibility."[42] Incapable of effecting policy change, presidents may step in, grab the reigns of government, and issue policy changes that members of Congress, left to their own devices, would not enact. When doing so, presidents do not always get everything that they want, for should they push too far, their actions may galvanize a congressional or judicial response. And in some instances, presidents might well prefer to have their policy inscribed in law rather than in a unilateral directive, if only to guard them against the meddling of future presidents (see note 20). But a window of opportunity nonetheless presents itself when members of Congress remain mired in gridlock—one that presidents can take without ever convincing a single member of Congress that they share the same interests or serve the same goals.

In both of these scenarios, the contours of executive influence are readily discernible. In the first, the counterfactual to a unilateral directive is a more radical policy shift by Congress—were it not for the president's actions, Congress would retain the votes of its more moderate members in support of sweeping legislative change. And in the second, the mark of presidential influence is not a public policy that is weaker (or stronger) than what Congress prefers—rather, it is the unilateral creation of a policy that otherwise would not

---

41. Cooper, *By Order of the President: The Use and Abuse of Executive Direct Action;* Mayer, *With the Stroke of a Pen: Executive Orders and Presidential Power.*

42. Joel Fleishman and Arthur Aufses, "Law and Orders: The Problem of Presidential Legislation," *Law and Contemporary Problems* 40 (Summer 1976): 24.

exist at all. For were it not for the president's ability to unilaterally change public policy, the federal government would appear incapable of changing public policy in either a liberal or conservative direction.

PROSPECTIVE INFLUENCE

Neustadt is sensitive to the downstream costs of policy change and the possibilities of alienating political allies when abruptly redirecting the doings of government. Influence, he argues, cannot be measured along each policy dimension taken one at a time. Rather, as he notes in personal correspondence, "I do distinguish between the president as a person and the institution of which he is a part. I have to do *that* because the first stated objective of my book is to pursue the question of how he, himself, can exert influence upon the outputs of that (and other) institutions in our separated system. And the second stated objective is to pursue that question *strategically,* in terms not of actual, momentary influence, but rather of *prospective* influence" (emphasis in original). Or, as Charles Jones puts it, "Critical . . . to the Neustadt formulation is the continuous calculation of the effects of a particular choice on personal influence for making the next and succeeding choices."[43] What gains achieved in one instance must be weighed against losses registered in others. And battles won today, it would seem, may foment opposition that will strike tomorrow, effectively undermining the president's longer-term prospects of effecting meaningful policy change.

On this matter, Neustadt's argument enjoys widespread appeal. Scholars continue to monitor the ways in which change can breed contempt, and there emerges, in John Mueller's phrase, "a coalition of minorities."[44] Stephen Skowronek has written one of the most nuanced examinations of the internal forces that drive the formation and decline of political coalitions.[45] Once

---

43. Charles Jones, "Richard E. Neustadt: Public Servant as Scholar," *Annual Review of Political Science* 6 (2003): 12.

44. John Mueller, "Presidential Popularity from Truman to Johnson," *American Political Science Review* 64, no. 1 (1970): 20. In some instances, though, change may breed newfound consensus. Jennifer Hochschild, for instance, has documented the ways in which some Southern communities turned to embrace the goals of desegregation once executive and judicial orders were handed down, often over the vocal objections of local community members. Jennifer Hochschild, *The New American Dilemma: Liberal Democracy and School Desegregation* (New Haven, CT: Yale University Press, 1984). In such instances, the interventions themselves subsequently engendered a measure of local support that could not be manufactured any other way. The following section discusses in further detail some of the issues surrounding the implementation of unilateral directives and laws.

45. Stephen Skowronek, *The Politics Presidents Make* (Cambridge, MA: Harvard University Press, 1993).

established, Skowronek argues, governing coalitions must balance competing interests against one another, and as commitments are made, so too are disaffected minorities. In success lie the seeds of a regime's undoing—for with great deeds come the creation, and eventual mobilization, of enemies. Such is the logic of coalition formation, Skowronek argues, and the logic of regime change more generally.

Unilaterally issued policies, however, are hardly unique in this regard. If presidents must proceed with care when issuing a unilateral directive, for fear that drastic action might alienate key constituents,[46] so too must members of the House and Senate proceed with caution before bringing a bill before their assemblies.[47] Moreover, it is not clear what presidents can, or should, do about this apparent dilemma. There may be instances when presidents ought to sacrifice their policy preferences today in order to maintain goodwill tomorrow. But if influence, ultimately, is measured by a political actor's ability to get things done, to redirect the doings of government, then they must take a stand. Lasting change does not always require that every vested interest buy into a proposed course of action. Often, it comes when unilateral powers are asserted and parties are forced to adapt to a new status quo not of their own making.

IMPLEMENTING PUBLIC POLICY

Many unilateral directives are, to borrow Neustadt's phrase, "self-executing." When presidents change an environmental rule on allowable pollutants, or when they require that firms contracting with the federal government retain some kind of affirmative action policy, or when they extend federal protections to public lands, their orders take immediate effect. Little light shines through the space between the language and implementation of these orders.

Presidents, however, do not always have it so easy. Issuing an order or command does not automatically make it so. When they set new mandates that require the active cooperation of other political actors who have their own independent sources of authority, presidents can have a difficult time effectuating their orders. Bureaucrats, who have their own independent sources of power, may read the president's mandates selectively, insert their own preferences when they think they can get away with it, and then report back incomplete, and sometimes false, information about the policy's successes and

---

46. Neustadt. *Presidential Power and the Modern Presidents,* pp. 27–28.

47. It is no coincidence that most of the quantitative research on the tradeoffs between the creation of policy and the maintenance of public support has focused on legislative processes. Douglas Rivers and Nancy Rose, "Passing the President's Program: Public Opinion and Presidential Influence in Congress," *American Journal of Political Science* 29, no. 2 (1985).

failures.[48] All presidents, and all politicians, struggle to ensure that those who work below them will faithfully follow orders. And to make the most of a difficult situation, persuasion can be helpful.[49]

Recognizing the slippages that occur between an order's issuance and its eventual implementation, however, neither "gives away much of the contested ground" nor "undercut[s] the substantive implications of [the] theory," as Matthew Dickinson suggests.[50] Four factors help explain why. First, it can be just as difficult to convince bureaucrats to execute laws as unilateral directives. If anything, laws may prove more difficult, if only because their mandates tend to be broader and their contents more ambiguous. In order to placate the required supermajorities within Congress, members often fill laws with loopholes and compromises, granting bureaucrats ample opportunities to substitute their own policy preferences for those of their political superiors. As presidents need not assemble a legislative coalition in order to issue a unilateral directive, their orders can be more direct. And as others have effectively argued, possibilities for shirking decline in direct proportion to clarity with which directions are handed down.[51]

Second, we need to be realistic about our expectations. Changes in systems of separated and federated powers almost always come in fits and starts, and policies submitted by any branch of government are regularly contested in others. Ours certainly is not a "presidency dominated" system of government, wherein Congress, courts, interest groups, and the media subvert their own independent interests in order to follow their Chief Executive.[52] No one who thinks seriously about unilateral powers argues as much. Instead, they attempt

---

48. Daniel Carpenter, *The Forging of Bureaucratic Autonomy: Reputations, Networks, and Innovations in Executive Agencies, 1862–1928* (Princeton, NJ: Princeton University Press, 2001).

49. Compliance, though, does not always (or even usually) come at the behest of persuasion, as defined by Neustadt. As a massive literature on delegation demonstrates, authority over budgets and hiring and firing decisions gives political authority considerable leverage over the bureaucracy. Knowing that their budgets might be cut, or that they might be transferred to another agency, or that they may simply be fired, bureaucrats often implement presidential orders even when no one has actively persuaded them to do so and even though they remain totally unconvinced that the president's interests are their own.

50. Dickinson, "Agendas, Agencies and Unilateral Action: New Insights on Presidential Power?" p. 103.

51. John Huber and Charles Shipan, *Deliberate Discretion? The Institutional Foundations of Bureaucratic Autonomy* (New York: Cambridge University Press, 2002).

52. Charles Jones, *The Presidency in a Separated System* (Washington, DC: Brookings Institution, 1994).

to determine whether presidents can draw upon these powers to change, if only marginally, the doings of government. And having framed the issue (and our expectations) appropriately, there is continued reason to believe that they can. Recall those instances when the legislative branch is mired in gridlock and the president strikes out on his own, altering policies in ways that Congress can neither replicate nor overturn. Bureaucrats may not implement a policy as vigorously as the president might desire and judges may interpret the order in ways he might not prefer, but the president still has set in motion changes that, over time, materially affect the rights and privileges afforded average citizens. Though their actions hardly revolutionized race relations overnight, it mattered greatly that Roosevelt introduced a formal ban on discrimination in the military in 1942, that Truman then desegregated the military in 1948, that Johnson issued the first affirmative action policy in 1965, and that Nixon instituted racial quotas in hiring in 1969. For in each of these actions, presidents identified new national priorities and redirected the government down new courses of action, and each thereby contributed to the gradual uplifting of blacks and other ethnic minorities in America.

Third, presidents are fully cognizant of the challenges of implementation, and they regularly take steps to reduce them. When they unilaterally create programs and agencies, presidents structure them in ways that augment executive control.[53] Between 1946 and 1997, fully 67 percent of administrative agencies created by executive order and 84 percent created by departmental order were placed either within the Executive Office of the President or the cabinet, as compared to only 57 percent of agencies created legislatively. Independent boards and commissions, which dilute presidential control, governed only 13 percent of agencies created unilaterally, as compared to 44 percent of those created through legislation. And 40 percent of agencies created through legislation had some form of restrictions on the kinds of appointees presidents can make, as compared to only 8 percent of agencies created unilaterally. Presidents do not suffer quietly under the weight of implementation problems. Rather, they actively participate in the "politics of bureaucratic structure," issuing orders that augment their control over and influence in administrative agencies scattered throughout the federal bureaucracy.[54]

---

53. Howell and Lewis, "Agencies by Presidential Design"; Lewis, *Presidents and the Politics of Agency Design.*

54. Terry Moe, "The Politics of Structural Choice: Toward a Theory of Public Bureaucracy," in Oliver Williamson, ed., *Organization Theory: From Chester Barnard to the Present and Beyond* (New York: Oxford University Press, 1990); Terry M. Moe and Scott A. Wilson, "Presidents and the Politics of Structure," *Law and Contemporary Problems* 57, no. 2 (1994).

Fourth, and finally, the relationship between a president who stands atop his governing institution and subordinates who ultimately are responsible to him differs markedly from that of a legislator who stands on roughly equal footing with 534 colleagues across two chambers. Assuredly, hierarchies reside in both the legislative and executive branches. And party leaders and committee chairs provide a modicum of order to their collective decision-making bodies, wherein no single member has the final word on which bills are introduced and which amendments are considered. In the executive branch, however, ultimate authority resides with a president who (fairly or not) is given credit or blame for the success or failure of public policies. While bureaucrats certainly retain a significant amount of discretion to do as they please, lines of authority converge upon the president.

To be sure, where implementation concerns arise, the influence afforded by unilateral powers is reduced. Just as presidents must anticipate the likely responses of Congress and the courts when issuing a directive, so too must they remain sensitive to the interests of their own administration. But it is equally important that scholars avoid overstating the case and resist the temptation of falling back into a world wherein all power is equated with bargaining and negotiating. Concerns about implementation pervade politics; but they do not eliminate opportunities for genuine influence. Unilateral powers do have limits for which any theory of unilateral action must account; but it is a mistake to equate these powers with persuasion, to dismiss them as merely epiphenomenal, or to conclude that because they do not allow presidents to secure everything they might like, these powers amount to little of consequence.

NEUSTADT'S THREE CASES
OF COMMAND

Neustadt is perfectly aware of the existence of these unilateral powers. Indeed, he begins his book with three such examples: Truman's decision to fire Douglas MacArthur in 1951; Truman's seizure of the steel mills in 1952; and Eisenhower's ordering of federal troops into Little Rock, Arkansas, in 1957. The lessons drawn, however, differ markedly from those outlined in this chapter. In each instance, Neustadt claims, commands were issued where efforts to persuade had faltered. The president proved incapable of convincing a general, a labor union, and a state governor to respect his wishes, and hence was left with no recourse but to holler in the hope that others would, at last, listen. For Neustadt, the exercise of these unilateral powers, as with virtually all formal powers, represents a "painful last resort, a forced response to the exhaustion of other remedies, suggestive less of mastery than of failure—the failure of attempts to gain an end by softer means."[55] Unilateral directives would seem to signal weakness, for when presidents issue them, they admit to having lost sway over other political actors and, by extension, the political system more generally.

Neustadt's caution that presidents do not automatically have their way every time they issue a command is a fair one. But for a variety of reasons, he overstates matters when he argues that presidents necessarily reveal weakness when they use their unilateral powers. Two stand out, the first of which concerns his case selection. It is misleading to characterize all unilateral actions as last-ditch efforts to salvage a policy that political actors elsewhere in the government are actively working to sabotage. When they alter a civil service rule or strengthen environmental regulation or send military troops to fight foreign armies, presidents are doing considerably more than expressing frustration at their inability to persuade. They are standing at the front end of the policy-making process, materially changing the doings of government, and challenging other lawmakers to catch up. Of course, presidents do not always get everything that they want. As emphasized from the outset, presidents who use these powers are well advised to respect their political and constitutional limitations. But Neustadt overlooks the many instances when presidents never attempted to persuade, when prior requests never went unheeded, and when political actors never overtly disavowed their president's wishes. Rather, seeing an opportunity, presidents struck, issued an order, and thereby set in motion a host of developments that otherwise would never have occurred.

Second, when measuring power, the standards of review cannot be whether presidents secure all aspects of their policy agenda, as all political actors freely cooperate in a set of shared pursuits. Rather, power is properly assessed by reference to conditions that would exist had powers not been exercised. And in all three cases that Neustadt considers, power is readily discernible. Had Truman not fired MacArthur, the general would have continued to wreak havoc on the president's war planning; had he not seized the steel mills, the workers' strike would have proceeded unabated; and had Eisenhower not sent the troops into Little Rock, Central High School would not have been integrated. Truman might well have preferred that MacArthur simply followed his order or that the unions abandon their strike, just as Eisenhower surely would have preferred that Arkansas Governor Orval Faubus would have followed the federal courts' desegregation orders. But it greatly misconstrues things to equate the mere issuance of commands as demonstrations of weakness. They may, in some instances, be second-best options, but they nonetheless yield influence that presidents, without them, would sorely miss.

---

55. Neustadt, *Presidential Power and the Modern Presidents*, p. 24.

A PRESIDENT STANDS APART

While writing *Presidential Power,* Neustadt struggled to see the world as the president sees it and to take inventory of the peculiar "vantage points in government" that the president holds.[56] As Jones notes, Neustadt intended to "settle into the head of the President so as to evaluate what is best for him, accepting who that President is and what his advantages are."[57] Though his immediate concern was the presidency, Neustadt discovered that the president's condition was hardly unique, and that the appropriate prescription for action, and the predictor of success, appeared to apply to politicians generally: Namely, marshal all available resources (personal and otherwise) in order to more effectively bargain, negotiate, and, with good fortune, persuade other political actors to do things that you cannot do for yourself. In his famous dictum, Neustadt observes that ours is a "government of separated institutions sharing power."[58] As powers are shared, and as members of Congress, judges, bureaucrats, and presidents all have independent means by which to check the actions of others, the importance of persuasion would appear to apply universally.

In one very important sense, Neustadt's argument does carry over to other political actors in other branches of government. To see why, it is useful to return to the context in which Neustadt was originally writing. During the 1940s and 50s, presidential power was conceived of largely in legalistic terms. Scholars dissected the Constitution for clues into the proper scope and content of presidential influence; they scrutinized the formal, enumerated powers bestowed upon the office; and they categorized the varied and various roles that presidents cast themselves in.[59] Politics, it seemed to Neustadt, were lost in these discussions. The sense that outcomes are not preordained, that power is always contested, that influence is always fleeting, was somehow missing from a literature that tried to piece together the formal powers of an officeholder, studied largely in isolation from the other political actors in other branches of government. The formal powers bestowed upon presidents do not automatically translate into influence over either the writing or the implementation of public policy. Neustadt correctly sought to insert politics into the study of the presidency; moreover, he wanted to offer counsel to presidents operating

---

56. Ibid., p. 150.

57. Jones, "Richard E. Neustadt: Public Servant as Scholar," p. 13.

58. Neustadt, *Presidential Power and the Modern Presidents,* p. 29.

59. Edward Corwin, *The President, Office and Powers, 1787–1948: History and Analysis of Practice and Opinion* (New York: New York University Press, 1957); Clinton Rossiter, *The American Presidency* (New York: Harcourt, Brace and World, 1956).

within a highly fragmented political system, one that retained strong biases in favor of the status quo. Neustadt's lessons for presidents, as such, resonate throughout politics, for the challenge that presidents face is a challenge that all political actors face: namely, how to alter the flavors and proportions of dishes served from a kitchen with many cooks. In this sense, Neustadt's legacy is strong and vibrant because he was considerably more than just a scholar of the American presidency; he spoke to the entirety of our discipline.

But a basic fact should not go overlooked: Presidential power is not the same as legislative power. And when equating the two, scholars give short shrift to one of the most important ways in which presidents effect policy change in the modern era—namely, by striking out on their own and leaving it to others to revise the new political landscape. Unlike any member of Congress, the president alone can send troops abroad, renegotiate the terms of a tariff agreement with another country, alter environmental or worker safety regulations, or revamp civil rights law *without ever constructing a coalition or holding it together through the legislative process.* To be sure, presidents must employ this tactic strategically, given that Congress and the courts, not to mention future presidents, can overturn a sitting president's orders. But while all members of Congress must rely upon their colleagues to accomplish anything at all, presidents can unilaterally issue public policies that would never survive the legislative process.

After acting unilaterally, presidents may choose to draw upon the resources (professional reputation and public prestige) that Neustadt identifies as being crucial to their eventual success. They do so, however, in order to protect orders already given, to block attempts at meddling with policies already in place. Persuasion may reenter the equation, as presidents may need to convince members of Congress to fund their programs and bureaucrats to implement them. But these two processes of change are not synonymous. It is misleading to suggest that unilateral powers are "but a method of persuasion."[60] That persuasion occasionally creeps back into unilateral action does not mean that the president's world always reverts back to the one Neustadt describes. For reasons previously outlined, the structure of negotiations over a policy that is up and running, rather than one that is strictly imagined, differs markedly. And in the end, precisely because they are able to unilaterally impose a new status quo, presidents have additional leverage when deliberations with Congress cannot be avoided.

Neustadt's essential arguments that persuasion is a component of power and that success is regularly fleeting certainly apply to politics generally. But not all politics consists of bargaining, not all bargaining frameworks are alike,

---

60. Neustadt, *Presidential Power and the Modern Presidents,* p. 28.

and opportunities to exert influence are not equally allotted across our system of governance. Power does not always find expression in deliberation, in the subtle push of adversaries, in the creation of new alliances, and the abandonment of old ones. And action—unsettling, calculating, and deliberate—is hardly the poor stepson to persuasion—decorous, reasoning, and humble. To the contrary, action often appears where persuasion cannot, reshaping and redirecting the doings of government in hugely important ways. The challenge that presidency scholars now face is to build upon Neustadt's central insight that politics matter greatly and that outcomes are not deterministic, in order to examine how different branches of government fare as they thrust and parry against one another, to identify the distinct advantages and disadvantages that presidents confront in this exchange, and to determine when presidents either succeed or fail in influencing the outcomes of government— sometimes by declaration, sometimes by persuasion, and occasionally by a combination of the two.

5

⚜

Presidential Decision Making

The Influence of Personality on George W. Bush's Decisions To Go to War

STEPHEN J. WAYNE
Georgetown University

Crisis decision making reveals much about presidents and their leadership styles: their eagerness to make decisions; their openness to diverse information and analyses; their methods for organizing information and applying it to the case at hand; the mindset they use to make sense of it all; the feelings that they and their advisers may have that affect the timing and substance of their decisions; and above all, their ability to make a sound judgment, to adhere to it if it works out well and to change it if it does not. For example,

- Do presidents wait for decisions or reach down for them?

- Do they encourage dissent or look for consensus among their advisers?

- Are they open to assumptions, inferences, facts, and advice that conflict with their own?

- How well do they deal with complexity, ambiguity, and conflict in the descriptions, explanations, and recommendations they receive?

- How long does it take them to decide?

- Do they agonize over the decisions they have made?

- Are they comfortable with own judgment?

- Do they move on, constantly evaluate their decisions, and/or second-guess themselves?

- Can they accept criticism and admit error?

- Can they reverse themselves if their decision results in an undesirable outcome?

- Do they take personal responsibility for their decision and the assumptions on which it was made, or do they attribute unsatisfactory or unexpected consequences to others?

The answers to these questions depend, in large part, on the presidents themselves, their character, work style, and world view. Personality drives the process although it does not necessarily dictate the results. It is one factor among many; it may not be the dominant one, but it is always present. And in crisis decision making, when the chips are down and the stakes are high, when presidents are stressed, when much is thought to ride on the decision, a president's personality is apt to be even more important than in routine decision making, when institutional processes largely condition presidential responses.

There is another reason to study the personality component in decision making. Situations change. People come and go. There is usually some variability in the political environment. But a personality, once established, is relatively stable over time; it is hard to change, as people who undergo psychotherapy usually find out. Thus, if a personality can be accurately assessed and if it impacts in much the same manner on most or all crisis decisions a president makes (a very big *if*), then a president's personality should be a useful explanatory tool.

The existence of a personality component in all but the most routine presidential decisions should motivate students of decision making to examine it closely. But political scientists have been reluctant to do so. Ironically, the behavioral revolution, which began in the 1950s, is partially to blame. Psychological variables are not directly observable. They must be inferred from observable phenomenon. From a scientific perspective, inferences are risky and ultimately speculative. Competing theories of personality contribute to the interpretive nature of the enterprise.

There's another problem. The complexity of the human personality and the need to be sensitive to that complexity require deep, idiosyncratic analysis that is not readily amenable to generalization, a goal of social science. Nor is psychological typecasting, from which hypotheses are often derived and tested, satisfactory from a psychological or political science perspective.[1]

---

1. An example of psychological typecasting and the methodological problems that result from it can be seen in James David Barber, *The Presidential Character* (Englewood Cliffs, NJ; Prentice Hall, 1972). For an effective critique of Barber's methodology, see Alexander George, "Assessing Presidential Character," in Aaron Wildavsky, ed., *Perspectives on the Presidency* (Boston: Little, Brown, 1975), 91–134.

Besides, the more comprehensive the personality component of the analysis, the more likely the tendency toward psychological reductionism, that is, explaining everything in terms of it.

What are the options? Can students of the presidency effectively incorporate the psychological dimension into their analyses without disregarding or downplaying situational and environmental factors that affect personal judgments? Professor Fred I. Greenstein thinks so. He has written a book, *The Presidential Difference,* in which he identifies six performance components of presidential leadership: public communication, organizational capacity, political skill, vision, cognitive style, and emotional intelligence.[2] Each of these components is character driven. Each is predicated in part on how presidents feel about themselves, their abilities to understand and explain the world around them, to interact with others, and to exercise good judgment.

Greenstein has applied his analytical framework to George W. Bush. He has described Bush as an effective but not eloquent communicator, a laid-back manager who delegates to others, seeks consensus from his advisers from whom complete loyalty is expected, is intelligent but not intellectually curious, personable but also highly partisan, visionary but not particularly flexible in his views, and emotional but self-contained.[3]

In another psychologically oriented analysis of George W. Bush, Hugh Heclo surmises that Bush is heavily invested in self-control. His confidence is buttressed by an unwillingness to challenge his own views. Heclo describes Bush's presidential mindset as purposive, disciplined, and goal-oriented: "In the internal schema, the purpose of politics is to identify one's mission, keep faith with that charge, and then move on to the next agenda item."[4]

Both Greenstein and Heclo support their analysis with the words and actions of George W. Bush before and during his presidency. By necessity, they draw conclusions on the basis of picking and choosing examples that led to and illustrate their judgment. Political scientists often find this type of analysis unconvincing. They point out that alternate explanations are possible for the same words, and that other words Bush may have uttered or behavior he may have exhibited, which the authors do not cite, could lead to very different psychological interpretations. Besides, presidents are scripted and choreographed by others; they make few decisions and take few public actions totally

---

2. Fred I. Greenstein, *The Presidential Difference* (New York: Free Press, 2000).

3. Fred I. Greenstein, "The Leadership Style of George W. Bush," in Fred I.
   Greenstein, ed., *The George W. Bush Presidency: An Early Assessment*
   (Baltimore, MD: Johns Hopkins Press, 2003), pp. 13–16.

4. Hugh Heclo, "The Political Ethos of George W. Bush," in Greenstein, ed.,
   The George W. Bush Presidency, p. 48.

on their own. Which words and actions are primarily theirs and which can be attributed individually or collectively to their staff?[5]

This chapter takes a slightly different approach. It examines two decisions in which the president was deeply and continually involved and which he has used to define his presidency and shape his legacy: his decisions to go to war first in Afghanistan and then in Iraq. It does so with the belief that case studies are a more appropriate format for assessing the impact of personality on performance than the pick-and-choose biographical approach that many presidential scholars adopt. Moreover, as this analysis is limited to Bush's war decisions, the words he uses tend to be more repetitive, making inferences about motives, assumptions, goals, and needs a bit easier. The extent to which these words and actions and the personal psychology underlying them are indicative of Bush's responses to other crises will have to be the subject of another inquiry.

My goal then is to demonstrate how George W. Bush's personality affected two of the most important and far-reaching decisions of his presidency. I rely wherever possible on seemingly unscripted remarks and actions, although I do cite some speeches and prepared comments to support my analysis. Over time, repetition makes unrehearsed remarks seem scripted and the script a consequence of the president's well-known rhetorical and policy preferences.

I begin my case studies with a prelude describing George W. Bush's psychological underpinnings: the Bush family legacy. I next discuss how that legacy and Bush's pre-presidential experiences helped shape his world views, work style, and personal attributes that he wished to demonstrate as president. The final part of the chapter applies Bush's conception of the presidency, mindset, and personal needs and desires to his decisions to go to war and his rationale for those decisions.

THE BUSH FAMILY LEGACY

As the oldest in a highly competitive family of smart female and male overachievers, George W. was expected to follow in the illustrious footsteps of those who had preceded him and who had achieved so much: economic success, social standing, and public service and elective office. George W. was aware,

---

5. David Frum, a former Bush speech writer states that he, not the president, was the creator of the "Axis of Evil" phrase that Bush employed in his 2002 State of the Union address. David Frum, *The Right Man* (New York: Random House, 2003), pp. 235–40. Bush claims that he, not his speech writers, was responsible for the line, "Freedom is not America's gift to the world. Freedom is God's gift to everybody in the world." Bob Woodward, *Plan of Attack* (New York: Simon and Schuster, 2004), pp. 88–89.

painfully aware, of his father as his male model. In his autobiography, he wrote, "My dad has never tried to influence me *except* [emphasis mine] through example, and it is a powerful one. I have his name, all but the Herbert, and people tell me I look a lot like him."[6]

But dad's was a tough act to follow and George W. knew it.

My problem was, "What's the boy ever done?" I have to make a fairly big splash in the pool because of who my Dad is. The advantage is that everybody knows who I am. The disadvantage is that no matter how great my accomplishments may be, no one is going to give me credit for them.[7]

Brother Jeb put it this way:

He [George W.] is the oldest and it is his namesake, and he more directly followed my dad's path. If he was openly honest about it, he might say that it had some effect, that it might define him in some way." Jeb went on to add, "[M]y estimation of my father is so powerful that if I felt like I had to follow his footsteps and follow a path that he has set for me, I would fail."[8]

George W. must also have felt some resentment in having his life's journey mapped out so clearly for him, much less being judged on the basis of the standards that his father and grandfather had set. Where was the adventure and self-discovery? How could he establish his own individuality in the light of such explicit expectations?

My guess is that young George had to deal with a lot of contradictory emotions and angry impulses. He also had to contend with more than his share of personal failures. His self-doubts and rebellious behavior prolonged his adolescence for almost two decades beyond his college years. Whether or not he had what would be required to travel the path his grandfather and father had

---

6. George W. Bush, *A Charge To Keep* (New York: William Morrow, 1999), p. 183. At the GOP convention that nominated his father, George W. told a reporter that he had no plans to run for office, but if he did, "I'd have to work hard at establishing my own identity . . . but if I were to think about running for office and he was president, it would be more difficult to establish my own identity. It probably would help me more if he lost . . . you know people have certain expectations from the son of a president, particularly the oldest one." Bill Minutaglio, *First Son: George W. Bush and the Bush Family Dynasty* (New York: Three Rivers Press, 1999), p. 230.

7. Minutaglio, *First Son,* p. 241.

8. Minutaglio, *First Son,* p. 101. Reflecting on the difficulty of living the family legacy, Elsie Walker, George H. W. Bush's cousin, commented: "This is not an easy family to grow up in. All of us had to come to grips with the fact that there are enormously successful people in it and a lot of pressure to be a big deal." Minutaglio, *First Son,* p. 158.

charted must have been a persistent anxiety, conscious or unconscious, during much of this period.

The contrast between father and son from the mid-1960s until 1980 was striking. The father was focused, upbeat, and goal-oriented—in an upward political trajectory; the son was unfocused, unsettled, and irresponsible—in a downward spiral. In the words of former speech writer, David Frum:

> He tried everything his father had tried—and well into his forties, succeeded at almost nothing. The younger Bush scraped through Andover and Yale academically, never made a varsity team, earned no distinction in the Air National Guard, and was defeated in a run for Congress in 1978. He lost millions in the oil business and had to be rescued by his father's friends in 1983. It was after that last humiliation that he began drinking heavily.[9]

Identity Crisis

During this period, George W. was struggling to find himself, "to reconcile who I was and who my Dad was, to establish my own identity in my own way."[10] Distinguishing himself from his father by his speech and manner, his dress, words, and general deportment set him apart from the upscale, New England preppies from whom he felt alienated. He talked, dressed, and acted as a stereotypical Texan. He stretched the coat and tie rules at Andover by wearing worn, wrinkled shirts, jeans, occasionally an Army jacket, sneakers, and no socks.[11] He disdained the "intellectual snobbery" he perceived at both schools and befriended the nonlibrary crowd of guys looking for a good time.[12]

George W. was an underachiever in a competitive atmosphere in which intellectual prowess and academic success were high on the list of school values. But he was also popular, witty, and fun, a person who had found his own element in an environment he undoubtedly perceived as pretentious and hostile. In a sense, George W. forsook the expectations of his career path by making a comparison with his father at a comparable stage in their lives, on its surface, ridiculous.

---

9. Frum, *The Right Man,* pp. 283–84.

10. Minutaglio, *First Son,* p. 97.

11. Nicholas Kristof, "Earning A's in People Skills at Andover," *New York Times,* June 10, 2000, p. A10.

12. George W. Bush, "In His Own Words," *Washington Post,* July 27, 1999, p. A11.

I would speculate as well that George W. Bush was also very angry. He had a temper that exploded frequently. Known as a "roman candle" by his family, he would vent his frustrations with outbursts that liquor often helped to ignite.[13]

After his graduation from Harvard Business School in 1974, George W.'s life continued to flounder. He went into the oil business in Texas without much success. A bachelor with many friends, he spent much of his leisure time during this period "drinking and carousing and fumbling around."[14] Although tobacco, alcohol, and womanizing filled the time, mollified the frustrations, and may have even numbed the feelings of inadequacy the younger George felt, none of this dysfunctional behavior succeeded in erasing the blueprint that had been etched into his psyche. Diane Paul, who dated George W. during his mid 20s, recalled that despite his behavior, he never gave up the models toward which he aspired: "The whole way he talked about his father and grandfather, it's no accident that he tried to repeat just what his dad did, in the same order . . . his goal was to see how he could step into those shoes, how he could live up to that family legacy. It was in his bones."[15]

The story of how he resurrected himself has been told elsewhere, but resurrect himself he did and pretty much on his own.[16] Religion was the crutch on which he leaned. Beginning in 1985, George W. participated in a bible study group with a small number of local businessmen who had received training in Community Bible Study, an organization based in California. The sessions in which a witty George W. learned to control his sharp tongue, tone

---

13. Tom De Frank, Presentation at White House Workshop, September 22, 2003. The most destructive of these explosions that has been reported occurred after George W., then 26, and his 15-year-old brother, Marvin, returned home inebriated from a friend's house. After banging into a neighbor's garage can and dragging it down the street, George parked the car. Marvin entered the house first. A very displeased father told Marvin to tell George that he wanted to see him. Moments later, George W. barged into his father's study and said, "I hear you're looking for me. You wanna go mano a mano right here?" Brother Jeb, also in the room at the time, interceded to save his older brother from further embarrassment with the news that George W. had been accepted into Harvard Business School. "You should think about that, son," his father advised. "Oh, I'm not going. I just wanted to let you know that I could get in," was George W.'s reply. Minutaglio, *First Son*, pp. 147–48.

14. Minutaglio, *First Son,* p. 173.

15. Nicholas Kristof, "A Father's Footsteps Echo throughout a Son's Career," *New York Times,* September 11, 2000, p. A18.

16. In his own words, see Bush, *A Charge to Keep;* Minutaglio, *First Son.*

down his sarcasm, and eventually gain inner tranquility contributed over time to a greater sense of self-control and, ultimately, self-respect.[17]

Bush's renewed faith—he does not refer to his enhanced religiosity as a rebirth—provided a foundation from which he took strength, gained confidence, and proved capable of reversing the dysfunctional behavior in which he had been engaged. And it enabled him to do so without enduring the pain of self-analysis, much less exploring the depths of his rebellion.[18]

Bush's reconfirmation of faith gave him the willpower to stop drinking and smoking.[19] The discipline and focus that he was now able to exert enabled him to exploit his social skills, compensate for his anti-intellectualism—probably fostered in part by his difficulties at Andover and Yale—and reaffirmed his conservative convictions while simultaneously demonstrating his compassion for the less fortunate. It gave him the encouragement, confidence, and finally, the strength to follow in his father's footsteps and control whatever demons had influenced his past behavior. His wife Laura and the birth of their twin daughters created an additional and compelling incentive to do so. What he needed was the will and strength, and his religious reconfirmation put both within reach. His religious beliefs provided him with the wherewithal to stand on his own feet without having to depend on alcohol to numb the pain of his failures. He was ready to strike out on his own.

His first challenge was to defeat Governor Anne Richards and then work with Texas Democratic legislative leaders to fashion public policy. The next challenge was to position himself as the most viable candidate for the 2000 Republican nomination, answering the call that he and his advisers helped to create, and then defeat an incumbent vice president whose great

---

17. Bush attributes some of the influence for his religious regeneration to the Rev. Billy Graham, a family friend and Kennebunkport guest who responded to questions from Bush and his siblings about spirituality and faith. In his book, George W. recalls a walk in the woods with Rev. Graham:

    Reverend Graham planted a mustard seed in my soul, a seed that grew over the next year. He led me to the path, and I began walking. And it was the beginning of a change in my life. I had always been a religious person, had regularly attended church, even taught Sunday school and served as an altar boy. But that weekend my faith took on new meaning. It was the beginning of a new walk where I would recommit my heart to Jesus Christ.

    Later on, he said: "My faith gives me focus and perspective." Bush, *A Charge to Keep,* p. 136–38.

18. George W. is not an introspective person. He regularly refers to psychologically oriented analysis as "psychobabble."

19. According to former White House staffer, David Frum, Bush told five religious leaders he had invited to the White House in September 2002, "You know, I had a drinking problem. Right now I should be in a bar in Texas, not the Oval Office. There is only one reason that I am in the Oval Office and not a bar. I found faith. I found God. I am here because of the power of prayer." Frum, *The Right Man,* p. 283.

personal ambition, deep policy interests, and ties to the Clinton administration made him a formidable political opponent. But Bush won the disputed outcome, which enabled him to face the challenge he was waiting for—to show that he could be a capable president, that he could meet, even exceed, his father's accomplishments in office.

THE PSYCHOLOGICAL DIMENSIONS OF THE GEORGE W. BUSH PRESIDENCY

Having won a controversial, nonplurality victory, George W. Bush's initial challenge was to show that he could do it, to act presidential and in doing so, overcome the negative stereotypes that plagued him from the campaign—that he was inarticulate, underinformed, unintelligent, and lacking in the skills to be president. Not only did he need to elevate his personal status, but he had to augment his political power. He did so by clothing himself in the garb of the office.[20] He also had to demonstrate that he, not Dick Cheney, was the real president, the final decision maker, the president in fact as well as title.

Much effort went into crafting George W.'s image in those first three months. His negative stereotype had to be replaced by a presidential demeanor. Rehearsed speeches reduced his verbal blunders; by detailing the policy of his administration, he was able to counter the informational deficiencies and cognitive inadequacies that shrouded his candidacy and marred his reputation in his pre-candidacy years. A nice-guy image was calibrated to conform to his promise to return civility to Washington and replace the strident, partisan rhetoric of the Clinton–Gingrich era. The president reached out to Democrats in a highly personal way, but he was not about to change his politics, compromise his political beliefs, or renege on his campaign promises. He remembered all too well the political grief his father suffered when he repudiated his "read my lips, no new taxes" promise. George W. Bush placed credibility high on the list of attributes he wished to demonstrate as president.

Much deference was paid to the majesty of the office. Business dress was required at all times in the White House; meetings started promptly; aides stood up when the president entered the room.[21] "Mr. President" became the

---

20. Charles O. Jones, "Capitalizing on Position in a Perfect Tie," in Greenstein, ed., *The George W. Bush Presidency,* pp. 173–96.

21. David Frum, a speechwriter in the Bush White House wrote in his book, *The Right Man,*

> I once asked George Stephanopoulos whether it was true, as I'd heard, that the Clinton staff did not rise when Clinton entered the room. He looked embarrassed and said, "Well, we had a lot of trouble at the beginning adjusting to the idea that Clinton was really the president."

No such trouble for the Bushies. (Frum, *The Right Man,* p. 15.)

only accepted appellation. Out of his presence, "the president" replaced the more informal references to "George."

The formality conformed to George W.'s normative conception of the office and his role in it. It also emphasized the hierarchy and the president's position atop it. Having witnessed his father's presidency first hand, George W. came to his presidency with a regal view of the office, the behavior he expected in it, and the deference to be paid to it.

Role, Control, and Self-Discipline

Bush's view of the presidency guided his own performance in it. He played the role of the CEO president, emphasizing command, professionalism, and delegation. Being president enhanced George W.'s sense of self; his confidence grew. He was determined to be the kind of president to which his father aspired but fell short, although George W.'s admiration and love for his father never allowed him to admit to any of his father's failings as president.

Not only did formality replace informality in the George W. Bush White House, but routine was encouraged over spontaneity. The unexpected was a potential threat; routine was more comfortable because the appropriate response was clearer. In the words of Frank Bruni, the *New York Times* reporter who covered George W. during the 2000 campaign, "his [George W. Bush's] almost obsessive adherence to the daily campaign schedule that had been laid out for him and his famous punctuality were not just about politeness; they reflected a desire to make his world as predictable—and manageable—as possible."[22]

Bush gave out clear-cut cues to those around him—what to say and how to behave. He desired his advisers to be concise, concrete, and direct; above all, he valued loyalty. He expected aides to toe the administration line in public; straying off the reservation was punishable by reprimand and ultimately, dismissal. Lieutenants imposed order; order reinforced Bush's leadership—hence the White House's "no-holds-barred" attack against former national security aide Richard Clarke, who questioned the direction and competency of Bush's decision making and his national security priorities.

Why the need for control? The answer lies in Bush's experience of being out of control for so many years. Transforming the dysfunctional behavior of his prolonged adolescence (to the age of 40) has required Bush to keep himself in check, to control the anger and the outbursts that had erupted so frequently in his past. According to David Frum, a White House speech writer in 2001:

> Id control was the basis of Bush's approach to the presidency. . . . Bush was a man of fierce anger. When he felt that he had been betrayed or

---

22. Frank Bruni, *Ambling into History* (New York: HarperCollins, 2001),
   pp. 65–66.

ill-used, his face would go hard, his voice would go cold, and his words would be scathing. Yet he did not allow the anger to govern him. His feelings were as disciplined as his legs. That is what we meant by "doing his duty": not gloopy niceness, but master of his emotions.[23]

Strength, Decisiveness, and Vision

Bush's penchant for self-control has not diminished his individuality as president. That individuality has been characterized by the attributes of strength, decisiveness, and vision he demonstrated in his response to the terrorists attacks of September 11, 2001. It is no coincidence that these attributes redress his father's publicly perceived character failings: weaknesses, vacillation, inconsistency, and lack of vision. [24]

In meeting the challenge that his father's political career posed for him, George W. was also determined not to fall victim to the deficiencies that afflicted his father's presidency: the elder Bush's failure to build and use political capital, give sufficient attention to public relations, impose loyalty on senior aides, and perceive the connection between electoral and governing politics.[25]

George W. is decisive to a fault. Reporter Bob Woodward, who was given access to the administration's decision making following the terrorist attacks of September 11, 2001, noted in his book, *Bush at War:* "Bush's leadership style bordered on the hurried. He wanted action, solutions. Once on a course, he directed his energy at forging on, rarely looking back, scoffing at—even ridiculing—doubt and anything less than 100 percent commitment. He seemed to harbor few, if any, regrets. His short declarations could seem impulsive."[26]

---

23. Frum, *The Right Man,* p. 57.

24. A *Newsweek* cover story in October 1988, headlined "The Wimp Factor," raised an issue that plagued George H. W. Bush throughout his presidency: Was he tough enough to do the job? Bush responded to the charge by overreacting: He launched a highly negative personal campaign against his opponent, Michael Dukakis, which many of his aides believed was out of character for him; in his first year in office, he sent 24,000 American troops to Panama to capture one man, Manuel Noriega; and he spoke and acted with certainty and resolve after Iraq invaded Kuwait. But as president, George H. W. Bush also repudiated his "read my lips, no new taxes" promise, expanded government's regulatory role, compromised the Reagan position on environmental legislation, and was reluctant to acknowledge, much less respond to, a recessed economy. To many, Democrats and conservative Republicans alike, he seemed out of it; "he just didn't get it" was the accusatory cry heard through the 1992 presidential campaign.

25. Richard L. Berke, "Bush Shapes His Presidency with Sharp Eye on Father's," *New York Times,* March 28, 201, pp. A1, A13.

26. Woodward, *Bush at War,* p. 256.

George W. admits to being an instinctive decision maker. "I'm not a text-book player. I'm a gut player."[27] Instinct for Bush substitutes for deep thinking about complex subjects and extended debate over policy options.

With respect to his actions following the terrorist attacks on September 11, 2001, the president noted, "I also had the responsibility to show resolve. I had to show the American people the resolve of a commander in chief that was going to do whatever it took to win. No yielding. No equivocation. No, you know, lawyering this thing to death, that we're after 'em."[28]

By his own admission, George W. is results-oriented, a decision maker who wants to get to the bottom line as soon as possible.[29] At a prime-time news conference in October 2001, Bush stated, "I'm a performance-oriented person. I believe in results."[30] As president, he strongly believed that other countries would be more influenced by his deeds than his words. He said to Woodward, "I know the world is watching carefully, would be impressed and will be impressed with results achieved."[31]

It all fit together: Results are concrete. Actions evidence strength. Strength is related to decisiveness. Waiting for more information, thinking about the complexity of a problem, engaging in lengthy debates on strategic and policy options are all impediments to swift and firm action. They also require skills that George W. had not demonstrated in his academic, business, and political days.

Bush is not curious, dislikes theoretical discussions, and is uncomfortable with ambiguity. Former antiterrorism adviser Richard Clarke put it this way: "When he [Bush] focused, he asked the kind of questions that revealed a results-oriented mind, but he looked for the simple solution, the bumper sticker description of the problem."[32] Former treasury secretary Paul O'Neill was even more critical, telling author Ron Suskind that he never heard George W. Bush "analyze a complex issue, parse opposing positions, and settle on a judicious path."[33]

Being strong and acting with resolve requires confidence and conviction, the belief that what one is doing is right. In George W.'s words, "We're

---

27. Woodward, *Bush at War*, p. 342.

28. Woodward, *Bush at War*, p. 96.

29. Richard A. Clarke, *Against All Enemies* (New York: Free Press, 2004), p. 244.

30. George W. Bush, "Interview with Claus Kleber of Ard," May 21, 2002.

31. Woodward, *Bush at War*, p. 341.

32. Clarke, *Against All Enemies,* p. 243.

33. Ron Suskind, *The Price of Loyalty* (New York: Simon and Schuster, 2004), p. 114. O'Neill describes the president in meetings as silent and expressionless, uninformed and unengaged: "The only way I can describe it is that, well, the President is like a blind man in a room of deaf people" (Suskind, *The Price of Loyalty,* p. 149).

never going to get people all in agreement about force and use of force. But action-confident action that will yield positive results provides kind of a slipstream into which reluctant nations and leaders can get behind and show themselves that there has been—you know, something positive has happened toward peace."[34]

Bush enjoys expressing strong convictions; he likes being seen as the tough guy. Here's how the president described his feelings during a speech at the United Nations on September 12, 2002, in which he urged the Security Council to enact new resolutions to compel Iraq to comply with previous resolutions or else face military sanctions: "When I walked up there and stood in front of that group, and by the way there's no expressions. It was dead quiet. And I can remember, the more solemn they looked to me, the more emotional I was in making the case. Not openly emotional, the more firm I was in making the case. It was a speech I really enjoyed giving."[35]

To fortify his belief structure, George W. relies on religion and ideology. Religion provides the foundation for doing what is right and for justifying actions on high moral grounds. He prays often. In the days leading up to the war in Iraq, the president recalled, "Going into this period, I was praying for strength to do the Lord's will. . . . I'm surely not going to justify war based upon God. Understand that. Nevertheless, in my case I pray that I be as good a messenger of His will as possible. And then, of course, I pray for personal strength and for forgiveness."[36]

Bush claimed that his decisions for taking military action in Afghanistan and later in Iraq were intended to extend God-given rights of freedom and human dignity to people denied them by two tyrannical governments.[37] In this sense, the president believed that he was doing God's work or, at least, proceeding in accordance with a basic and intuitively correct moral belief that all human beings have inherent and inalienable rights.

Ideology provides a clear vision for Bush. It enables him to perceive and understand events and actions within a larger world view. It is a tool for cognition, comprehension, and consistency as well as a shortcut for quick and decisive decision making. It is a mindset that serves operationally as a guide for action.

Believing in the correctness of his actions makes admitting error difficult and apologies almost impossible for George W. In fact, it is hard for him to even

---

34. Woodward, *Bush at War*, p. 96.

35. Woodward, *Plan of Attack*, p. 184.

36. Woodward, *Plan of Attack*, p. 379.

37. "There is a human condition that we must worry about in times of war. There is a value system that cannot be compromised—God-given values. These aren't United States-created values. These are values of freedom and the human condition . . ." (Woodward, *Bush at War*, p. 131.)

think of mistakes, as was evident in his news conference of April 13, 2004. When asked by a reporter to indicate his biggest mistake after September 11, Bush replied:

> I wish you had given me this question ahead of time, so I could plan for it. John, I'm sure historians will look back and say, gosh, he could have done it better this way, or that way. You know, I just—I'm sure something will pop into my head here in the midst of this press conference, with all the pressures of trying to come up with an answer, but it hasn't yet.[38]

The president's difficulty in thinking about his mistakes is not surprising. Bush does not look back. Questioning the policy-based actions upon which he has chosen to define his presidency would undercut the confidence Bush has had in going with his gut. Revisiting decisions and actions could lead to self-doubt, hesitation, even inaction in the future, the antithesis of the style and the attributes he wants to demonstrate as president.

Religion and ideology thus constitute the vision that George W. believes is so important for a president to have. Vision matters—another lesson that he learned from his father's failings.[39]

Role playing stylizes the response. Presidents are supposed to act with strength, conviction, and decisiveness in times of crisis. The public expects it. History illustrates it. The "great" presidents are those who responded to the crises they faced in this manner.

The terrorist attacks of September 11, 2001, demanded no less. "If America is under attack, my job as the President is to protect the homeland, to find out the facts, and to deal with it in a firm way," a point that Bush reiterated often in the aftermath of the attacks.[40]

> My job is to protect America, and that is exactly what I'm going to do. People can ascribe all kinds of intentions. I swore to protect and defend the Constitution; that's what I swore to do. I put my hand on the Bible and took that oath, and that's exactly what I am going to do.[41]

Repetition is a tactic Bush uses frequently in spontaneous expression. It serves a dual purpose: emphasizing what he wants others to know and giving himself more time to think. In an interview with *Washington Post* reporter,

---

38. George W. Bush, "Presidential Press Conference," April 13, 2004.

39. Woodward, *Bush at War*, p. 341.

40. George W. Bush, "Interview with Claus Kleber of Ard," May 21, 2002.

41. George W. Bush, "Presidential Press Conference," March 6, 2003.

Bob Woodward, Bush said, "I know it is hard for you to believe, but I have not doubted what we're doing. I have not doubted. . . . There is no doubt in my mind we're doing the right thing. Not one doubt."[42]

The repetition is also a form of thought control that Bush imposes on himself. Making and remaking the same point keeps him focused and on course; it's safe; it protects him from making a thoughtless remark that could get him into trouble, particularly with the "gotcha" journalists looking for any presidential miscue. Repetition also relaxes cognitive processing; the words reinforce the beliefs, convincing the speaker that he is right.

In short, strength, decisiveness, and vision are three attributes that George W. Bush values and demonstrates in his presidency. They are evident in his decisions to go to war, first in Afghanistan and then Iraq. These decisions provided the younger Bush with the opportunity to take his father's challenge to a higher and more definitive level, to pursue the universal values of freedom and human dignity. What more could any father ask of his son? What more could any president ask of himself?

GEORGE W. BUSH'S DECISIONS TO GO TO WAR

While reading to second-graders in a Florida classroom, the president was interrupted, not once but twice, by aides who told him about the planes hitting the World Trade Center in New York. According to Bob Woodward, the president's immediate reaction was that "they had declared war on us, and I made up my mind at that moment that we were going to war."[43] An overreaction or one that resembled his father's 11 years earlier? Meeting with the press 45 minutes after the first plane hit, Bush said: "Terrorism against our nation will not stand." His father had used the very same words, "this will not stand," in his first declaration after the Iraqi attack against Kuwait.

George W. later told Bob Woodward, "We didn't just sit around massaging the words. I got up there and just spoke. What you saw was my gut reaction coming out."[44] Thus, the younger Bush had quickly seized the gauntlet as his father had done 11 years earlier. He saw the attack as a challenge from which he could not shirk. There was no ambiguity in his response, no indecision. The reaction was immediate, guttural, and determined.

---

42. Woodward, *Bush at War*, p. 256.

43. Woodward, *Bush at War*, p. 15.

44. Woodward, *Bush at War*, p. 16.

After telephoning Vice President Cheney from Air Force One and telling him, "We're at war," the president turned to his staff and said: "That's what we're paid for boys. We're going to take care of this. And when we find out who did this, they're not going to like me as president. Somebody is going to pay."[45] To reporters the next day, he added, "The deliberate and deadly attacks which were carried out yesterday against our country were more than acts of terror. They were acts of war . . . This will be a monumental struggle between good and evil. But good will prevail." At the prayer service at the Washington Cathedral, the president reiterated, "Our responsibility to history is already clear . . . to answer these attacks and rid the world of evil."[46]

The president's rhetoric remained strong, consistent, committed, even defiant, and above all, highly personal. Bush told aides preparing his address to a joint session of Congress on September 20, 2001, that he wanted to make a personal pledge to all Americans. According to author Bob Woodward, he ended his instructions to his staff with words to this effect: "This is my mission, my purpose; this is the nation's purpose. This is what my presidency is about."[47] The actual words he delivered in the speech were: "I will not forget this wound to our country and those who inflicted it. I will not yield; I will not rest; I will not relent in waging this struggle for freedom and security for the American people."[48]

Bush had personalized the challenge the country faced, a challenge that assumed almost divine proportions for him.[49] He seemed to relish his role as a war-time president, as protector and defender of the American people, as the nation's father figure. The divine connection elevated the struggle, justifying

---

45. Woodward, *Bush at War*, p. 17.

46. Woodward, *Bush at War*, pp. 45, 67.

47. Woodward, *Bush at War*, p. 102.

48. George W. Bush, "Address to a Joint Session of Congress," September 20, 2001.

49. George W. saw it as an act of Providence, a call to defend God's gift of freedom against those who threaten it. In a speech at the University of Pittsburgh, he said:

   History has called us into action, here at home and internationally. We've been given a chance to lead, and we're going to seize the moment in this country. . . . I view this as an opportunity to secure the peace for a long time coming. I view this as a struggle of tyranny versus freedom, of evil versus good. And there's no in-between as far as I'm concerned. Either you are with us or against us. (George W. Bush, "Address at the University of Pittsburgh," February 5, 2002.)

   Later to religious broadcasters at a national prayer dinner, he sounded a similar refrain: "Events aren't moved by blind change and chance. Behind all of life and all of history, there's a dedication and purpose, set by the hand of a just and faithful God." (Laurie Goodstein, "A President Puts His Faith in Providence," *New York Times*, February 9, 2003, p. 4.)

the battle and the loss of life that would inevitably result from it; that connection clearly distinguished right and wrong for him. It gave him the strength and conviction to proceed on his course. The president saw the terrorist attacks and his administration's response to them as "a monumental struggle between good and evil," much the same way his father had seen the Iraqi invasion of Kuwait and America's response to it. [50]

The distinction between right and wrong, between good and evil, seemed self-evident to the younger Bush. In fact, he expressed utter amazement that others did not see it that way:

> I'm amazed that there is such misunderstanding of what our country is about, that people would hate us . . . like most Americans, I just can't believe it. Because I know how good we are. . . . We are fighting evil. And these murderers have hijacked a great religion in order to justify their evil deeds. And we cannot let it stand. [51]

By invoking religion against terrorists who killed in the name of God, the president implicitly claimed superiority for his own moral views. He saw his task as a divine mission. "This crusade, this war on terrorism is going to take a while," Bush stated several days after the attacks. When Muslims objected to the

---

50. On the eve of the Persian Gulf War, George H. W. Bush wrote in his diary:

> *At some point it came through to me that this was not a matter of shades of gray, or of trying to see the other side's point of view. It was good versus evil, right versus wrong. I am sure the change strengthened my determination not to let the invasion stand and encouraged me to contemplate the use of force to reverse it. This was how I worked it out in my mind, which made the choice before me clearer. It also made it a little easier to speak to the families of our troops and explain why their loved ones might have to sacrifice themselves. (George H. W. Bush and Brent Scowcroft,* A World Transformed *(New York: Vintage, 1998), pp. 374–75.)*

51. George W. Bush, "Presidential Press Conference," September 16, 2001. Bush frequently reiterated the good/evil refrain in his references to terrorism and to the need for a strong military response to it. In an address to U.S. troops in Alaska in February 2002, the president said: "Out of evil will become America more resolved not only to defend freedom, more resolved to sacrifice, if necessary, to defend the freedom, but America resolved to show the world our true strength, which is the compassion, decent heart of the American people." ("Speech to U.S. Military in Alaska," February 16, 2002).

   On the first anniversary of the Iraq war, March 19, 2004, the president repeated the theme to diplomats gathered in the White House:

> *We do love life, the life given to us and to all. We believe in the values that uphold the dignity of life, tolerance, and freedom, and the right of conscience. And we know that this way of life is worth defending. There is no neutral ground—no neutral ground—in the fight between civilization and terror, because there is no neutral ground between good and evil, freedom and slavery, and life and death. ("Address to Diplomats at the White House," March 19. 2004.)*

word *crusade,* Bush dropped it from his public vocabulary but continued to proclaim his moral beliefs as justification for taking resolute action, not only in Afghanistan but also in Iraq.[52] In his 2002 commencement speech at West Point, the president stated as a matter of fact: "Moral truth is the same in every culture, in every time, and in every place."[53] Moreover, he invoked democratic principles, human rights, and freedom, as if they were universally-accepted articles of faith.

Like his father, George W. believed that the use of force was the only possible response that would deter despots from imposing their will on others. On the eve of the Persian Gulf War, George H. W. Bush had written his children:

> How many lives might have been saved if appeasement had given way to force earlier on in the late '30's or earliest '40s? How many Jews might have been spared the gas chambers, or how many Polish patriots might be alive today? I look at today's crisis as "good" vs. "evil"—Yes, it is that clear.[54]

The father's teachings were not lost on the son.[55] George W. Bush repeated the same argument in a prime-time news conference on March 6, 2003, two weeks before military hostilities got under way.

> The risk of doing nothing, the risk of hoping that Saddam Hussein changes his mind and becomes a gentle soul, the risk that somehow— that will make the world safer is a risk I'm not willing to take for the American people . . .I think the threat is real. And so do a lot of other people in *my* [emphasis mine] government. And since I believe the threat is real, and since my most important job is to protect the security of the American people, that's precisely what we'll do.[56]

---

52. "My faith sustains me because I pray daily. I pray for guidance and wisdom and strength. If we were to commit our troops [to Iraq]—if we were to commit our troops—I would pray for their safety, and I would pray for the safety of innocent Iraqi lives, as well" ("Presidential Press Conference," March 6, 2003).

53. "Address at West Point," June 1, 2002.

54. George H. W. Bush, *All the Best* (New York: Scribner, 1999), p. 497.

55. George W. used similar logic in urging the United Nations to support the military action against Saddam Hussein.

> *Failure to act would embolden other tyrants, allow terrorists access to new weapons, new resources, and make blackmail a permanent feature of world events. The United Nations would betray the purpose of its founding, and prove irrelevant to the problems of our time. And through its inaction, the United States would resign itself to a future of fear. ("Presidential Address in Cincinnati," October 7, 2002.)*

56. "Presidential Press Conference," March 6, 2003.

For George W., the terrorist attacks demanded forceful leadership, as did Saddam Hussein's support of terrorism. George W. saw Saddam as a despot, just as his father had.[57] There was no nuance. He quickly dismissed criticisms as too late, naïve, or beside the point. *Assumptions became facts.* In his new conference on March 6, 2003, two weeks before the beginning of hostilities in Iraq, George W. stated, as fact, that Saddam Hussein possessed weapons of mass destruction.[58] He and his advisers had made a leap of faith in their interpretation of the intelligence they had seen and perhaps even shaped with the clarity of their belief that Iraq's weapons of mass destruction threatened the national security of the United States.[59]

The absence of ambiguity not only reinforced the correctness of the decision but also helped to suppress any anxieties the president may have felt at the outset of hostilities. According to White House aides, Bush made the final decision to go to war with no equivocation.[60] After he had ordered the invasion, his friends reported that he was "far less frustrated now than he was in the protracted period of prewar diplomacy that ultimately failed."[61]

---

57. Bob Woodward, *The Commanders* (New York: Simon and Schuster, 1991), pp. 299–302.

58. "This is a regime [Iraq] that has already used poison gas to murder thousands of its own citizens—leaving the bodies of mothers huddled over their dead children. This is a regime that agreed to international inspections—then kicked out the inspectors. This is a regime that has something to hide from the civilized world."

    Later on, in the same press conference, he repeated the fact that Iraq has WMD: "Iraqi operatives continue to hide biological and chemical agents to avoid detection by inspectors. In some cases, these materials have been moved to different locations every 12 to 24 hours, or placed in vehicles that are in residential neighborhoods."

    And again: "The American people know that Saddam Hussein has weapons of mass destruction. . . . he declared he didn't have any—[Resolution] 1441 insisted that he have a complete declaration of his weapons; he said he didn't have any weapons. Secondly, he's used these weapons before. I mean, that is—we're not speculating about the nature of man. We know the nature of the man. ("Presidential Press Conference," March 6, 2003.)

59. Woodward, *Plan of Attack,* pp. 83–84; Clarke, *Against All Enemies,* pp. 231–46; Suskind, *The Price of Loyalty,* pp. 73–73.

60. Elisabeth Bumiller, "Another President Bush Watches on the Sidelines," *New York Times,* April 7, 2003, p. B1.

61. Bumiller, "Another President Bush Watches on the Sidelines," p. B11. "But they said that he is weighed down by reports of the dead and prisoners of war, particularly by specialist Shoshana Johnson, the only woman among seven troops taken captive last week." Referring to the capture of the troops, Roland W. Betts, a close friend of George W. Bush from their days at Yale, who was with the president in the days following his decision to commence hostilities, stated: "That troubled him. But is he thinking, did I do the wrong thing? Not at all." (Bumiller "Another President Bush Watches on the Sidelines," p. B11.)

If the president was anxious during this period, he did not show it publicly. The *Washington Post* reported that he "told visitors he is sleeping well and exercising regularly."[62] In fact, he exercised with a vengeance, stuck to his routine, prayed daily, and went to bed early.[63] Stated one senior administration official, "In these types of times, he becomes even more disciplined than usual."[64]

Although father and son had frequent contact, mostly by telephone, during the period leading up to the 2003 war in Iraq, George H. W. Bush was very careful not to impose his views on his son.[65] In the words of George W. Bush:

> I talk to him, of course. I cannot remember a moment where he said, "Don't do this" or "do this." I can't remember a moment where I said to myself, maybe he can help me make the decision . . . The discussions would be more on the tactics. How are we doing, How are you doing with the Brits? He is following the news now. And so I am briefing him on what I see. *You know, he is the wrong father to appeal to in terms of strength. There is a higher father that I appeal to.* [Italics mine][66]

George W. Bush met the enemies and defeated them on the battlefield so that he himself could stand tall in the eyes of the world, particularly those of his father, his God, and himself. Iraq had been liberated from Saddam Hussein but, as subsequent events were to prove, not from itself.

CONCLUSION

The terrorist attacks on September 11, 2001, gave George W. Bush his greatest challenge, one that he did not anticipate but one that he accepted with relish. It was the perfect challenge for him. It gave him the opportunity to show what he was made of, that he was up to the task, and, most importantly, to finish the

62. Mike Allen and Karen DeYoung, "Bush's Posture: A Leader Apart," *Washington Post*, March 22, 2003, p. A26.

63. Elisabeth Bumiller, David E. Singer, and Richard W. Stevenson, "How Three Weeks of War in Iraq Looked from the Oval Office," *New York Times*, April 14, 2003, p. B11.

64. Allen and DeYoung, "Bush's Posture: A Leader Apart," p. A26. George W. spent most of the weekends at Camp David as his father had done during the Persian Gulf War. Elisabeth Bumiller, "For a President at War, Refuge at Camp David," *New York Times,* November 11, 2001, p. B11.

65. *New York Times* reporter Elisabeth Bumiller writes, "The 41st and 43rd presidents talk at least several times a week, but advisers to each man insist that the father never directly tells the son what to do." (Bumiller, "Another President Bush Watches on the Sidelines," p. B1.

66. Woodward, *Plan of Attack,* p. 421.

job his father had begun. If he did so successfully, he would not only prove himself to be the legitimate heir to the Bush family legacy, but he would take that legacy a step beyond where his father had left it. In other words, he would extend and perfect his father by demonstrating the attributes of strength, decisiveness, and vision—attributes his father was perceived to lack—and thereby fulfill a natural wish to surpass his father's accomplishments.

From the outset, George W. saw Iraq and the issue of fighting terrorism as clearly connected; in retrospect, perhaps too clearly. There was little hesitation on policy direction—"Axis of Evil," "regime change," then the ultimatum followed by the attack. The only hesitation was on the tactics of coalition building at home and within the international community, and the timing, generated in large part by the public campaign of his father's top foreign policy advisers to touch all bases—Congress and the United Nations—before implementing the military option.

Was George W. Bush *totally* motivated by his inner needs? Probably not. A variety of factors pushed him in the direction of war: his own predilections; the advice he received from his closest advisers; the support of Congress and the American people; his father's unfinished business as far as Iraq was concerned; and Saddam Hussein's attempt to assassinate the elder Bush when the former president visited Kuwait. Policy considerations also affected both decisions. The need to stand up to terrorism; the despotic governments in Afghanistan and Iraq that denied their citizens basic human rights; more effective use of U.S. military power as an instrument of diplomacy; with respect to Iraq, the continued availability of oil from the Middle East; and the threat to the United States that Iraq's weapons of mass destruction posed all also contributed in one way or another to Bush's decisions. The point is that Bush's policy goals and psychological needs pushed him in the same direction.

Would a president with different psychological needs and policy judgments have responded differently? Probably, particularly in the case of Iraq. In my opinion, Bush's psychological needs, as reinforced by loyal, and for the most part, like-minded advisers, accelerated his rush to war and downplayed the problems of the occupation that would follow. The expectation was that the Americans would be treated as liberators (as they were in Kuwait) and that grateful Iraqis would embrace democracy and human rights (as the Japanese and Germans did following World War II). It was a case of self-deception, pure and simple, to which Bush and his advisers succumbed.

PART III

The President and the Public

6

❧

Do Presidents Lie?

JAMES P. PFIFFNER
George Mason University

The answer to the question posed in the title is, "of course, presidents lie," just as virtually all human beings lie throughout our lives. We often engage in flattery when we compliment someone on a new haircut or new suit of clothes when we really think that they are tacky. As children most of us are taught to thank Aunt Minnie for her gift of garish socks that she knitted for us. Often, telling the literal truth can get you into trouble—at least in social relationships or diplomacy. But these "white lies" that smooth social relationships are most often not seen as breaches of honesty or integrity.

People do, however, occasionally tell serious lies, and politicians are often tempted to shade the truth when they try to knit together coalitions from opposing parts of the political spectrum. Nevertheless, politicians have a greater obligation to tell the truth when they speak about public policy because their statements may have broad public consequences. Democracy is based on the premise that citizens have the right to choose their governmental leaders. And the only way voters can make informed choices is if political leaders tell the truth. Thus, lying about important matters of public policy is incompatible with democracy, except in narrow, special circumstances.

Just as most people lie, so do most presidents. But presidents are in a special position because of the power they wield in the name of the electorate and because of the far-reaching consequences of their actions. They have the responsibility to make life and death decisions that affect millions of people throughout the world. Besides the duties of office, they also have the responsibility of the high expectations placed upon them by the American people; that is, they are seen by many as role models as well as decision makers. Because of the great power vested in them and the leadership responsibility entrusted to them, we have the right to expect a high level of ethical behavior by the presidents we elect. Telling the truth, particularly with respect to public policy, is an important ethical imperative for presidents. That presidents do not always tell the truth is evident, but that does not mean that all untruths are equally wrong.

This essay will examine a number of lies by presidents over the course of the modern presidency. It will argue that not all lies are equal; some are more serious than others, and in judging presidents, citizens ought to consider the context and consequences of presidential lies. The analysis will proceed from justifiable lies to lies to avoid embarrassment to more serious lies of policy deception.

JUSTIFIABLE LIES

When Jimmy Carter was running for president in 1976, he wanted to remind voters of the deception and lies of President Nixon in the Watergate scandal, and he stated, "I will never lie to you."[1] This may have been reassuring, and it may even have won him some votes, but if one takes a promise like this seriously, it should actually undermine one's confidence in the candidate. If the candidate is telling the truth, it must mean that he or she cannot conceive of a situation in which a president would be obligated to tell a public lie.

For instance, in April of 1980 the Carter administration had sent a secret team of special military forces to attempt to free U.S. hostages in Iran. If a reporter had asked President Carter at a press conference if U.S. troops were going to attempt a hostage rescue, the president would have been obligated to lie in order to protect the lives of the hostages and rescuers (a "no comment" to such a pointed question would have compromised the mission). But if the candidate were intelligent enough to imagine such a situation, the blanket promise never to lie would be disingenuous. That is, the candidate would be saying something he knew not to be true in order to win votes. Such a candidate would be either naïve or deceptive. Neither is reassuring in a presidential candidate.

It is not difficult to imagine situations in which a president might be obliged to lie in order to protect national security operations. But this is not a blanket pass for presidents to lie whenever national security is involved. The lies must be clearly justified by the circumstances and not merely used to avoid embarrassment. Thus, protecting covert operations can justify lying. But covert policies almost never justify lying. Covert operations are secret actions meant to support legitimate, that is, constitutionally justified, foreign policies. Covert policies, on the other hand, include instances when the president says the government is doing X when in fact it is doing Y. This type of lie breaks the bonds of accountability in a democracy, for if the people do not know what policies the president is pursuing, they cannot make informed

---

1. Jules Witcover, *Marathon: The Pursuit of the Presidency* (New York: Viking Press, 1977), p. 320.

decisions about how to vote. For instance, if the government is publicly supporting opposition to the Soviet occupation of Afghanistan, secret operations
(and lying about them) in support of this policy are justified. But if the government publicly opposes giving arms to Iran, it is not legitimate to give
arms to Iran and lie to the American public about it, except in very narrow
operational circumstances.

An example of a justified lie occurred during the 1960 campaign for
the presidency. U.S. policy toward Cuba was an important issue, and John
F. Kennedy was criticizing the Eisenhower administration for not giving
enough support to the Cubans who opposed Fidel Castro and his revolu-
tionary government. This put Vice President Nixon, who was running
against Kennedy for the presidency, in a difficult situation. He knew that the
government was actively involved in support of the Cuban exiles, but the
operation was covert and could not be publicly acknowledged for fear of
disclosing its existence and putting Castro on guard. So he could not come
out and say that he agreed with Kennedy and that such operations were
already under way. He had to preserve the secrecy of the operation, and so
Nixon concluded that the only responsible action was for him to attack
Kennedy's proposal as being reckless and irresponsible, which he did.[2]

Thus, Nixon in this situation was telling a blatant lie, saying exactly the
opposite of what he believed and covering up the actual actions of the
Eisenhower administration. But from his perspective, his statement has to
be seen as a legitimate, justified, and even necessary lie. The United States was
undertaking a covert operation against what was seen as a Communist
enemy, and disclosure of the operation could have led to its failure. Setting
aside what we now know about the Cold War and the future consequences
of U.S. actions toward Cuba, we have to admit that Nixon's lie was ethical,
even courageous, since he may have jeopardized his chance of being elected.

MINOR LIES AND LIES TO AVOID EMBARRASSMENT

A number of presidents have told minor lies, usually to embellish their own
stature or reputation. For instance, Lyndon Johnson told audiences that his
great-grandfather had died at the Alamo (a touchstone of Texas history), and
when this was shown to be untrue, he changed it to the Battle of San Jacinto.
But this was not true either.[3] John F. Kennedy lied about his ability to

2. Richard M. Nixon, *Six Crises* (Garden City, NY: Doubleday, 1962), p. 355.

3. Doris Kearns, *Lyndon Johnson and the American Dream* (New York: New
    American Library, 1976), p. 15.

speed-read through documents (speed-reading was a fad in the 1960s).[4] More importantly, Kennedy also lied when he denied that he had Addison's disease.[5]

Ronald Reagan told a number of untrue stories as a candidate and as president. He was fond of telling the story about a "welfare queen" who lived in Chicago and had defrauded the government of thousands of dollars. He continued to tell the story even after it had been shown to be grossly exaggerated.[6] Another story Reagan often told was about his football-playing days at Dixon High School, in which his honesty cost Dixon the game. The game was against Mendota, and Reagan recounted how he had committed an infraction of the rules that the referee did not see. When the referee asked Reagan whether he had broken the rules, Reagan recalled, "But truth-telling had been whaled into me. . . . I told the truth, the penalty was ruled, and Dixon lost the game." The only time that Dixon lost to Mendota when Reagan was on the varsity team was in 1927, and Mendota won 24 to 0.[7] The ironic point here is that Reagan seems to have told the story to demonstrate how truthful he was, yet he was telling an untruth to make the point.

More serious lies by presidents concern public policy, often national security policy. Since national security often involves secrecy and can sometimes justify lying to the public, presidents are tempted to use the national security excuse to lie in order to save themselves from embarrassment.

---

4. Richard Reeves, *President Kennedy: Profile of Power* (New York: Simon and Schuster, 1993), p. 280. Reeves cites page 35 of Hugh Sidey's oral history statement at the Kennedy Library.

5. Reeves, *President Kennedy,* p. 24.

6. See Lou Cannon, *President Reagan: The Role of a Lifetime* (New York: Simon and Schuster, 1991), pp. 518–20. During his 1976 campaign, Reagan said that a Chicago woman "has eighty names, thirty addresses, twelve Social Security cards and is collecting veterans' benefits on four nonexisting deceased husbands. . . . Her tax-free cash income alone is over $150,000." But the woman was convicted in 1977 for having two aliases and receiving unauthorized benefits of $8,000. For another account of Reagan's Welfare Queen stories, see David Zucchino, *Myth of the Welfare Queen* (New York: Scribner, 1997), pp. 64–65.

7. The account of Reagan's often-used story is in Lou Cannon, *Reagan* (New York: G. P. Putnam's Sons, 1982), p. 36. In the account, which Cannon got from the *Rockford Morning Star,* Reagan said: "I finally wrote a story about it [the football incident he just related] and sold it to a national boys magazine. That sale just about turned the tide for me away from professional sports and coaching on the one hand and acting on the other." Cannon's account continues: "There are no contemporary accounts of any incident of this sort, and Dixon High lost to Mendota only once when Reagan was a member of the varsity team. In that game, when Reagan was a senior in 1927, Mendota won 24–0."

Eisenhower and the U-2 Incident

In the spring of 1960, President Eisenhower had proposed to negotiate with the Russians a test-ban treaty that would end the testing of nuclear weapons. Despite the potential risk to the talks, Eisenhower allowed the CIA to fly one last mission to photograph Soviet military installations, and Gary Powers took off in a U-2 the morning of May 1. When the plane did not return for several days, it was presumed to be destroyed and the pilot dead because of self-destruct mechanisms built into the plane and the likelihood that the pilot could not have survived.[8] According to Eisenhower, the CIA had assured the White House that "in the event of a mishap the plane would virtually disintegrate," and that it was highly unlikely that a U-2 pilot would survive.[9]

On May 5, Khrushchev announced that the Soviet Union had shot down an American spy plane and denounced the United States for "aggressive provocation." Ike knew that the Soviets were aware of the U-2 overflights, but he presumed that Powers was dead and the plane destroyed. So he approved a statement by NASA that the plane was not a spy plane but instead a weather research plane that had been over Turkey "to obtain data on clear air turbulence," and might have strayed into Soviet airspace.[10] Then, after the administration had lied about the plane, Khrushchev announced on May 7 that he had the pilot, Gary Powers, "alive and kicking," as well as wreckage from the plane.[11] Faced with this incontrovertible evidence, Eisenhower compounded the lie by having the State Department say that the pilot could have lost consciousness from lack of oxygen and that the automatic pilot might have taken the plane "for a considerable distance . . . accidentally violating Soviet airspace."[12]

Finally Eisenhower had to admit publicly that the United States had been spying on the Soviet Union and that the administration had authorized the flights. Eisenhower felt personally mortified and told his secretary, Anne Whitman, on the morning of May 9, "I would like to resign."[13] Thus,

---

8. See the account by Fred Greenstein, *The Hidden-Hand Presidency* (New York: Basic Books, 1982), p. 253.

9. Dwight D. Eisenhower, *Waging Peace, 1956–1961* (New York: Doubleday, 1965), p. 546.

10. Eisenhower, *Waging Peace,* p. 548.

11. James Bamford, *Body of Secrets* (New York: Doubleday, 2001), p. 52.

12. Eisenhower, *Waging Peace,* p. 549. See also Stephen Ambrose, *Eisenhower: Soldier and President* (New York: Simon and Schuster), p. 510.

13. Michael R. Beschloss, *Mayday: Eisenhower, Khrushchev and the U-2 Affair* (New York: Harper and Row, 1986), p. 254.

Eisenhower's hopes for a test-ban treaty to crown his eight years in office were dashed, and he was severely disappointed.

The irony, as pointed out by historian Stephen Ambrose, was that the U-2 overflights were no secret to the Soviets, whose frustration had been growing for four years because of their inability to shoot down the planes, which were flying at an altitude of up to 70,000 feet, out of the range of their missiles or fighter planes (that is, until the Powers flight). Nor were the flights secret to U.S. allies in Britain, France, Norway, Turkey, or Taiwan. Those who did not know about the U-2 flights were members of Congress and the American people. Thus, Eisenhower undermined his most important asset, his "reputation for honesty," and undermined the trust of the American people in their government because he thought there was no evidence to prove the administration was lying.[14]

Nixon and Watergate

Although Richard Nixon told Republican delegates in 1968 that "Truth will become the hallmark of the Nixon Administration," his more realistic judgment was reflected in a statement to a political associate earlier in his career: "You don't know how to lie. If you can't lie, you'll never go anywhere."[15] Nixon lied numerous times concerning his knowledge of the cover-up of the Watergate break-in in June of 1972. For instance, on May 21, 1973, he said in a public statement that he had "no part in, nor was I aware of, subsequent efforts that may have been made to cover up Watergate."[16] He repeated similar statements often during 1973 and 1974 as he tried to avoid public disclosure of the Watergate cover-up and other illegal activities sponsored by the White House.

Perhaps the most important lie was recorded on the "smoking gun" tape from June 23, 1972, in which Nixon told his chief of staff, H. R. Haldeman, to have the CIA call the FBI to tell them to stop pursuing the trail of Watergate money because it would make public a CIA covert operation. Nixon told Haldeman to tell Richard Helms, "The president believes that it is going to open the whole Bay of Pigs thing up again. And . . . that they

---

14. When asked about the reason for Eisenhower's actions, General Andrew Goodpaster, one of his top aides, said that they had prepared a "cover story" based on the premise that the plane and pilot would have been destroyed if the mission went amiss. Their mistake, he said, was to use the cover story. Conversation with the author, March 21, 2000, Washington, DC.

15. Quoted in Stanley I. Kutler, *The Wars of Watergate* (New York: Alfred A. Knopf, 1990), p. 619. Also quoted in Fawn M. Brodie, *Richard Nixon: The Shaping of His Character* (New York: W. W. Norton, 1981), p. 504.

16. Quoted in Kutler, *The Wars of Watergate,* p. 347.

[the CIA] should call the FBI in and [unintelligible] don't go any further into this case period!"[17] This order to the CIA to lie to the FBI, when disclosed to the House Judiciary Committee, was the turning point in the impeachment proceedings against Nixon. The committee voted for impeachment articles, and Nixon resigned before the full House could vote on them.

Clinton and Lewinsky

In the late fall of 1995, President Clinton began a sexual affair with a White House intern, Monica Lewinsky. In 1998, when his affair came to public attention, he falsely denied his affair to the American public, but he also lied about it under oath in the Paula Jones sexual harassment case and in his grand jury appearance.

Although Clinton was embarrassed about his affair, he was also calculating the political repercussions of any admission of an extramarital affair while he was in the White House. On January 21, 1998, the story of the Linda Tripp tapes of her conversations with Lewinsky became public, and the media began a feeding frenzy about all aspects of the scandal. Clinton adviser Dick Morris said he told the president that his polls indicated that the public would not accept his lying about it under oath. President Clinton then made a strong statement, publicly denying that he had a sexual relationship with Lewinsky. "I want you to listen to me. I'm going to say this again. I did not have sexual relations with that woman, Miss Lewinsky. I never told anybody to lie—not a single time, never. These allegations are false. And I need to go back to work for the American people."[18]

On August 17, 1998, President Clinton testified before a grand jury that was investigating his actions, and he again denied that he had engaged in a sexual relationship with Lewinsky. His testimony was under oath, compounding his lie. The House of Representatives impeachment managers made a powerful argument that our system of justice depends upon the assumption of truth-telling under oath and that to lie under oath is therefore an offense serious enough to impeach the president, regardless of the subject of the lie. The House impeached Clinton in December 1998, and in the spring of 1999, the Senate voted not to remove him from office.

Clinton's lie was wrong in several ways. Lying under oath undermines the assumptions upon which the judicial system is based and sends a message that

---

17. The selection from the tape is reprinted in Michael Nelson, *Congressional Quarterly's Guide to the Presidency* (Washington, DC: CQ Press, 1989), p. 1389. Also, see the discussion in Kutler, *The Wars of Watergate*, pp. 534–35.

18. Quoted in Jeffrey Toobin, "Circling the Wagons," *The New Yorker*, July 6, 1998), p. 29.

the president thinks that he is not subject to the law. In addition, Clinton cynically used others in his lie by lying to his staff and cabinet with the expectation that they would innocently repeat his lies. This violation of the confidence of his friends led to their feelings of betrayal and to large legal fees for some. In addition, the president undermined his responsibility as a role model by his public lying.

Despite his many denials, President Clinton did lie under oath about his relationship with Monica Lewinsky; he lied in intent and spirit, as well as literally. In a statement issued on his last day in office, he said: "I tried to walk a fine line between acting lawfully and testifying falsely, but I now recognize that I did not fully accomplish this goal and that certain of my responses to questions about Ms. Lewinsky were false."[19]

Although we might argue that even presidents ought to have some privacy and we might deplore the tactics that Kenneth Starr used to obtain evidence of Clinton's sexual affair with Lewinsky, the president did in fact lie about it, and the lie was wrong. Whether the lies rose to the level of high crimes and misdemeanors for which a president ought to be impeached and removed from office is a separate question.[20]

LIES OF POLICY DECEPTION

At the most serious level are lies of policy deception in which a president deceives the public about important matters of public policy. The most basic premise of democratic government is that the government ought to do what the people want and that during elections the voters can choose whom they want to govern them. Misleading the public about government policy does not allow the electorate to make an informed choice and undermines the premise of democratic government. In the words of philosopher Sissela Bok, "Deception of this kind strikes at the very essence of democratic government. It allows those in power to override or nullify the right vested in the people to cast an informed vote in critical elections."[21] Policy deception lies include

---

19. Quoted in John F. Harris and Bill Miller, "In a Deal, Clinton Avoids Indictment," *Washington Post,* January 20, 2001, p. 1.

20. For an argument that Clinton's lies did not constitute the "high crimes or misdemeanors" necessary for impeachment, see James P. Pfiffner, *The Modern Presidency,* 3rd ed. (New York: Bedford St. Martin's, 2000), chap. 8; and Pfiffner, "President Clinton's Impeachment and Senate Trial," in James P. Pfiffner and Roger Davidson, eds., *Understanding the Presidency* (New York: Addison Wesley Longman, 2000).

21. Sissela Bok, *Lying: Moral Choice in Public and Private Life* (New York: Vintage Books, 1978), p. 182.

Lyndon Johnson's lies about U.S. military involvement in Vietnam, Richard Nixon's secret bombing of Cambodia, Ronald Reagan's statements about Iran–Contra, and some of George W. Bush's statements in the run-up to the war in Iraq.

LBJ and Vietnam

One of Johnson's most far-reaching deceptions was his orchestration of the Gulf of Tonkin Resolution in August of 1964. On the stormy night of August 4, the *Maddox* reported that it had been attacked by North Vietnamese gun boats. But subsequent reports came in that there was serious doubt about whether there had been any attack. Nevertheless, Johnson pushed ahead by ordering retaliatory raids, addressing the American people, and getting Congress to pass a resolution of support for his reaction to the doubtful attack.

On August 6, 1964, Walt Rostow, Johnson's national security advisor, said at a State Department luncheon that the supposed attack on August 4 probably did not take place.[22] Several days after the resolution passed, Johnson himself admitted to George Ball, "Hell, those dumb, stupid sailors were just shooting at flying fish!"[23] On September 18, Johnson said privately to McNamara, "When we got through with all the firing, we concluded maybe they hadn't fired at all."[24] In early 1965, Johnson said, "For all I know, our Navy was shooting at whales out there."[25] But Johnson publicly continued to present the second attack to Congress as completely true and confirmed and used the congressional resolution to justify his military actions in Vietnam.

Later, in the fall of 1964 in his campaign for election, Johnson downplayed any hint of an expanding U.S. involvement in Vietnam. He told a campaign

---

22. Edwin E. Moise, *Tonkin Gulf and the Escalation of the Vietnam War* (Chapel Hill: University of North Carolina Press, 1996), p. 243.

23. George W. Ball, *The Past Has Another Pattern* (New York: W. W. Norton, 1982), p. 379. For an analysis sympathetic to Johnson, see Robert Dallek, *Flawed Giant*, pp. 147–56; for a critical account, see Stanley Karnow, *Vietnam: A History* (New York: Penguin Books, 1983), p. 367–75; Joseph Goulden, *Truth Is the First Casualty: The Gulf of Tonkin Affair* (Chicago: Rand McNally, 1969); Neil Sheehan, *A Bright Shining Lie* (New York: Vintage Books, 1988). See also Larry Berman, *Planning a Tragedy: The Americanization of the War in Vietnam* (New York: W. W. Norton, 1982), pp. 31–34; and H. R. McMaster, *Dereliction of Duty* (New York: Harper Collins, 1997), pp. 107–08, 121–23.

24. Michael Beschloss, *Reaching for Glory: Lyndon Johnson's Secret White House Tapes, 1964–1965* (New York: Simon and Schuster, 2001), pp. 37–39. At this point Johnson wanted to resist Barry Goldwater's calls for more aggressive military action in Vietnam.

25. Goulden, *Truth Is the First Casualty: The Gulf of Tonkin Affair*, p. 160. The context of this quote was that Johnson was implying that he was misled by the Pentagon.

audience on September 25, 1964, "We don't want our American boys to do the fighting for Asian boys. We don't want to get involved in a nation with seven hundred million people and get tied down in a land war in Asia." Later, on October 21 in Akron, Ohio, he declared, "But we are not about to send American boys nine or ten thousand miles away from home to do what Asian boys ought to be doing for themselves."[26]

In December, after his election, Johnson authorized planning for air strikes against the North. But he was also planning his Great Society legislative program for the next year, and he sought to conceal increasing U.S. involvement in Vietnam from the public. Johnson sent a memo to his national security advisors ordering that his decision to approve the military plans for escalation should be kept secret. Johnson said that it was "a matter of the highest importance that the substance of the decision should not become public except as I specifically direct" and that knowledge of the plans be kept "as narrowly as possible to those who have an immediate working need to know."[27] In December of 1964, General Harold K. Johnson predicted that it would take 500,000 men and five years to achieve victory in Vietnam, but Johnson did not allow this to become public.[28]

On January 21, 1965, Johnson's first full day as an elected president, he and McNamara met with a bipartisan group of members of Congress from both Houses. He misled them by presenting the bombing of Laos and covert operations against North Vietnam as being successful and misrepresented his military advisers' pessimistic judgment about the status of South Vietnamese military readiness.[29] Johnson told the congressional leaders that he had "decided that more U.S. forces are not needed in South Vietnam short of a decision to go to full-scale war . . . war must be fought by the South Vietnamese. We cannot control everything that they do and we have to count on their fighting their war."[30] He did not tell them of his plans to begin bombing North Vietnam. On March 8, 1965, the first combat troops, 3,500 Marines, arrived at Danang in South Vietnam.

These troops, although engaged in combat, were supposed to be assisting the South Vietnamese in defensive operations. But in April an increase of 18,000–20,000 in Marine forces was authorized, and their mission was

26. Both quotes from David Wise, *The Politics of Lying* (New York: Vintage Books, 1973), p. 65–66.

27. Quoted in Fredrik Logevall, *Choosing War: The Lost Chance for Peace and the Escalation for War in Vietnam* (Berkeley: University of California Press, 1999), p. 273.

28. McMaster, *Dereliction of Duty*, p. 247.

29. See Logevall, *Choosing War*, p. 315.

30. McMaster, *Dereliction of Duty*, p. 211.

changed by National Security Action Memorandum [NSAM] 328, which authorized the offensive utilization of U.S. ground troops against the Viet Cong. NSAM 328 stated explicitly that the change in mission was to be kept secret: "Premature publicity [should] be avoided by all possible precautions. The actions themselves should be taken as rapidly as practicable, but in ways that should minimize any appearance of sudden changes in policy. . . . changes should be understood as being gradual and wholly consistent with existing policy."[31] Ambassador Maxwell Taylor sent a cable to Secretary of State Dean Rusk saying, "We believe that the most useful approach to press problems is to make no, repeat, no special public announcement to the effect that U.S. ground troops are now engaged in offensive combat operations. . . ."[32]

At the same time, the mission of the U.S. Marines had changed to "offensive killing operations."[33] And McNamara had requested a Joint Chiefs of Staff (JCS) schedule for deploying two or three divisions to Vietnam "at the earliest practicable date."[34] On June 8, Johnson's press secretary, George Reedy, stated, "There has been no change in the mission of U.S. ground combat units in Viet Nam in recent days or weeks."[35]

By July 28 of 1965, authorized U.S. troop strength would increase to 125,000 along a gradual escalation to a peak of 500,000 troops.[36] Johnson had succeeded in concealing from Congress and the American public the escalating military commitment of the United States in Vietnam. In the end, Johnson destroyed his presidency and put the United States through a divisive war during which 58,000 U.S. soldiers lost their lives, in addition to several million Vietnamese.

Nixon and the Secret Bombing of Cambodia

When President Nixon came to office in 1969, he decided that North Vietnamese supply routes through the jungles of Cambodia should be attacked. But he thought that publicly expanding the war would be politically dangerous, so he decided to proceed surreptitiously. The secret bombing of Cambodia in 1969 involved elaborate deception and falsification of reports.

Nixon decided to pursue a systematic bombing campaign to attack North Vietnamese supply routes in Cambodia. But in order to do this

---

31. Quoted in Larry Berman, *Planning a Tragedy,* p. 57.

32. Quoted in Larry Berman, *Planning a Tragedy,* p. 57.

33. Quoted in McMaster, *Dereliction of Duty,* p. 261.

34. McMaster, *Dereliction of Duty,* p. 263.

35. McMaster, *Dereliction of Duty,* p. 291.

36. Berman, *Planning a Tragedy,* p. xii.

secretly, a dual reporting system had to be developed. Nixon ordered that a cable be sent to U.S. Ambassador to South Vietnam, Elsworth Bunker, saying that all discussion of possible bombing of North Vietnamese targets in Cambodia were suspended. At the same time, he had a separate, backchannel message sent to the commander of American forces in Vietnam, General Creighton W. Abrams. Abrams was instructed to disregard the cable to Bunker and to plan for the Cambodian bombing campaign.[37]

The pilots of the B-52s were briefed on missions in South Vietnam, but a subset of the pilots were told that they would get special orders while they were in flight. Once on the mission, they would then be instructed to leave the other planes and deliver their bombs to specific coordinates in Cambodia. After dropping the bombs, they returned to their bases and reported as if they had been bombing in South Vietnam. These reports were the official reports recorded in the Air Force and Defense Department records. The secret reports of the actual bombings went through backchannels to the White House. Not even the Secretary of the Air Force knew of the secret bombings.[38] Official reports of the bombing targets were falsified at the president's order. But the larger deception was that the United States was secretly bombing a neutral country without the knowledge of Congress, to which the Constitution gives the power to declare war.

The question arises as to the purpose of the secrecy. Originally, Secretary of Defense Melvin Laird favored making the bombing public, but he was overruled by Nixon and Kissinger. After all, the North Vietnamese knew they were being bombed, the Cambodians knew bombs were dropping on their country, and the Communist allies of the North Vietnamese were informed of the bombing. The only implicated parties who did not know were the U.S. Congress and the American people. Nixon argued that diplomatically, if the bombing were acknowledged, the Cambodian government might have felt compelled to protest or the North Vietnamese might have protested. But the real reason was probably revealed by Nixon in his memoirs: "Another reason for secrecy was the problem of domestic antiwar protest. My administration was only two months old, and I wanted to provoke as little public outcry as possible at the outset."[39]

---

37. This analysis is based on Seymour Hersh, *The Price of Power* (New York: Summit Books, 1983), pp. 60–65.

38. Robert Seamans was Secretary of the Air Force and was not told of the bombing missions in Cambodia. His morning briefing indicated that the bombs were dropped in Vietnam. He signed documents about the location of the bombing targets based on his misunderstanding of the actual location of some of the targets. Conversation with the author, September 4, 1991, Washington, DC.

39. Richard Nixon, *RN: The Memoirs of Richard Nixon* (New York: Grosset and Dunlop, 1978), p. 382.

Nixon's deception about the secret bombing of Cambodia was wrong because it was a significant (legally and militarily) expansion of the war into a neutral country (even though the North Vietnamese were not respecting its neutrality). The war at that point was controversial, and its expansion would have increased political opposition to it and President Nixon (as did the public invasion of Cambodia in May 1970). Thus, the lies and secrecy were intended to pursue a significant foreign policy change without the knowledge of Congress or the American people.

President Reagan and Iran-Contra

The Iran–Contra affair consisted of two parts: the sale of arms to Iran for the purpose of freeing U.S. hostages held in Lebanon, and the diversion of funds from the sale of those arms to support the Contras in Nicaragua when public law forbade aid to the Contras. The sale of arms to Iran was first conducted through Israel in 1985 and later came directly from the United States. The secret sales were disclosed by the Lebanese newspaper *Al-Shiraa* on November 3, 1986, and became public. In December, President Reagan issued an executive order (No. 12575) establishing a Special Review Board, known as the Tower Commission, to investigate the matter. The Commission interviewed President Reagan about various aspects of the Iran–Contra affair.

Although the sale of arms to Iran was probably illegal under the Arms Export Control Act,[40] the largest political problem for President Reagan was that he did not want the American public to believe that he had traded arms for hostages. On November 13, 1986, after the arms deals had been revealed, President Reagan addressed the nation and said:

> The charge has been made that the United States has shipped weapons to Iran—as ransom payment for the release of American Hostages in Lebanon. . . . Those charges are utterly false. . . . Our government has a firm policy not to capitulate to terrorist demands. That "no-concessions" policy remains in force in spite of the wildly speculative and false stories about arms for hostages and alleged ransom payments. We did not— repeat—we did not trade weapons or anything else for hostages.[41]

But as more information about the arms-for-hostages deal with Iran came out in congressional hearings and testimony, President Reagan reconsidered his position. Just as President Eisenhower was forced to admit the U-2 overflight after Khrushchev had the evidence, and President Clinton was forced to admit that he had sex with Monica Lewinsky when evidence proved that he

---

40. See George Shultz, *Turmoil and Triumph* (New York: Charles Scribners, 1993), p. 811.

41. *Washington Post*, July 16, 1987, p. A15.

had, President Reagan had to admit what the evidence showed. In a March 4, 1987 address to the nation, he said: "I told the American people I did not trade arms for hostages. My heart and my best intentions still tell me that's true. But the facts and the evidence tell me it is not. . . . What began as a strategic opening to Iran deteriorated in its implementation into trading arms for hostages."[42] President Reagan made two other untrue public statements during the Iran–Contra affair.[43]

George W. Bush and the War in Iraq

After the war in Iraq, a number of pundits and political adversaries accused President George W. Bush of lying in some of his statements.[44] These charges were often based on the failure of U.S. forces to find weapons of mass destruction (WMD) in Iraq after the war of March–April 2003. The following discussion will examine several potential lies of President Bush and his administration concerning the war in Iraq.

In the run-up to the war in Iraq, the Bush administration claimed with some certainty that Iraq possessed chemical and biological weapons. President Bush said on September 26, 2002, that "the Iraqi regime possesses biological and chemical weapons. The Iraqi regime is building the facilities necessary to make more biological and chemical weapons."[45] That Iraq had chemical and biological weapons in the 1980s is certain, in part because some of the materials came from the United States and because Saddam used chemical weapons against Iran and against the Kurds in northern Iraq.[46] But serious questions about the administration's claims were raised when U.S. forces were not able to

---

42. *Washington Post,* July 16, 1987, p. A15.

43. See James P. Pfiffner, *The Character Factor* (College Station: Texas A&M University Press, 2004), pp. 56–60.

44. For polemical books, see Al Franken, *Lies (and the Lying Liars Who Tell Them)* (New York: Dutton, 2003); and David Corn, *The Lies of George W. Bush* (New York: Crown, 2003). For more carefully argued and sourced books, see John W. Dean, *Worse Than Watergate* (Boston: Little Brown, 2004); and John Prados, *Hoodwinked* (New York: New Press, 2004). For a scholarly analysis, see James P. Pfiffner, "Did President Bush Mislead the Country in His Arguments for War with Iraq?," *Presidential Studies Quarterly* 34 (March 2004): 25–46.

45. Dana Priest and Walter Pincus, "Bush Certainty on Iraq Arms Went beyond Analyst's Views," *Washington Post,* June 7, 2003, pp. A1, A17.

46. In the 1980s, the U.S. Department of Commerce authorized the sale to Iraq of biological agents such as anthrax and bubonic plague. According to a memo to Secretary of State George Shultz in 1983, the Iraqis were using chemical weapons against the Iranians on an "almost daily basis." The Commerce Department also approved the sale by Dow Chemical of insecticides that were thought to be used for chemical weapons. Reported by Michael Dobbs, "U.S. Had Key Role in Iraq Buildup," *Washington Post,* December 30, 2002, p. 1, A12. See also Kenneth M. Pollack, *The Threatening Storm* (New York: Random House, 2002), pp. 20–21, 170.

find evidence of Iraq's chemical and biological weapons after the war, despite the diligent searching of U.S. military forces and the 1200-member Iraq Survey Group headed by David Kay.[47]

Two other aspects of the president's claims turned out to be problematic: the implied connection between Saddam Hussein and the atrocities of September 11, and the implication that Iraq had nuclear weapons.

A Saddam–al Qaeda Link? On September 12, 2001, in the Situation Room in the White House, President Bush asked Richard Clarke to look for a link between Saddam Hussein and the terrorists attacks of the previous day. When Clarke replied that it was known that al Qaeda was responsible, although Iran, Pakistan, Saudi Arabia, or Yemen might have been implicated in minor ways, the president "testily" ordered: "Look into Iraq, Saddam."[48] After a meeting among intelligence agencies, "all agencies and departments agreed, there was no cooperation between the two," and a memorandum reporting the conclusion was sent to the president. Nevertheless, from 2002 to 2004, President Bush and his administration strongly implied that there was a significant link between Saddam and the al Qaeda hijackers, despite Osama bin Laden's contempt for Saddam as the head of a secular state.[49]

In early October 2002, President Bush was trying to convince Congress to pass a resolution to give him unilateral authority to go to war with Iraq. In a major address to the nation on October 7, he said, "We know that Iraq and al Qaeda have had high-level contacts that go back a decade. . . . We've learned that Iraq has trained al Qaeda members in bomb-making and poisons and deadly gasses." In the same speech, the president closely connected the need to attack Iraq with the September 11 attacks: "Some citizens wonder, 'after 11 years of living with this [Saddam Hussein] problem, why do we need to confront it now?' And there's a reason. We have experienced the horror of September the 11th." Thus, the terrorist attacks of September 11 were a major reason for attacking Iraq. Vice President Cheney said on *Meet the Press* in late 2001 that a meeting between Mohamed Atta and an Iraqi official in Prague in 2000 was "pretty well confirmed."[50]

The problem was that evidence for a connection between Saddam and al Qaeda was not very solid. Neither the FBI nor the CIA was able to establish

---

47. Walter Pincus and Dana Priest, "Iraq Weapons Report Won't Be Conclusive," *Washington Post,* September 25, 2003, p. 1, A24.

48. Richard A. Clarke, *Against All Enemies* (New York: Free Press, 2004), p. 32.

49. In a tape urging Muslims to fight against the United States, Osama bin Laden said that the fighting should be for God, not for "pagan regimes in all the Arab countries, including Iraq. . . . Socialists are infidels wherever they are, either in Baghdad or Aden." Transcript posted on website: www.indybay.org (accessed April 10, 2003).

50. Dana Milbank and Claudia Deane, "Hussein Link to 9/11 Lingers in Many Minds," *Washington Post,* September 6, 2003, p. 1.

that the September 11 terrorist Mohamed Atta had been in Prague to meet with an Iraqi official as the Bush Administration had asserted.[51] And a UN terrorism committee could find no link between al Qaeda and Saddam.[52] Despite the lack of solid evidence, President Bush continued to connect the war in Iraq with al Qaeda and September 11. In his victory speech on May 1, 2003, on an aircraft carrier off the coast of California, he said: "The battle of Iraq is one victory in a war on terror that began on September the 11, 2001. ... We've removed an ally of al Qaeda, and cut off a source of terrorist funding. ... With those attacks [of September 11], the terrorists and their supporters declared war on the United States. And war is what they got."[53]

In a defense of the administration's policies in Iraq, on September 14, 2003, Vice President Cheney said: "If we're successful in Iraq ... then we will have struck a major blow right at the heart of the base, if you will, the geographic base of the terrorists who had us under assault now for many years, but most especially on 9/11."[54] But on September 18, 2003, President Bush conceded: "No, we've had no evidence that Saddam Hussein was involved with September the 11th."[55] He gave no explanation as to why the previously implied connection was abandoned.[56]

When the staff reports of the 9/11 Commission were released in June of 2004, the analysis further undermined the statements by the Bush administration implying that Saddam Hussein supported al Qaeda in its attacks on the United States. The staff report concluded that although Osama bin Laden had sought space for training camps and assistance with weapons procurement in Sudan in 1994, "Iraq apparently never responded." Echoing the UN report on the same issue, they concluded, "We have no credible evidence that Iraq and al Qaeda cooperated on attacks against the U.S."[57] Thomas H. Kean,

---

51. Dana Milbank and Walter Pincus, "Cheney Defends U.S. Actions in Bid to Revive Public Support," *Washington Post,* September 15, 2003, p. 1, A19. Milbank and Deane, "Hussein Link to 9/11 Lingers," p. 1.

52. Associated Press, "U.N. Panel Finds No Evidence to Link Iraq, Al-Qaeda" [online version], TruthOut.org (accessed June 26, 2003).

53. Quoted in Milbank and Deane, "Hussein Link to 9/11 Lingers," p. 1.

54. Milbank and Pincus, "Cheney Defends U.S. Actions, p. 1, A19.

55. Dana Milbank, "Bush Disavows Hussein–Sept. 11 Link," *Washington Post,* September 18, 2003, p. A18; David E. Sanger, "Bush Reports No Evidence of Hussein Tie to 9/11," *New York Times,* September 18, 2003, p. A18.

56. For a full analysis of the misleading statements of President Bush on the link between Saddam and September 11, and Saddam's nuclear capacity, see Pfiffner, "Did President Bush Mislead the Country in his Arguments for War with Iraq?"

57. "Overview of the Enemy: Staff Statement No. 15," Commission Investigating the September 11 Attacks (The 9/11 Commission), Quoted in *The New York Times,* June 17, 2004, p. A15.

a Republican and chair of the 9/11 Commission, summarized the staff report's finding: "What our staff statement found is there is no credible evidence that we can discover, after a long investigation, that Iraq and Saddam Hussein in any way were part of the attack on the United States."[58]

How can we judge this systematic pattern of implication and the sudden reversal by the president? It is difficult to show that there was an outright lie in the president's rhetoric because his use of language was too careful. Some of his early statements might have been based on claims that he thought were true when he implied the connection between Saddam and September 11 was serious. But as it became clear that the evidence was dubious, the president continued to imply that the connection was significant. But as time went by, there was enough coverage in the press of the failure of intelligence agencies to substantiate the claim, that the president could not credibly claim ignorance.

It thus seems that President Bush did exploit and encourage the common public belief that Saddam was connected to the attacks of September 11, and his strong implications served his purpose of achieving public support for war with Iraq. We can conclude that his statements were misleading and deceptive, though not outright lies.

Nuclear Claim. In 2002, President Bush and his administration also made a number of assertions about Saddam Hussein's potential nuclear capacity. The claim was that Saddam Hussein had reconstituted his nuclear weapons program and was potentially less than a year away from possessing nuclear weapons. This was a powerful argument that deposing Saddam Hussein was important for U.S. national security. Even those who thought Saddam could be deterred from using chemical and biological weapons (as he had been in 1991) might be persuaded that an attack was necessary if they were convinced that Saddam was closing in on a nuclear weapons capability. Thus, the claim about Saddam's nuclear capacity was one of the strongest arguments that President Bush could make for war with Iraq.

Before the president's campaign to convince Congress of the necessity of war with Iraq, the White House asked the CIA to prepare a National Intelligence Estimate (NIE) on Iraq, that is, an authoritative statement of the consensus of intelligence agencies about the potential threat from Iraq.[59] This NIE was used as a basis for President Bush's speech in Cincinnati on October 7, 2002, to convince Congress to give him the authority to go to

---

58. Dana Milbank, "Bush Defends Assertions of Iraq-al Qaeda relationship," *Washington Post,* June 18, 2004, p. A9.

59. Central Intelligence Agency, "Key Judgments [from October 2002 NIE] Iraq's continuing Programs for Weapons of Mass destruction," (2003), declassified excerpts published on the CIA website: www.odci.gov/nic/pubs/research (accessed October 10, 2003), pp. 5–6.

war with Iraq and convince the nation of the immediacy of the threat from Saddam Hussein. In the speech President Bush said:

> We agree that the Iraqi dictator must not be permitted to threaten America and the world with horrible poisons and diseases and gasses and atomic weapons. . . . The evidence indicates that Iraq is reconstituting its nuclear weapons program. . . . he could have a nuclear weapon in less than a year. . . . Facing clear evidence of peril, we cannot wait for the final proof, the smoking gun that could come in the form of a mushroom cloud.

Then, in his State of the Union Speech on January 28, 2003, President Bush said: "The British Government has learned that Saddam Hussein recently sought significant quantities of uranium from Africa." The African country in question was Niger.

The problem with these statements was that the evidence upon which the president's claims were based turned out to be questionable. Two claims of evidence for Saddam's nuclear capacity that the administration relied upon were of dubious authenticity: the claim that Iraq sought large amounts of uranium oxide, "yellowcake," from Niger; and that aluminum tubes shipped to Iraq were intended to be used as centrifuges to create the fissile material necessary for a nuclear bomb.

But the British claim that Saddam sought uranium oxide from Niger turned out to have been based on forged documents. The CIA had serious doubts about the accuracy of the claim and even had convinced NSC aides to take the claim out of the president's October 7, 2002 speech to the nation.[60] How it got into the 2003 State of the Union address was not clear.

In addition to the Niger yellowcake claim, the administration also adduced, as evidence for Iraq's reconstituting its nuclear program, reports of large numbers of aluminum tubes purchased by Iraq. President Bush said in his September 12, 2002 speech to the United Nations: "Iraq has made several attempts to buy high-strength aluminum tubes used to enrich uranium for a nuclear weapon. Should Iraq acquire fissile material, it would be able to build a nuclear weapon within a year."[61]

The evidence of the aluminum tubes was also featured in the NIE issued in early October 2002, which played an important role in convincing members of Congress to vote for the resolution giving the president the authority to take the United States to war with Iraq. The State Department's Bureau of Intelligence and Research (INR), however, registered its dissent in the NIE

---

60. Associated Press, "White House Official Apologizes for Role in Uranium Claim," *New York Times*, July 22, 2003, nytimes.com (accessed July 22, 2003).

61. President Bush's Address to UN, printed in the *New York Times*, September 13, 2003, p. A31.

itself: "INR is not persuaded that the tubes in question are intended for use as centrifuge rotors. . . . INR considers it far more likely that the tubes are intended for another purpose, most likely the production of artillery rockets."[62] The physical characteristics of the tubes—diameter, length, composition, coating—matched closely the dimensions of aluminum tubes used in Medusa rockets but did not track as closely with the dimensions of centrifuge rotors.[63] The State Department concluded: "The activities we have detected do not, however, add up to a compelling case that Iraq is currently pursuing what INR would consider to be an integrated and comprehensive approach to acquire nuclear weapons."[64]

In his interim report to Congress in the fall of 2003, David Kay told Congress that Iraq's nuclear program was in "the very most rudimentary" state: "It clearly does not look like a massive, resurgent program, based on what we discovered."[65] According to Kay's report, Iraqi scientists said, "To date we have not uncovered evidence that Iraq undertook significant post-1998 steps to actually build nuclear weapons or produce fissile material."[66]

The Bush administration's inference that Saddam Hussein was continuing his previous weapons programs was not an unreasonable conclusion. The problem was that there was little evidence to support their conclusions about Saddam's nuclear capacity, and they used claims of dubious validity to make their case to the American people about nuclear weapons and a connection between Saddam and the atrocities of September 11.

"No War Plans on My Desk." In the spring of 2002, President Bush did come close to lying when he publicly said several times that he had no war plans on his desk. President Bush was concerned with Iraq from the

---

62. Central Intelligence Agency, "Key Judgments [from October 2002 NIE] Iraq's continuing Programs for Weapons of Mass destruction," (2003), declassified excerpts published on the CIA website: www.odci.gov/nic/pubs/research (accessed October 10, 2003), p. 9.

63. Barton Gellman and Walter Pincus, "Depiction of Threat Outgrew Supporting Evidence," *Washington Post,* August 10, 2003, p. 1, A9.

64. Central Intelligence Agency, "Key Judgments [from October 2002 NIE] Iraq's continuing Programs for Weapons of Mass destruction," (2003), declassified excerpts published on the CIA website: www.odci.gov/nic/pubs/research (accessed October 10, 2003), p. 8–9.

65. Dana Priest and Walter Pincus, "Search in Iraq Finds No Banned Weapons," *Washington Post,* October 3, 2003, p. 1.

66. David Kay, "Report on the Activities of the Iraq Survey Group to the House Permanent Select Committee on Intelligence and the House Committee on Appropriations, Subcommittee on Defense and the Senate Select Committee on Intelligence," p. 7. The page reference is to the unclassified report published on the CNN website: http://cnn.allpolitics (accessed October 10, 2003) p. 7.

beginning of his administration.[67] Immediately after the terrorist attacks on September 11, President Bush resolved to do something about Iraq, and on September 17, 2001, he directed the Department of Defense to begin general planning for a possible war with Iraq.[68] The president decided to take more concrete action on November 21, 2001, when he told Secretary Rumsfeld to develop operational plans for a possible war with Iraq.[69] Rumsfeld ordered General Tommy Franks to work on the plans, and Franks presented his first formal plans to Rumsfeld on December 4, 2002.

After two more iterations of the plans, on December 12 and 19, Franks went to Crawford, Texas, to present his plans to the president, and after that meeting, Franks set up top-secret planning teams in the Pentagon to further develop the plans. On January 17, 2003, Franks presented the fourth iteration of the plans to Secretary Rumsfeld, and the fifth on February 1. On February 7, General Franks presented to President Bush the formal plan that was in operational form; that is, rather than a working draft, it was an operational set of plans that could be carried out.[70]

After the elaborate planning for war in Iraq at the president's orders, it is striking that on the weekend of April 6–7 at Crawford, Texas, when he was hosting Tony Blair, President Bush told a British news reporter, "And I have no plans to attack on my desk." Later, on May 23 and 26, he repeated at press conferences, "I have no war plans on my desk.[71]

In what way might these statements be considered not to be lies? One might take a literalist approach and say that at the time the president made the statements, in fact no physical documents were on his desk in the Oval Office or in Crawford that included plans for war. In this literalist sense, the

---

67. Ronald Suskind, *The Price of Loyalty* (New York: Simon and Schuster, 2004), pp. 82–86; Woodward, *Plan of Attack,* pp. 1–3, 9–10, 26 and Woodward, *Bush at War* (New York: Simon and Schuster, 2003), pp. 84–91.

68. Glen Kessler, "U.S. Decision on Iraq has Puzzling Past," *Washington Post,* June 12, 2003, pp. A1, A20. President Bush wanted to keep his decision secret because public knowledge of it would engender "enormous international angst and domestic speculation. I knew what would happen if people thought we were developing a potential [sic] or a war plan for Iraq," Woodward, *Plan of Attack,* p. 3.

69. Woodward, *Plan of Attack,* pp. 30–31.

70. Woodward, *Plan of Attack,* pp. 77, 80, 96, 98. On March 21, 2003, General Franks told his top commanders who would be waging the war that the United States was going to war with Iraq unless Saddam left the country. To emphasize his seriousness, he said: "You know, if you guys think this is not going to happen, you're wrong." CIA Director George Tenet in March also told Kurdish leaders that there would be a military attack in Iraq. Woodward, *Plan of Attack,* pp. 115, 117.

71. Woodward, *Plan of Attack,* pp. 120, 127. General Franks also stated on May 21 that "my boss has not yet asked me to put together a plan to do that [attack Iraq]," p. 130.

truthfulness of the president's statement depends on the meaning of the word "desk."[72] But President Bush was clearly using a metaphor and clearly meant to convey that although he was considering going to war with Saddam, his intention was not firm enough to have drawn up serious plans for an attack. It is ironic that the president could easily have avoided lying and evaded the question by saying something like "all of my options are open, and I have made no final decision." But he chose not to do that and instead several times made the untrue categorical statement.

One might argue that the consequences of this lie were not serious. In retrospect, there were many signs that President Bush intended to go to war to depose Saddam Hussein, beginning publicly with his 2002 State of the Union Speech that included Iraq in what he termed an "Axis of Evil." One might also argue that this lie was not as consequential as the administration's misleading references to Saddam's nuclear capacity or the connection between Saddam and September 11 in its arguments for war with Iraq. Nevertheless, these statements were not true, and the president knew that they were not true when he said them. It seems reasonable to conclude that the president intended to deceive the public about the level of planning he was doing in preparation for war.

Assessing Bush's Statements. In trying to assess the truthfulness of President Bush in his arguments for the war in Iraq, we must take into account what he himself believed as well as the evidence for the accuracy of his claims. With respect to Iraq's chemical and biological weapons capacity, President Bush's statements were incorrect, but he cannot be fairly accused of deliberately lying. There was no convincing evidence that the weapons Iraq had used in the 1980s were destroyed during the 1990s, and there was an international consensus among the intelligence agencies of Western Europe as well as the United States and the United Nations that Saddam still had them. In light of this almost universal consensus that Saddam had a chemical and biological weapons capacity, President Bush cannot be blamed for coming to the same conclusion, even if the conclusion was factually incorrect.

With respect to the implied link between Saddam and September 11, the president was surely aware that little direct evidence was available. Neither the FBI nor the CIA had been able to verify the alleged Prague meeting between Mohamed Atta, the leader of the hijackers, and an Iraqi intelligence agent. The president's statement of August 17, 2003, shows that he did not believe there was a direct link. Thus, we can conclude that the

---

72. This might bring to mind President Clinton's convoluted reasoning when he denied that he had had sex with Monica Lewinsky, "It depends on what the meaning of the word 'is' is."

systematic series of statements by him and his administration before and after the war was intentionally misleading in implying the link but did not constitute direct lies.

With respect to Saddam's possession of nuclear weapons, the deliberate rhetorical conjuring of "mushroom clouds" and claims about the near-term potential for an Iraqi nuclear capacity can also be considered systematically misleading. The president may have believed that Saddam was close to possessing a nuclear capacity, but he ignored conflicting arguments and evidence presented by the Departments of State and Energy in the National Intelligence Estimate of October 2002. If the president did not fully understand the tenuousness of the evidence, he should have.[73] Thus again, the president and his administration were systematically misleading in their public arguments for war by strongly implying that Saddam was close to having a nuclear capacity despite the lack of compelling evidence and the considered opinions of the International Atomic Energy Agency and the U.S. Departments of State and Energy.

With respect to his statement, "I have no war plans on my desk," however, it seems that President Bush made a statement that he knew to be untrue. His probable intention was to reassure the American public and other nations that war with Iraq was neither imminent nor inevitable. But given the series of plans, promises, and assurances that the administration had given to allies, war was becoming increasingly probable.

If the president had wanted to avoid the issue or give a reassuring statement, he could have chosen another formulation, but he did not choose to take a truthful way to evade the question. But even though this direct statement (repeated) can be considered to be a direct lie, the consequences of it were considerably less momentous than his misleading statements about Saddam's nuclear capacity and the link between Saddam and September 11. Thus, a concerned citizen might be more legitimately upset about the misleading statements than the direct lies.

---

73. On December 21, 2002, CIA Director George Tenet and his deputy John McLaughlin went to the Oval Office to brief the president on Iraq's WMD. After McLaughlin had presented the strongest evidence they had, the president was not enthusiastic. His response was, "Nice try," but "I don't think this is quite—it's not something that Joe Public would understand or would gain a lot of confidence from. . . . I've been told all this intelligence about having WMD and this is the best we've got?" Then Tenet reassured the president, "Don't worry, it's a slam dunk." The president left Tenet with the instructions: "Make sure no one stretches to make our case." After this briefing it is not obvious that the evidence for WMD in Iraq ever improved. The vice president's staff collected a lot of allegations and threads of evidence, but Colin Powell rejected most of them before his February 5, 2003 presentation to the United Nations of the U.S. case for war with Iraq. See Woodward, *Plan of Attack*, pp. 249–50, 299–301.

CONCLUSION

Presidential lying undercuts the democratic link between citizens and their government; it undermines trust in government and all public officials, and it sets a bad example that may lead others to justify their own lying. But not all lies are equal; that is, some are worse than others. The argument that "they all do it," so there is no point in evaluating lies, is insidious and undermines moral responsibility. So we must avoid this cynical approach. But we must also avoid the excuse of moral relativism, which holds that moral judgments are hopelessly subjective and that we ought not to judge others' behavior at all.

When presidents tell lies for reasons of state, they often justify their lies by arguing that their deception is intended for hostile foreign governments. The problem is that such lies may also be intended to deceive the American public. Presidential deception tends to undermine democracy, and thus the threshold for justifying lies ought to be quite high. It is the argument of this essay that presidential deception of the American public is only justified in exceptional circumstances, such as when legitimate national security interests are at stake. Otherwise, the presumption must be against lying.

We must also keep presidential lying in perspective. Lies are not the most important aspect of what presidents do, either in a negative or a positive sense. Lyndon Johnson's lies about Vietnam were not as damaging as the broader, flawed policies that got us into a land war in Asia. President Nixon's lies about Watergate were not as insidious as the broader aspects of his lack of scruples (for example, using the IRS to harass his enemies, campaign "dirty tricks," creating the "Plumbers," wiretaps on citizens without warrants, the Huston plan, and so on). President Reagan's lies or misstatements about Iran–Contra were not as bad as the deliberate breaking of the law by his administration. President Bush's misleading statements in the run-up to the war in Iraq were less important than his strategic decisions that took the United States into that war, whether or not one thinks those were wise decisions.

From the evidence presented here, it is clear that presidents do occasionally lie about important issues of public policy. When one is evaluating presidential performance or deciding for whom to vote, one should take into account presidential lies, but one should also keep lying in perspective.

7

⚜

The Limits
of the Bully Pulpit

GEORGE C. EDWARDS III
Texas A&M University

No president ever invested more in attempting to mold public opinion than Bill Clinton. His was a presidency based on a perpetual campaign to obtain the public's support[1]—a campaign fed by public opinion polls, focus groups, and public relations memos. The White House even polled voters on where it was best for the First Family to vacation. In 1995, the White House spent an unprecedented $18 million in advertising on behalf of the president—a year *before* the presidential election.[2]

Public leadership dominated the policy-making process in the Clinton White House, serving as both the focus of the president's energies and the criterion by which it evaluated itself. In a typical year, Clinton spoke in public 550 times,[3] and he traveled around the country every fourth day.[4] Equally important, the administration repeatedly interpreted its setbacks, whether in elections or on such policies as health care reform, in terms of its failure to communicate[5] rather than in terms of the quality of its initiatives or its strategy for governing.

The Clinton administration's focus on public leadership was characteristic of the modern presidency. Ronald Reagan took office oriented to using his

---

1. See Samuel Kernell, *Going Public,* 3d ed. (Washington, DC: Congressional Quarterly Press, 1997).

2. Bob Woodward, *The Choice* (New York: Simon & Schuster, 1996), p. 344. These funds were spent through the Democratic National Committee.

3. Michael Waldman, *POTUS Speaks* (New York: Simon & Schuster, 2000), p. 16. See also Marc Lacey, "Guarding the President's Words and, Maybe, His Legacy," *New York Times,* January 24, 2000, p. A12.

4. Kernell, *Going Public,* p. 121.

5. Woodward, *The Choice,* pp. 54, 126; Elizabeth Drew, *Showdown: The Struggle between the Gingrich Congress and the Clinton White House* (New York: Simon & Schuster, 1996), pp. 19, 34–35.

communications skills to persuade the public and thus the Congress to do his bidding.[6] Much to the surprise of many political observers, George W. Bush launched a massive public relations campaign on behalf of his priority initiatives soon after taking office, and the White House's pace has never slackened.[7] Presidents clearly believe that they need to lead the public, and they "go public" more than ever, depending on a steadily expanding White House public relations infrastructure to take their messages to the American people.[8]

Leading the public is at the core of the modern presidency. Even as they try to govern, presidents are involved in a permanent campaign. Both politics and policy revolve around presidents' attempts to garner public support, both for themselves and for their policies. The division between campaigning and governing has become obscured. Indeed, governing often seems little more than an extension of the campaign that won the president his office in the first place.

At the base of this core strategy for governing is the premise that through the permanent campaign, the White House *can* successfully persuade or even mobilize the public. Commentators on the presidency in both the press and the academy often assume that the White House can move public opinion if the president has the skill and will to effectively exploit the "bully pulpit." In Sidney Blumenthal's words, in the permanent campaign "the citizenry is viewed as a mass of fluid voters who can be appeased by appearances, occasional drama, and clever rhetoric."[9]

Equally important, those in the White House share the premise of the potential of presidential leadership of the public. David Gergen, an experienced White House communications adviser, favorably cites Winston Churchill's assertion that "of all the talents bestowed upon men, none is so precious as the gift of oratory. He who enjoys it wields a power more durable than that of a great king. He is an independent force in the world." He adds that Ronald Reagan turned television "into a powerful weapon to achieve his legislative goals."[10] Sidney Blumenthal agreed, declaring that Reagan had "stunning success in shaping public opinion," which in turn was central to transforming his ideas into law.[11]

---

6. Lou Cannon, *Reagan* (New York: Putnam, 1982), p. 319.

7. For more on this topic see George C. Edwards III, "The Strategic Presidency of George W. Bush," in *New Challenges for the American Presidency* (New York: Longman, 2004).

8. See, for example, Kernell, *Going Public.*

9. Sidney Blumenthal, *The Permanent Campaign,* rev. ed. (New York: Simon & Schuster, 1982), p. 24. See also pp. 297–298.

10. David Gergen, *Eyewitness to Power: The Essence of Leadership* (New York: Simon & Schuster, 2000), pp. 210, 348.

11. Blumenthal, *The Permanent Campaign,* p. 284.

Similarly, in interviews in the 1990s, Lawrence Jacobs and Robert Shapiro found among both White House and congressional staff widespread confidence in the president's ability to lead the public. Evidently President Clinton shared this view, as his aides reported that he exhibited an "unbelievable arrogance" regarding his ability to change public opinion and felt he could "create new political capital all the time" through going public—a hubris echoed by his aides.[12]

The assurance with which presidents, scholars, and journalists accept the assumption of the potential of presidential public leadership belies our lack of understanding of that leadership. We actually know very little about the effect of the president's persuasive efforts because we have focused on what the president says rather than how the public responds to his words.

One of the crowning ironies of the contemporary presidency is that at the same time that presidents increasingly attempt to govern by campaigning—"going public," public support for presidential policies is elusive, perhaps more than ever before. President Clinton was not alone in his frustration with communicating with the public. In the century since Theodore Roosevelt declared the White House a "bully pulpit," presidents have often found the public unresponsive to issues at the top of the White House's agenda and unreceptive to requests to think about, much less act on, political matters. When asked about his "biggest disappointment as president," George Bush replied, "I just wasn't a good enough communicator."[13]

In his memoirs, Ronald Reagan—the "Great Communicator"—reflected on his efforts to ignite concern among the American people regarding the threat of communism in Central America and mobilize them behind his program of support for the Contras. "For eight years the press called me the 'Great Communicator'," he wrote. "Well, one of my greatest frustrations during those eight years was my inability to communicate to the American people and to Congress the seriousness of the threat we faced in Central America."[14]

If the frustration that presidents often experience in their efforts to obtain the public's support were nothing more than an irritating cost of doing the job, then public leadership would be a topic of only passing interest to political scientists, historians, and journalists. Governing by campaigning is much more important than that, however. The way presidents attempt to govern, and their success in doing so, has profound consequences for politics and public policy.

---

12. Lawrence R. Jacobs and Robert Y. Shapiro, *Politicians Don't Pander* (Chicago: University of Chicago Press, 2000), pp. 45, 106, 136.

13. Quoted in Victor Gold, "George Bush Speaks Out," *The Washingtonian* (February 1994): 41.

14. Ronald Reagan, *An American Life* (New York: Simon & Schuster, 1990), p. 471.

If there is substantial potential for presidents to govern through leading the public, then it is reasonable to evaluate them on their success in public leadership. If presidents do not succeed in obtaining the public's support, it is a failure of leadership for which they should be held accountable. However, if the premise of the potential of public leadership is false, then we may be evaluating presidents and presidential candidates on the wrong criteria.

If the conventional wisdom is wrong and presidents are not able to persuade, much less mobilize, the public, then presidents may be wasting their time and adopting governing styles that are prone to failure. For example, the massive Clinton health care reform plan of 1993–1994 was based on the underlying, and unquestioned, assumption within the White House that the president could sell his plan to the public and thus solidify congressional support. Because the administration believed it could move the public, Clinton and his aides felt they could focus on developing their preferred option in health care policy in 1993. In the process, they discounted centrist opinion and underestimated how opponents could criticize their plan as big government. Moreover, even as the bill's fortunes soured, the White House refused to compromise. As Jacobs and Shapiro put it, "The White House's unquestioned faith that the president could rally Americans produced a rigid insistence on comprehensive reforms."[15]

In the end, Clinton was not able to obtain even a vote in either house of Congress on what was to have been his centerpiece legislation. Not long after, the Democrats lost majorities in both the House and the Senate for the first time in four decades. The administration's health care proposal was the prime example of the Republicans' charge that the Democrats were ideological extremists who had lost touch with the wishes of Americans. Summing up the health care reform debacle, Jacobs and Shapiro conclude that the "fundamental political mistake committed by Bill Clinton and his aides was in grossly overestimating the capacity of a president to 'win' public opinion and to use public support as leverage to overcome known political obstacles—from an ideologically divided Congress to hostile interest groups."[16]

This is not the lesson that Clinton learned, however. Indeed, the premise of the power of the presidential pulpit is so strong that each downturn in the bill's progress prompted new schemes for going public rather than a reconsideration of the fundamental framework of the bill or the basic strategy for obtaining its passage.[17] Ultimately, the president concluded that health care reform failed because "I totally neglected how to get the public informed. . . . I have to get

---

15. Jacobs and Shapiro, *Politicians Don't Pander,* pp. 76, 81–83, 105, 115–116, 136, 149, 152.

16. Jacobs and Shapiro, *Politicians Don't Pander,* p. 115.

17. Jacobs and Shapiro, *Politicians Don't Pander,* pp. 115, 149.

more involved in crafting my message—in getting across my core concerns."[18] In other words, his strategy was not inappropriate, only his implementation of it. The premise of the potential of presidential public leadership seems to be nonfalsifiable.

The Clinton White House was not alone in its myopia regarding the effectiveness of the permanent campaign. The Reagan administration suffered from the same malady. For example, one of the president's highest priorities was obtaining congressional support for the Contras in Nicaragua. The White House launched a full-scale public relations campaign portraying the conflict in Nicaragua as a crucial confrontation between the United States and the Soviet Union. The public was not persuaded. Nevertheless, one White House official concluded that the problem was not in the potential of presidential leadership of the public but rather in "[the] packaging of the activity, in terms of policy and presentation to the public. It wasn't well staged or sequenced."[19]

It is appropriate, then, that we reevaluate presidential public leadership. To do so, I focus on a sample of issues during the tenures of two recent presidents, Ronald Reagan and Bill Clinton. Republican Reagan and Democrat Clinton are best-test cases for presidential leadership of the public. Each president displayed formidable rhetorical skills, and both supporters and detractors frequently commented on their unusual rapport with the public. Each president overwhelmingly won a second term in office, and they became the only presidents since Eisenhower's tenure in the 1950s to win and complete two terms. If we cannot find successful public leadership during the tenures of Reagan and Clinton, we are unlikely to find it anywhere. I also examine two issues central to our most recent president, George W. Bush.

BILL CLINTON

An articulate and energetic speaker, Bill Clinton displayed an impressive mastery of public policy as well as a unique ability to empathize with his audience. The president's political resurrection following the dramatic Democratic losses in the 1994 midterm elections and his *rise* in public esteem in the face of clear evidence of lying to the public and engaging in what most people saw as immoral behavior in the Oval Office left an indelible imprint on pundits and politicians alike.

---

18. Drew, *Showdown,* p. 66.

19. Quoted in Blumenthal, *The Permanent Campaign,* pp. 292–293.

Economic Program

Bill Clinton's 1992 presidential election campaign kept a clear focus on the economy. On February 15, 1993, the new president addressed the nation on his economic program. Two days later he delivered a much more detailed address to the Congress on his policy plans. His economic proposals included spending for job creation, a tax increase on the wealthy, investment incentives, and aid to displaced workers. In the same month, he introduced his first major legislative proposal, a plan to spend more than $16 billion to stimulate the economy. It immediately ran into strong Republican opposition. During the April 1993 congressional recess, Clinton stepped up his rhetoric on his bill, counting on a groundswell of public opinion to pressure moderate Republicans into ending the filibuster on the bill. (Republicans, meanwhile, kept up a steady flow of sound bites linking the president's package with wasteful spending and Clinton's proposed tax increase.) The groundswell never materialized, and the Republicans found little support for any new spending in their home states. Instead, they found their constituents railing against new taxes and spending.[20] The bill never came to a vote in the Senate.

The figures in Table 7–1 show that public support for the president's economic plan peaked immediately following his speech on February 17 and then dropped dramatically a few days later. (Clinton's chief speechwriter reports that the speech was viewed in Washington as a failure.[21]) During the period when the president needed support the most and when he worked hardest to obtain it, it diminished to the point that by May a plurality of the public *opposed* his plan.

Health Care Reform

Health care reform was to be the centerpiece of the Clinton administration. In September 1993, the president delivered a well-received national address on the need for reform. Yet the president was not able to sustain the support of the public for health care reform. The White House held out against compromise with the Republicans and conservative Democrats, hoping for a groundswell of public support for reform. But it never came.[22] In the meantime, opponents of the president's proposal launched an aggressive counterattack, including running negative television advertisements. Clinton's tendency to carry the campaign mode to governance by demonizing opponents such as the medical profession and the drug and insurance industries

---

20. "Democrats Look to Salvage Part of Stimulus Plan," *Congressional Quarterly Weekly Report* (April 24, 1993): 1002–1003.

21. Waldman, *POTUS Speaks,* p. 41.

22. "Health Care Reform: The Lost Chance," *Newsweek* (September 19, 1994): 32.

Table 7–1 Public Support for Clinton's Economic Plan

Date	Support	Oppose	Mixed	No Opinion
2/17/93*	79%	16%	2%	5%
2/26–2/28/93	59	29	6	6
3/22–3/24/93	54	34	6	6
4/22–4/24/93	55	39	2	4
5/21–5/23/93	44	45	5	5
6/29–6/30/93	44	49	2	5

SOURCE: Gallup/CNN/*USA Today* Poll question, "Do you generally support or oppose Bill Clinton's economic plan?"

*"Do you generally support or oppose the economic plan that President (Bill) Clinton outlined tonight (in his speech February 17, 1993)?"

Table 7–2 Public Support for Clinton's Health Care Reform

Date	Favor	Oppose	Don't Know
9/24–9/26/93	59%	33%	8%
10/28–10/30/93	45	45	10
11/2–11/4/93	52	40	8
11/19–11/21/93	52	41	7
1/15–1/17/94	56	39	6
1/28–1/30/94	57	38	5
2/26–2/28/94	46	48	5
3/28–3/30/94	44	47	9
5/20–5/22/94	46	49	5
6/11–6/12/94	42	50	8
6/25–6/28/94	44	49	8
7/15–7/17/94	40	56	5

SOURCE: Gallup Poll question, "From everything you've heard or read about the plan so far . . . do you favor or oppose President Clinton's plan to reform health care?"

probably exacerbated his problems in obtaining public support. As the figures in Table 7–2 show, by mid-July 1994, only 40 percent of the public favored the president's health care reform proposals, and 56 percent opposed them. The bill did not come to a vote in either chamber of Congress.

Haiti

One hallmark of foreign policy during the Clinton administration was a series of military interventions. One of these interventions occurred in Haiti in September 1994. On September 15, the president addressed the nation on a military buildup for a possible intervention in Haiti, explaining

Table 7–3 Public Approval of Clinton's Handling of Haiti

Date	Approve	Disapprove	Don't Know
7/15–7/17/94*	28%	56%	16%
9/6–9/7/94	27	58	15
9/14/94	35	49	15
9/15/94**	53	43	4
9/23–9/25/94*	48	48	4
10/11/94	43	49	9

SOURCE: Gallup Poll question, "Do you approve or disapprove of the way (President) Bill Clinton is handling . . . the situation in Haiti?"

* Same question, different lead-in: "Now thinking of some issues, ..."

**Reinterview of 400 respondents from the previous day after the president's speech.

U.S. involvement. Three days later, on September 18, Clinton addressed the nation again, this time on the resolution of the Haitian conflict. The figures in Table 7–3 show that the president received a short-term increase in support for his handling of the situation in Haiti following his speech to the nation on September 15, 1994,[23] but this support quickly deteriorated into plurality disapproval less than a month later. Indeed, Clinton faced near-majority disapproval only five days after his September 18 speech announcing a peaceful resolution of the crisis.

Bosnia

Conflict within the former Yugoslavia posed a problem throughout Clinton's tenure in office. On November 27, 1995, the president gave a nationally televised address seeking the public's support for deploying U.S. peacekeeping troops to Bosnia. As the figures in Table 7–4 show, the president's plea met with little success. In fact, public support for sending U.S. troops to Bosnia dropped steadily as the president implemented this policy. It was not until two years later that a plurality of the public supported the deployment of U.S. troops in Bosnia.

Kosovo

On March 24, 1999, Clinton gave a nationally televised address informing the public that he was ordering bombing on Serbia to stop the ethnic cleansing of ethnic Albanians in Kosovo province. From the beginning, the public supported the president's handling of Kosovo, with little variation in public

---

23. Caution is appropriate in interpreting the figures for the September 15 poll because only 400 people were reinterviewed after the president's September 15 speech.

Table 7–4 Public Support of Deployment of Troops in Bosnia

Date	Approve	Disapprove	Don't Know
9/19–9/22/95*	50%	44%	6%
11/6–11/8/95*	47	49	4
11/27/95**	46	40	14
12/15–12/18/95	41	54	5
1/5–1/7/96	36	58	6
5/28–5/29/96	42	51	7
6/26–6/29/97	39	53	8
12/18–12/21/97	49	43	8
1/16–1/18/98	53	43	5

SOURCE: Gallup Poll question, "Do you approve or disapprove of the presence of U.S. (United States) troops in Bosnia?"

*Gallup/CNN/*USA Today* Poll question, "There is a chance a peace agreement could be reached by all the groups currently fighting in Bosnia. If so, the Clinton Administration is considering contributing U.S. (United States) troops to an international peacekeeping force. Would you favor or oppose that?"

**Gallup/CNN/*USA Today* Poll question, "Now that a peace agreement has been reached by all the groups currently fighting in Bosnia, the Clinton Administration plans to contribute U.S. (United States) troops to an international peacekeeping force. Do you favor or oppose that?" A total of 632 respondents were interviewed after the president's speech.

Table 7–5 Clinton's Handling of Kosovo

Date	Approve	Disapprove	No Opinion
3/25/99	58%	32%	10%
4/6–4/7/99	58	35	7
4/13–4/14/99	61	34	5
4/26–4/27/99	54	41	5
4/30–5/2/99	54	41	5
5/7–5/9/99	55	35	10
6/4–6/5/99	56	39	5
6/10/99	55	35	10
6/11–6/13/99	57	38	5

SOURCE: Gallup Poll question, "Do you approve or disapprove of the way President Clinton is handling the situation in Kosovo?"

opinion over the entire period of the bombing (see Table 7–5). The public appears more willing to support bombing than the use of troops on the ground. At the same time, the public never agreed that the president had a clear and well-thought-out policy on the Kosovo situation (see Table 7–6). Indeed, for most of the period of the bombing, a majority of the public thought that he did *not* have such a policy.

Table 7–6 Clinton's Kosovo Policy

Date	Clear and Well-Thought-Out Policy	Not Clear and Well-Thought-Out	No Opinion
3/30–3/31/99	46%	47%	7%
4/6–4/7/99	39	50	11
4/13–4/14/99	41	51	8
4/26–4/27/99	38	54	8
6/11–6/13/99	43	52	5

SOURCE: Gallup Poll question, "From what you have heard or read, do you think the Clinton administration has a clear and well-thought-out policy on the Kosovo situation, or don't you think so?"

Table 7–7 Public Support for NAFTA

Date	Favor	Oppose	Don't Know
6/21–6/24/93	43%	45%	12%
8/2–8/3/93	35	46	19
8/8–8/10/93***	41	44	15
9/10–9/12/93***	35	40	25
9/16–9/19/93*	33	40	27
11/2–11/4/93*	38	46	16
11/8–11/9/93*	34	38	29
11/11–11/14/93**	37	41	22
11/15–11/16/93***	38	41	21

SOURCE: Gallup/CNN/*USA Today* Poll, CBS News/*New York Times* Poll, and NBC/*Wall Street Journal* Poll question, "Do you favor or oppose the proposed North American Free Trade Agreement—called NAFTA—with Mexico and Canada that eliminates nearly all restrictions on imports, exports, and business investment between the United States, Mexico, and Canada?"

*Gallup/CNN/*USA Today* Poll, "Do you favor or oppose the North American Free Trade Agreement between the United States and Mexico and Canada, sometimes known as N.A.F.T.A.?"

**CBS News/*New York Times* Poll question, "Would you say you (Favor/Oppose) N.A.F.T.A. (North American Free Trade Agreement) strongly or not so strongly?" [strongly and not strongly responses combined in the table]

***Gallup/CNN/*USA TODAY* Poll question: "Do you favor or oppose the proposed free trade agreement between the United States and Mexico?"

NAFTA

Free trade was another hallmark of Clinton's foreign policy. The first major free trade agreement to reach Congress during the Clinton administration was the North American Free Trade Agreement (NAFTA). The White House fought hard for the agreement but the figures in Table 7–7 show that the White House never achieved plurality support for NAFTA before Congress's decision to pass it.

On the Defense: Impeachment

The presidency of Bill Clinton was a tumultuous one. Congress was highly polarized, and the Republican majorities he faced for six of his eight years in office were eager to bring about change to which the president was opposed. Under such conditions, Clinton frequently had to defend both himself and his policies. The burden of moving public opinion in such cases was on his opponents, who had to build support to change the status quo. The White House's task was to *maintain* existing support. Under these circumstances, we would expect the White House to have more success than when it wished to change opinion. In other words, we would expect the president to do better on defense than on offense.

Certainly the most dramatic issue of the Clinton administration was its successful effort to fight the president's removal from office following the Monica Lewinsky scandal. The media attention devoted to the impeachment controversy and thus the issue's visibility make it unique.

The results in Table 7–8 show that the public did not support the impeachment and conviction of the president. In a brief nationally televised speech on August 17, 1998, the president admitted lying to the public about his relationship with Monica Lewinsky. Over the five and one-half months between the poll on August 21–23, 1998, and the final poll on February 9, 1999, public opinion barely changed at all. Despite, or because of, the enormous volume of commentary from advocates on both sides of the issue, the public did not budge from opinions it had reached *before* the issue came to a head. Opinions were shaped before the issue was joined and before the president and his spokespeople took to the airways to combat the Republican impeachment effort. The president's task was to maintain the strong support he enjoyed on the issue, and he seems to have done an effective job. It is difficult to determine whether Clinton's success was the result of his leadership of the public or the result of public reaction against what it saw as the overreaching of the Republicans.

Clinton in Perspective

Bill Clinton based his strategy of governing on moving the public to support his policy initiatives. Despite his impressive political and communications skills, the evidence is clear that the president typically failed to obtain public support. He did succeed in defending the status quo against radical departures proposed by his Republican opponents, but he could not rally the public behind his own initiatives. Given his experience with attempting to lead the public, it is no wonder that at the middle of his first term Clinton lamented that "I've got to . . . spend more time communicating with the American people about what we've done and where we're

Table 7–8 Support for Clinton's Impeachment and Conviction

Poll Date	Remove From Office	Not Remove From Office	No Opinion
6/5–6/7/98	19%	77%	4%
8/7–8/8/98	23	75	2
8/10–8/12/98	20	76	4
8/17/98	25	69	6
8/18/98	26	70	4
8/21–8/23/98	29	67	4
9/10/98	31	63	6
9/11–9/12/98	30	64	6
9/13/98	31	66	3
9/20/98	35	60	5
9/21/98	32	66	2
9/23–9/24/98	29	68	3
10/6–10/7/98	32	65	3

SOURCE: Gallup Poll, "Based on what you know at this point, do you think that Bill Clinton should or should not be impeached and removed from office"?

Poll Date	Vote in Favor of Impeaching	Vote Against Impeaching	No Opinion
10/9–10/12/98	31%	63%	6%
10/23–10/25/98	30	63	7
11/13–11/15/98	30	68	2
11/20–11/22/98	33	64	3
12/4–12/6/98	33	65	2
12/12–12/13/98	35	61	4
12/15–12/16/98	34	63	3

SOURCE: Gallup Poll, "As you may know, removing a president from office involves two major steps in Congress. First, the House of Representatives must vote on whether there is enough evidence to bring a president to trial before the Senate. This step is called impeachment. Next the Senate must vote on whether to remove the president from office, or not. What would you want your member of the House of Representatives to do?

1. Vote in favor of impeaching Clinton and sending the case to the Senate for trial

2. Vote against impeachment of Clinton

3. Don't know/refused answer

Poll Date	Vote in Favor of Convicting	Vote Against Convicting	No Opinion
12/19–12/20/98	29%	68%	3%
1/6/99	33	63	4
1/8–1/10/99	32	63	5

(Continued)

Table 7–8 (*Continued*)

Poll Date	Vote in Favor of Convicting	Vote Against Convicting	No Opinion
1/18/99	33%	63%	4%
1/22–1/24/99	33	64	3
2/4–2/7/99	36	62	4
2/9/99	31	66	3

SOURCE: Gallup Poll, "As you may know, the House has now impeached [Bill] Clinton and the case has been sent to the Senate for trial. What do you want your Senators to do—vote in favor of convicting Clinton and removing him from office, or vote against convicting Clinton so he will remain in office?"

going."[24] Although he often declared that he needed to do a better job of *communicating*, it seems never to have occurred to him or his staff that his basic strategy may have been inherently flawed.

RONALD REAGAN

In contrast to his immediate predecessors, the public viewed Ronald Reagan as a strong leader, and his staff was unsurpassed in its skill at portraying the president and his views in the most positive light. This seeming love affair with the public generated commentary in both academia and the media about the persuasiveness of "The Great Communicator." Reagan's views were notable for their clarity, and there is little doubt that the public knew where the president stood on matters of public policy. The question for us is the degree to which the public moved in Reagan's direction.

Aid to the Contras

In his memoirs, Reagan reflects on his efforts to ignite concern among the American people regarding one of his principal preoccupations: the threat of communism in Central America. At the core of his policy response to this threat was an effort to undermine the Sandinista government of Nicaragua through support of the opposition Contras. Reagan required congressional support to obtain aid for the Contras, and he made substantial efforts to

---

24. White House transcript of interview of President Clinton by WWWE Radio, Cleveland, OH, October 24, 1994.

mobilize the public behind his program of support for the Contras. Yet he consistently failed.[25] As he lamented in his memoirs,

> Time and again, I would speak on television, to a joint session of Congress, or to other audiences about the problems in Central America, and I would hope that the outcome would be an outpouring of support from Americans who would apply the same kind of heat on Congress that helped pass the economic recovery package.

> But the polls usually found that large numbers of Americans cared little or not at all about what happened in Central America—in fact, a surprisingly large proportion didn't even know where Nicaragua and El Salvador were located—and, among those who did care, too few cared enough about a Communist penetration of the Americas to apply the kind of pressure I needed on Congress.[26]

The problem of which Reagan spoke is reflected in Table 7–9, which shows the responses to questions inquiring about support for aiding the Contras during Reagan's second term. No matter how the question was worded, at no time did even a plurality of Americans support the president's policy of aiding the Contras. Because the questions represented in the table have somewhat different wording, we must be cautious about inferring trends in opinion. Nevertheless, it is difficult to conclude that Reagan's rhetorical efforts moved opinion in his direction. (The unusually low level of support in January 1987 polls is undoubtedly the result of the Iran–Contra scandal that had just broken.)

Richard Wirthlin provides additional evidence of the limits of Reagan's persuasive powers on aid to the Contras. In a memo to the president on April 20, 1985—at the height of Reagan's popularity—Wirthlin advised against Reagan taking his case directly to the people through major speeches. The president's pollster told him that doing so was likely to lower his approval and generate more public and congressional opposition than support.[27]

---

25. Ronald Reagan, *An American Life* (New York: Simon & Schuster, 1990), pp. 471, 479; Richard Sobel, ed., *Public Opinion in U.S. Foreign Policy: The Controversy over Contra Aid* (Lanham, MD: Rowman and Littlefield, 1993); Benjamin I. Page and Robert Y. Shapiro, *The Rational Public* (Chicago: University of Chicago Press, 1992), p. 276. See also CBS News/*New York Times* Poll, December 1, 1986, table 5; CBS News/*New York Times* Poll (news release, October 27, 1987), table 17; "Americans on Contra Aid: Broad Opposition," *New York Times*, January 31, 1988, sec. 4, p. 1.

26. Reagan, *An American Life,* p. 479.

27. Memo from Richard Wirthlin to Ronald Reagan, April 10, 1985. My thanks to Lawrence R. Jacobs and Robert Y. Shapiro for sharing a copy of the memo.

Table 7–9 Public Support for Aid to the Contras

Date	Support Aid	Oppose Aid	Don't Know
6/85[1]	34%	59%	6%
7/85[1]	28	64	7
3/86[2]	34	59	8
3/86[2]	30	54	16
3/86[3]	35	60	4
3/86[4]	42	53	5
3/86[5]	37	44	19
4/86[6]	33	62	5
4/86[7]	39	54	7
4/86[8]	28	65	7

SOURCES:

1. Harris Poll question: "Recently, President Reagan has had some serious disagreements with Congress. Now who do you think was more right—Reagan or Congress—in their differences over sending military aid to the Contra rebels in Nicaragua, which is favored by Reagan and opposed by Congress?"

2. ABC News Poll question: "President Reagan is asking Congress for new military aid for the Nicaraguan rebels know as the 'Contras.' Do you agree or disagree with Reagan that Congress should approve that money?"

3. ABC News question: "The House of Representatives has refused Reagan's request for 100 million dollars in military and other aid to the contra rebels in Nicaragua. Do you approve or disapprove of that action by the House?" [Because the question asks respondents whether they approve of the House's negative action, a response of "approve" means opposing aid to the Contras. Thus, we have reversed the results to make them consistent with the portrayal of the results from the other questions.]

4. ABC News Poll question: "As you may know, President Reagan has asked Congress for new military aid for the Nicaraguan rebels known as the 'contras.' Do you agree or disagree with Reagan that Congress should approve that money?"

5. *USA Today* Poll question: "Do you favor or oppose military aid to the Contras fighting the Sandinista government in Nicaragua?"

6. ABC News/*Washington Post* Poll question: "Do you generally favor or oppose the U.S. granting $100 million in military and other aid to the Nicaraguan rebels known as the 'contras'?"

7. Harris Poll question: "Do you favor or oppose the U.S. sending $100 million in military and non-military aid to the Contra rebels in Nicaragua?"

8. Harris Poll question: "Do you favor or oppose the U.S. sending just $30 million in non-military aid to the Contra rebels in Nicaragua?"

Date	Approve	Disapprove	Don't Know
1/87	22%	70%	7%
7/87	43	46	12

(Continued)

Table 7–9 (*Continued*)

Date	Approve	Disapprove	Don't Know
7/87	35%	54%	14%
7/87	41	49	11
8/87	36	59	5
8/87	40	56	4
9/87	33	61	5
10/87	33	63	4

SOURCE: ABC News/*Washington Post* Poll question: "Do you generally favor or oppose the U.S. Congress granting military aid to the Nicaraguan rebels known as the 'Contras'?"

Date	Approve	Disapprove	Don't Know
1/87	28%	60%	12%
7/87	33	51	16
7/87	40	49	12
8/87	33	49	18
10/87	35	53	12
1/88	30	58	12
3/88	39	48	14

SOURCE: CBS News/*New York Times* Poll question: "Do you approve or disapprove of the United States government giving military and other aid to the Contras who are fighting against the government of Nicaragua?"

Defense Spending

One of Ronald Reagan's highest priorities was increasing defense spending. Indeed, during his first term, he oversaw the greatest peacetime increase in defense spending in U.S. history. In Table 7–10, we find that public support for defense expenditures was decidedly *lower* at the end of his administration than when he took office.[28]

Upon closer examination, the data are even more interesting. Support for increased defense spending was unusually high *before* Reagan took office. The Reagan defense buildup represented an acceleration of change initiated late

---

28. This may have been the result of the military buildup that did occur, but the point remains that while Reagan wanted to continue to increase defense spending, the public was unresponsive to his wishes. Larry M. Bartels, "The American Public's Defense Spending Preferences in the Post-Cold War Era," *Public Opinion Quarterly* 58 (Winter 1994): 479–508; Seymour Martin Lipset, "Beyond 1984: The Anomalies of American Politics," *PS* 19 (1986): 229; William G. Mayer, *The Changing American Mind* (Ann Arbor: University of Michigan Press, 1992), pp. 51, 62, 133. See also "Defense," *Gallup Report* (May 1987): 2–3; "Opinion Outlook," *National Journal* (June 13, 1987): 1550; CBS News/*New York Times* poll, October 27, 1987, table 15.

Table 7–10 Public Support for Defense Spending

Date	Too Little	About Right	Too Much	Don't Know
1/80	49%	24%	14%	13%
1/81	51	22	15	12
3/82	19	36	36	9
3/83	14	33	45	8
1/85	11	36	46	7
3/86	13	36	47	4
4/87	14	36	44	6

SOURCE: Gallup Poll question: "There is much discussion as to the amount of money the government in Washington should spend for national defense and military purposes. How do you feel about this: do you think we are spending too little, too much, or about the right amount?"

Date	Decrease	About the Same	Increase
1980	11%	18%	71%
1982	34	33	33
1984	32	32	36
1986	39	29	32
1988	35	32	33

SOURCE: National Election Study question: "Some people believe that we should be spending much less on money for defense. Others feel that spending should be greatly increased. Where would you place yourself on this scale?"
Note: Decrease = 1–3, About the Same = 4, Increase = 5–7 on NES 7-point scale.

in the Carter administration. A number of conditions led to broad partisan support of the defense buildup in both the Carter and Reagan administrations, including the massive Soviet increase in their strategic nuclear forces; a series of communist coups in Third World countries, followed by revolutions in Nicaragua and Iran; and the Soviet invasion of Afghanistan. American hostages held in Iran, Soviet troops controlling a small neighbor, and communists in power in the Western hemisphere created powerful scenes on television and implied that American military power had become too weak.

Nevertheless, public support for increased defense expenditures dissipated by 1982, only a year after Reagan took office. Indeed, in his second term, a plurality of the public thought the United States was spending *too much* on defense. It is possible that the decline in support for defense spending may have been the unintended consequence of the military buildup that did occur.[29] Opinion changed by 1982, long before increased

---

29. This view is articulated in Christopher Wlezien, "Dynamics of Representation: The Case of U.S. Spending on Defense," *British Journal of Political Science* 26 (January 1996): 81–103.

defense spending could have influenced the nation's military security, however. In addition, pressures inevitably increase to spend on butter after periods of spending on guns. The point remains, however, that while Reagan wanted to continue to increase defense spending, the public was unresponsive to his wishes. As a result, Reagan suffered another disappointment, as Congress did not increase defense spending in real dollars during his entire second term.

Interestingly, when Reagan's chief public relations adviser, Michael Deaver, wrote his memoir of the Reagan years, he presented quite a different picture of the president's leadership of the public on defense spending. According to Deaver, distressed about the lack of public support for defense spending, "Reagan pulled me aside one day; 'Mike,' he said, 'these numbers show you're not doing your job. This is your fault; you gotta get me out of Washington more so I can talk to people about how important this policy is.' I did, and he would systematically add his rationale for more military spending to nearly every speech, and eventually his message would get through to the American people."[30] One does not have to challenge the sincerity of the author's memory to conclude that such commentary contributes to the misunderstanding of the potential of the permanent campaign.

Domestic Policy Spending

Limiting spending on domestic policy was at the core of Reagan's domestic policy. For many programs, spending *is* policy. The amount of money spent on a program determines how many people are served, how well they are served, or how much of something (land, employees, vaccines, and so on) the government can purchase. Because, as he often declared, "government is the problem," Reagan was eager to limit government spending. Table 7–11 provides responses to a question on spending for government services that specifies by way of example health and education policy. As the data in the table show, Reagan never obtained majority support for reducing spending. Only in 1982 did a plurality of the public favor reducing spending (despite the recession of that year). Indeed, support for Reagan's preference for reducing spending declined during his tenure, and in his second term pluralities actually favored *increasing* spending.

Numerous national surveys of public opinion have found that support for regulatory programs and spending on health care, welfare, urban problems, education, environmental protection, and aid to minorities increased, rather

---

30. Michael K. Deaver, *A Different Drummer: My Thirty Years with Ronald Reagan*
     (New York: HarperCollins, 2001), p. 154.

Table 7–11 Public Support for Government Spending

Date	Reduce Spending	Spend the Same	Increase Spending
1980	34%	20%	47%
1982	41	29	33
1984	34	36	30
1986	26	28	46
1988	32	29	39

SOURCE: National Election Study question: "Some people think that government should provide fewer services, even in areas such as health and education, in order to reduce spending. Other people feel that it is important for the government to provide many more services even if it means an increase in spending. Where would you place yourself on this scale?"

Note: Reduce spending = 1–3; Spend the same = 4; Increase spending = 5–7 on NES 7-point scale.

than decreased, during Reagan's tenure.[31] In each case, the public was moving in the *opposite* direction to that of the president. Increasing majorities of the public wanted the federal government to spend more on health care, education, and environmental protection, and substantial pluralities supported spending more on food stamps.[32]

Environmental Protection

A hallmark of Reagan's domestic policy was his administration's antagonism to environmental protection legislation.[33] One of the first scandals of the administration focused on the director of the Environmental Protection Agency and her close relationship with regulated interests. The data in Table 7–12, which covers only Reagan's first term, show that the public did not follow Reagan's lead on

31. Seymour Martin Lipset, "Beyond 1984," pp. 228–229; Mayer, *The Changing American Mind,* chapters 5, 6; Page and Shapiro, *The Rational Public,* pp. 133, 136, 159; William Schneider, "The Voters' Mood 1986: The Six-Year Itch," *National Journal* (December 7, 1985): 2758. See also "Supporting a Greater Federal Role," *National Journal* (April 18, 1987): 924; "Opinion Outlook," *National Journal* (April 18, 1987): 964; "Federal Budget Deficit," *Gallup Report* (August 1987): 25, 27; Davis, "Changeable Weather in a Cooling Climate." See also CBS News/*New York Times* poll, October 27, 1987, tables 16, 20; Robert Y. Shapiro and John T. Young, "Public Opinion and the Welfare State: The United States in Comparative Perspective," *Political Science Quarterly* 104 (Spring 1989): 59–89.

32. See Edwards, *On Deaf Ears,* pp. 60–64.

33. See, for example, Robert F. Durant, *The Administrative Presidency Revisited* (Albany: SUNY Press, 1992); Dan B. Wood, "Principals, Bureaucrats, and Responsiveness in Clean Air Enforcement," *American Political Science Review* 82 (March 1988): 213–234.

Table 7–12 Public Support for Environmental Protection

Date	Favor	Oppose	Unsure
3/11/82	83%	14%	3%
7/09/82	85	10	5
12/27/83	84	13	3
3/08/84	88	9	3
5/16/84	84	10	6
7/02/84	85	9	6
7/20/84	84	10	6

SOURCE: Harris question, "Do you favor or oppose . . . strict enforcement of air and water pollution controls as now required by the Clean Air and Water Acts?"

environmental protection. Instead, the public never wavered from its strong support for strictly enforcing laws designed to protect the environment.

Ideology

Presidents are also interested in influencing people's general ideological preferences. Success in affecting ideological preferences may translate into changing the premises on which citizens evaluate policies and politicians and thus be especially significant. Ideological self-identification may also influence the kinds of political appeals to which one is attuned.

Reagan did no better in moving citizens' general ideological preferences to the right than he did in influencing their views of specific policies.[34] The data in Table 7–13 represent how individuals characterized their own ideology and how they viewed liberals and conservatives more generally. The readings of public opinion were taken at the time of Reagan's first election in 1980, his reelection in 1984, at the end of his term in 1988, and the midpoints of each term. It is clear that there was very little change in either dimension between 1980 and 1988.

One prominent study concluded that rather than conservative support swelling once Reagan was in the White House, there was a movement away from conservative views almost as soon as he took office.[35] According to

---

34. See, for example, John A. Fleishman, "Trends in Self-identified Ideology from 1972 to 1982: No Support for the Salience Hypothesis," *American Journal of Political Science* 30 (1986): 517–541; Martin P. Wattenberg, "From a Partisan to a Candidate-Centered Electorate," in Anthony King, ed., *The New American Political System* (Washington, DC: American Enterprise Institute, 1990), pp. 169–171; Wattenberg, *The Rise of Candidate-Centered Politics*, pp. 95–101.

35. James A. Stimson, *Public Opinion in America* (Boulder, CO: Westview, 1991), pp. 64, 126–127.

Table 7–13 Trends in Political Ideology

Self-placement scale	1980	1982	1984	1986	1988
Conservative	23.1%	22.5%	20.8%	19.3%	23.6%
Slightly conservative	21.0	19.8	20.1	20.1	21.7
Moderate	30.6	34.9	33.4	36.9	31.3
Slightly liberal	13.5	11.7	12.9	14.2	13.1
Liberal	11.8	11.1	12.7	9.5	10.3
Mean feeling thermometer ratings of					
Conservatives	62.7	53.3	59.9	58.6	61.1
Liberals	51.7	45.7	55.9	53.3	51.7

SOURCE: National Election Studies ideological self-placement question: "We hear a lot of talk these days about liberals and conservatives. Here is a seven-point scale on which the political views that people might hold are arranged from extremely liberal to extremely conservative. Where would you place yourself on this scale, or haven't you thought much about this?"

The National Election Studies "feeling thermometer" question: "I'd like to get your feelings toward some of our political leaders and other people who are in the news these days. I'll read the name of a person and I'd like you to rate that person using this feeling thermometer. You may use any number from 0 to 100 for rating. Ratings between 50 degrees and 100 degrees mean that you feel favorable and warm toward the person. Ratings between 0 and 50 mean that you don't feel too favorable toward the person. If we come to a person whose name you don't recognize, you don't need to rate that person. Just tell me and we'll move on to the next one. If you do recognize the name, but don't feel particularly warm or cold toward that person, you would rate that person at the 50 degree mark."

Note: In order to reduce the NES ideology scale from seven to five points, "Liberal" combines those who selected themselves to be either "extremely liberal" or "liberal"; "Conservative" combines those who indicated they were either "extremely conservative" or "conservative."

another scholar, "Whatever Ronald Reagan's skills as a communicator, one ability he clearly did not possess was the capacity to induce lasting changes in American policy preferences."[36]

Defensive Efforts: Iran–Contra

Like Bill Clinton, sometimes Ronald Reagan's public relations focus was defensive. Was The Great Communicator more successful in resisting criticism than he was in creating positive support?

The greatest crisis of the Reagan administration began in November 1986, when it was revealed that the president had decided to sell weapons to Iran secretly in return for its aid in freeing American hostages. Many saw this move as foolish (it did not work) and contrary to long-standing U.S. policy of not negotiating with terrorists. Soon, officials also learned that National Security Council staffer Oliver North led an illegal effort to divert some of the money from the sale of missiles to funding the Contras in Nicaragua. The president's

---

36. Mayer, *The Changing American Mind,* p. 127.

Table 7–14 Reagan's Truthfulness on the Iran–Contra Affair

Date	Yes	No	Don't Know
11/25/86*	40%	56%	4%
12/2/86*	47	49	4
1/11–11/13/87**	42	53	5
1/18–1/20/87**	33	60	7
7/15/87*	34	60	6
8/12/87*	39	58	4
8/16–8/17/87**	42	55	3
9/19–9/22/87**	37	60	3

SOURCES:

*ABC News/*Washington Post* Poll question: "Generally speaking, do you think Reagan has been telling the public the truth about the Iran/Contra situation or not?"

**Wirthlin question, "As you may know, Ronald Reagan said he knew nothing about funding the Contra effort with money from the Iranian arms deal. From what you have heard and read, do you believe he is telling the truth?"

approval rating in the Gallup Poll dropped 16 percentage points after the scandal was unearthed and did not rise to his pre-Iran–Contra heights until two years later, after the election of his successor.

Clearly, the White House had some explaining to do. How convincing was it to the public? In the post-Watergate period, it is not surprising that two important questions regarding the Iran–Contra scandal were whether the president was telling the truth and whether he was involved in a cover-up of the scandal. The White House protested its innocence during four nationally televised addresses on November 13, 1986; December 2, 1986; March 4, 1987; and August 12, 1987.

Table 7–14 shows public responses to questions about Reagan's truthfulness. Over the period of the heart of the scandal, public opinion changed little, and the percentage of the public who felt the president was telling the truth did not increase. Similarly, Table 7–15 shows that the president did not make much headway in convincing the public that he had not engaged in a cover-up. Over the same period covered in the table, Gallup found that 75 percent of the public felt that Reagan was withholding information on the Iran–Contra affair.[37]

Reagan in Perspective

Ronald Reagan was less a public relations phenomenon than the conventional wisdom indicates. He had the good fortune to take office on the crest of a compatible wave of public opinion, and he effectively exploited the

37. "Do you feel that President Reagan has told the public everything he knows about the Iran–Contra affair or that he is holding back certain information?" in polls of January 16–19, 1987, and August 24–September 2, 1987.

Table 7–15 Reagan's Covering Up the Iran–Contra Affair

Date	Yes	No	No Opinion
2/26/87	38%	57%	5%
3/5–3/9/87	48	48	4
5/28–6/1/87	51	47	2
6/25–6/29/87	50	48	2
7/11–7/12/87	45	49	6
7/15/87	45	49	6
8/3–8/5/87	43	52	5

SOURCE: ABC News/*Washington Post* Poll question: "Do you think Ronald Reagan himself participated in an organized attempt to cover up the facts about the Iran/Contra arms affair or not?"

opportunity the voters had handed him. Yet when it came time to change public opinion or mobilize it on his behalf, he typically met with failure. As press secretary Marlin Fitzwater put it, "Reagan would go out on the stump, draw huge throngs and convert no one at all."[38]

Clearly, there was a disjunction between what the polls said and what the press and Washington insiders believed about Reagan's relationship with the public. Perhaps those inside the beltway had such a strong belief in the power of a person of Reagan's skill and charm on television and were so impressed with Reagan's communications skills that they took it for granted that he was able to move the American people. These premises made it easy to attribute the president's early legislative victories to his skill as a communicator. On closer examination, the insiders appear to have been wrong. Once the themes had been established, however, they were difficult to adjust to the reality of years of stalemate and budgets declared "Dead on Arrival." In retrospect, Reagan's image as The Great Communicator appears to owe more to his early success with Congress than to his ability to move the public in a reliable fashion.

GEORGE W. BUSH

Much to the surprise of many political observers, George W. Bush launched a massive public relations campaign on behalf of his priority initiatives soon after taking office in 2001. At the core of this effort was the most extensive domestic travel schedule of any new president in American history. Bush

---

38. Quoted in R. W. Apple, "Bush Sure-Footed on Trail of Money," *New York Times*, September 29, 1990, p. 8.

Table 7–16 Public Support for Bush Tax Cut

Date	Favor	Oppose	No Opinion
2/9–2/11/01	56%	34%	10%
2/19–2/21/01	53	30	17
3/5–3/7/01	56	34	10
4/20–4/22/01	56	35	9

SOURCE: Gallup Poll, "Based on what you have read or heard, do you favor or oppose the federal income tax cuts George W. Bush has proposed?"

spoke in 29 states by the end of May, often more than once. The president also used his Saturday radio addresses to exhort members of the public to communicate to Congress their support for his tax cut and education plans.

As we have seen with Bill Clinton and Ronald Reagan, it is one thing to go public. It is something quite different to succeed in moving public opinion. Table 7–16 shows responses to Gallup Poll questions on the president's tax cut proposal, the central domestic and economic program of his administration. The results show that public opinion did not change in response to the president's efforts.

No issue was more important to George W. Bush's presidency than the war with Iraq. The context in which Bush sought this support was certainly favorable. In surveys conducted over the previous 10 years, stretching back to the end of the Gulf War, majorities had generally supported U.S. military action in Iraq to remove Saddam Hussein from power. The American public has long held strongly negative perceptions of Iraq and its leader. In a December 1998 poll, Saddam Hussein received the worst rating of any public figure tested in Gallup poll history—1 percent positive and 96 percent negative.[39] In early 2002, the country of Iraq received a 6 percent favorable and 88 percent unfavorable rating, the worst of any of the 25 countries tested in that poll.[40] Since 1991, Iraq had never received even a 10 percent favorable rating.[41] Asked in February 2001 what country was America's worst enemy, Americans named Iraq significantly more often than any other country.[42]

In September 2002, Gallup reported that most Americans believed that Iraq had developed or was developing weapons of mass destruction. Many

---

39. Gallup poll, December 28–29, 1998.

40. Gallup poll, February 4–6, 2002.

41. Chris Chambers, "Americans Most Favorable toward Canada, Australia and Great Britain; Iran, Libya and Iraq Receive the Lowest Ratings," Gallup Poll News Release, February 16, 2001.

42. Gallup poll, February 1–4, 2001.

Table 7–17 Support for War with Iraq

Date	Worth Going to War	Not Worth Going to War	No Opinion
6/27–6/29/03*	56%	42%	2%
7/18–7/20/03*	63	35	2
7/25–7/27/03*	63	34	3
8/25–8/26/03*	63	35	2
9/8–9/10/03*	58	40	2
9/19–9/21/03*	50	48	2
10/6–10/8/03*	55	44	1
10/24–10/26/03*	54	44	2
11/3–11/5/03*	54	44	2
11/14–11/16/03*	56	42	2
12/5–12/7/03*	59	39	2
1/9–1/11/04	59	38	3
1/29–2/1/04	49	49	2
3/5–3/7/04	55	43	2
3/26–3/28/04	56	41	3
4/5–4/8/04	50	47	3
5/21–5/23/04	45	52	3
6/3–6/6/04	46	52	2

SOURCE: Gallup Poll question: "All in all, do you think it was worth going to war in Iraq, or not?"

*"All in all, do you think the situation in Iraq was worth going to war over, or not?"

Americans felt that if left alone, Iraq would use those weapons against the United States within five years. Most Americans felt that Saddam Hussein sponsored terrorism that affected the United States. A little more than half of Americans took the additional inferential leap and concluded that Saddam Hussein was personally and directly involved in the September 11, 2001, terrorist attacks.[43]

The war itself was over in a matter of weeks, but the pacification, reconstruction, and democratization of Iraq was to take much longer. The president needed to sustain support for his policy, especially as he sough reelection. Table 7–17 shows public support for the war with Iraq. Public opinion did not change in response to the administration's blitzkrieg. Unfortunately for the president, the public was less supportive of the war after a year, with a plurality concluding the war was not worth fighting.

---

43. Frank Newport, "Public Wants Congressional and U.N. Approval before Iraq Action," Gallup Poll News Release, September 6, 2002.

DISAGGREGATING PUBLIC OPINION

The focus in this article has been on the president moving public opinion in his direction. The data are all the aggregate results of national polls. In addition to national totals, the president may be especially interested in moving opinion in certain states or congressional districts, those in which he has the best chance of influencing a member of Congress. It is possible that the absence of aggregate national change may mask significant change in only a few, but critical, geographic areas.

Systematic data on opinion on policies within a state or congressional district are not available, so it is not possible to provide a definitive answer to the question of targeted impact. We can say that there is simply no evidence for this kind of effect. Moreover, even the White House lacks a mechanism for attempting to directly influence public opinion in delineated areas. How could it? In the electronic age, the bully pulpit is not a precision tool. When the president speaks, anyone can listen. In addition, even a presidential visit is unlikely to be repeated often, especially to a House district. If the White House wants to focus on a particular congressional constituency, it is much more likely to attempt quietly to mobilize campaign contributors, local elites, and interest groups than it is to employ the bully pulpit.

It is possible that despite the limitations of targeting his message, the president's rhetoric could have a disproportionate effect in certain constituencies. This is unlikely, however, as public opinion tends to swing in national trends. For example, Robert Erikson, Michael MacKuen, and James Stimson found that public opinion tends to move similarly across a broad range of groups within the country.[44] Page and Shapiro reached the same conclusion. They found that although demographic groups may start from different levels of support, the direction and extent of opinion change within them is similar.[45] Moreover, if there is movement in some constituencies that is not captured by the national totals, and these totals typically do not move in the president's direction, then there must be an even greater countermovement elsewhere. It is much more likely that the national totals have captured whatever opinion change occurs.

An alternative view is that the president primarily seeks to influence those segments of the population that may be most attuned to his appeals. Of course, there is no way for the president to segment his appeals so that only a select but sizable audience hears them. It is possible, however, that the president is more successful in influencing some groups than others and that the aggregate

---

44. Robert S. Erikson, Michael B. MacKuen, and James A. Stimson, *The Macro Polity* (New York: Cambridge University Press, 2002), pp. 219, 369.

45. Page and Shapiro, *The Rational Public,* chap. 7.

national data mask movement that occurs among subgroups of the population, such as those most predisposed to support him. In a separate analysis, I present a detailed analysis of disaggregated opinion on a selection of issues from the Reagan and Clinton years and find results similar to those for national totals.[46]

RECONSIDERING PRESIDENTIAL LEADERSHIP OF THE PUBLIC

The failure of presidents to change the public's mind does not mean that presidents should not go public. This essay focuses on the president's efforts to use the bully pulpit to influence public opinion regarding their performance (including answering charges of misconduct) and their policies—ranging from legislative initiatives to military interventions. The president speaks out for other purposes as well, such as trying to influence the national agenda, satisfy a constituency with symbolic benefits, neutralize critics, or prepare the public for a policy shift. It is possible that the White House enjoys more success in these endeavors.

Nevertheless, the evidence is clear that even able communicators like Ronald Reagan and Bill Clinton do not move the public much. This finding poses a direct challenge to the faith that many have in the broad premise of the potential of presidential leadership of the public. At the very least, it is appropriate to rethink the theory of governing based on the principle of presidential success in exploiting the bully pulpit to achieve changes in public policy. Presidents should not base their strategies for governing on the premise of substantially increasing the size of their public support. Such strategies are prone to failure. As historian E. H. Carr put it, "the men who are popularly said to 'make history' are dealing with highly intractable material, . . . which includes the wills of their fellow men, [which] can be moulded only in accordance with certain existing trends, and . . . the statesman who fails to understand, and refuses to comply with, those trends dooms himself to sterility."[47]

Presidents not only fail to create new political capital by going public, but their efforts at persuading the public may also *decrease* their chances of success in bringing about changes in public policy. The way presidents attempt to govern has important consequences for public policy. When political leaders take their cases directly to the public, they have to accommodate the limited attention spans of the public and the availability of space on television. As a result, the president and his opponents often reduce choices to stark

---

46. Edwards, *On Deaf Ears,* pp. 228–238.

47. E. H. Carr, *Conditions of Peace* (New York: Macmillan, 1942), p. 6.

black-and-white terms. When leaders frame issues in such terms, they typically frustrate rather than facilitate building coalitions. Such positions are difficult to compromise, which hardens negotiating positions as both sides
posture as much to mobilize an intense minority of supporters as to persuade
the other side. *The permanent campaign is antithetical to governing.*

Indeed, as Hugh Heclo argues, campaigning to govern is antideliberative.
Campaigning focuses on persuasion, competition, conflict, and short-term victory. Campaigns are waged in either/or terms. Conversely, governing involves
deliberation, cooperation, negotiation, and compromise over an extended
period. Campaigns prosecute a cause among adversaries rather than deliberate
courses of action among collaborators. Campaign communications are
designed to win rather than to educate or learn. Thus, the incentives for
leaders are to stay on message rather than to engage with opponents and to
frame issues rather than inform their audience about anything in detail.
Similarly, campaigning requires projecting self-assurance rather than admitting
ignorance or uncertainty about complex issues, and counterattacking and
switching the subject rather than struggling with tough questions. It is better
to have a campaign issue for the next election than deal with an issue by
governing. Thus, Heclo concludes, the more campaigning infiltrates into governing, the more we should expect the values of a campaign perspective to
dominate over values of deliberation.[48]

Similarly, David Brady and Morris Fiorina argue that governing by campaigning too often revolves around destroying enemies rather than producing
legislative products broadly acceptable to the electorate. The tendencies are for
civility to lose out to conflict, compromise to deadlock, deliberation to sound
bites, and legislative product to campaign issues.[49] Norman Ornstein and
Thomas Mann add that in the permanent campaign, political leaders do not
look for ways to insulate controversial or difficult policy decisions from their
vulnerability to demagoguery and oversimplification.[50]

Given the nature of White House efforts at public persuasion, it is not the
case that even a failed effort at going public will be useful for educating the
public and thus pave the way for eventual passage of proposals. There is little
evidence that public relations campaigns, as they are currently executed, actually do much educating. The public is more likely to respond to what they

---

48. Hugh Heclo, "Campaigning and Governing: A Conspectus" in Norman
     Ornstein and Thomas Mann, eds., *The Permanent Campaign and Its Future*
     (Washington, DC: American Enterprise Institute and Brookings Institution,
     2000), pp. 11–15, 34.

49. David Brady and Morris Fiorina, "Congress in the Era of the Permanent
     Campaign," in *The Permanent Campaign and Its Future,* p. 156.

50. Norman J. Ornstein and Thomas E. Mann, "Conclusion: The Permanent
     Campaign and the Future of American Democracy," in *The Permanent
     Campaign and Its Future,* p. 225.

experience in their everyday lives than to the urgings of the chief executive in the permanent campaign.

These narrowing and antideliberative propensities of the permanent campaign are exacerbated by the increasing ideological distinctiveness of the two major parties, which encourage presidents and members of Congress to view those on the other side of the aisle as enemies to defeat rather than opponents with whom to compromise. Moreover, the media is oriented toward viewing politics as a game and more likely to cover communications that are critical and conflictual, providing additional incentives to publicity hungry officials.

Traditionally, presidents attempted to build coalitions in Congress through bargaining. The core strategy was to provide benefits for both sides, allowing many to share in a coalition's success and to declare victory. Going public is fundamentally different. The core strategy is to *defeat the opposition,* creating winners and losers in a zero-sum game. In going public, the president tries to intimidate opponents by increasing the political costs of opposition rather than attracting them with benefits. If going public is not a successful strategy and actually makes coalition building more difficult, polarization, gridlock, and public cynicism, which characterize American politics today, are the likely results.

PART IV

The President
and the Press

8

⚜

The Changing Presidential
Media Environment

MARTIN P. WATTENBERG
University of California, Irvine

I f the power of the presidency is the power to persuade, then the ability to
communicate with the American public is one key tool in exercising that
power. When presidents speak to the nation, they expect to garner a large
viewing audience and for their message to continue to permeate the public
consciousness through news reports in the days following their address. But
a series of changes in the mass media environment have made it much less
likely that these expectations will be fulfilled today compared to just several
decades ago. A tale of two presidential speeches concerning foreign military
actions in 1971 and 2003 provides a good illustration of the profound
changes discussed in this paper.

President Richard Nixon spoke to the nation during prime time on the
evening of April 7, 1971 to defend his policies in Vietnam and to announce
further troop withdrawals during the coming months. Nixon's speech was
covered live on CBS, NBC, and ABC and garnered a Nielsen rating of 51.2,
meaning that just over half of the American public watched it. As Matthew
Baum and Samuel Kernell show, this was a typical rating for Nixon's televised
addresses and press conferences.[1] Furthermore, Nixon's ability to communicate his message extended beyond the enormous size of his live audience—
he could also expect most people to be reading and viewing news about his
remarks soon afterward. The next day, at least 69 percent of the public could
be expected to pick up a newspaper containing stories about the president's
speech, as surveys back then found this percentage reported reading a newspaper every day. Later that evening, at least 58 percent of the public could be
expected to watch one of the three nightly news broadcasts, as this percentage said they watched these programs frequently.

---

1. Matthew A. Baum and Samuel Kernell, "Has Cable Ended the Golden Age
   of Presidential Television?" *American Political Science Review* (March 1999):
   99–114.

The situation was markedly different when President George W. Bush went on TV on the evening of September 7, 2003 to brief the public about the Iraqi situation and to request $87 billion from Congress for troop deployments and the rebuilding of Iraq. Even with the addition of a fourth broadcast network (FOX), Bush's talk received a combined TV rating of just 20.5. Adding in the viewing audience on the cable news channels and C-SPAN would add a few points to this rating, but these channels typically get such low ratings that they are rarely reported. In the age of narrowcasting, with so many choices available to most viewers, large audiences are increasingly rare—and even presidents usually do not achieve them. Not only was the audience rating for Bush's speech at best half of Nixon's but he also could not count on a regular audience of news consumers learning about his remarks the next day. Whereas 69 percent of the public read a newspaper every day in the early 1970s, by the time Bush assumed office only about 40 percent did so. And the percentage who said they regularly watched the nightly news had plummeted to just 32 percent, compared to 58 percent who said they frequently watched these programs during the Nixon era.

These contrasting audience figures between the current era and that of President Nixon are noteworthy in and of themselves. The diminishing size of the audience for presidential messages, as well as for national news, means that presidents now face a significantly more difficult task in getting messages through to the entire public than at any time since the birth of the mass media.

But perhaps even more important is that the nature of the audience no longer befits the ideal notion of a nationally elected officer who is president of *all* the people. The presidential audience is now highly skewed in terms of age, with young adults less and less likely to follow what the president is doing. Such a bias may not seem too serious because everyone eventually gets older. But it is a bias that degrades representation, as young people do clearly have interests and policy priorities that are distinct from their elders. Furthermore, the age bias in the presidential audience is one that is likely to get more pronounced in the foreseeable future, as the time series data show this to be a clear case of generational change whose effects will continue to be felt for quite some time.

THE DECLINING AUDIENCE
FOR PRESIDENTIAL SPEECHES

Like all other regularly occurring live events shown on television, presidential speeches have been viewed by a smaller percentage of the American public in recent decades as compared to the 1960s and 1970s. In experiencing declining ratings, presidential speeches are in good company with other categories of

Table 8–1 Average Nielsen Ratings of Televised Presidential Addresses and Press Conferences From Nixon to Clinton

President	Average Nielsen Rating
Nixon	47
Ford	48
Carter	49
Reagan	38
Bush	34
Clinton (through January 1998)	29

SOURCE: http://weber.ucsd.edu/~skernell/files/APSR.htm (accessed April 12, 2004).

events that have regularly drawn big audiences, such as the World Series, the Oscars, and the Miss America Pageant. For many years, the three major networks dominated the airwaves, controlling the only channels available in many areas. During the Nixon years, for example, prime-time ratings for the three major networks from September to May were an incredible 56.9. In 2002, the comparable ratings for the four major networks were just 28.9. One result of this change in the TV environment is that the notion of a captive audience is a concept that no longer applies. When President Nixon went on TV to give a speech or hold a press conference, many viewers had little choice but to watch him if they had their TV on at that time. Today, not only do the major networks control substantially less of the audience but there are numerous alternatives available, what with the average viewer having a remote control and 62 channels from which to choose. As Baum and Kernell conclude, "The cumulative evidence indicates that cable technology has allowed the public to become strategically discriminating in its viewing decisions."[2]

Baum and Kernell's data on ratings over time for presidential addresses and press conferences are shown in Table 8–1. The average ratings for Nixon, Ford, and Carter's appearances were strikingly consistent, at nearly half of the population. The change occurred right at the beginning of the Reagan presidency, as cable started to make inroads into the viewing audience. In Reagan's first year in office, his TV audiences were roughly the same proportion of the population as his three predecessors, with an average Nielsen rating of 48. But after 1981, the mean rating for his appearances was just 37, with little variation during his seven years in office. The size of presidential audiences slid further under Reagan's two immediate successors, with Clinton's speeches and press conferences drawing a mere 29 percent of the population.

---

2. Ibid., p. 100.

Why did presidential audiences start to decline in the 1980s? Surely, the rising number of homes with cable TV during this period explains much about the timing of this trend. However, this is probably just part of the story, as the proportion of households with cable TV only increased from 20 to 56 percent during the 1980s. It was not just the rise of cable subscriptions that made a difference but also the proliferation of channels available on cable. People were signing up for cable for a good reason—namely, that new and interesting channels were regularly being added to cable TV packages. But perhaps most important of all during this period was the rise of video recorders. Only 1 percent of homes owned a VCR in 1980, but by 1990 this device had nearly saturated the market and could be found in 69 percent of homes. VCRs freed viewers from the standard question of asking what's on tonight, allowing them to watch shows whenever they had the time. In sum, when regular programming is preempted on the major networks for a presidential address, most people now can turn to either the many alternatives offered via cable TV or to a videotape if they are not interested in seeing what the president has to say.

It should be kept in mind that these changes in the media environment do not preclude presidential messages from ever being seen by a large proportion of the American public. On occasions of high drama many people will inevitably be interested in what the president is expected to say. For example, President Clinton's 1998 State of the Union address received a rating of 37 due to the extraordinary attention he received in the preceding week as the result of the breaking news about the Monica Lewinsky scandal. And in 2003, President George W. Bush's State of the Union speech garnered a rating of 40 due to interest in what he might say about the impending war against Saddam Hussein's regime. But these are exceptions to the rule in the current media environment, as demonstrated by the combined rating of 28 for Bush's 2004 State of the Union address shown on four major networks and four cable news channels.

THE GENERATION GAP IN WATCHING THE PRESIDENT

A whole generation has now grown up in the narrowcasting age. Political scientists were slow to realize the impact of television—as late as 1980 there was surprisingly little literature on this subject. Today, a similar shortcoming is the lack of research concerning how the shift from broadcasting to narrowcasting has dramatically altered the amount of exposure to politics young adults receive while growing up. Because of the narrowcasting revolution, today's youth have grown up in an environment in which presidential actions have not been as readily visible as in the recent past. It has become particularly difficult to

Table 8–2 Percent Watching President Carter's Crisis of Confidence Speech, July 1979

18–29	60
30–44	69
45–64	71
65+	73

SOURCE: *New York Times*/CBS News poll, July 26, 1979.

convince a generation that has channel-surfed all their lives that they ought to tune in to what the president has to say. Presidential pronouncements were once shared national experiences. However, the current generation of young adults is the first to grow up in a media environment in which there are few such shared experiences. Young people have therefore never known a time when most citizens paid attention to major political events, such as presidential addresses. It is thus likely that the decline in the presidential audience over the last two decades has been in part due to the influx of a new generation of citizens who pay much less attention to the presidency than their elders. This section will test this theory as best as possible with the available survey data.

Academic polls do not typically ask about current events, such as a recent presidential speech. Thus, most of the analysis in this section is drawn from data gathered by media organizations, such as the *New York Times*/CBS News polls and the *Washington Post*/ABC News polls. These polls were initiated in the late 1970s, and they are all archived at the Inter-University Consortium for Social and Political Research (ICPSR). It is a simple matter to search the ICPSR website to determine which polls asked about a presidential speech. In addition to these polls, George Edwards has uncovered relevant data from internal polls conducted for the Reagan White House, and the 2000 National Annenberg Election Survey asked people whether they watched Clinton's State of the Union address that year.

Tables 8–2 to 8–6 display a variety of data gathered between 1979 and 2003 regarding the percentage of different age groups who watched miscellaneous presidential speeches. The earliest speech for which I was able to get viewing data was Jimmy Carter's famous "crisis of confidence" speech in July 1979. The actual rating of this speech was just 36, substantially below the average of 49 for Carter's appearances. The relatively low Nielsen rating for this speech was probably due to the fact that it took place during the summer reruns, when TV viewing is generally down. But given the tremendous stir this speech caused, both pro and con, it should not be surprising that roughly 70 percent of people interviewed by the *New York Times*/CBS News poll the next day reported they had watched or listened to it. No doubt some people

Table 8–3 Average Viewing for 22 Reagan Televised Addresses by Age (in percents)

	Watched All	Watched Part	Heard or Read About Later	Heard or Read Nothing About
18–24	8	24	15	54
25–34	13	24	18	46
35–44	15	23	19	43
45–54	20	26	17	38
55–64	30	23	15	32
65+	40	21	12	27

SOURCE: George C. Edwards III, *On Deaf Ears: The Limits of the Bully Pulpit* (New Haven, CT: Yale University Press), 2003.

interpreted this question as asking whether they had seen any part of the speech, including news summaries of it. In any event, there was a distinct lack of age bias in President Carter's reported audience. Aside from the 18- to 29-year-olds being about 10 percent less likely to have watched the speech, there are no age differences at all. In this speech, given at the tail end of the age when the three networks had a largely captive audience, the president's audience was pretty well representative along age lines.

The Reagan years coincided with the rise of narrowcasting. Consequently, we should expect to find that younger people were less attentive to his speeches than older Americans. Indeed, Table 8–3 verifies this hypothesis based on George Edwards' analysis of Richard Wirthlin's private polls for the Reagan White House. People over 65 years of age were about twice as likely to view the typical Reagan speech than those under 35. And older people who tuned in were also much more attentive to President Reagan. When senior citizens said they watched a speech, two out of every three said they watched the whole thing. In contrast, less than one out of every three young viewers said they watched a typical speech in its entirety. Channel surfing, as facilitated by the widespread diffusion of TV and cable remote controls during the 1980s, apparently caught on more quickly with young adults—who used them to switch away from President Reagan's speeches.

The pattern of young people being less attentive to presidential messages is again found in data from an Annenberg survey that asked respondents whether they had seen President Clinton's 2000 State of the Union address (see Table 8–4). Younger people were not only less likely to have seen the speech but also much less likely to have watched a good portion of it. Of young people who watched at least some of Clinton's rather lengthy speech, just six percent said they were glued to their sets; two-thirds said they watched just some of it. It is important to note, though, that even among older viewers about half said

Table 8–4 Viewing Percentages for Clinton's 2000 State of the Union Address

	Watched All	Watched Most	Watched Some	Did Not Watch
18–34	2	10	26	61
35–59	7	8	21	63
60+	16	12	28	44

SOURCE: 2000 National Annenberg Survey.

Table 8–5 Percent Watching or Listening to Bush's Post-September 11 Speech on Terrorism

18–34	67
35–59	82
60+	86

SOURCE: ABC/*Washington Post* poll, September 20, 2001.

they only watched some of it. Clearly, Clinton had a lot of trouble holding on to his audience given the absence of any big news in his remarks. Presidents need high drama to get the nation—and especially young citizens—to pay attention to what they have to say in today's mass media environment.

Such drama was certainly provided by the events of September 11, 2001. President Bush's speech to Congress nine days later drew a Super-Bowl–sized audience rating of 53. A *Washington Post*/ABC News poll conducted that night found that 79 percent of those interviewed said they had watched or listened to some of the speech. Table 8–5 shows that Bush's audience even penetrated into the very hard to reach young audience, with two-thirds of those under 35 years of age saying they saw or heard his speech on terrorism. Yet even in the case of this extremely high profile presidential address, older citizens were about 20 percent more likely to tune in to hear the president. An astonishingly high 86 percent of those over 60 years of age saw or heard this post-September 11 speech.

Similarly, there are clear age-related patterns in data presented in Table 8–6 on attentiveness to two key speeches that drew large audiences prior to the 2003 Iraq war—Bush's 2003 State of the Union speech and Colin Powell's speech to the United Nations. Overall, 57 percent said they watched or listened to Bush deliver the State of the Union, and 64 percent said they had heard something about Powell's UN speech. One might expect that young people would be especially attentive to speeches regarding the onset of a war that their cohort would be asked to fight. Yet, this was not the case. Young

Table 8–6 Percent Watching Bush and Powell's Speeches on Iraq in February 2003

	Percent Reporting Watching Bush's 2003 State of The Union Address	Percent Reporting They Had Heard a Lot About Powell's United Nations Speech	Percent Reporting They Had Heard Some About Powell's United Nations Speech	Percent Reporting They Had Not Heard About Powell's United Nations Speech
18–29	48	22	30	48
30–44	52	23	39	38
45–65	58	35	32	33
65+	76	46	32	22

SOURCE: *New York Times*/CBS News poll, February 5–6, 2003.

people were about 25 percent less likely to have tuned in to Bush's speech, and the same was true for Powell's speech. Senior citizens were more than twice as likely as those under 30 to have heard a lot about Powell's speech, which attempted to lay out the detailed evidence concerning allegations that Iraq was hiding weapons of mass destruction.

In sum, the audience for presidential speeches is now unrepresentative of the general adult public in terms of age. Presidents in the narrowcasting era should expect that when they use the mass media to ostensibly address the nation they are likely to reach a much larger percentage of older than younger citizens. Whether or not this was true in what Baum and Kernell label the "golden age of presidential television" cannot be ascertained for certain, given the fragmentary nature of the available data. Perhaps some day the Nielsen Company will open up their data archive to scholars, and this theory can be adequately tested by analyzing TV ratings by demographic groups. Fortunately, there is plenty of available data over time to assess whether an age gap in following the news has emerged over the past several decades.

THE GENERATION GAP IN WATCHING
THE NIGHTLY NEWS

Presidential speeches have a political life well beyond the actual time it takes to give them. Their importance rests in large part on how they are received and interpreted in the following days. In particular, when people say they've seen something about a presidential speech, it often merely means they have seen a sound bite or two from it on the nightly news. In most cases, one would certainly expect a nationally televised presidential address to be reviewed and analyzed in network news broadcasts the following night. Thus, if some age groups are more likely to watch the nightly news than others, then these groups will inevitably be learning more about the president's message.

For a time, the anchors of the three nightly news broadcasts were major figures in American political life. As Jeff Alan writes, "For all of us who grew up with the evening news anchors in our living rooms and family rooms five nights a week, it's fair to say that we saw more of the anchors than we saw of most of our neighbors, and even some of our close friends and relatives."[3] In 1974, the National Election Studies actually asked people to rate them on a feeling thermometer, just like they did for major political leaders. All but 7 percent were able to rate Walter Cronkite of CBS, and all but 17 percent rated John Chancellor of NBC and Howard K. Smith of ABC. By comparison, 39 percent could not rate Senator Jackson, 52 percent could not rate Senator Mondale, and 65 percent could not rate Senator Bentsen—all of whom were prominent senators gearing up for a run at the presidency. By the end of 1980, one could make a legitimate argument that network newscasts had played a significant role in the political downfall of Presidents Johnson, Nixon, and Carter due to the way they drew attention to these presidents' shortcomings. As Barbara Matusow wrote about the stars of the evening news in 1983, "They have taken their place beside presidents, congressmen, labor leaders, industrialists, and others who shape public policy and private attitudes."[4]

Over the last quarter century, however, the NBC, CBS, and ABC nightly news broadcasts have gone from being instrumental in setting the nation's agenda to the TV equivalent of dinosaurs on their last legs. During the 1980–1981 TV season, these three network broadcasts had an average Nielsen rating of 37.3; by the 2002–2003 season, their ratings were down to 20.8. As *New York Times* media critic Frank Rich recently wrote, "The No. 1 cliché among media critics is that we're watching the 'last hurrah' of network news anchors as we have known them for nearly half a century."[5]

It doesn't take much analytical ability these days to recognize that the network news broadcasts are barely hanging on by relying on older viewers who got into the habit of viewing these shows decades ago. Just as one can easily guess the types of people most likely to watch the Super Bowl by the many advertisements for beer and chips, so one can easily see that the network news audience is quite elderly by keeping an eye on the ads. For example, on one randomly chosen night (January 13, 2004) the *CBS Nightly News* contained

---

3. Jeff Alan, *Anchoring America: The Changing Face of Network News* (Chicago: Bonus Books, 2003), p. xiii.

4. Barbara Matusow, *The Evening Stars: The Making of the Network News Anchor* (Boston: Houghton Mifflin, 1983), p. 1.

5. Frank Rich, "The Weight of an Anchor," *New York Times,* May 19, 2002.

Table 8–7 Age and Viewing of TV Network News: 1967, 1974, and 2002 Compared

1967	Every Day	Few Times a Week	Once a Week or Less	Never
18–29	66	22	7	5
30–44	69	21	6	4
45–64	74	16	5	5
65+	78	9	4	9
1974	**Frequently**	**Sometimes**	**Rarely**	**Never**
18–29	45	32	13	10
30–44	50	27	12	12
45–64	68	17	8	7
65+	71	18	5	6
2002	**Regularly**	**Sometimes**	**Hardly Ever**	**Never**
18–29	19	29	22	30
30–44	22	36	17	25
45–64	40	25	11	24
65+	53	24	8	16

SOURCES: 1967 Political Participation in America Study; 1974 National Election Study; 2002 Pew Center Media Study.

commercials for the following products: Pepto Bismol, Ambien, Ex-Lax, Pepcid Complete, Imitrex, Ester-C, Dulcolax, Maalox, Wellbutrin XL, Detrol LA, and Benefiber. If one doesn't know what some of these products are, one is probably best off that way—suffice it to say that these ads are not for anything that one would buy for pleasure. Even products that could theoretically appeal to all age groups were advertised so as to appeal to senior citizens. An ad for dinner rolls from Pillsbury featured an elderly couple who raved about how the package allowed them to use only a few at a time, which was great now that their kids had moved out. Coricidon was portrayed not just as a cold remedy but also as one that would be appropriate for someone with high blood pressure. And Quaker Oatmeal was described as a good food for reducing cholesterol.

Table 8–7 compares responses from 1967, 1974, and 2002 surveys that asked national samples how frequently they viewed the nightly news on the three major networks. As would be expected from the lower Nielsen ratings, there is clear decline among all age groups in the regularity of viewing these news programs. This trend has been particularly pronounced among younger viewers. In the 1960s and 1970s, TV news producers could hardly write off young people, as at least three out of four adults under 30 years of age reported watching the nightly news either frequently or sometimes. In 2002, only senior citizens reported watching the TV news this frequently, and the majority of young adults said they hardly ever or never watched these shows.

The survey data from 2002 probably underestimate the current age gap in watching network nightly news. It is hard to believe that if so many young adults really watched the nightly news that the sponsors of these programs—who have access to the Nielsen rating data by demographics—would be so focused on products of particular interest to the elderly. According to the *New York Times,* Nielsen Media Research reports that the median age of viewers of the CBS, ABC, and NBC news broadcasts from September 2003 through early February 2004 was almost exactly 60 years of age—roughly 5 years older than the median viewer age for these shows in 1991.[6] The recent Nielsen numbers are substantially higher than one would estimate from the survey data in Table 8–7. Presumably, Nielsen ratings should be more accurate because they rely on actual viewing behavior of a sample rather than reported viewing patterns.

A Pew Center survey from January 2004 casts further light on young adults' relative lack of reliance on broadcast news programs. Respondents were asked how often, if ever, they learned something about the presidential campaign or the candidates from a variety of media sources. Among respondents under 30 years old, 23 percent said they regularly learned something from network newscasts as compared to 21 percent from comedy TV shows. Given how little one can learn about politics from comedy shows, the degree to which network news reaches young adults is clearly quite minimal.

Of course viewers now have an alternative to the 30-minute network news shows in the form of round-the-clock news on CNN, MSNBC, and Fox News Channel. The January 2004 Pew Center survey found that more Americans say they regularly learn about the presidential campaign from the cable news networks than from the nightly network news. Among young adults, this pattern is particularly pronounced. On the positive side, there can be little doubt that there is a good deal of *potential* for learning about politics from watching a substantial amount of political coverage on the cable news networks. Indeed, the recent Pew Center survey found that the seven percent of the sample who scored highest on political engagement reported more reliance on cable news channels for political information than any other source. However, there is reason to be skeptical about how much the *typical* person with only limited political interest actually learns from these channels. The combined rating for the three hour-long news shows on cable (*Newsnight* with Aaron Brown, *Special Report* with Brit Hume, and *Countdown* with Keith Olbermann) is currently a minuscule 2.1. Thus, the audience size of these programs is a mere tenth of the ABC, NBC, and CBS evening news programs.

---

6. "A Graying, Ailing Audience," *New York Times,* February 9, 2004, p. C6.

Given that so few people watch an entire news program on the cable news channels, when most people say they are relying on these channels for political information, it means they've caught a snippet or two in a spare moment. It is unlikely that these channels are the source for much detailed learning about a president's actions. In particular, the fact that young people are relying on cable news as opposed to network news probably means that they are just getting quick snippets as opposed to full stories that could allow them to grasp the details. The changes over the last few decades in watching TV news have led to diminished opportunities for the public to learn about presidential actions.

THE GENERATION GAP
IN READING NEWSPAPERS

If one really wants to be informed about political matters, decades of research support the conclusion that newspapers are the best media source.[7] Thus, when President George W. Bush told Brit Hume on September 23, 2003 that he doesn't read newspapers, many pundits and scholars gasped.[8] Long-time White House correspondent Helen Thomas, who has long been known for her objectivity, wrote a widely cited critical piece about this revelation from Bush entitled "No Wonder Bush Doesn't Connect with the Country." In this piece, Thomas argued that "anyone who wants to stay in touch with national, international and local events looks forward to reading the newspaper every day. The variety and breadth of newspaper stories make Americans the best-informed people in the world."[9] Of course, President Bush maintained that he did not need to read newspapers because his Chief of Staff and National Security Advisor briefed him on the news every day. But this satisfied few critics, who wondered whether even the most trusted aides could be expected to relay a full sense of the news of the day to the commander in chief. For example, Tom Rosenstiel of the Project for Excellence in Journalism wrote, "It makes you wonder if the only people he is talking to are people who work for him or agree with him and whether everything he sees about America he learns through them or through the window of a

---

7. See Doris Graber, *Mass Media and American Politics,* 6th ed. (Washington, DC: Congressional Quarterly Press, 2002).

8. See http://www.foxnews.com/story/0,2933,98111,00.html (accessed February 7, 2004).

9. See Helen Thomas, "No Wonder Bush Doesn't Connect with the Rest of the Country." *Hearst Newspapers,* October 15, 2003. See http://seattlepi.nwsource. com/opinion/143851_thomas15.html (accessed February 7, 2004).

motorcade. One of the few ways to not do that is to read a newspaper or watch TV."[10]

Left unsaid in this hullabaloo was the hard fact that the percentage of the American public that reads a daily newspaper has been declining for quite some time, a trend that has been—and likely will continue to be—driven by generational replacement. Whether Bush's avoidance of newspapers is a good practice for a president or not, the fact that so many people in the electorate no longer bother to read a newspaper has made it easier for a president to say he doesn't either. A few decades ago it probably would have seemed outlandish for a president to say this; today, given the decline of American newspapers, it is not.

Table 8–8 displays survey data from 1957 to 2002 regarding the percentage of the American public that reported reading a newspaper every day of the week. The data are presented this way partly to simplify the presentation but also due to a theoretical perspective that newspaper paper reading is a habit that either people develop early and continue throughout their lifetime or they do not. Of course, most people who do not read a paper every day will occasionally pick one up and leaf through it. In all likelihood, President Bush sometimes reads a newspaper; when he said he did not what he probably meant was that it wasn't a habit for him. As can be seen from the survey data, it is no longer a daily habit for three-fifths of Americans either.

In contrast, a 1957 survey of news media usage found that 76 percent of the U.S. adult population (then defined as over 21 years of age) read a paper every day. Not shown in the data in Table 8–8 is the fact that this survey asked people how many papers they read as well as how often. Amazingly, 21 percent said they read two papers daily and another 4 percent said they read three papers every day. Most of these people who read more than one paper a day were probably reading a morning and an afternoon paper. In the absence of the ability to turn on the TV in the evening and get the news, getting a paper that was published in the late afternoon was a good way for a news junkie to keep abreast of late-breaking events. As late as 1970, afternoon papers accounted for 58 percent of daily newspapers sold; by 2001, this figure had fallen to a mere 16 percent.[11]

Table 8–8 shows that in the 15 years between 1957 and 1972, there was only a slight decline in daily newspaper reading, though probably far fewer people were reading more than one newspaper a day by the early 1970s. Since the early 1970s, though, the decline in daily newspaper reading has been precipitous. In the 30 years from 1972 to 2002, this habit has declined at the rate of approximately one percent a year. Should this trend continue unabated, no

10. Quoted in "Bush's Disdain for the News Media Puzzles, Angers Many Journalists, *USA Today,* December 21, 2003.

11. *Statistical Abstract of the United States,* 2002, p. 700.

Table 8–8 Percent Reading a Newspaper Every Day, 1957–2002

1957	76.3
1958	75.3
1967	73.4
1972	69.3
1973	——
1974	——
1975	66.7
1976	——
1977	63.2
1978	57.7
1980	——
1982	53.0
1983	56.2
1984	——
1985	53.0
1986	53.9
1987	55.9
1988	50.9
1989	49.6
1990	52.7
1991	51.9
1993	46.7
1994	50.4
1996	42.4
1998	42.9
2000	36.5
2002	42.5

SOURCES: 1957 News Media Study; 1958 Omnibus Survey of Consumer Attitudes and Behavior; 1967 Political Participation in America Study; 1972–2002 General Social Surveys.

one will be reading a newspaper every day by the year 2042. Of course, such long-term projections can hardly be taken seriously given all the impossible-to-anticipate factors that might intervene to accelerate or reverse this trend over the next 40 years. But clearly, people in the newspaper business are concerned that they are losing their customers and that the process of generational replacement makes it likely this trend will continue for at least the near future.

The generational nature of the decline of daily newspaper reading is shown dramatically in the cohort data displayed in Table 8–9. Looking across the rows, one sees a good deal of stability within each cohort in terms of the percentage reading a newspaper every day. For example, of people born in my cohort

Table 8–9 Cohort Analysis: Percent Reading the Newspaper Every Day

Born in:	1998–2002 Data	1987–1989 Data	1972–1977 Data	1967 Data	1957 Data
1978–1982	19				
1973–1977	22				
1968–1972	23	22			
1963–1967	30	30			
1958–1962	33	37			
1953–1957	39	43	42		
1948–1952	48	53	50		
1943–1947	49	58	56	57	
1938–1942	59	57	65	64	
1933–1937	62	65	72	75	70*
1928–1932	73	66	74	79	74
1923–1927	67	74	79	75	78
1918–1922		74	79	79	76
1913–1917		72	79	77	82
1908–1912			78	79	80
1903–1907			79	76	82
1898–1902			77	78	77
1893–1897				75	75

* only 1933 to 1936 here

SOURCES: 1957 News Media Study; 1967 Political Participation in America Study; 1972–2002 General Social Surveys.

(1953–1957), 42 percent said they read a newspaper every day in the mid 1970s, 43 percent in the late 1980s, and 39 percent in the 1998–2002 period. This compares poorly to the steady 75 percent rate of daily newspaper readings among my parents' cohort. Such a generational difference is hardly unusual, as Table 8–9 clearly shows that since the beginning of the TV age, new cohorts have become increasingly less likely to report reading a newspaper every day. Thus, the habit of reading a newspaper every day is not evident at nearly the same rate among new cohorts as compared to the age groups that are currently dying out. At present, what we are seeing is that 7 out of 10 of the most-elderly adults have read a newspaper every day throughout their lives. In contrast, among the young adults who are replacing them in the electorate, only about 2 in 10 have thus far developed this media consumption habit.

The financial viability of the printed newspaper delivered to your front door every morning is therefore surely in doubt. Many people believe the future of the newspaper business lies with the Internet. Today, most major

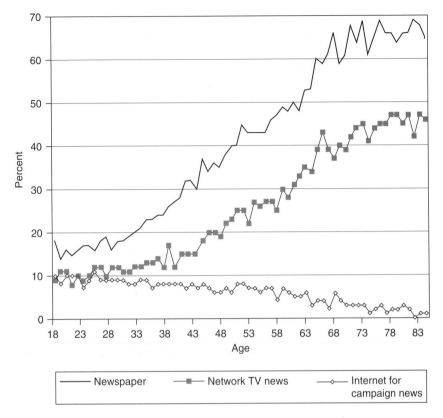

Figure 8–1 Percent Using Medium Every Day in the Past Week, 2000.

SOURCE: 2000 National Annenberg Election Study.

newspapers have an online edition. It is certainly conceivable that as a younger generation accustomed to receiving news electronically comes of age that the newspaper business will make a successful transition to an Internet-based medium. However, the data on internet usage to follow politics are thus far are not terribly promising. A January 2004 Pew survey found that only 20 percent of people under 30 years old said they regularly learned something about the campaign from the Internet. And in 2000, the National Annenberg Election Study found that relatively few people said they had used the Internet to follow the campaign every day in the past week. The Annenberg study allows researchers to analyze media usage patterns by age with a great deal of precision because over 94,000 respondents were asked the same questions over the course of the year. Figure 8–1 displays the findings on daily use of the Internet, newspapers, and network TV news. As expected, the trend line for using the Internet to follow the campaign differs markedly from usage patterns of traditional media sources, with young people being more likely to use the web. Yet even among young adults, regular use of the Internet to follow the campaign was fairly rare in 2000. It would appear that the Internet has a long way to go as a source of political information before it can be said to take the place of newspapers and/or broadcast TV news. Today's young adults can potentially learn a tremendous amount about presidential actions from the Internet, *if they so choose,* but it would appear that very few are choosing to do so.

CONCLUSION

The changing media environment in the United States over the past several decades has had numerous consequences for the American presidency. In some sense, the presidency is a less powerful position than it used to be as presidents have lost the ability to communicate their messages to a broad cross-section of the American public anytime they see fit. In the so-called "golden age of presidential television," the president could expect airtime anytime he asked for it, have a high percentage of the public hear what he had to say, and have most people learn more about his message the following day via newspapers and TV news. This power to communicate directly with the American public was long thought to be an invaluable asset. As Fred Friendly of CBS wrote years ago, "No mighty King, no ambitious Emperor, no Pope, no prophet ever dreamt of such an awesome pulpit, such a magic wand."

Yet this power rested on a president successfully persuading people that his policies were wise. All of the presidents who had the opportunity to use this power found that getting a big and attentive audience was much easier than getting a positive reception for their message. President Johnson was the first to have cameras set up in the White House to allow him to go on nationwide TV at virtually a moment's notice, but ultimately he could not convince the American public of the wisdom of his Vietnam War policy. President Nixon's speeches and press conferences on Watergate drew high audiences but failed to derail the movement to drive him out of office before the end of his term. President Ford had no problem in getting people to hear about his WIN plan, standing for "Whip Inflation Now," but the slogan was widely ridiculed and ineffective. And President Carter's address in a cardigan succeeded in getting many people to hear his plea that fighting the energy crisis was the "moral equivalent of war" but convinced few that it was of such importance, and his call to action was largely ignored.

One of the reasons why the president's power to communicate has been so highly prized is that it theoretically enables presidents to shape the nation's political agenda. It certainly seems logical that the bigger the presidential audience, the more likely the president will be able to control what topics are talked about. In practice, however, the presidents who had the most opportunity to exercise this power found it short-lived. For example, President Carter's famous "crisis of confidence" speech got people talking about the topic for a few days, but the public agenda quickly turned to other issues.

President Carter, like other presidents who served during the era when three TV networks dominated the airwaves, found that he had strong competition in controlling the public agenda from the nightly news broadcasts. As Shanto Iyengar and Donald Kinder aptly put it in their classic book entitled *News That Matters,* "The networks can neither create national problems where there are none nor conceal national problems that actually exist. What television news does instead is alter the priorities Americans attach to a circumscribed set of problems, all of which are plausible contenders for public concern."[12] When Walter Cronkite ended every night's *CBS Evening News* with a count of the number of days American hostages had been held in Iran, it certainly had a crucial impact on Jimmy Carter's presidency. Cronkite didn't intentionally try to bring Carter down, but by keeping this problem on the public agenda, he and others in the media primed voters to evaluate the Carter presidency by its failure to deal with the problem.

For presidents, the positive side of the changing media environment is surely the decreased competition from the media in setting the agenda. Declining audiences for the nightly network news and the fact that fewer people are reading newspapers have made it far more difficult for just a handful of media outlets to shape the national agenda. A fragmented media with a smaller audience reach is a less powerful media. Such a change does not necessarily mean that a president will be able to successfully direct the nation's agenda, but at least the media are now less of an obstacle. The proliferation of media sources with different political points of view also makes it easier to find a receptive outlet for delivering partisan presidential pronouncements.

Smaller audiences for the news have also made the job of targeting presidential messages to the attentive public somewhat easier. In particular, presidents who can tailor their policies to please the elderly stand to be in much better shape than those fail to do so. Although it would be hard to argue that the age bias in presidential audiences is a positive development for representative democracy, it is unfortunately always easier to please some of the people than all of the people.

The changing media environment for presidents has contributed to the polarization phenomenon that is currently much discussed with regard to President Bush. When Bush recently appeared on *Meet the Press,* one of the questions posed by Tim Russert was, "Why do you think you are perceived as such a divider?" Bush did not even bother to try to dispel this image,

---

12. Shanto Iyengar and Donald R. Kinder, *News That Matters* (New Haven, CT: Yale University Press, 1987), pp. 118–119.

responding, "Gosh, I don't know, because I'm working hard to unite the country." He then went on to reflect that "as a matter of fact, it's the hardest part of being the president. I was successful as the governor of Texas for bringing people together for the common good, and I must tell you it's tough here in Washington, and frankly it's the biggest disappointment that I've had so far of coming to Washington."[13] Yet based on trends over time in presidential support approval, he really should not have been surprised. As Gary Jacobson has argued, "By every measure, national politics has become increasingly polarized along partisan and ideological lines over the decades between the Nixon and G. W. Bush administrations."[14] Among the factors that have contributed to this polarization are the changes in the media environment. As news audiences have shrunk, those who are attentive to what the president is doing are more likely to be locked into a favorable or unfavorable predisposition. The key to a successful White House political communication strategy today is keeping one's base of supporters satisfied. Reaching out more broadly is unfortunately quite difficult when so few people with marginal political interest are paying much attention.

---

13. Transcript of February 8, 2004 *Meet the Press,* http://www.msnbc.msn.com/id/4179618/ (accessed February 20, 2004).

14. Gary C. Jacobson, "Partisan Polarization in Presidential Support: The Electoral Connection." Paper presented at the 2002 Annual Meeting of the American Political Science Association, p. 1.

9

News That Doesn't Matter

Presidents, the News Media,
and the Mass Public in an Era
of New Media[1]

JEFFREY E. COHEN
Fordham University

B y almost any standard, 1998 was a horrible year for any president. Bill
Clinton's affair with Monica Lewinsky became public, leading to his
impeachment. The Republican-controlled Congress heartily attacked
him, and the news media, never easy on the administration,[2] escalated the
degree to which it challenged and criticized the president. Figure 9–1 traces
the percentage of news stories about the president and the administration
from 1981 that were coded as clearly negative or more negative than positive.[3]

---

1. With apologies to Shanto Iyengar and Donald R. Kinder, *News That Matters:
   Television and American Opinion* (Chicago: University of Chicago Press, 1987)
   for my irreverent title. An earlier version of this paper was presented at the
   Conference on Researching the Public Presidency, Bush Presidential Library
   Conference Center, Texas A&M University, February 27–28, 2004. I want to
   thank Tom Patterson and Lyn Ragsdale for allowing me to use data they
   have collected. This paper would not be possible without their data.

2. Howard Kurtz, *Spin Cycle: Inside the Clinton Propaganda Machine* (New York:
   Free Press, 1998).

3. These data come from Thomas Patterson's random sample of 5000 stories
   from Lexus-Nexus service from 1981 through 1998. His data cast a wide net
   beyond stories on the presidency; I only present presidential news stories
   here, about 20 percent of the entire sample. The number of presidential stories per year is often modest, which precludes making definitive statements
   about news coverage of the presidency. Yet because of the long span of time
   and the random selection of stories, we can gather a sense of the comparative tone of news reporting on the presidency across these nearly two
   decades. See Thomas E. Patterson, "Doing Well and Doing Good: How Soft
   News and Critical Journalism are Shrinking the News Audience and
   Weakening Democracy—And What News Outlets Can Do About It" (Joan
   Shorenstein Center for Press, Politics, and Public Policy, John F. Kennedy
   School of Government, Harvard University, 2000).

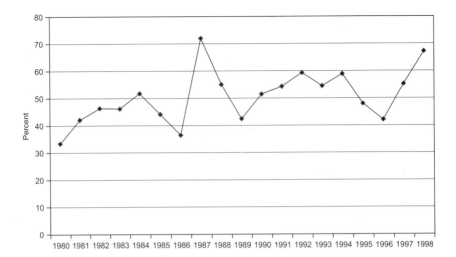

FIGURE 9–1 Percentage of Negative News Stories about the President, 1980–1998.

SOURCE: Patterson, 2000, Lexis-Nexis sample of news stories.

As the figure demonstrates, 1998 stood out in its degree of negative news reports. Only 1987, the year of the Iran–Contra scandal, produced a higher percentage of negative news stories on the president.[4] Even 1994, the year of Clinton's ill-fated health care initiative, itself a bad press year for Clinton at 58 percent, is still less negative than 1998 by nearly 10 percent. Not surprisingly, nearly 22 percent of all news stories in 1998 about the president and administration focused on the scandal, and nearly all of those stories were negative. Without the scandal stories, only 47 percent of the news stories about Clinton would have been negative, which is similar to the amount of negative news he received in any given year.

⌈What is so remarkable about these figures is not that Clinton received so much bad press but that his job approval polls rose that year.⌉Fifty-six percent of those polled in the last Gallup poll of 1997 approved of the job that Clinton

---

4. We should not overly interpret the 1987 figure because of the modest number of stories coded that year (25).

5. In a perceptive analysis, Brian Newman finds that the scandal actually hurt Clinton's ratings. Had the scandal not existed, Clinton's polls would have been about 2–3 points higher. Still, this is a meager effect of scandal on presidential polls in light of Ostrom and Simon's analysis of the impact of Watergate and Iran–Contra. See Brian Newman, "Bill Clinton's Approval Ratings: The More Things Change, the More they Stay the Same," *Political Research Quarterly* 55 (December 2002): 781–804; and Charles W. Ostrom, Jr., and Dennis M. Simon, "The Man in the Teflon Suit? The Environmental Connection, Political Drama, and Popular Support in the Reagan Presidency," *Public Opinion Quarterly* 53 (Autumn 1989): 353–87.

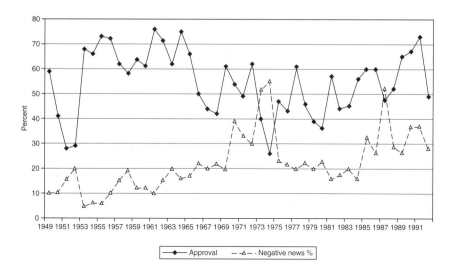

FIGURE 9–2 Trends in Presidential Approval and News Tone, *New York Times,* 1949–1992.

SOURCE: News tone data come from the *New York Times,* supplied to the author by Lyn Ragsdale; approval data from Gallup.

was doing. By the end of July 1998, his job approval rating had risen to 65. It remained at about that level throughout the remainder of the year, before spiking upward in very late 1998 and early 1999, reaching a peak of 73 percent in Gallup's poll of December 19–20, 1998.

That Clinton's polls did not plummet in the face of such bad press challenges many widely held assumptions about the role of news in shaping opinions. Richard Brody's seminal book argues that the balance of positive and negative news about the president will affect public attitudes toward the president.[6] When the news leans in a negative direction, presidential approval should too. Brody's perspective suggests that Clinton's approval polls should have declined in 1998, yet they rose! Our existing theories and understandings of the relationship among the news, the presidency, and public opinion cannot explain why Bill Clinton's approval rose in 1998.

Nor do our exiting theories explain the general decoupling of news from presidential approval. Figure 9–2 plots data on the annual tone of presidential news and Gallup approval from 1949 through 1992.[7] The two series diverge, as expected, until about the mid-1970s; then they began to track together.

---

6. Richard Brody, *Assessing the President: The Media, Elite Opinion, and Public Support* (Stanford, CA: Stanford University Press, 1991).

7. Lyn Ragsdale, "Disconnected Politics: Public Opinion and Presidents," in Barbara Norrander and Clyde Wilcox, eds., *Understanding Public Opinion* (Washington, DC: CQ Press, 1997), pp. 229–51.

Regression analysis reveals that the two series are negatively related ($b = -.40$; $se = .16$; $t = 2.52$; $p = .02$). However, if we bisect the series into two subsets (1949–1976 and 1977–1992), we find the expected negative relationship for the 1949–1976 segment ($b = -.68$, $p = .000$) but no relationship for the 1977–1992 segment ($b = .31$, $p = .28$). In fact, if we drop 1987, the year of Iran–Contra, from the 1977–1992 segment, we find a strong positive relationship between negative news and presidential popularity ($b = .90$, $p = .000$)! In other words, bad news leads to higher presidential polls, barring major negative events like Iran–Contra. I do not want to make such a claim, but obviously our traditional understanding of the relationship between news and public regard for the president needs rethinking.

The presidential news subsystem, the set of interrelationships among the president, the news media, and the public, underwent a major transformation over the past 20–25 years. In this paper I identify the major aspects of this transformation and discuss the implications of this transformation for politics and presidential leadership in the late 20th and early 21st centuries. Four changes are especially important. Briefly, (1) the news media have become increasingly competitive and decentralized; (2) reporting styles have changed as stories became softer and increasingly negative; (3) the public's consumption of news from traditional outlets declined; and (4) public regard toward the news media plummeted. In the next section, I describe the presidential news subsystem during television's "golden age" of the 1960s and 1970s.[8] Then I trace the four trends. I conclude by discussing the implications of these trends on modern American politics and presidential leadership and return to the paradox of the rise in Clinton's polls in 1998 despite a heavy barrage of bad news about the president.

THE PRESIDENTIAL NEWS SYSTEM IN THE GOLDEN AGE OF TELEVISION

Matthew Baum and Samuel Kernell colorfully call the period of the late 1950s through 1970s the "golden age of presidential television."[9] In that era, the president enjoyed a number of major advantages. But that system also posed grave threats to presidential leadership. During the golden era, the public received the

---

8. Matthew A. Baum and Samuel Kernell, "Has Cable Ended the Golden Age of Television?" *American Political Science Review* 93 (March 1999): 99–114; and Timothy E. Cook and Lyn Ragsdale, "The President and the Press: Negotiating Newsworthiness in the White House," in Michael Nelson, ed., *The Presidency and the Political System,* 5th ed. (Washington, DC: CQ Press, 1998), pp. 323–57.

9. Baum and Kernell, "Has Cable Ended the Golden Age of Television?"

bulk of its news from the three nightly news broadcasts, and the audience for the nightly broadcasts was large. Through television, presidents had easy access to the mass public, a major advantage for presidents bent on leading the public.

News content during this era also advantaged the president. The president was the dominant news story of the age, crowding rivals and other political leaders off the news.[10] Additionally, news was reported objectively and tended to portray the president in a positive light.[11] While the seeds of interpretive and cynical news reporting were sown during this era, such a style was not yet the norm. Still, this news system could pose a danger to a president if it turned against him, as it occasionally did. Two administrations, Johnson's and Nixon's, were cut short in part because the press turned against the president.

The Public and Television News

In the 1950s, television emerged as the most popular entertainment and news medium for American citizens. For instance, in 1952, 79 percent of ANES respondents claimed to have read something about the presidential campaign in newspapers, whereas only 51 percent said that they had watched a television program about the campaign.[12] By 1956 the pattern had shifted. Newspaper reading declined to 68 percent, while TV watching rose to 73 percent. From then on, more people would claim to have received news about the campaign from TV than from newspapers (see Figure 9–3).

Moreover, the percentage of people who relied only on TV for news increased from about 8 percent in 1952 to 18 percent in 1956, ranging between 14 and 19 percent through 1968 (Figure 9–4). From one-sixth to one-fifth of the public claimed that television was its sole source of news. At the same time,

---

10. Robert E. Gilbert, "Television and Presidential Power," *Journal of Social, Political, and Economic Studies* 6, no. 1 (1981): 75–93; and Robert E. Gilbert, "President Versus Congress: The Struggle for Public Attention," *Congress and the President* 16, no. 1 (1989): 91–102.

11. Michael Baruch Grossman and Martha Joynt Kumar, *Portraying the President: The White House and the News Media* (Baltimore, MD: Johns Hopkins University Press, 1981).

12. We need to take these numbers with caution. People seem to inflate their news exposure, as they overreport turnout. Given that surveys indicate that some people consider programs like *Entertainment Tonight* and reality crime shows like *Cops* to be news, people may overstate their news consumption when all they have done is watch an entertainment program. Similarly, newspaper reading attention to the campaign may be inflated as sports readers glance at the news headlines about the campaign. Still, despite these sources of measurement error, assuming that such problems are relatively constant across years, we can track some trends. But it is quite likely that these numbers understate those who are inattentive to either medium. Other data suggest that the percentage of the population that is inattentive to all forms of hard news has increased. See Patterson, "Doing Well and Doing Good."

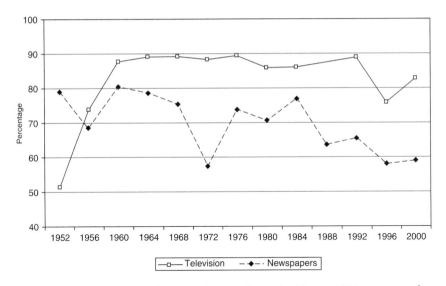

FIGURE 9–3 Percentage of Respondents Using Television and Newspapers for Presidential Campaign News, 1952–2000.

SOURCE: ANES, 1948–2000. No data for TV watching in 1988.

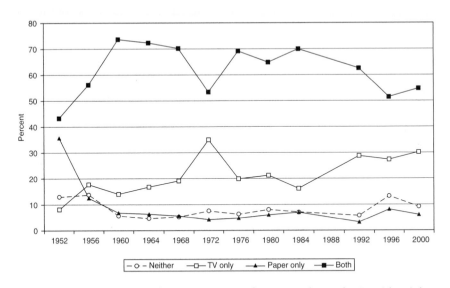

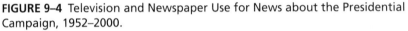

FIGURE 9–4 Television and Newspaper Use for News about the Presidential Campaign, 1952–2000.

SOURCE: ANES, 1952–2000. No data for 1988.

the percentage of the public that only used newspapers dwindled precipitously from over 35 percent in 1952 to 12 percent four years later. Thereafter, it never rose above 10 percent. As Figure 9–4 illustrates, the public had bifurcated into two groups by the late 1950s, those who only watched TV for news about the campaign and those who used both TV and newspapers.

Presidents and Reporters in the Golden Age

The three broadcast networks dominated the dissemination of both entertainment and news programming to the public by the late 1950s. It was not until John F. Kennedy became president in 1961, however, that the presidency understood and attempted to harness the power and reach of television. Although both Truman and Eisenhower occasionally appeared on television, they focused the bulk of their attention on print journalists. Broadcast journalists were decidedly second-class citizens among reporters. The status differences between print and broadcast reporters narrowed with the arrival of the Kennedy administration. Kennedy viewed the new medium as one to exploit rather than one to fear. It offered him access to the mass public unlike any previous means of communication. He innovated its use, appearing to the public directly, over the heads of the news media, but he also made it easier for broadcast journalists to cover him.

Unlike his predecessors, Kennedy offered live press conferences in prime time, a departure from past press conference practice. Over the course of the 20th century, journalists had come to expect press conferences. Through press conferences, journalists received content for their news stories, which made the journalists key transmitters of information from government to the mass public. Kennedy's televised press conferences, however, altered the press–public connection. If people could watch the press conference, they no longer needed the newspaper story to fill them in on what transpired. Kennedy and subsequent White Houses began to favor the electronic over the print media, figuring that it could transmit its message directly to the public.[13] They also figured that television would be satisfied with film showing the president and in this way would become relatively passive transmitters of news that presidents manufactured. Across the 1960s, because of the public's appetite for television and the growing stature of television journalists, the system worked to the advantage of the president and television journalists.

News Reporting Styles
in the Golden Age of Television

During the golden age of television, the president dominated the news. News tended to be reported objectively, although early signs of a new interpretive news style were emerging. The news also tended to portray the president in a positive light. The combination of these news reporting attributes conferred advantages on the president, enhancing his ability to lead.

From the late 1800s on, the presidential image in the news had been expanding. Long before television was invented, presidents were beginning to

---

13. John Anthony Maltese, *Spin Control: The White House Office of Communications and the Management of Presidential News* (Chapel Hill: University of North Carolina Press, 1992).

receive more news coverage than Congress, something unheard of previously, except during presidential election years.[14] Television enhanced this trend, garnering the president an even larger share of the news.

Measuring the quantity of news is complicated because of the numerous news outlets and the sheer volume of news. Consequently, most studies of presidential news look at only the number of presidential news stories and perhaps collect similar figures for news about Congress. But rarely do such studies attempt to calculate the percentage of news about the president as a proportion of the total amount of news. Frank Baumgartner and Bryan Jones's Agendas Project provides one data source that can give us a glimpse at the comparative volume of presidential news.

Their Agendas Project randomly sampled news stories from the index of the *New York Times* from 1946 into the mid-1990s. Figure 9–5, traces two trend lines using these data: presidential mentions as a percentage of all news stories and presidential mentions as a percentage of news stories about government. Both trend lines display an unmistakable and similar pattern, a growth of presidential news from the 1940s into the 1970s. The two are highly correlated in spite of their differing bases (Pearson's $r = .87$, $p = .000$). From 1946 to 1959, presidents received on average about 5 percent of all news and 12 percent of government/policy news. These figures jumped to 8 and 17 percent in the 1960s, growth rates of 60 and 42 percent respectively. The growth in presidential news continued in the 1970s, with the president receiving 11 percent of all news and 23 percent of governmental/policy news during that decade.

Comparable data do not exist on television news coverage of the president, but indications suggest that the president was an even more pronounced figure there than in newspapers. Still, these newspaper data probably reflect a similar trend in television news. Feeling competition from television, major national newspapers would likely have followed suit and increased their coverage of the president. Plus, through interaction on the beat, training, and other processes, journalists have tended to develop a consensual understanding of what is news. The president was the star news attraction across news media during the golden age of the 1960s and 1970s.

News reporting on the president also tended to be objective and positive. The best data on these attributes come from Grossman and Kumar.[15] They ambitiously content-analyzed news stories about the president from three

14. Alan P. Balutis, "Congress, the President, and the Press," *Journalism Quarterly* 59 (Autumn 1976): 505–509; Alan P. Balutis, "The Presidency and the Press: The Expanding Public Image," *Presidential Studies Quarterly* 7 (Fall 1977): 244–51; Elmer E. Cornwell, Jr., "Presidential News: The Expanding Public Image," *Journalism Quarterly* 36 (Summer 1959): 275–83; and Samuel Kernell and Gary C. Jacobson, "Congress and the President as News in the Nineteenth Century" *Journal of Politics* 49 (November 1987): 1016–35.

15. Grossman and Kumar, *Portraying the President*, pp. 253–272.

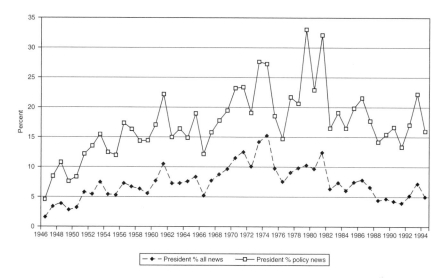

FIGURE 9–5 Presidential News Volume, *New York Times,* 1946–1994.

SOURCE: Baumgartner and Jones, Agendas Project.

news sources: *Time* magazine, the *New York Times,* and CBS News. The *Time* and *New York Times* data span from 1953 through August 1978. The CBS data begin with August 1968, when the Vanderbilt Television Archives began collecting tapes of the broadcasts.

All three news organizations reported more favorable than unfavorable news about the president. Approximately 60 percent of *Time*'s stories were favorable, with about 11.8 percent neutral and 28.2 percent negative. The *New York Times'* breakdown is similar, with 48.7 percent positive, 24.1 percent neutral, and 27.2 percent negative. CBS, which spans a shorter time frame, displays a balance between positive (38.5 percent) and negative (38.6 percent) news, with 22.9 percent neutral.

The shorter data gathering period for CBS allows Watergate to weigh more heavily in CBS's totals, which accounts for the difference between CBS's tonality in news about the president and the two print outlets. From 1953 to 1965, both *Time* and the *New York Times* gave the president a ratio of favorable to unfavorable news of approximately 5 to 1. From 1966–1974, news from both print outlets was more negative than positive, as was the case for CBS. In the post-Watergate years, 1975–1978, news for all three news organizations shifted, with positive news again outweighing negative news, often by hefty margins (see Table 9–1). What is so remarkable is that even during the Watergate years, the news was not extraordinarily negative. Thus, other than when extraordinary events led the press to view the president in a negative light, presidents during the golden age could count on favorable news.

Table 9–1 Tone of News about the President from Three News Organizations, 1953–1978

Date	Time Positive	Time Negative	New York Times Positive	New York Times Negative	CBS News* Positive	CBS News* Negative
1953–1978	60	28.2	48.7	27.2	38.5	38.6
1953–1965	58.9	10.9	50	11	na	na
1966–1974	28.7	31.6	28.5	35.2	23.5	38.2
1974–1978**	43.3	19.4	37.5	23.4	44.8	23.6

* only from 1968–1978.
** begins when Ford assumes office.

SOURCE: Grossman and Kumar, 1981, pp. 256, 265.

Summary

The presidential news subsystem of the golden age, roughly the 1960s and 1970s, was one in which people watched television for news, and three major networks were their major news sources. The president was the dominant news story across all forms of news media, with nontelevision news copying television's emphasis on the president in order to compete with television. Furthermore, the news, except in extraordinary times, was generally positive towards the president. The large television news audience, the amount of presidential coverage, and its positive tone all should have enhanced the ability of the president to lead the public.

The great danger for the president was when events turned sour and the press began portraying him in a negative light. In an age when negative news about the president was uncommon, a surge in bad press came as a shock and often would lead people to rethink their approval and support of the president. The centralization of the news delivery system, in which news providers offered the public essentially the same news, reinforced the opinion-shaping effects of news. In other words, the system of news delivery during this era was essentially a one–message system, to use John Zaller's term.[16] The public received essentially one message about the president, no matter the news source that a person used. Two presidents, Johnson and Nixon, were arguably driven from office in part because of this dynamic. In the main, however, this news system worked to the president's advantage because the news tended to be favorably disposed toward him.

All this would begin to change in the late 1970s. The news media decentralized. Competition and other forces led to a new style of news reporting that was more interpretive and negative than the style of the golden age.

---

16. John R. Zaller, *The Nature and Origins of Mass Opinion* (New York: Cambridge University Press, 1992).

The audience for news also shrank and people, perhaps because of the new style of news, became more cynical toward the news media itself, which likely muted the impact of news on public opinion.[17] Together these trends blunted the impact of the news on public attitudes toward the president. They also lessened the ability of the president to lead the public.

THE PRESIDENTIAL NEWS SUBSYSTEM IN THE NEW MEDIA AGE

Competition among the news media, the rise of soft news, increasing negativity in hard news, a shrinking news audience, and declining public regard for the news media characterize the presidential news subsystem in the new media age. Such a news subsystem ironically limits the damage that the news media can do to a president, while also limiting the president's ability to lead the public. In response to the changes in the structure of the presidential news subsystem, presidents have changed their style of "going public." Instead of focusing attention on leading the broad mass public, much presidential activity now targets select constituencies, which are often already presidential allies.

The Decline of Network Monopoly and the Rise of Competition

In the golden age, three national networks and a handful of other national news organizations dominated the production, definition, and dissemination of the news. All news outlets offered essentially the same basic portrait of the president, except that television could not portray the president in as much depth as the print media. Technological and economic forces came together in the late 1970s and 1980s to crack the control that these elite news organizations had over the news.[18] By the 1990s, the news production system had decentralized and splintered. Many news organizations competed for a shrinking news audience: To create a market niche, news programs and producers tried to differentiate themselves from their competitors by presenting distinctive voices and perspectives on the news.[19]

---

17. See Patterson, "Doing Well and Doing Good," pp. 2–3.

18. James T. Hamilton, *All the News That's Fit to Sell: How the Market Transforms Information into News* (Princeton, NJ: Princeton University Press, 2003).

19. Centralization was occurring in the newspaper sector as many papers failed, leaving only a handful of cities with more than one daily paper, and as corporate chains took over many other newspapers. Yet, as Hamilton argues, the newspaper sector was not immune to competitive pressures. Corporate offices were often highly sensitive to the economic implications of their news product and altered daily papers to reflect these new economic considerations. See Hamilton, *All the News That's Fit to Sell.*

Cable television, the Internet, new printing technologies, handheld cameras, and satellite systems all worked together to break the monopoly of the elite press of the golden age. Lightweight, handheld cameras and satellite technology allowed local broadcast stations to produce their own news from almost any location. Although they tended to center their activities within their localities, some local broadcasters would send production teams to Washington to follow events of local interest in the nation's capitol, as well as to give a local spin to a national story. Similarly, new printing technologies, desktop publishing, and computer-assisted customer lists allowed smaller, specialized magazines, newspapers, and so on to proliferate and prosper during this decade.

Cable television had perhaps the greatest impact on the presidential news subsystem. It spawned dedicated news networks, like CNN, Fox, and MSNBC, offering news around the clock. No longer did news-hungry viewers have to wait until the nightly broadcast to learn of events. Each cable network also tried to differentiate itself. CNN prides itself on international coverage. Fox offers viewers news with a conservative tilt, or so it proclaims. All have increased the amount of political commentary, with programs like *Crossfire* that mix theater and political opinion. More importantly, the big-three networks now faced competition from the 24/7 cable news outlets.

Cable had another, perhaps more profound effect. Cable programming offered viewers a choice of shows to watch besides what the three major networks offered. By and large, the public of the golden age had little programming choice. In the early evening, all three networks broadcast their national nightly news programs, sandwiched between local news broadcasts. If one was to watch television during these hours, one had to tune into a news program. The structure of television during the golden age effectively captured the public. People without an interest in news had little choice but to watch such programs, unless they decided to turn off the television.

With cable, people's tastes were better served. Reluctant news viewers had a myriad of entertainment offerings to watch in lieu of the network nightly news (and network entertainment fare). Across the board, the ratings of network programs, news and entertainment alike, eroded. VCRs allowed people to tape a show and watch it when they wanted, as well as rent or buy a copy of a film to watch whenever they felt like it. It is highly unlikely that many people taped news programs for later viewing. The Internet may similarly peel away the television audience, as some early data indicate it is doing. All traditional news organizations, from television stations to newspapers and news magazines, have a presence on the Internet. The news hungry may peruse the web pages of these established news media outlets, which some seem to be doing.

Less traditional news providers are also springing up on the Internet, challenging the dominance of the traditional media, redefining news, and affecting public regard for news organizations in the process. The prime example of this phenomenon is Matt Drudge, who came to national prominence in late 1997, when he published on his web page the allegations that President Clinton was having an affair with Monica Lewinsky. *Newsweek* purportedly also had the story but refused to publish it because the news magazine could not find a second source to confirm it. Drudge turned the hand of the traditional news media, much as print tabloids had been doing for the past 10–15 years, forcing the news media en masse to cover the scandal.

The Rise of Negative News and the Decline of Political News

The decentralization of the news media and the ability of almost anyone to become a "journalist" and publish a web page (for example, Matt Drudge) threatened the traditional norms of news publishing, such as source protection and confirmation of information, norms that had evolved over the course of the 20th century. Whereas news in the golden age was primarily objective and positive toward the president, news in the age of new media became softer and more sensational.[20] The boundary between entertainment and news blurred, and journalist voices began to appear in the news in greater quantity than the voices of politicians. Two trends have special relevance to the president and his relationship with the mass public: the decline in the volume of news and the rise of negativity in news reporting.

Many commentators have noted the decline of traditional hard news, such as reporting on government and public policy, as crime stories, entertainment and celebrity profiles, and personal health, and so on replaced traditional hard news.[21] Many factors are alleged to have stimulated these shifts, including the rise of market-driven journalism, greater competition among news organizations, and the rise of cable television. Here we need not detain ourselves with the causes of these trends, however interesting they may be. Instead, I just want to review some relevant evidence on this trend.

Declining Volume of Hard News. The Project for Excellence in Journalism conducted a study that content-analyzed the news of seven major media outlets (the three major networks, *Time*, *Newsweek*, the *New York Times*, and the *Los Angeles Times*) for three time points—1977, 1987, and 1997. These data reveal a dramatic decline in traditional hard news across almost all media

---

20. Patterson, "Doing Well and Doing Good"; and Larry J. Sabato, *Feeding Frenzy: How Attack Journalism Has Transformed Politics* (New York: Free Press, 1991).

21. Patterson, "Doing Well and Doing Good," pp. 3–5; and Stephen Hess, "Federalism and News: Media to Government: Drop Dead," *Brookings Review* 18 (Winter 2000): 28–31.

Table 9–2 Percentage of News Stories on Government, Military, Domestic and/or Foreign Affairs, 1977–1997

Media Organization	1977	1987	1997
ABC	71.6	60.3	44.9
CBS	67.8	54.4	40.3
NBC	62.6	60.1	38.8
Los Angeles Times*	74.8	77.6	62.0
New York Times*	63.8	63.8	69.3
Time Magazine**	48.1	51.9	19.2
Newsweek**	46.1	42.3	25.0

*Front page stories.

**Cover stories.

SOURCE: Project for Excellence in Journalism. "Changing Definitions of the News," March 6, 1998, http://www.journalism.org/resources/research/reports/definitions/subjects.asp. The coding period for all years was the month of March for each year.

(see Table 9–2). The Project coded entire network broadcasts, the front pages of the newspapers, and cover stories of the news weeklies.[22]

Here I use the Project's definition of traditional hard news—it is news about the government, military, domestic policy, and foreign policy. Their other subject categories are entertainment/celebrities, lifestyle, celebrity crime, personal health, other crime, business and commerce, science, technology, arts, religion, sports, weather and disasters, science fiction, and the supernatural. As Table 9–2 displays, only the major newspapers seemed to have resisted the trend of replacing government and policy-related news with other types of content. The decline among the three networks is striking, from about two-thirds or more of broadcast new stories dealing with government and policy in 1977 to about 40 percent in 1997. Similarly, the weekly news magazines, *Time* and *Newsweek,* which in the 1970s ran government and policy-related figures and stories on about half of their covers, ran such stories on their covers only about 20–25 percent of the time in 1997, a reduction rate of approximately 50 percent. The *Los Angeles Times* displays a minor drop in government and policy news on its front page, from about three-quarters to two-thirds of stories. Still, the bulk of the *Los Angeles Times'* front page is given to hard news. Only the *New York Times* seems to have resisted the trend of declining news coverage on its front page, with about two-thirds of front-page stories given to traditional news items for all three time points.

---

22. For more details of their study, see http://www.journalism.org/resources/research/reports/definitions/subjects.asp.

The Project's data are limited in several regards. They provide us with only three time points. They code only one month per year. Either of these data collection decisions may have skewed results. For the news magazines, exclusive attention to the cover story may overstate the decline in news coverage between the covers, as covers are used primarily to attract newsstand purchasers.

The Baumgartner and Jones Agendas Project data give us another vantage point from which to look at trends in news coverage in the *New York Times*. Figure 9–5 presents the percentage of presidential news as a fraction of all news and governmental news. Unlike the Project for Excellence data, these data span a much longer time frame (1946–1994) but also contain more than just front-page stories. Unfortunately, the sampling system of Baumgartner and Jones just does not provide enough front-page stories to render reliable temporal comparisons.

In these data, we see the rise in presidential news through the mid to late 1970s, followed by a steady decline thereafter, which comports well with Project for Excellence data. Thus, while the *New York Times,* according to the Project data, may have resisted the pressures to replace "hard" news on its front page, the *Times* may not have been so able to resist such trends in the rest of the publication. Perhaps the most important point made by these data is that from several different vantage points, coverage of traditional government and policy news has declined across a variety of news media. Moreover, the networks, still the medium with the largest news audience, show the steepest decline in government and policy news.

Increasing Negativity in Presidential News.   At the same time that the volume of governmental news, much of it about the presidency, has been ebbing, the lion's share of presidential news is no longer positive.[23] Again, the Project for Excellence provides some useful data. They compared nightly network news coverage of Presidents Bill Clinton and George W. Bush during their first 100 days.[24] In his first 100 days, Bill Clinton received positive coverage 22 percent of the time, compared to 28 percent negative and 49 percent neutral coverage. George W. Bush's news coverage was similar: 27 percent positive, 28 percent negative, and 44 percent neutral. While not extraordinarily negative, the fact that the figures are not lopsidedly positive is notable given that this is the president's traditional honeymoon period. If the honeymoon represents a period when presidents can expect

23. Tim Groeling and Samuel Kernell, "Is Network News Coverage of the President Biased?" *Journal of Politics* 60 (November 1998): 1063–87.

24. "The First 100 Days: How Bush Versus Clinton Faired in the Press," http://www.journalism.org/resources/research/reports/100days/default.asp.

their best overall news coverage, these figures do not bode well for the rest of the administration's time in office. These numbers differ markedly from the ones reported previously that Grossman and Kumar collected for the 1953–1977 period, and they differ dramatically from the high degree of positive news that presidents received on average in the 1950s and early 1960s.[25] Yet it is hard to compare the Grossman–Kumar data with the Project for Excellence data.

Fortunately, Lyn Ragsdale has taken Grossman and Kumar's *New York Times* data and extended the series forward to 1949 and through 1992. Her efforts provide us with a long annual time series, displayed in Figure 9–2. The figure plots the percentage of negative news, which shows a clear upward trend.[26] From 1949 through 1959, about 12 percent of presidential news was negative. In the 1960s, this percentage rose to 17.5, climbing to nearly 32 percent in the 1970s and 28 percent in the 1980s. Obviously, Watergate had a huge impact on the average amount of negative news in the 1970s, with over half of news about the president negative in 1973 and 1974. If we remove 1973 and 1974 from the average of the 1970s, we find about 26 percent of presidential news being negative in the remaining years of that decade. In the 1980s and 1990s, presidents could expect news to be more negative than it was in the 1960s and 1970s, and on average, presidential news in the 1980s and 1990s tended to be more negative than positive.[27]

The Declining Audience for News

At the same time that the amount of political and presidential news declined and negative news rose, the news audience was shrinking. Commentators offer several explanations for the declining size of the news audience. Patterson attributes the decline to changing reporting styles.[28] The rise of sensationalistic and soft news, according to Patterson, alienated some of the news audience, especially those who preferred hard news. Baum and Kernell point to

---

25. Grossman and Kumar, *Portraying the President*, pp. 253–272..

26. A regression of negative news on a time counter (1949 = 1) is strongly statistically significant and suggests that each year that the series progresses the president will receive about a half a percentage point more negative news. The regression equation (standard errors in parentheses) is $y = 10.10$ (2.93) Constant + .54 (.11) Counter; $R^2 = .35$. A similar regression for positive news finds a near mirror result. Each additional year subtracts about .4 percentage points of positive news. The resulting equation is $y = 50.41$ (2.83) Constant − .39 (.11) Counter; $R^2 = .23$.

27. This judgment is made by comparing the percent of positive news and negative news. For almost every year of the 1980s and 1990s, there was more negative than positive news.

28. Patterson, "Doing Well and Doing Good."

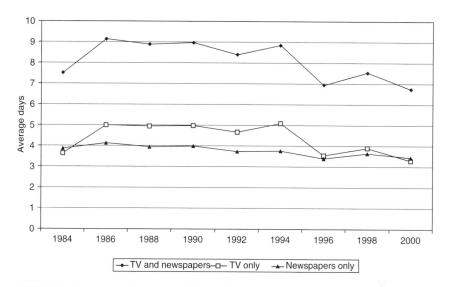

FIGURE 9–6 Average Number of Days That Respondents Watched TV News and/or Read the Daily Newspaper Last Week, 1984–2000.

SOURCE: ANES, 1984–2000. Each point represents the average days during the past week that the respondent watched TV news and read a daily newspaper.

the effects of changes in the structure of the mass media.[29] The arrival of cable television offered viewing choices besides the network nightly news. Instead of watching the network broadcasts, television viewers with cable access could watch entertainment, sports, and other non-news fare. Indications are that large numbers of viewers left the networks for cable offerings, as well as other media, such as VCRs and the Internet.

Whatever the source of the decline in the audience for news, we see it in some of the data presented earlier on Figure 9–4. Figure 9–6 presents the average number of days per week that respondents used various news media from the mid-1980s forward, when ANES began collecting such data. All news media show declines in average usage from the 1980s to the 1990s. In the late 1980s and early 1990s, people on average watched the nightly network news broadcast from 4.6 to 5 days a week. Their news viewing dropped to less than 4 days a week from 1996 through 2000. On average, people now claim to watch the nightly network news about one day a week less than they did a decade ago. Coupling this decline with the decline in hard news content may lead to the conclusion that the public overall, which relies mainly on these broadcasts for news, is much less informed about public affairs than it was two decades ago.

---

29. Baum and Kernell, "Has Cable Ended the Golden Age of Television?,"
      pp. 99–100.

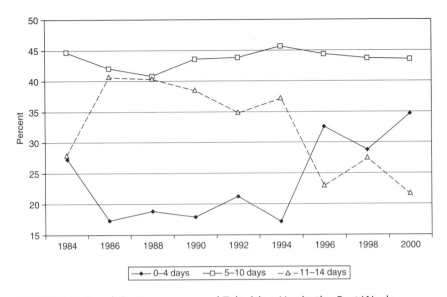

FIGURE 9–7 Trends in Newspaper and Television Use in the Past Week, 1984–2000.

SOURCE: ANES, 1984–2000. Each time point represents the percentage of individuals whose combined use of TV and newspapers during the past week totaled either 1–4 days (light media news consumers), 5–10 days (moderate media news consumers), or 11–14 days (heavy media news consumers).

Newspaper consumption has also declined, although not as steeply. On average, people claimed to read a daily newspaper nearly 4 days a week from 1984 through 1994. From 1996 through 2000, they decreased their newspaper reading about half a day per week to about 3.5 days per week, or about every other day, although we cannot say whether the mix of stories they read during the time frame changed or not. Given that the Baumgartner and Jones *New York Times* data and the Project for Excellence data on the *Los Angeles Times* front page suggest a decline of hard news as a percentage of overall newspaper content across the last two decades or so, it would not be surprising if newspaper readers also were less informed than two decades ago, given these changes in news content and reader habits.

The ANES data are displayed in a different way in Figure 9–7. Here the number of people who are heavy media users—that is, those whose combined use of television news and newspapers per week totals at least 11 days over the past week,[30]—declined as a percentage of the population from about 35–40 percent in the 1980s and early 1990s to 20–25 percent in the late 1990s

---

30. This is calculated by summing the number of days in the past week that respondents claimed to have read the newspaper and watched the evening network news.

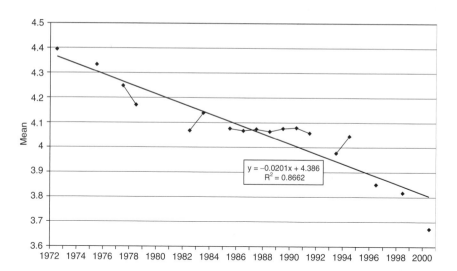

FIGURE 9–8 Newpaper Reading Habits, Mean Days per Week, 1972–2000, GSS.

SOURCE: General Social Survey, 1972–2000.

(1996–2000). At the same time, light media users, those whose combined consumption totaled no more than 4 days a week, increased as a percentage of the population from 15–20 percent across the 1980s and early 1990s to 30–35 percent in the second half of the 1990s.

Other ANES data, which can be traced back to the 1950s, suggest a long-term decline in news consumption. Figure 9–3, presented previously, plots the percentage of the public who claim to use newspapers and television for news about presidential election campaigns. The utility of this measure is its series length. The deficit of this measure is that it does not seem to discriminate well among heavy and light media users. As Figure 9–3 shows, and as reported earlier, television viewing increased in the 1950s, peaking at 80–90 percent by the 1960s, where it settled until the early 1970s. A small decline is noticeable in the mid-1970s, but a break in the series in 1988 makes it hard to specify the trend's shape in the mid-1980s. The mid-1990s drop is easily seen in these data. The newspaper trend suggests a decline from the late 1950s onward, with of course some upward and downward spikes along the way.

General Social Survey (GSS) data, which use a more discriminating question by asking people to classify how many days per week they use the newspaper, is plotted in Figure 9–8. The classification scheme and resulting figure require some explanation. GSS has asked people since 1972 how many days a week they read a daily newspaper: every day, a few times a week, once a week, less than once a week, or never. I scored these categories 5, 4, 3, 2, and 1 respectively. The figure plots the averages of these individual scores, which should not be read as literal averages but as category averages. The trend line shows a decline in which the average was between every day and several times a week of newspaper reading in the 1970s. A steady state appears in the 1980s, when people seemed to read the newspaper on average several times a week. In the 1990s, their newspaper reading habits deteriorated even more to between once a week and several times a week. Like the ANES data, the GSS data indicate a steep step-like decline in the mid to late 1990s.

Overall, these data indicate a shrinking audience for news in both television and newspapers. Moreover, not only is there a long-term deterioration in news consumption that begins for newspapers in the 1960s and television in the 1970s but a steeper decline sets in sometime in the mid 1990s. The 1990s decline appears not to be just a short-term trough but appears to be a step-like drop.

The combination of the decline in news content with the shrinking news audience points to the conclusion that the public today is less informed than was the case in the 1950s and 1960s. Whether the increased amount of negative news can influence public opinion about the president, considering today's small audience for news, is another question. Whether negative news about public figures and government can have much impact on public opinion when public confidence in that institution has also declined raises still another question.

Declining Trust in News Media

A fourth trend of significance is the declining public confidence in the news media. Considerable debate exists over whether declining confidence in the news media is just a function of overall confidence declines in all major institutions[31] or whether some aspect of the decline is particular to the news media itself.[32]

The GSS has been asking people off and on since 1972 about their confidence in those running television and the press. Although the press question clearly points to the news media, the television question is more ambiguous. Many people may think of television entertainment executives as well as news executives. But as the data in Figure 9–9 indicate, both series display a downward trend of similar magnitude from the 1970s through the 1990s. Linear trend lines have been added to the figure to highlight the downward trend and make the series, which are often broken due to missing data, more easily

---

31. Stephen Earl Bennett, Staci L. Rhine, and Richard S. Flickinger, "Assessing Americans' Opinions about the News Media's Fairness in 1996 and 1998," *Political Communication* 18 (April 1998): 163–183.

32. Timothy E. Cook and Paul Gronke, "Dimensions of Institutional Trust: Is Public Confidence in the Media Distinct from Other Institutions?" (paper presented at the Annual Meeting of the Midwest Political Science Association, 2001, Chicago, IL).

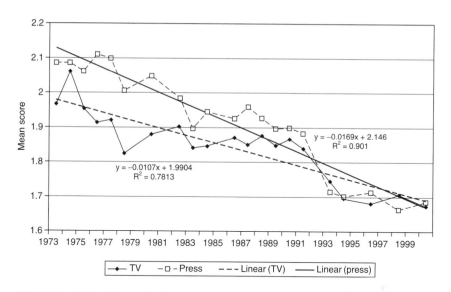

FIGURE 9–9 Confidence in the Press and TV, 1973–2000, GSS.

SOURCE: GSS, 1972–2000. Question: "I am going to name some institutions in this country. As far as the people running these institutions are concerned, would you say you have a great deal confidence, only some confidence, or hardly any confidence at all in them? Press? TV? The figure is constructed by coding "great deal" = 3, "only some" = 2 and "hardly any" = 1, and then taking the average for each year.

interpretable. Patterson argues that the content and style of modern journalism has alienated many viewers and readers.[33] One casual path linking news styles, confidence, and consumption is that the modern news style erodes confidence and trust in the news, which in turn leads people to abandon the news.

Summary

In this essay, I have documented major trends in the style of news and the audience for news. Since the 1970s, the heyday of the golden age of television and news, the amount of news devoted to traditional news about government, public policy, and the presidency has plummeted. At the same time, presidential news has turned increasingly negative. Now the news is more likely to be negative than positive toward the presidency. While these news content trends have been taking place, public habits and attitudes toward the news have also been changing. The public consumes less news than it did two decades ago, and it has less confidence and trust in the news media than it once did. What are the implications of these changes for the press, the presidency, and public opinion?

---

33. Patterson, "Doing Well and Doing Good," pp. 7–9; also see Joseph N. Capella and Kathleen Hall Jamieson, *Spiral of Cynicism: The Press and the Public Good* (Oxford, England: Oxford University Press, 1997).

IMPLICATIONS FOR PRESIDENTS, THE NEWS MEDIA, AND THE PUBLIC

Based on existing understanding of the impact of news on public opinion, one would expect the increase in negative news to have a dampening effect on public support for the president.[34] Not only does the case of Bill Clinton during 1998 belie this expectation but the positive correlation between negative news and presidential approval since the late 1970s also confounds traditional understanding of the connections between news and public support for the president.

Several factors about the new news media may blunt its impact on public opinion. First, it is harder for the news media to reach and consequently affect public thinking because the news audience has shrunk. Fewer people are attentive to the news than was once the case. Furthermore, there is less news content for them to be attentive to. Although it is true that people may encounter the news indirectly, through conversations with friends and family, such indirect or two-stage flows of information may weaken the impact of the news, as content is filtered in the course of communication. Moreover, some people's social networks may be nearly apolitical and lacking much news content, due to the degree of shrinkage in the news audience. Such a social network context will further blunt the impact of news on public opinion.

The rise of public discontent with the news media may blunt the impact of news reporting on the public even more than the shrinking news audience. Source credibility is an important ingredient in opening a person to communication effects. As source credibility declines, communication effects should also diminish. If the increasing levels of distrust and lack of confidence in the media measure the credibility of the press, then we can conjecture that the news has less impact on the public because the source that the information came from has lost some of its credibility.

A closely related fact that the news now is regularly negative may also undermine the ability of news content to affect public support for the president. In the golden age of broadcast television, negative news about the president was potent because it was rare. Its rarity signaled to the public that something was truly amiss in the White House. When all news about the president is negative, the signaling value of news to the public declines. The public can no longer tell if there are problems with the president and the administration that it needs to consider or if the negative news is just the same old story the news media always seem to be reporting. When the signal from the news media is so noisy, the public discounts it heavily.

---

34. For instance, see Brody, *Assessing the President.*

The combination of a smaller news audience, the loss of credibility of the news media, and the noisiness of the news signal to the public all have undermined the ability of the media to affect public attitudes about the president compared to the impact of the news during the golden age. If my argument is logical, there are even more profound implications. In a mass-mediated age, the public relies heavily on the news media to act as its eyes and ears about government. The information the public receives from the news media is indispensable in the public's ability to hold its leaders accountable. As such, the news media play a vital role in democratic processes. When the public pays little attention to the news, when it views the news as incredible and the news as noise rather than information, then this linkage that binds the governed and the governors together is weakened.

This new system also has important consequences for the president and his ability to lead the public. One may read from the previous comments that the president may be somewhat immunized from bad news. This is one way to read the Clinton example. But this new system is a double-edged sword for the president too. It also limits his ability to lead the public.[35] Rather than trying to build widespread support across a national mass public, in this new environment the president must build support a different way.

A smaller news audience means that the president can reach fewer people through the news media than he once could. Moreover, his ability to go public directly is undermined, as the audience for presidential addresses has declined.[36] As George Edwards argues, one of the barriers to presidential leadership is gaining public attention.[37] This barrier has always been in place, given the relatively low levels of public awareness and interest that polls have noted across the last 50 years. But the news system described here has raised the height of that barrier. First, presidents have increasing difficulty even getting the news media to pay attention to them, as the declines in news content indicate. And even when presidents make the front page and nightly news broadcast, stories are more likely to be about scandals and less likely to be about policy making than was the case several decades ago. Moreover, when the president wants to address the nation on prime time, the networks have been increasingly likely to deny his request, and sometimes when access is granted, only one of the

---

35. Robert E. DiClerico, "The Role of Media in Heightened Expectations and Diminished Leadership Capacity," in Richard W. Waterman, ed., *The Presidency Reconsidered* (Itasca, IL: F. E. Peacock, 1993), pp. 115–43.

36. Baum and Kernell, "Has Cable Ended the Golden Age of Television?," pp. 107–110; and Reed L. Welch, "Is Anybody Watching? The Audience for Televised Presidential Addresses," *Congress and the Presidency* 27 (Spring 2000): 41–58.

37. George C. Edwards, III, *On Deaf Ears: The Limits of the Bully Pulpit* (New Haven, CT: Yale University Press, 2003).

networks will broadcast the presidential address.[38] The lack of news attention by average citizens adds to the barrier between the president and the public.

In place of building public support through appealing to the public at large, the president engages in a more selective approach, targeting specific groups. We see this in the increase of public presidential speeches, but not to the nation as a whole. Usually presidents target friends, gunning up their enthusiasm for the president. Presidential opponents counter with appeals to opposition groups.

Neither the president nor his opponents have much incentive to moderate their rhetoric or policy proposals in such a system. The moderate middle of the public is effectively left out of the picture. Instead presidents and political elites in general try to mobilize already committed and loyal constituencies composed of people whose political beliefs tend to veer far from the middle. This system of leadership and opposition further polarizes an already-polarized politics.

Thus, while the new system may immunize presidents to some degree from negativity in the news, this new system also limits opportunities for presidential leadership. Great events, like September 11, that galvanize the public, must exist for presidents to lead the nation. Rather than being the nation's leader with one *national constituency*, presidents in this new system act more as the leader of *many constituencies*.

Democracy suffers in such a system. Presidents are to a degree uncoupled from the mass public but are tethered to special interests. The news media seem unable to act as a true watchdog for the reasons expressed here. The linkages once meant to bind governed and governors have come undone. And of course, the public feels increasingly dispossessed. The irony in all of this is that presidents may actually enjoy solid popularity levels. We may characterize this new system as "popularity without responsibility or accountability."

A CODA: HOW DID CLINTON SURVIVE 1998?

I opened this paper with the puzzle of how Bill Clinton's popularity could have risen while being pummeled with so much bad news emanating from a hostile press. This is only puzzling if we look at politics in the late 1990s as structurally similar to politics 25 years ago. It is not the same structurally.

Bill Clinton survived 1998, a scandal with a young White House intern and a congressional impeachment as well as uniformly bad press because

---

38. Joe S. Foote, *Television Access and Presidential Power: The Networks, the Presidency, and the "Loyal Opposition"* (New York: Praeger, 1990).

(1) much of the public was not paying much attention to what was going on, and (2) much of the public discounted what the press had to say about the president because the public had gotten use to the press knocking presidents. Bill Clinton's polls rose in part because of a good economy and in part because of a counterreaction of the public to the extreme negativity of the press.[39]

But it is also likely that Bill Clinton's public relations strategy, built on a system fully expressed by Ronald Reagan, had a role to play in explaining Clinton's rising polls. If the public refused to pay much attention to what the press said about the president, the public may have paid some attention to what the president had to say about himself. Clinton's public relations strategy was to emphasize his leadership and the effectiveness of his policies.

Unwittingly, the press may have enabled Clinton's strategy to reach the public by showing film of the president acting presidential and touting his accomplishments. In news stories, journalists would routinely comment on the "presidential strategy" in cynical terms. But if my ideas are correct, the public discounted, if not ignored, what the journalists had to say, instead absorbing some of the president's message. We did not see a groundswell of support behind the president; the audience was too small for that and many people's political attitudes were too hardened to change. But we did see a modest increase in presidential support across 1998. The president reached a modest number of people through his public relations campaign, driving up his polls. Ironically, despite access to a large audience, he might not have been able to do this in the golden age of broadcast television.

---

39. Samuel Popkin, "When the People Decline to be Spun," *New York Times,* November 10, 1998, p. A29.

PART V

The President
and the Government

10

⚜

What Is the Appropriate Role of Congress in National Security Policy?*

LOUIS FISHER
Congressional Research Service

ickey Edwards, who served as a Republican member of the House of Representatives from 1977 to 1993, was advised by one of his staff that it would be important for him to make a floor statement that defended the president's independent power to take the country to war. Edwards, seeing an opportunity to educate his aide, suggested that the speech would be more effective if he had a chart, to be mounted on an easel, that identified the constitutional language that gave the president this power. At a later point, an embarrassed aide returned to report to Edwards that the language did not exist.[1]

A friend of mine, who teaches at a law school, tells his students at a certain point in the semester to prepare for the following class by carefully reading Articles I and II of the Constitution, paying particular attention to provisions that allocate the powers over foreign affairs and war. The students expect to find, somewhere in Article II, language that vests those powers solely in the president. To their surprise, they discover that most of the powers over foreign affairs and war are granted to Congress under Article I.[2]

Why is there such a gap between what the Constitution provides and what many people believe? There has not always been this level of confusion and misconception. From 1789 to 1950, all three branches understood that the powers over foreign affairs and war had been placed primarily with

---

* The views expressed in this article are personal, not institutional, and do not reflect the views of the Congressional Research Service or the Library of Congress.

1. I heard this anecdote from Edwards, who served as a representative from Oklahoma.

2. The friend is Neal Devins, who teaches at the William and Mary School of Law.

members of Congress. It is only with the initiative by President Harry Truman in 1950, in taking the country to war against North Korea without receiving authority from Congress, that the scope of presidential power began to climb toward its current breadth. What accounts for this growth? What are the implications for democratic control, constitutional government, the rule of law, and individual freedoms? What fundamental changes have occurred with the system of checks and balances, the doctrine of separated powers, and the framers' radical experiment in creating a republican form of government?

THE FRAMERS' DESIGN

Had the framers wanted to concentrate foreign affairs and military actions in the president, they could have borrowed freely from the English model. The respected John Locke identified foreign affairs with the executive. He advocated three branches of government: legislative, executive, and "federative." The latter consisted of "the power of war and peace, leagues and alliances, and all the transactions with all persons and communities without the commonwealth." To Locke, the federative power (what we would today call foreign policy) was "always almost united" with the executive. Any effort to separate the executive and federative powers, he warned, would invite "disorder and ruin."[3]

William Blackstone, the distinguished 18th-century jurist, treated all of external affairs as part of the King's prerogative. He defined the prerogative as "those rights and capacities which the king enjoys alone." Some of those rights and capacities are "rooted in and spring from the king's political person," including the right to send and receive ambassadors and the power to make war or peace. Through the prerogative, the King could make "a treaty with a foreign state, which shall irrevocably bind the nation." He could issue letters of marque and reprisal (authorizing private citizens to undertake military actions). The King was "the generalissimo, or the first in military command," who possessed "the sole power of raising and regulating fleets and armies."[4]

The Constitution does not transfer a single one of those powers to the president. They are either assigned solely to Congress or granted to the president acting with the consent of the Senate. Article I gives to Congress, not the president, the powers to declare war, issue letters of marque and reprisal, and to raise and regulate the military. With the consent of the

---

3. John Locke, *Second Treatise on Civil Government* §§ 146–48 (1690).

4. William Blackstone, *Commentaries on the Laws of England* 238, 239, 251, 262 (1803 ed.).

Senate, the president can appoint ambassadors and enter into treaties. The president's power as commander in chief is carefully circumscribed. Vesting that power in the president, instead of a member of the military, preserves the important principle of civilian supremacy. As explained by Attorney General Edward Bates in 1861, the president is commander in chief not because he is "skilled in the art of war and qualified to marshal a host in the field of battle," but to underscore that whatever soldier leads a U.S. army to victory against an enemy, "he is subject to the orders of the civil magistrate, and he and his army are always 'subordinate to the civil power.'"[5] Also, placing the commander-in-chief power in the president assures that the command over military forces will be undivided and successful.[6]

The Constitution also vests in Congress the power to regulate foreign commerce, an area that Locke and Blackstone would have assigned to the executive. The framers understood the relationship between foreign commerce and the war power. Commercial conflicts between nations, they knew, often led to war. In a major case in 1824, Chief Justice John Marshall said that the commerce power—especially the decision to impose embargoes—"may be, and often is, used as an instrument of war."[7] Guided by history and newly fashioned principles of republican government, the framers placed the power over foreign commerce with Congress.

At the Philadelphia convention in 1787, the delegates clearly broke with English precedents that vested the war power and foreign affairs in the executive. Charles Pinckney said he was for "a vigorous Executive but was afraid the Executive powers of [the existing] Congress might extend to peace & war &c which would render the Executive a Monarchy, of the worst kind, towit an elective one." John Rutledge wanted the executive power placed in a single person, "tho' he was not for giving him the power of war and peace." James Wilson, stating his preference for a single executive, "did not consider the Prerogative of the British Monarch as a proper guide in defining the Executive powers. Some of these prerogatives were of a Legislative nature. Among others that of war & peace &c."[8]

The delegates at Philadelphia realized that the president needed certain defensive powers over war, but not offensive powers. An early draft of the Constitution empowered Congress to "make war." Pinckney objected that legislative proceedings "were too slow" for the safety of the country in an emergency, since he expected Congress to meet but once a year. James

---

5. 10 Ops. Att'y Gen. 74, 79 (1861) (emphasis in original).

6. *United States v. Sweeny,* 157 U.S. 281, 284 (1895).

7. *Gibbons v. Ogden,* 22 U.S. (9 Wheat.) 1, 192 (1824).

8. Max Farrand, ed., *The Records of the Federal Convention of 1787,* vol. 1 (New Haven CT: Yale University Press, 1937), pp. 64–66.

Madison and Elbridge Gerry moved to insert "declare" for "make," leaving to the president "the power to repel sudden attacks." Their motion carried.[9] The duty to repel sudden attacks represented a limited power that enabled the president to respond to foreign attacks, either against the mainland of the United States or against American forces abroad. The president never received a general power to initiate war against other nations.

Reactions to the Madison–Gerry amendment illustrate the narrow grant of authority to the president. Pierce Butler wanted to give the president the power to make war, arguing that he "will have all the requisite qualities, and will not make war but when the Nation will support it." Roger Sherman objected: "The Executive shd. be able to repel and not to commence war." Gerry said he "never expected to hear in a republic a motion to empower the Executive alone to declare war." George Mason spoke "agst giving the power of war to the Executive, because not <safely> to be trusted with it; . . . He was for clogging rather than facilitating war."[10]

Delegates to the state ratifying conventions expressed similar views. In Pennsylvania, James Wilson told his colleagues that the system of checks and balances "will not hurry us into war; it is calculated to guard against it. It will not be in the power of a single man, or a single body of men, to involve us in such distress; for the important power of declaring war is vested in the legislature at large."[11] In North Carolina, James Iredell compared the limited powers of the president with those of the British monarch. The King of Great Britain was not only the commander in chief "but has power, in time of war, to raise fleets and armies. He has also authority to declare war." In sharp contrast, the president "has not the power of declaring war by his own authority, nor that of raising fleets or armies. These powers are vested in other hands."[12]

The framers restricted the president's power to go to war because they were creating a republican form of government and knew from history the dangers of unchecked executive power. They believed that presidents, in their search for fame and personal glory, would have an appetite for war.[13] John Jay warned in Federalist No. 4 that "absolute monarchs will often make war when their nations are to get nothing by it, but for purposes and

---

9. Ibid., vol. 2, pp. 318–19.

10. Ibid.

11. Jonathan Elliot, ed., *The Debates in the Several State Conventions, on the Adoption of the Federal Constitution*, vol. 2, (Washington, DC: 1836–45), p. 528.

12. Ibid., vol. 4, page 107. See also the comments of Charles Pinckney in South Carolina; ibid., vol. 4, p. 287.

13. William Michael Treanor, "Fame, the Founding, and the Power to Declare War," *Cornell Law Review* 82 (1997): 695.

objects merely personal, such as a thirst for military glory, revenge for personal affronts, ambition, or private compacts to aggrandize or support their particular families or partisans. These and a variety of other motives, which affect only the mind of the sovereign, often lead him to engage in wars not sanctified by justice or the voice and interests of the people."[14]

Madison expressed many of these values in his writings. In 1793, he called war "the true nurse of executive aggrandizement.... In war, the honours and emoluments of office are to be multiplied; and it is the executive patronage under which they are to be enjoyed. It is in war, finally, that laurels are to be gathered; and it is the executive brow they are to encircle. The strongest passions and most dangerous weaknesses of the human breast; ambition, avarice, vanity, the honourable or venial love of fame, are all in conspiracy against the desire and duty of peace."[15] Writing to Thomas Jefferson five years later, Madison said that the Constitution "supposes, what the History of all Govts demonstrates, that the Ex. is the branch of power most interested in war, & most prone to it. It has accordingly with studied care, vested the question of war in the Legisl."[16]

Joseph Story, who served on the Supreme Court from 1811 to 1845, explained why fundamental republican principles vested in Congress the decision to go to war:

> The power of declaring war is not only the highest sovereign prerogative; ... it is in its own nature and effects so critical and calamitous, that it requires the utmost deliberation, and the successive review of all the councils of the nations. War, in its best estate, never fails to impose upon the people the most burthensome taxes, and personal sufferings. It is always injurious, and sometimes subversive of the great commercial, manufacturing, and agricultural interests. Nay, it always involves the prosperity, and not infrequently the existence, of a nation. It is sometimes fatal to public liberty itself, by introducing a spirit of military glory, which is ready to follow, wherever a successful commander will lead; ... It should therefore be difficult in a republic to declare war; but not to make peace.... The cooperation of all the branches of the legislative power ought, upon principle, to be required in this the highest act of legislation.[17]

---

14. Benjamin Fletcher Wright, ed., *The Federalist* (Cambridge, MA: Harvard University Press, 1961), p. 101.

15. Gaillard Hunt, ed., *The Writings of James Madison (1900–1910),* vol. 6 (1906), p. 174.

16. Ibid., p. 312.

17. Joseph Story, *Commentaries on the Constitution of the United States,* vol. 3 (1833 ed.), pp. 60–61.

For the first century and a half, presidential use of force closely conformed to the expectations of the framers. The decision to go to war against other nations was reserved to Congress. Presidents accepted that principle for all wars: declared or undeclared. The president's latitude was confined to certain defensive operations and to relatively small uses of military force.

THE CONSTITUTION AS APPLIED

The first exercise of the Commander-in-Chief Clause involved actions by President George Washington against certain Indian tribes. Those actions were explicitly authorized by Congress. Legislation enacted on September 29, 1789, anticipated the protection of inhabitants "of the frontiers of the United States from the hostile incursions of the Indians." To provide that protection, Congress authorized the president "to call into service from time to time, such part of the militia of the states respectively, as he may judge necessary for the purpose aforesaid."[18] Washington and his executive officers understood that military operations against Indians were limited to defensive actions, and that anything of an offensive nature would have to await congressional authorization.[19] Washington's military action against the Whiskey Rebellion of 1794 faithfully followed the procedures set forth in a congressional statute.[20]

When President John Adams decided it was necessary to use military force against France in 1798, he never argued that he could act on his own. He presented the matter to Congress and asked for legislative authority.[21] Presidents Jefferson and Madison sought legislative authority from Congress before acting militarily against the Barbary pirates.[22] Jefferson took certain initiatives in the Mediterranean to protect U.S. vessels against attacks from Tripoli but told Congress afterward that he was "unauthorized by the Constitution, without the sanctions of Congress, to go beyond the line of defense." It was up to Congress to authorize "measures of offense also."[23] In 1805, he notified Congress about tension between the United States and

---

18. 1 Stat. 96, sec. 5 (1789). See also 1 Stat. 121, sec. 16 (1790); 1 Stat. 222 (1791).

19. Louis Fisher, *Presidential War Power* (Lawrence: University Press of Kansas, 2004), pp. 18–19.

20. Ibid., pp. 22–23.

21. Ibid., pp. 23–24.

22. Ibid., pp. 35–36.

23. James D. Richardson, ed., *A Compilation of the Messages and Papers of the Presidents,* vol. 1 (New York: Bureau of National Literature, 1897–1920), p. 315 (hereafter Richardson).

Spain, acknowledging that "Congress alone is constitutionally invested the power of changing our condition from peace to war."[24]

Other statements made during this period by lawmakers, presidents, and federal courts reflect this understanding. In 1806, a federal appellate court reviewed a Neutrality Act violation by someone who claimed that his military enterprise "was begun, prepared, and set on foot with the knowledge and approbation of the executive department of our government."[25] The court rejected the idea that executive officials—even the president—could somehow waive the provisions of the Neutrality Act. The court asked: "Does [the president] possess the power of making war? That power is exclusively vested in congress. . . . [I]t is the exclusive province of congress to change a state of peace into a state of war."[26]

When presidents had to seek an increase in army and naval forces from Congress, the legislative branch had a decisive advantage. Once a semblance of a standing army existed, presidents could move troops to disputed areas and provoke a military confrontation, as President James Polk did with Mexico. He told Congress that "war exists." It was up to Congress, however, to decide whether war with Mexico was necessary or desirable. Polk had to await legislative deliberations and decisions. Congress could have decided that hostilities, not war, existed, and that the hostilities could be remedied with measures that fell short of war. In the end, Congress recognized that "a state of war exists."[27]

President Abraham Lincoln took many decisive initiatives after the outbreak of Civil War. He issued proclamations calling forth the state militia, suspending the writ of habeas corpus, and placing a blockade on the rebellious states. He had genuine doubts about the legality of his actions, advising Congress upon its return that his actions, "whether strictly legal or not, were ventured upon under what appeared to be a popular demand and a public necessity, trusting then, as now, that Congress would readily ratify them."[28] He conceded that his actions probably stepped over the line and invaded legislative prerogatives. As he put it, the emergency orders (especially suspending the writ) were not "beyond the constitutional competency of Congress."[29] Congress passed legislation "approving, legalizing, and making valid all the acts, proclamations, and orders of the President, etc., as

24. *Annals of Cong.*, 9th Cong., 1st Sess. (1805), p. 19.

25. *United States v. Smith*, 27 Fed. Cas. 1192, 1229 (C.C.N.Y. 1806) (No. 16,342).

26. Ibid., p. 1230.

27. 9 Stat. 9 (1846); see Fisher, *Presidential War Power*, pp. 39–44.

28. Richardson, vol. 7, p. 3225.

29. Ibid.

if they had been issued and done under the previous express authority and direction of the Congress of the United States."[30] During congressional debate, it was clear that lawmakers concluded that Lincoln's actions, standing alone, were illegal.[31]

The Supreme Court upheld Lincoln's blockade in 1863. Justice Robert Grier said that the president as commander in chief had no power to initiate war but when faced with foreign invasion or internal insurrection was "bound to resist force by force."[32] Such actions were well within the president's defensive, not offensive, duties. The president "has no power to initiate or declare a war against either a foreign nation or a domestic State."[33] Richard Henry Dana, Jr., serving as legal counsel for Lincoln, used the same language when addressing the Court. Lincoln's actions had nothing to do with "the right *to initiate a war, as a voluntary act of sovereignty.* That is vested only in Congress."[34]

Toward the end of the 19th century, the executive branch again recognized that the power of taking the country to war against another nation lay with Congress, not the president. England had called upon the United States to supply naval forces in a military action against China. In a case before the Supreme Court, it was understood that offensive operations required congressional authority: "As this proposition involved a participation in existing hostilities, the request could not be acceded to, and the Secretary of State in his communication to the English government explained that the warmaking power of the United States was not vested in the President but in Congress, and that he had no authority, therefore, to order aggressive hostilities to be undertaken."[35]

Congress declared or authorized all of the major wars over the first century and a half: the Quasi-War against France in 1798, the Barbary Wars, the War of 1812 against England, the Mexican War, the Spanish–American War, and World Wars I and II. On a number of other occasions, presidents used military force without seeking authority from Congress, but as constitutional scholar Edward S. Corwin explained, the list of these incidents largely covered "fights with pirates, landings of small naval contingents on barbarous or semi-barbarous coasts, the dispatch of small bodies of troops to chase bandits or cattle rustlers across the Mexican border, and the like."[36]

---

30. 12 Stat. 326 (1861).

31. *Cong. Globe,* 37th Cong., 1st Sess (1861), p. 393 (Senator Howe).

32. *The Prize Cases,* 67 U.S. 635, 668 (1863).

33. Ibid.

34. Ibid., p. 660 (emphasis in original).

35. *The Chinese Exclusion Case,* 130 U.S. 581, 591 (1889).

36. Edward S. Corwin, "The President's Power," *New Republic* (January 9, 1951): 16.

THE *CURTISS-WRIGHT* CASE

The current scope of presidential power over foreign affairs owes much to a case decided by the Supreme Court in 1936, *United States* v. *Curtiss-Wright Corp.* The Court was asked to decide whether Congress had delegated too broadly when it empowered the president to declare an arms embargo in South America. The statute allowed the president to impose an arms embargo whenever he found that it "may contribute to the establishment of peace" between belligerents. The scope of independent presidential power was never at stake. Rather, the question before the Court was whether *Congress,* in determining the extent of *its* power, had granted the president too much discretion.

Nevertheless, the author of *Curtiss-Wright,* Justice George Sutherland, decided to highlight the president's independent powers. He said that the president "*makes* treaties with the advice and consent of the Senate; but he alone negotiates. Into the field of negotiation the Senate cannot intrude; and Congress itself is powerless to invade it."[37] Clearly the case had nothing to do with the treaty power or the president's capacity to negotiate without Congress. The case involved the extent to which Congress, *by statute,* could direct and empower the president to monitor military threats abroad.

Sutherland spoke about "this vast external realm, with its important, complicated, delicate and manifold problems." As a consequence, he said, legislation over the international field must often accord to the president "a degree of discretion and freedom from statutory restrictions which would not be admissible were domestic affairs alone involved."[38] That is all that the Court needed to do: recognize that *Congress* could delegate *its powers* more broadly in foreign affairs than in domestic affairs. Yet Sutherland went further, straying from statutory grants of authority to inherent presidential power. He claimed that the exercise of presidential power does not depend solely on an act of Congress because of the "very delicate, plenary and exclusive power of the President as the sole organ of the federal government in the field of international relations."[39] That issue was never before the Court, never briefed, and never argued.

Sutherland's flowery language consisted of pure dicta: extraneous matter that had nothing to do with the legal dispute before the Court. As Justice Jackson later observed in the Steel Seizure Case of 1952, the most that can be drawn from *Curtiss-Wright* is the intimation that the president "might act in external affairs without congressional authority, but not that he might act contrary to an act of Congress."[40] Jackson noted that "much of the

---

37. 299 U.S. 304, 319 (1936) (emphasis in original).

38. Ibid., pp. 319, 320.

39. Ibid., p. 320.

40. *Youngstown Co. v. Sawyer,* 343 U.S. 579, 636 n. 2 (1952).

[Sutherland] opinion is dictum."[41] In 1981, a federal appellate court cautioned against placing undue reliance on "certain dicta" in Sutherland's opinion: "To the extent that denominating the President as the 'sole organ' of the United States in international affairs constitutes a blanket endorsement of plenary Presidential power over any matter extending beyond the borders of this country, we reject that characterization."[42]

What is meant by "sole organ"? It seems to suggest that when it comes to foreign policy, the president is the exclusive policymaker. The term carries special weight because it appears in a speech given by John Marshall in 1800 when he served in the House of Representatives. Given his elevation a year later to the position as Chief Justice of the Supreme Court, and Marshall's dominant position in the history and development of constitutional law, Sutherland appeared to draw from an impeccable, authoritative source. In fact, Sutherland took Marshall's statement wholly out of context to argue for a position that Marshall never took. At no time, in 1800 or in any other period, did Marshall suggest that the president possessed exclusive and unreviewable power to make foreign policy.

During the debate in 1800, some House members objected to the decision by President John Adams to turn over to England someone charged with murder in an American court. These lawmakers thought that Adams should be impeached and removed from office because he had encroached on the judiciary and violated the doctrine of separation of powers. It was at that point that Marshall took to the floor to deny that there was any basis for impeachment. Adams returned the individual to England to carry out an extradition treaty that the United States and England had agreed to. Adams wasn't making foreign policy single-handedly. He was carrying into effect a policy made jointly by the president and the Senate through the treaty process. Only after foreign policy had been made to reflect the collective judgment of the executive and legislative branches, either by treaty or by statute, did the president become the "sole organ" of the nation. Here is Marshall's full sentence: The president "is the sole organ of the nation in its external relations and its sole representative with foreign nations."[43] After the two branches make policy, the president announces and implements it. It was only in that sense that Marshall called the president the "sole organ."

There are other problems with Sutherland's opinion. He argued that foreign and domestic affairs are different "both in respect of their origin and their nature" because the powers of external sovereignty "passed from the

---

41. Ibid.

42. *American Intern. Group v. Islamic Republic of Iran,* 657 F.2d 430, 438 n. 6 (D.C. Cir. 1981).

43. *Annals of Congress,* 6th Cong. (1880), p. 613.

Crown not to the colonies severally, but to the colonies in their collective and corporate capacity as the United States of America."[44] This was poor history. External sovereignty did not bypass the colonies and the states and come directly to an independent executive. At the time of independence in 1776, there was no president and no separate executive branch. All of the national powers were vested in a single branch: the Continental Congress, which carried out legislative, judicial, and executive duties. Moreover, the states in 1776 operated as sovereign bodies rather than as parts of a collective body. The creation of the Continental Congress did not disrupt the sovereign power of the states to make treaties, borrow money, solicit arms, lay embargoes, collect tariff duties, and conduct separate military campaigns.[45] When the American colonies broke with England, they acquired certain elements of sovereignty.[46]

After the power of external sovereignty passed from the English Crown to the United States, it did not reside only in the presidency. The Constitution allocates the sovereign power both to Congress and the president. The treaty power belongs to the president and the Senate. The president receives ambassadors from other countries, but the Senate must approve U.S. ambassadors. Congress has the power to declare war, raise and support the military forces, make rules for their regulation, and provide for the calling up of the militia to suppress insurrections and repel invasions. The Constitution empowers Congress to lay and collect duties on foreign trade, regulate commerce with foreign countries, and establish a uniform rule of naturalization.

Throughout U.S. history, there has been difficulty in drawing a crisp line between foreign and domestic affairs. Scholars have written on the substantial overlap between these two domains.[47] In 1991, President George H. W. Bush remarked: "I guess my bottom line . . . is you can't separate foreign policy from domestic."[48] Two years later President Clinton made the same observation: "There is no longer a clear division between what is foreign and what is domestic."[49] For both constitutional and practical reasons, it makes

---

44. 299 U.S. 315–16.

45. Charles Lofgren, "United States v. Curtiss-Wright Export Corporation: An Historical Reassessment," *Yale Law Journal* 83 (1973): 1; David M. Levitan, "The Foreign Relations Power: An Analysis of Mr. Justice Sutherland's Theory," *Yale Law Journal* 55 (1946): 467; Claude H. Van Tyne, "Sovereignty in the American Revolution: An Historical Study, *American Historical Review* 12 (1907): 529.

46. *United States v. California,* 332 U.S. 19, 31 (1947); *Texas v. White,* 74 U.S. 700, 725 (1869).

47. Bayless Manning, "The Congress, the Executive and 'Intermestic' Affairs: Three Proposals," *Foreign Affairs* 55 (1977): 306.

48. *Public Papers of the Presidents, 1991,* II, p. 1629.

49. *Public Papers of the Presidents, 1993,* I, p. 2.

no sense to argue that either Congress or the president exercise exclusive power over foreign affairs. For the most part they must act jointly and develop a consensus.

Notwithstanding the historical and conceptual errors in Sutherland's opinion, *Curtiss-Wright* has become a popular citation for Court decisions and academic writings that argue in favor of broad presidential powers. The case is frequently cited to support not only broad delegations of legislative power to the president but even the existence of independent, implied, inherent, and exclusive powers for the president.[50]

TRUMAN'S INITIATIVE IN KOREA

A major contribution to unilateral presidential power in military affairs is the decision by President Harry Truman to take the country to war against North Korea. At no time, either before or after, did he come to Congress for statutory authority. On June 26, 1950, he announced to the American public that he had conferred with the secretaries of state and defense, their senior advisers, and the Joint Chiefs of Staff to discuss the problem of North Korea crossing over the 38th parallel into the territory of South Korea. He said that a resolution adopted by the United Nations Security Council ordered North Korea to withdraw its forces.[51] At that point he made no reference to the commitment of U.S. military forces.

The next day, Truman announced that North Korea had failed to cease hostilities and withdraw its forces, and that a Security Council resolution "called upon all members of the United Nations to render every assistance to the United Nations in the execution of this resolution. In these circumstances I have ordered United States air and sea forces to give the [South] Korean Government cover and support."[52] Over the coming months, Truman continued to send additional U.S. forces, calling the military operations "a police action under the United Nations."[53] How could a resolution of the Security Council become a substitute for congressional authority?

---

50. For broad delegation arguments, see *Ex parte Endo*, 323 U.S. 283, 298 n.21(1944), *Zemel v. Rusk*, 381 U.S. 1, 17 (1965), and *Goldwater v. Carter*, 444 U.S. 996, 1000 n.1 (1979). Inherent powers are discussed in *United States v. Pink*, 315 U.S. 203, 229 (1942), *Knauff v. Shaughnessy*, 338 U.S. 537, 542 (1950), *United States v. Mazurie*, 419 U.S. 544, 566–67 (1975), and *Dames & Moore v. Regan*, 453 U.S. 654, 661 (1982).

51. *Public Papers of the Presidents, 1950*, p. 491.

52. Ibid. p. 492.

53. Ibid., p. 504.

The Senate passed the UN Charter in 1945 to create an international organization capable of keeping the peace. Chapter VII of the Charter dealt with UN responses to threats to peace, breaches of the peace, and acts of aggression. It established procedures to permit the United Nations to employ military force to deal with these threats. All UN members would make available to the Security Council, "on its call and in accordance with a special agreement or agreements," armed forces and other assistance for the purpose of maintaining international peace and security. The agreements, concluded between the Security Council and member states, "shall be subject to ratification by these signatory states in accordance with their respective constitutional processes." Thus, each nation would have to decide under its constitutional system the manner in which political institutions would ratify these agreements.

During Senate debate, it was understood that these agreements would require some kind of advance legislative approval. There was sharp opposition to the idea that approval would be needed only from the Senate. Constitutional passages were discussed to demonstrate that the powers to raise and support armies, declare war, and appropriate funds for the military belonged to both Houses of Congress.[54] Truman, who was in Potsdam during the debate, wired a note to Senator Kenneth McKellar (D–Tenn.) on July 27, 1945, in which he pledged: "When any such agreement or agreements are negotiated it will be my purpose to ask the Congress for appropriate legislation to approve them."[55] By "Congress," the senators understood that approval would have to come from both Houses.[56] With that understanding, the Senate approved the UN Charter by a vote of 89 to 2.[57]

Congress then passed legislation to set forth the procedures to implement military action under the United Nations. Section 6 of the UN Participation Act of 1945 requires that the agreements "shall be subject to the approval of the Congress by appropriate Act or joint resolution."[58] Statutory language could not be more clear. The president would have to seek approval from both Houses in advance. Amendments to the UN Participation Act in 1949 placed specific restrictions on presidential power. The amendments allowed the president, on his own initiative, to provide military forces to the United Nations for "cooperative action," but the forces could serve only as observers and guards, perform only in a noncombatant capacity, and not exceed 1,000 in number.[59] Neither in the UN Participation Act nor its amendments in

---

54. 91 *Cong. Rec.* 8021–24 (1945).

55. Ibid., p. 8185.

56. Ibid. (Senator Donnell).

57. Ibid., p. 8190.

58. 59 Stat. 621, sec. 6 (1945).

59. 63 Stat. 735–36, sec. 5 (1949).

1949 was there any opportunity for the president to engage unilaterally in large-scale military actions.

Yet five years after the UN Participation Act and one year after the clarifying amendments, Truman went to war on his own under the UN banner. How could Truman act in this manner? The short answer is that he ignored the procedure for special agreements that was the mechanism for assuring congressional control. No special agreement was drawn up in 1950, and there has been no special agreement at any other time. Truman gave consideration to presenting a joint resolution to Congress, to permit lawmakers to voice their approval, but the draft resolution never left the administration.[60]

In the years since the Korean War, presidents have several times sought approval from the UN Security Council—rather than Congress—for military actions. Under the urging of President George H. W. Bush, the Security Council on November 29, 1990, passed a resolution authorizing member states to use "all necessary means" to force Iraqi troops out of Kuwait. The phrase "all necessary means" is diplomatic talk for military force. Bush and his top executive advisers believed that the UN resolution was sufficient legal authority and that it was not necessary to seek approval from Congress. Only at the eleventh hour, in January 1991, did Bush come to Congress for authority and then argued, after it was granted, that he could have acted without Congress.[61]

In 1994, President Bill Clinton obtained from the Security Council a resolution "inviting" all states, particularly those in the region of Haiti, to use "all necessary means" to remove the military leadership on that island. Clinton never sought authority from Congress to invade Haiti. He announced: "Like my predecessors of both parties, I have not agreed that I was constitutionally mandated to obtain the support of Congress."[62] Also in 1994, Clinton relied on Security Council resolutions and NATO decisions to conduct air strikes in Bosnia against the Serbs. When the Security Council refused to grant authority for a war against Yugoslavia, Clinton relied solely on NATO. He never sought authority from Congress.[63]

Through these precedents, the UN Security Council and mutual security pacts (such as NATO) have become substitutes for congressional authority. The UN Charter and NATO are treaties entered into by the president and the Senate. One would be hard-pressed to argue, at least in a convincing

---

60. *Foreign Relations of the United States, 1950*, vol. 7, pp. 282–83, nn. 1 and 2; 287–91 (Washington, DC: Government Printing Office, 1976). See Louis Fisher, "The Korean War: On What Legal Basis Did Truman Act?" *American Journal of International Law* 89 (1995): 21.

61. Fisher, *Presidential War Power*, pp. 169–72.

62. *Public Papers of the Presidents, 1994*, II, at 1419.

63. Fisher, *Presidential War Power*, pp. 183–86, 198–201.

manner, that a treaty can strip the House of Representatives of its war powers under the Constitution. Yet that has been the result, and neither the House nor the Senate have mounted a counterattack to protect their prerogatives.[64] Instead, congressional leaders regularly side with presidential power instead of protecting the constitutional interests of the legislative branch.

CONGRESSIONAL ACQUIESCENCE

When President Truman decided to use military force against North Korea, lawmakers offered little resistance. Senator James P. Kem (R–Mo.) responded to Truman's initiative by asking: "Does that mean that he has arrogated to himself the authority of declaring war?" Senate Majority Leader Scott Lucas replied: "I do not care to debate that question. . . . I do not believe that it means war but the Senator can place his own interpretation on it." When Kem persisted, asking Lucas to identify on what legal or constitutional authority a president could mount an armed attack, Lucas stated that "history will show that on more than 100 occasions in the life of this Republic the President as Commander in Chief has ordered the fleet or the troops to do certain things which involved the risk of war."[65] However, none of the incidents referred to by Lucas approached the magnitude of the Korean War.

Senator Leverett Saltonstall (R–Mass.), the minority whip, came to Truman's support, remarking that "it seems to me the responsibility of the President of the United States to protect the security of the United States." What was the constitutional responsibility of Congress? Senator Arthur Watkins (R–Utah) asked why Truman failed to notify Congress first, drawing this response from Lucas: "I am willing to leave what has been done in the hands of the Commander in Chief."[66] It would be difficult to craft a more pure form of legislative abdication. To Senator George Malone (R–Nev.), the Constitution "leaves determinations of foreign policy to the President."[67] One of the few lawmakers to challenge Truman's legal authority was Representative Vito Marcantonio, a member of the American Labor Party from New York. He denied that a president could rely on a Security Council resolution: "[W]hen we agreed to the United Nations Charter we never agreed to supplant our Constitution with the United Nations Charter."[68]

---

64. Louis Fisher, "Sidestepping Congress: Presidents Acting under the UN and NATO," *Case Western Reserve Law Review* 47 (1997): 1237.

65. 96 *Cong. Rec.* 9228–29 (1950).

66. Ibid., p. 9229.

67. Ibid., p. 9240.

68. Ibid., p. 9268.

Some lawmakers advised Truman that he could use military force against another country without coming to Congress. For example, Senator Lucas saw no need for Congress to authorize the intervention in Korea.[69] When Truman asked congressional leaders on July 3, 1950, whether he should submit a joint resolution to Congress seeking legislative authority, Lucas argued against that choice.[70] That is an interesting comment by a Senate majority leader, but nothing Lucas or Truman could say in private or public could alter the text and intent of the Constitution, the UN Charter, or the UN Participation Act.

In 1995, when President Clinton planned to send 20,000 American troops to Bosnia, Congress actively debated whether to adopt legislative restraints. Much would turn on the position taken by Bob Dole, the Senate majority leader. He made it clear that legislative prerogatives were no match for presidential decisions, saying that Clinton had "the authority and the power under the Constitution to do what he feels should be done regardless of what Congress does."[71] All that mattered was what a president *felt* should be done. There was no need to cite constitutional or statutory authority. And it mattered not what Congress did, according to Dole. Instead of examining legislative prerogatives or exerting leadership, he looked to public opinion: "We need to find some way to be able to support the President and I think we need to wait and see what the American reaction is."[72] In an interview with CBS News, Dole remarked: "No doubt about it, whether Congress agrees or not, troops will go to Bosnia."[73]

Representative James B. Longley (R-Maine), having announced that it would be a "terrible mistake" to put U.S. ground troops in Bosnia, nonetheless deferred to Clinton: "I have to respect the authority of the Commander in Chief to conduct foreign policy. . . . I think there is no greater threat to American lives than a Congress that attempts to micromanage foreign policy."[74] Respect for the president is warranted, but there is a greater need for lawmakers to respect the Constitution, their prerogatives, and the system of checks and balances. Also, the deployment of 20,000 ground troops to

---

69. Robert F. Turner, "Truman, Korea, and the Constitution: Debunking the 'Imperial President' Myth," *Harvard Journal of Law & Public Policy* 19 (1996): 574.

70. Louis Fisher, *Congressional Abdication on War and Spending* (College Station: Texas A&M University Press, 2000), p. 45.

71. 141 *Cong. Rec.* S17529 (daily ed., November 27, 1995).

72. "As Dole Equivocates on Troop Deployment, Most GOP Rivals Oppose Plan," *Washington Post,* November 28, 1995, p. A9.

73. "U.S. Troops Vital to Bosnia Peace, Clinton Says," *Washington Post,* November 28, 1995, p. A1.

74. 141 *Cong. Rec.* 33835 (1995).

Bosnia did not represent an issue of micromanagement. It marked a fundamental national commitment of funds and armed forces to a dangerous region, a decision that called for legislative action. Finally, congressional participation was not a "threat to American lives." The lives of American soldiers are threatened when a president decides to put them in harm's way.

Hearing these statements of legislative abdication, Representative David Skaggs (D-Colo.) rebuked both Clinton and Congress for violating the war power provisions of the Constitution. Clinton, he said, "acted in violation of the Constitution in ordering these attacks without authority of Congress." The decision to go to war "is vested in Congress and not in the Commander in Chief." Lawmakers shared the blame for violating the Constitution: "We have time and again defaulted in our responsibility and obligation to insist on our proper constitutional role."[75]

The War Powers Resolution of 1973 represents what many regard as a serious legislative effort to reassert congressional prerogatives. The statute claims as its purpose an attempt "to fulfill the intent of the framers of the Constitution of the United States and insure that the collective judgment of both the Congress and the President will apply to the introduction of United States Armed Forces into hostilities, or into situations where imminent involvement in hostilities is clearly indicated by the circumstances, and to the continued use of such forces in hostilities or in such situations."[76] In truth, the statute neither fulfills the framers' intent nor does it ensure collective judgment of the branches.

First, the statute recognizes that the president on his own can use military force against other nations for up to 60 days (with an extension up to 90 days) at whatever time and for whatever reason. The framers would have been astonished at that grant of power. Second, there is no requirement for collective judgment during that period. The statute merely requires that the president "in every possible instance" consult with Congress before introducing troops into hostilities,[77] and to submit a report to Congress within 48 hours.[78] For the clock to begin to tick for the 60- to 90-day period, the President needs to report under Section 4(a)(1), but presidents regularly report in a more general manner ("consistent with" the War Powers Resolution). Thus, it is uncertain what happens if a president's military commitment were to exceed 90 days.

The bill that cleared the Senate was fairly restrictive on presidential wars, but the House endorsed a weaker version. When the bill emerged

---

75. 144 *Cong. Rec.* H11727 (daily ed., December 17, 1998).

76. 87 Stat. 555, sec. 2(a) (1973).

77. Ibid., sec. 3.

78. Ibid., sec. 4.

from conference committee, a number of lawmakers who had supported the War Powers Resolution now voiced their opposition. Senator Tom Eagleton (D-Mo.), a principal sponsor of the resolution, denounced the conference bill as a "total, complete distortion of the war powers concept."[79] The bill, he pointed out, gave the president "carte blanche" authority to use military force for up to 90 days, constituting a startling surrender of legislative prerogatives. Eagleton said that the bill, after being nobly conceived, "has been horribly bastardized to the point of being a menace."[80]

The bill survived a veto by President Richard Nixon. The Senate margin on the override vote was substantial (75 to 18), but the House narrowly gathered the two-thirds margin (284 to 135). How the House managed the override is significant. Fifteen members of the House had voted against the House bill and the conference version because it gave the president too much power. To be consistent, they should have voted to sustain the veto to prevent the bill from being law. Yet they voted for the override for a variety of reasons, some of them related to the move to impeach Nixon.[81] Thus, a key group of House members decided that the short-term effort to discredit or remove Nixon was more important than the long-term interest of maintaining legislative prerogatives and protecting the Constitution.

MILITARY ACTIONS
AFTER SEPTEMBER 11

On September 11, 2001, terrorists from the Middle East hijacked four U.S. commercial airliners, flying two into the World Trade Center with the loss of almost 3,000 people. Another plane crashed into the Pentagon. The fourth, apparently destined for the White House or the Capitol, was forced down by passengers in rural Pennsylvania, killing all aboard. Two days later, President George W. Bush issued a proclamation that called the terrorist attacks "acts of war."[82]

As military responses, Bush went to war against Afghanistan and Iraq, coming to Congress both times for statutory authority. The Use of Force Act, which passed Congress on September 14, was directed against the Taliban and al Qaeda terrorist structures in Afghanistan. It passed the Senate 98 to 0 and the House 420 to 1. The statute authorized the president to use "all necessary

---

79. 119 *Cong. Rec.* 36177 (1973).

80. Ibid., p. 36178.

81. Fisher, *Presidential War Power,* p. 147.

82. *Weekly Compilation of Presidential Document,* vol. 37, p. 1308.

and appropriate force against those nations, organizations, or persons he determines planned, authorized, committed or aided" the September 11 attacks.[83] In a speech to Congress on September 20, Bush issued an ultimatum to the Taliban: "Deliver to United States authorities all the leaders of al Qaeda who hide in your land" and close the terrorist training camps.[84]

The Taliban rejected those conditions, leading to U.S. military action. When Bush reported to Congress on his planned combat operation, he referred to the Use of Force Act as "support," not authority, relying instead on his "constitutional authority to conduct U.S foreign relations as Commander in Chief and Chief Executive."[85] Military action against Afghanistan drew broad support from the American public and other nations. The rapid military victory was followed with guerrilla tactics by the surviving remnants of the Taliban and al Qaeda, producing a pattern that would reappear in Iraq.

The Iraq Resolution, which passed Congress in October 2002, granted Bush authority to use "the Armed Forces of the United States as he determines to be necessary and appropriate in order to (1) defend the national security of the United States against the continuing threat posed by Iraq; and (2) enforce all relevant United Nations Security Council resolutions regarding Iraq."[86] In signing the legislation, Bush referred to it as a "resolution of support" only, explaining: "While I appreciate receiving that support, my request for it did not, and my signing this resolution does not, constitute any change in the long-standing positions of the executive branch on either the President's constitutional authority to use force to deter, prevent, or respond to aggression or other threats to U.S. interests or on the constitutionality of the War Powers Resolution."[87]

Unlike the military operations against Afghanistan, the Iraq Resolution triggered substantial opposition in Congress, the American public, and the international community. The Bush administration, finding it difficult to present a credible and consistent argument for war, regularly indulged in exaggeration and loose claims. The meaning of "regime change" varied over time. On April 4, 2002, Bush said he made up his mind "that Saddam needs to go."[88] He stated the same position on August 1.[89] Yet when he appeared at the United Nations on September 12, he set forth five conditions for a

---

83. 115 Stat. 224 (2001).

84. *Weekly Compilation of Presidential Documents,* vol. 38, p. 1348.

85. Ibid., pp. 1447–48.

86. 116 Stat. 1501, sec. 3 (2002).

87. *Weekly Compilation of Presidential Documents,* vol. 38, p. 1779.

88. Ibid., p. 573.

89. Ibid., p. 1295.

peaceful resolution. If Iraq complied with the five demands, Saddam Hussein could stay in power.[90] On October 21, after Congress had passed the Iraq Resolution, Bush again said that Hussein could stay. If Hussein complied with every UN mandate, "that in itself will signal the regime has changed."[91]

After the September 12 UN speech, Iraq agreed to unconditional inspections. Having requested this level of cooperation, the Bush administration now began to make light of inspections. Pentagon spokeswoman Victoria Clarke warned that inspections would be difficult, if not impossible to carry out.[92] If that were so, why have Bush go to the United Nations to place that demand on Iraq and international inspectors?

The administration made repeated efforts to establish a connection between Iraq and al Qaeda, but these claims could never be substantiated. On September 25, Bush stated that Saddam Hussein and al Qaeda "work in concert."[93] On the following day he said that the Iraqi regime "has long-standing and continuing ties to terrorist organizations, and there are Al Qaida terrorists inside Iraq."[94] White House spokesman Ari Fleischer tried to play down Bush's remark, saying he was talking about what he feared *could* occur."[95] Which was it? Did the ties and links exist, as Bush claimed, or were they merely future possibilities? News accounts in 2004 continued to dispute any operational ties between Iraq and al Qaeda.[96]

Following the vote on the Iraq Resolution, the Bush administration promoted a story about Mohamed Atta, the leader of the September 11 attacks, meeting with an Iraqi intelligence officer in Prague in April 2001. Czech President Vaclav Havel and the Czech intelligence service said that there was no evidence that the meeting ever took place. CIA Director George Tenet told Congress that his agency had no information that could confirm the meeting.[97] Subsequent news stories in 2003 and 2004 cast

---

90. Ibid., p. 1532.

91. David E. Sanger, "Bush Declares U.S. Is Using Diplomacy to Disarm Hussein," *New York Times,* October 22, 2002, p. A15.

92. Todd A. Purdum and David Firestone, "Chief U.N. Inspector Backs U.S., Demanding Full Iraq Disclosure," *New York Times,* October 5, 2002, p. A1.

93. *Weekly Compilation of Presidential Documents,* vol. 38, p. 1619.

94. Ibid., p. 1625.

95. Mike Allen, "Bush Asserts That Al Qaeda Has Links to Iraq's Hussein," *Washington Post,* September 26, 2002, p. A29.

96. Walter Pincus and Dana Milbank, "Al Qaeda-Hussein Link Is Dismissed," *Washington Post,* June 17, 2004, p. A1; Susan Jo Keller, "9/11 Panel Members Debate Qaeda-Iraq 'Tie,'" *New York Times,* June 21, 2004, p. A11.

97. James Risen, "Prague Discounts an Iraqi Meeting," *New York Times,* October 21, 2002, p. A1; James Risen, "How Politics and Rivalries Fed Suspicions of a Meeting," *New York Times,* October 21, 2002, p. A9; Peter S. Green, "Havel Denies Telephoning U.S. on Iraq Meeting," *New York Times,* October 23, 2002, p. A11.

doubt that the meeting ever occurred.[98] The 9/11 Commission concluded that "available evidence" does not support Atta's meeting with the Iraqi officer in Prague in April 2001.[99]

On September 7, 2002, President Bush cited a report by the International Atomic Energy Agency (IAEA) that the Iraqis were "6 months away from developing a weapon. I don't know what more evidence we need."[100] More evidence was needed because the report did not exist.[101] In an October 7 speech, Bush claimed that satellite photographs revealed that Saddam Hussein was "rebuilding facilities at sites that have been part of his nuclear program in the past."[102] Two hundred reporters visited the site, the Al Furat manufacturing facility, but could not substantiate the claim about a weapons program.[103] When the UN inspection teams reached Iraq in November 2002, they could find no evidence of a nuclear weapons program at Al Furat or anywhere else in Iraq.[104]

The Bush administration claimed that Iraq had bought aluminum tubes and planned to use them to enrich uranium to produce nuclear weapons. Specialists from UN inspection teams concluded that the specifications of the tubes were consistent with tubes used for rockets. The tubes could have been modified to serve as centrifuges for enriching uranium, but the modifications would have had to be substantial. Moreover, there was no evidence that Iraq had purchased materials needed for centrifuges, such as motors, metal caps, and special magnets.[105]

In his statement to the UN Security Council on February 5, 2003, as part of the effort to justify war, Secretary of State Colin Powell claimed that Iraq had mobile production facilities "used to make biological agents."[106]

---

98. James Risen, "Iraqi Agent Denies He Met 9/11 Hijacker in Prague before Attacks on the U.S.," *New York Times,* December 13, 2003, p. A8; James Risen, "No Evidence of Meeting with Iraqi," *New York Times,* June 17, 2004, p. A14.

99. *The 9/11 Commission Report* (New York: W. W. Norton, 2004), pp. 228–29.

100. *Weekly Compilation of Presidential Documents,* vol. 38, p. 1518.

101. Dana Milbank, "For Bush, Facts Are Malleable," *Washington Post,* October 22, 2002, pp. A1, A22.

102. *Weekly Compilation of Presidential Documents,* vol. 38, p. 1718.

103. John Burns, "Iraq Tour of Suspected Sites Gives Few Clues on Weapons," *New York Times,* October 13, 2002, p. A1.

104. "Nuclear Inspection Chiefs Reports Finding No New Weapons," *New York Times,* January 28, 2003, at A11.

105. Michael R. Gordon, "Agency Challenges Evidence against Iraq Cited by Bush," *New York Times,* January 10, 2003, p. A10; Joby Warrick, "U.S. Claims on Iraqi Nuclear Program Is Called into Question," *Washington Post,* January 24, 2003, p. A1.

106. Michael Dobbs, "Powell Lays Out Case against Iraq," *Washington Post,* February 6, 2003, pp. A1, A25.

After hostilities were over, U.S. forces discovered two mobile labs in Iraq but no evidence that they were related to any program for biological warfare.[107] A May 28, 2003 report on the mobile labs, jointly authored by the CIA and the Defense Intelligence Agency, conceded that the labs could have been used to produce hydrogen for artillery weather balloons.[108] The consensus now is that the labs were used for the weather balloons, prompting Powell in 2004 to ask the CIA why he received misleading information.[109]

In his State of the Union address on January 28, 2003, President Bush said that the British government "has learned that Saddam Hussein recently sought significant quantities of uranium from Africa."[110] Why did he rely on British intelligence instead of American intelligence? Part of the answer may have been that the U.S. intelligence agencies were divided. In the end, the documents about Iraq seeking uranium ore from Niger turned out to be a fabrication. They contained crude errors that undermined their credibility.[111] On July 7, 2003, the White House acknowledged that President Bush should not have alleged that Iraq had sought to buy uranium in Africa.[112]

A few days later, however, Defense Secretary Donald Rumsfeld and National Security Adviser Condoleezza Rice argued that Bush's claim in the State of the Union address was "technically correct" because the British government believed it to be true.[113] If the claim was technically correct, why did the White House issue an apology? The Rumsfeld–Rice position was undermined within weeks when it was publicly revealed that the CIA had notified Stephen Hadley, Rice's deputy in the National Security Council, that the evidence about Iraqi trying to purchase uranium in Africa was weak.[114] After Hadley took the blame, Rice announced that she felt

---

107. Walter Pincus and Michael Dobbs, "Suspected Bioweapon Mobile Lab Recovered," *Washington Post,* May 7, 2003, p. A1.

108. CIA and DIA, "Iraqi Mobile Biological Warfare Agent Production Plans," May 28, 2003, http://www.cia.gov

109. David E. Sanger, "Powell Says C.I.A. Was Misled about Weapons," *New York Times,* May 17, 2004, p. A8; Douglas Jehl and David E. Sanger, "Powell Presses C.I.A. on Faulty Intelligence on Iraq Arms," *New York Times,* June 2, 2004, p. A12.

110. *Weekly Compilation of Presidential Documents,* vol. 39, p. 115.

111. Joby Warrick, "Some Evidence on Iraq Called Fake," *Washington Post,* March 8, 2003, p. A1.

112. Walter Pincus, "White House Backs Off Claim on Iraqi Buy," *Washington Post,* July 8, 2003, p. A1.

113. James Risen, "Bush Aides Now Say Claim on Uranium Was Accurate," *New York Times,* July 14, 2003, p. A7.

114. David E. Sanger and Judith Miller, "National Security Aide says He's to Blame for Speech Error," *New York Times,* July 23, 2002, p. A11; Dana Milbank and Walter Pincus, "Bush Aides Disclose Warnings from CIA," *Washington Post,* July 23, 2003, p. A1.

"personal responsibility."[115] Subsequent news reports faulted the White House for including the claim in the State of the Union address.[116]

VOTING ON THE IRAQ RESOLUTION

A few days before Congress was scheduled to vote on the Iraq Resolution, the CIA released a classified report on "Iraq's Weapons of Mass Destruction Programs." At this same time, President Bush announced on October 2 a bipartisan agreement on a joint resolution to authorize armed force against Iraq. He stated that Iraq "has stockpiled biological and chemical weapons."[117] On October 7, in an address in Cincinnati, he said that Iraq "possesses and produces chemical and biological weapons."[118]

These dramatic statements reflect the views contained in the CIA report. The unclassified version, available on the CIA website (www.cia.gov), states unequivocally: "Baghdad has chemical and biological weapons." This sentence appears in the opening paragraph, yet when one reads the 100-page report, it fails to substantiate this claim. Instead, the sentences are much more cautious and qualified. Iraq "has the ability to produce chemical warfare (CW) agents within its chemical industry." That speaks to potential, not actual, production. Iraq "probably has concealed precursors, production equipment, documentation, and other items necessary for continuing its CW effort." *Probably,* not actually. Baghdad "continues to rebuild and expand dual-use infrastructure that it could divert quickly to CW production." This is not evidence of chemical weapons. It indicates that certain infrastructure, currently employed for a legitimate and benign use, could be switched to a second (lethal) use. Iraq "has the capability to convert quickly legitimate vaccine and biopesticide plants to biological warfare (BW) production and already may have done so." *May have done so* is not the same as "has," and reference to conversion capability is just another way of restating the dual-use potential. None of the statements in the analytical section of the report supports the striking claim that Iraq "has chemical and biological weapons."

What seems clear about this CIA report is that professional analysts did their work with care and balance, adding necessary caveats and qualifications, after which someone else decided that the report lacked the punch to

---

115. Richard W. Stevenson, "President Denies He Oversold Case for War with Iraq," *New York Times,* July 31, 2003, pp. A1, A11.

116. Walter Pincus, "White House Faulted on Uranium Claim," *Washington Post,* December 24, 2003, p. A1.

117. *Weekly Compilation of Presidential Documents,* vol. 38, p. 1670.

118. Ibid., p. 1716.

influence congressional votes. Thus, it was decided to rewrite the lead to make it dramatic and eye-catching, even if the analytical section did not support the assertion. A change of this nature goes beyond being "misleading." It is a deliberate falsification, done with the purpose of influencing a congressional vote.

It was under these conditions that lawmakers were asked to vote on the Iraq Resolution. Both Democrats and Republicans took account of the political stakes, with the congressional elections a month off. Legislative action on the eve of an election invited partisan exploitation of the war issue. Several Republican nominees in congressional contests made a political weapon out of Iraq, comparing their "strong stand" on Iraq to "weak" positions by Democratic campaigners. Some of the key races in the nation appeared to turn on what candidates were saying about Iraq.[119]

It was never clear why Democrats were worried about being viewed as antiwar. They had supported the statute authorizing military operations against Afghanistan. It could certainly be argued that a second war against Iraq might weaken the effort in Afghanistan to eliminate existing Taliban and al Qaeda cells, and that the occupation of Iraq by American soldiers might lead to easier recruitment of new terrorists. Legitimate grounds could be presented that a war against Iraq, at least in the near term, was not in the interest of the United States or in the war against terrorism.

There was no evidence that the public, in any broad sense, supported immediate war against Iraq. A *New York Times* poll published on October 7, 2002, indicated that 69 percent of Americans believed that Bush should be paying more attention to the economy. Two-thirds of the public approved U.S. military action against Iraq, but when it was asked, "Should the U.S. take military action against Iraq fairly soon or wait and give the U.N. more time to get weapons inspectors into Iraq?," 63 percent preferred to wait. To the question "Is Congress asking enough questions about President Bush's policy toward Iraq?," only 20 percent said too many, while 51 percent said not enough.[120]

The Democrats could have pointed to the precedent established by Bush's father. In 1990, after Iraq had invaded Kuwait, the administration did not ask Congress to vote for authorizing legislation before the November elections. The administration first went to the Security Council to seek a resolution of support for military action. Only in January 1991, after lawmakers returned, did they debate and pass legislation to authorize war against Iraq. They were not forced to vote in the shadow of an election.

---

119. Jim VandeHei, "GOP Nominees Make Iraq a Political Weapon," *Washington Post,* September 18, 2002, p. A1.

120. Adam Nagourney and Janet Elder, "Public Says Bush Needs to Pay Heed to Weak Economy," *New York Times,* October 7, 2002, pp. A1, A14.

For various reasons, the Bush administration in 2002 decided to press for a vote in October. President Bush gained important bipartisan support when House Minority Leader Dick Gephardt (D-Mo.) broke ranks with many in his party to announce support for a slightly redrafted resolution. He said: "We had to go through this, putting politics aside, so we have a chance to get a consensus that will lead the country in the right direction."[121] Partisanship might be put aside, but not politics. Gephardt's interest in running for president was well known, as was his vote against the January 1991 resolution to go to war against Iraq. His support for Bush in 2002 could be interpreted as an effort to bolster his national security credentials. Democratic Senators John Edwards, John Kerry, and Joseph Lieberman, all interested in a 2004 bid for the presidency, decided to support the Iraq Resolution of 2002.

Notwithstanding Gephardt's statement, the vote on the Iraq Resolution would be a quintessential political decision, quite likely the most important congressional vote of the year. Lawmakers would be asked to vote on a multiyear military and economic commitment that could cost several hundred billion dollars. U.S. intervention in Iraq would stabilize or destabilize the Middle East, strengthen or weaken the war against terrorism, bolster or undermine America's relations with allies, and enhance or debase the nations' prestige.

The House passed the Iraq Resolution, 296 to 133. Following this vote, Senate Majority Leader Tom Daschle announced that he would support the resolution, again providing President Bush with important bipartisan backing. Daschle suggested that the Senate might want to "go back and tie down the language a little bit more if we can" but insisted that "we have got to support this effort. We have got to do it in an enthusiastic and bipartisan way." Senator Kerry, after raising serious doubts about the need for war against Iraq, now accepted presidential superiority over congressional power: "We are affirming a president's right and responsibility to keep the people safe, and a president must take that grant of responsibility seriously."[122]

The decision to go to war against another country can, at times, justify what might be called enthusiasm, or at least confidence that the end is just and necessary. Such a spirit is possible when the facts show that military action is in the nation's interest. However, it was never clear, in the run-up to the vote on the Iraq Resolution, why lawmakers should be enthusiastic about the war. At almost every turn were disturbing reports about misconceptions, unfounded assertions, and faulty claims. No one from either party

---

121. "For Gephardt, Risks and a Crucial Role," *Washington Post,* October 3, 2002, p. A15.

122. Helen Dewar and Juliet Eilperin, "Iraq Resolution Passes Test, Gains Support," *Washington Post,* October 10, 2002, p. A16.

could feel comfortable that the administration possessed reliable sources of intelligence or that a military plan would assure not only a quick victory but also a successful occupation. The array of doubts and misgivings made enthusiasm unlikely.

Senator Robert C. Byrd watched the congressional debate drift from an initial willingness of lawmakers to analyze issues and weigh the merits to wholesale legislative abdication to the president. To Byrd, the fundamental question of why the United States should go to war was replaced by "the mechanics of how best to wordsmith the president's use-of-force resolution in order to give him virtually unchecked authority to commit the nations' military to an unprovoked attack on a sovereign nation." Byrd did not find the threat from Iraq "so great that we must be stampeded to provide such authority to this president just weeks before an election."[123]

On October 10, the Senate voted 77 to 23 for the resolution. The only Republican voting against the resolution was Lincoln Chafee of Rhode Island. An independent, James Jeffords of Vermont, also voted no. It would be incorrect to say that lawmakers, in voting for the resolution, decided on war. Because of the way it was worded, they decided only that President Bush should decide the crucial question of using military force against another nation. A question of that magnitude the framers placed in Congress, not the president. After seeking resolutions of support from the Security Council, succeeding with one but failing with the second, President Bush ordered military operations against Iraq in March 2003.

Following a swift, month-long military victory, teams of experts conducted careful searches to look for the weapons of mass destruction that President Bush had offered as the principal justification for war. He claimed that the weapons represented a direct and immediate threat. Months after active hostilities had ended, little evidence had been found nor was there any reason to expect anything significant to emerge. Having conducted a skillful military campaign, the administration was unprepared for predictable looting, violence, and military counterattacks from insurgents. After the recent experience in Afghanistan, it should have been obvious that a military victory must be followed quickly by a secure environment and visible reconstruction efforts. Inadequate and fanciful planning resulted in heavy casualties, mounting financial costs, and political instability.

Congress failed to discharge its constitutional duties when it passed the Iraq Resolution. Instead of making a decision about whether to go to war and spend billions for a risky, multibillion-dollar, multiyear commitment, it decided to shift those legislative judgments to President Bush. Legislators washed their hands of the key decisions to go to war and for how long.

---

123. Robert C. Byrd, "Congress Must Resist the Rush to War," *New York Times,* October 10, 2002, p. A35.

Congress should not have voted on the resolution before the midterm elections, which colored the votes and the political calculations. Voting under that pressure benefited the president. It would have been better for Congress as an institution, and for the country as a whole, to first wait for President Bush to request the Security Council to authorize inspections in Iraq. Depending on what the Security Council did or did not do, and on what the inspectors found or did not find, Congress could then have made an informed choice about going to war. There was no need for Congress to act when it did. Instead of deciding on war, lawmakers agreed to ambivalent language that left the decisive judgment to initiate war in the hands of the president, which is what the framers thought they had avoided.

CONGRESSIONAL POWER
BUT NO WILL?

The record of the past half-century calls into question Madison's assumption about separation of powers and checks and balances. Government powers were to be divided and checked as a means of protecting individual rights and liberties, but Madison knew that it was not enough to separate powers on paper. As he explained in Federalist No. 48, the separation of powers adopted by the state constitutions turned out to consist of mere "parchment barriers" that were incapable of preventing one branch from taking power from the others. It was never Madison's intention that the branches "be wholly unconnected with each other." Unless the branches "be so far connected and blended as to give to each a constitutional control over the others, the degree of separation which the maxim requires, as essential to a free government, can never in practice be duly maintained."

By the late 1780s, the concept of checks and balances had gained dominance over the doctrine of separated powers, which one contemporary pamphleteer called a "hackneyed principle" and a "trite maxim."[124] Madison devoted Federalist No. 51 to expounding on checks and balances. How shall the branches be kept separate? The only answer, he said, is "by so contriving the interior structure of the government as that its several constituent parts may, by their mutual relations, be the means of keeping each other in their proper places." For that system to be effective in preserving liberty, it was necessary that "each department should have a will of its own." The "great security against a gradual concentration of the several powers in the same department, consists in giving to those who administer each department the

---

124. M. J. C. Vile, *Constitutionalism and the Separation of Powers* (Oxford, England: Clarendon Press, 1967), p. 153.

necessary constitutional means and personal motives to resist encroachments of the others." The provision for defense must be made "commensurate to the danger of attack." Here Madison introduces his key principle: "Ambition must be made to counteract ambition." The interest of a member of a branch "must be connected with the constitutional rights of the place." In arranging for this system of checks and balances, he cautioned that "it is not possible to give to each department an equal power of self-defense. In republican government, the legislative authority necessarily predominates."

These constitutional principles endured in America for the first century and a half. For the last half century they have been in retreat. The presumption in favor of the legislative branch and republican government has been replaced by a preference for presidential military initiatives that the framers would have loathed. Few members of Congress "have a will of [their] own" or possess the "personal motives" to resist encroachments by other branches, especially the president. Few have a commitment to and understanding of the prerogatives of their branch and a determination to protect its separateness and coequality. Repeatedly, especially in the area of the war power, legislators have championed executive over legislative power. There is little appreciation in Congress, the executive branch, academia, the media, or the general public for the dependence of individual liberty on checks and balances and the maintenance of legislative prerogatives. However politically convenient, unilateral military commitments by presidents are unlikely to succeed. To endure, they require the collective judgment, support, and understanding of both branches.

11

⚜

Is Congress Gridlocked?

BARBARA SINCLAIR
University of California, Los Angeles

C*ongressional Quarterly*, a highly respected publication for congressional insiders, headlined an article on the then just-concluded 108th Congress (2003–2004) "Capitol Hill gridlock."[1] President George W. Bush and congressional Republicans called the 108th a highly productive congress and touted bill after bill enacted into law. "From tax cuts to intelligence reform, the 108th Congress has tackled big issues and made great strides . . . ," Senate Republican leader Bill Frist declared. "The 108th was truly an historic period in our legislative history."[2] Is this just journalistic cynicism versus partisan hype or is the question my essay title asks really that difficult to answer?

Perhaps a look at what the 108th Congress did and did not produce can help us decide whether or not Congress is indeed gridlocked. Congress failed to pass Bush's signature energy program; a massive and important transportation bill; reauthorizations of the Head Start program and of the welfare program; bankruptcy legislation that has been on the agenda for a number of years; and tort reform of any sort through bills dealing with medical malpractice suits and class action lawsuits was considered at length. On the other hand, Congress did pass a $330 billion tax cut in 2003 and, in 2004, a $137 billion corporate tax cut and a $146 billion extension of middle-class tax breaks; a bill banning partial birth abortion that had been long stymied; and a hugely consequential bill adding prescription drug benefits to Medicare as well as beginning the restructuring of the Medicare program. In addition, Congress finished its essential work of funding the national government through the appropriations process—although in both 2003 and 2004, Congress passed catch-all omnibus spending bills rather

---

1. Alex Wayne and Bill Swindell, "2004 Legislative Summary: Capitol Hill Gridlock Leaves Programs in Limbo," *Congressional Quarterly Weekly* (December 11, 2004): 2834.

2. Press release, December 15, 2004, frist.senate.gov (accessed December 16, 2004).

than the 13 separate bills the regular process dictates. So does this amount to gridlock or to an admirable record of productivity?

DEFINING GRIDLOCK
AND MEASURING PRODUCTIVITY

Determining whether Congress is gridlocked is complicated by the different meanings people give to the term. If we simply mean "Does Congress pass legislation?," then Congress is not gridlocked. About 500 bills per two-year session have been enacted on average during recent congresses.[3] Congress does not pass a large percentage of the bills that are introduced, but that is not a new phenomenon.[4] Nor would we expect or want every bill introduced to be extensively considered, much less enacted. There are far too many introduced—over 5,000 per congress in the House and about 3,000 in the Senate—and members introduce bills for many different reasons. In the 108th Congress, for example, Democrat Charlie Rangel, who represents Harlem, introduced a bill reinstating the draft; his purpose was to highlight that the poor and minorities were bearing the brunt of the war in Iraq.

If we mean "Does Congress get its essential legislative work done?," then the answer is also that Congress is not gridlocked. Congress's absolutely essential work is passing the appropriations necessary to keep the government from shutting down many of its services and programs. Not since Christmas 1995 has Congress let that happen. However, as I discuss later, one can argue about how Congress goes about appropriating and about other tasks that, while not so catastrophic in impact if left undone, Congress is charged with carrying out but does not always do.

When people say Congress is gridlocked, they most often mean that Congress fails to pass important legislation. But since the determination of what is important is to some extent subjective, the differences of opinion evident on the 108th Congress may well be more than journalistic cynicism versus partisan boasting. At minimum we need a definition of importance and some comparative data to determine what is a good record and what is a bad one.

To begin, I define as "important" the legislation that *Congressional Quarterly* contemporaneously lists as major legislation under consideration

---

3. Norman Ornstein, Thomas Mann, and Michael Malbin, *Vital Statistics on Congress 2001–2002* (Washington, DC: AEI Press, 2002) p. 149.

4. *Vital Statistics,* pp 146–47.

Table 11–1 The Rate of Bills Becoming Law 1961–2004 (major legislation)

Congress	Years	% Enacted
87	1961–1962	81
89	1965–1966	77
91	1969–1970	82
94	1975–1976	58
95	1977–1978	69
97	1981–1982	68
100	1987–1988	84
101	1989–1990	64
103	1993–1994	65
104	1995–1996	52
105	1997–1998	50
106	1999–2000	44
107	2001–2002	67
108	2003–2004	59

SOURCE: Author's computations.

by Congress, and I augment that with bills on which a key vote occurred, again according to *CQ's* contemporaneous judgment.[5] This produces about 40 to 50 major measures per congress which can be considered Congress's active agenda; they are the bills that close contemporary observers considered major and under active consideration. For selected congresses from the early 1960s to the 108th, I have examined each of these measures and determined whether or not it was enacted.

As one can see from Table 11–1, Congress never enacts all of the major measures on its agenda. The legislative process in a division-of-powers system is an obstacle course, with many stages where bills can be killed.[6] A bill must survive the complex, multistage legislative process in both the House and the Senate. Then, if the two chambers have passed the bill in different forms, which given their different make-ups is likely, proponents from the two chambers must agree on a single bill and get approval for that version from both chambers. Finally, the president must agree to the bill, or if he vetoes it, two-thirds of each chamber must vote to override his veto to

5. The measures are mostly, but not all, ordinary bills; budget resolutions that do not require the president's signature are included as are a few constitutional amendments that require a two-thirds vote. "Enactment" in those cases is defined as successfully completing the process.

6. See Barbara Sinclair, *Unorthodox Lawmaking,* 2nd ed. (Washington, DC: CQ Press, 2002).

enact the bill. It would thus be unrealistic to expect that every major measure would be enacted.

Table 11–1 also reveals considerable variability across congresses in the rate of enactment, with a low of 44 percent and a high of 84 percent—almost double the low. Furthermore, although the rate of enactment does not simply decline from high to low over time, there is a noticeable trend toward lower rates of enactment later in the period under study. Four of the five lowest rates occur from the mid-1990s forward.

From the president's point of view—and that is often the one adopted by journalists when they make judgments about success—the rate of enactment of major measures overall is far less important than the rate of enactment of bills that carry his program. The congressional agenda may well include priorities that the president's opponents have managed to place there; for example, partial birth abortion was constantly on the congressional agenda during the late 1990s, but it certainly was not part of President Clinton's agenda, just as campaign finance reform was not on President George W. Bush's agenda but was a prominent part of the congressional agenda until it was enacted in 2002. In these two cases, the president opposed the legislation at issue; in many instances, the president does not oppose some form of the legislation, but it is much lower on his list of priorities than his own program.

Because we expect the president's success on his program to vary across his term, comparisons must take that into account. Specifically, a newly elected president should be most successful during his first two years in office; this is when a honeymoon or a mandate, should he enjoy either or both, will have its effect.[7] The president's program can be ascertained by examining his State of the Union address, other major messages to Congress, and important presidential speeches.

Presidential success in enacting his program has declined marginally; the average success rate for Kennedy, Nixon, Carter, and Reagan in their first congresses was 74 percent; the average for George H. W. Bush, Clinton, and George W. Bush was 69.8 percent. The rates for the latter three presidents are remarkably similar: 70 percent of George H. W. Bush's program was enacted in some form during his first two years in office; the comparable figure for Clinton was 68 percent; and for George W. Bush, it was 71.4 percent. Since we tend to remember those congresses as very different in terms of presidential success, further examination is called for.

A more detailed look at these three congresses resolves this puzzle and introduces my arguments about the determinants of legislative productivity

---

7. Paul Light, *The President's Agenda* (Baltimore, MD: Johns Hopkins University Press, 1983).

Table 11–2 Three Presidents' Success on their Programs

President's Success on His Enacted Agenda	George H. W. Bush	Bill Clinton	George W. Bush
% won	29	100	80
% mixed	43	0	7
% lost	29	0	14
Agenda size	10	25	21
% enacted	70	68	71

SOURCE: Author's computations.

and so, conversely, the determinants of gridlock. The rate of enactment may be similar for Clinton and the two Bush presidents, but the rate tells us nothing about how ambitious the president's agenda was and whether or not the bills that got to the president's desk were in a form he was happy with. Using *CQ*, I coded for each of the measures whether the president won, clearly or on balance; lost, clearly or on balance; or fell into an intermediate category, where he got some of but far from all he asked for. The judgment was based on how far from the president's proposal the final bill was, as well as his expressed attitudes about the final bill.

As Table 11–2 shows, the first Bush's agenda was small compared to those of the other two presidents. Probably the most ambitious item on the agenda was a rewrite of the Clean Air Act. Furthermore, many of the agenda items that got to George H. W. Bush's desk got there in a form he did not much like; Congress had changed the bills extensively and made them less to his liking. Thus, the Clean Air bill that made it to Bush's desk and that he signed was much stronger than his initial proposal.

Clinton, in contrast, had a much bigger agenda and one that was much more ambitious in content. A bold economic program, a massive reform of the health care system so as to provide universal coverage, and NAFTA received the most attention, but the agenda also included issues such as parental leave, motor voter (easing voting registration), and national service legislation. When Congress sent bills to Clinton, the bills were always in a form that he found at least satisfactory. However, about a third of the president's agenda never reached his desk. Health care reform is the most notorious example, but other presidential priorities also died in Congress. These prominent cases account for the very negative assessment of the 103rd Congress (1993–1994) by the media and much of the public.[8]

8. See Barbara Sinclair, "Trying to Govern Positively in a Negative Era: Clinton and the 103rd Congress," in Colin Campbell and Bert A. Rockman, eds., *The Clinton Presidency: First Appraisals* (Chatham, NJ: Chatham House Publishers, 1996), pp. 88–125.

George W. Bush's agenda was almost as large and certainly as ambitious as Clinton's, including huge tax cuts, a major revision of education legislation, and a big energy program that represented major change in policy direction. As was the case for Clinton, though not to the same extent, when legislation came to Bush, it was in a form he liked. But Bush, too, suffered a number of defeats when Congress did not pass his program in any form, energy legislation being perhaps the most prominent.

LEGISLATIVE PRODUCTIVITY OR GRIDLOCK: WHAT EXPLAINS THE PATTERNS?

Three systematic factors go a long way toward explaining the patterns identified. In the sections that follow, I show that whether control of Congress and the presidency is unified or divided, the increase in partisanship and party leadership strength, especially in the House, and how senators use extended debate are important determinants of what is enacted. Of course, there are occasional "wild cards"—exogenous events, September 11 for example—that can have huge, if usually temporary, effects.

Divided versus Unified Control

Our system of government makes possible divided partisan control of the presidency and one or both houses of Congress. As even at their least programmatic, the two major parties have represented different constituencies and different policy thrusts, one would expect more policy conflict between the president and congress when control is divided, and thus expect divided-control congresses to be less productive. However, David Mayhew, a prominent political scientist, has shown that for the period he studied (1947–1990), the number of significant enactments per congress did not vary with divided versus unified control.[9] Mayhew argues that so many other factors are at work that control simply does not matter. A quick glance at Table 11–1 might tend to support Mayhew's generalization for the rate of enactment as well. True, the four least productive congresses measured by the rate of enactment of major legislation were the 94th, when Republican Gerald Ford confronted a congress with big Democratic majorities, and the 104th through 106th, when Clinton was in the White House but a new Republican majority controlled both chambers. On the

---

9. David Mayhew, *Divided We Govern* (New Haven, CT: Yale University Press, 1991).

other hand, some divided-control congresses were among the most productive, such as the 91st, when Nixon was president, and the 100th, when Reagan was president; in both instances Democrats controlled the House and the Senate.

The relationship between presidential success and divided versus unified control is much clearer. Presidents do much better when their party controls Congress. Considering all major bills, presidents have supported the final bill as it came to them 83 percent of the time and opposed it 4 percent of the time when control was unified; they supported it 40 percent of the time and opposed it 31 percent of the time when control was divided.[10] And the impact of divided versus unified control is much greater earlier in the legislative process; for example, presidents under unified control supported the legislation reported by the House committee 85 percent of the time and opposed it 5 percent of the time; contrast that with circumstances under divided control when the president supported the legislation the House committee reported only 28 percent of the time and opposed it 52 percent of the time.[11]

As one would expect, presidents do considerably better in enacting their program in a form they like when control is unified than when it is divided. Under unified control, presidents won, either clearly or on balance, on 63 percent of their agenda items; under divided control, the presidents won on only 39 percent of their agenda items.

In sum, the differences among the first congresses of the three most recently elected presidents can in part be attributed to the character of control. George H. W. Bush faced a House and a Senate solidly controlled by Democrats. He did not propose a large and ambitious agenda, in part because divided control made the passage of such an agenda unlikely; in addition, one may argue that since Bush followed eight years of Reagan, the parts of the Republican agenda that had a chance of passing a Democratic congress had long since been enacted. Bush's limited win rate on those parts of his program that did pass can also be attributed to the congress being in Democratic hands. Clinton, by contrast, had a solidly Democratic congress during his first congress, and this accounts for his high win rate on those of his priorities that were enacted; it does not, of course, explain why a third of his policy priorities were killed in Congress. Finally, George W. Bush began with unified control but lost the Senate about halfway through his

---

10. The two congresses when there was split control of the House and Senate—the 97th and 107th—are excluded.

11. See Table 5 in Barbara Sinclair, "Leading and Competing: The President and the Polarized Congress," in George Edwards III and Philip John Davies, eds., *New Challenges for the American Presidency* (New York: Pearson Longman, 2004).

first year, when Jim Jeffords of Vermont switched from Republican to independent, making expectations less clear.

Divided versus unified control, then, seems to be part of the explanation but far from all of it.

Partisan Polarization and Strong Party Leadership in the House

The congressional parties of today are polarized along ideological lines, that is, policy preference lines. Most congressional Republicans are conservatives; most Democrats, liberals or moderates. Figure 11–1 displays the difference in the parties' medians over time in the Poole–Rosenthal DW-nominate scores, which can be interpreted as locating members of Congress on a left–right dimension.[12] The current partisan polarization, as the figure illustrates, is a relatively recent phenomenon. The middle years of the 20th century were a period of low intraparty ideological agreement, especially within the majority Democratic party. The late 1960s and early 1970s saw cohesion reach a nadir, with numerous congressional Democrats, mostly conservatives from the southern states, voting more often with opposition Republicans than with their party colleagues.[13]

Partisan polarization can be traced to an alteration in the constituency bases of the parties. The change in southern politics that the Civil Rights movement and the Voting Rights Act set off resulted in conservative southern Democrats, so common in the 1960s and before, being replaced either by even more-conservative Republicans or by more-mainstream Democrats. As African Americans became able to vote and as more conservative whites increasingly voted Republican, the supportive electoral coalitions of southern Democrats began to look similar to those of their northern party colleagues. As their constituencies became more alike, the legislative preferences of northern and southern congressional Democrats also began to converge.[14]

The increasing proportion of House Republicans elected from the South made the Republican party more conservative but accounts for far

---

12. Scores are available at Keith Poole's website: http://voteview.com. See Keith T. Poole and Howard Rosenthal, *Congress: A Political-Economic History of Roll Call Voting,* (New York: Oxford University Press, 1997).

13. Barbara Sinclair, *Congressional Realignment* (Austin: University of Texas Press, 1982.)

14. David Rohde, *Parties and Leaders in the Postreform House* (Chicago: University of Chicago Press, 1991); Jeffery Stonecash, Mark Mariani, and Mark Brewer, *Diverging Parties: Social Change, Realignment, and Party Polarization* (Boulder, CO: Westview Press, 2002); Stanley Berard, *Southern Democrats in the House of Representatives* (Norman: University of Oklahoma Press, 2001).

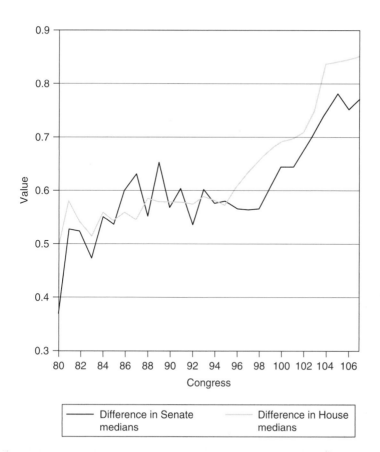

FIGURE 11–1 Ideological Polarization in the House and Senate (difference between Democratic and Republican median DW-Nominate scores).

SOURCE: DW-Nominate scores taken from Keith Poole's website: http://voteview.com. Difference scores were computed by the author.

from all of the change in the party's ideological cast. A resurgence of conservatism at the activist and primary voter level resulted in the nomination of fewer moderates; increasingly, the Republicans who won nominations and election, especially to the House, were hard-edged, ideological or Movement conservatives. Perhaps in response to the polarization of the parties' elected officials and party activists, party identifiers also became more polarized on policy issues.[15] Thus, constituency sentiment at both the

---

15. Gary C. Jacobson, "Party Polarization in National Politics: The Electoral Connection," in Jon Bond and Richard Fleisher, eds., *Polarized Politics: Congress and the President in a Partisan Era* (Washington, DC: CQ Press, 2000).

activist and voter level underlies congressional partisan polarization, especially in the House with its smaller and more homogeneous districts.

In the House of Representatives, greater ideological homogeneity made possible the development of a stronger and more activist party leadership.[16] The House is a majority-rule institution; decisions are made by simple majorities and opportunities for minorities to delay, much less block, action are exceedingly limited. The Speaker is both the presiding officer of the chamber and the leader of the majority party. When the majority party is homogeneous, its members have the incentive to grant the Speaker significant new powers and resources and to allow the Speaker to use them aggressively because the legislation the Speaker will use them to pass is broadly supported in the party. By the mid-1980s, majority party members had granted their party leadership such new authority, and the leadership did, in fact, employ it assertively to pass legislation the members wanted.

Over the course of the 1980s and 1990s, both parties organized themselves for joint action and for member participation. By the late 1990s, with a highly ideologically cohesive Republican party controlling the House, the incentives for House members to be team players had become enormous. Members' House lives now take place mostly within their party. The party affords them many opportunities to participate through the party, while bipartisan participation opportunities are fewer and often fraught with difficulty. Advancement within the chamber (getting good committee assignments and committee or subcommittee chair positions, and, of course, rising in the party hierarchy) depends on the member's reputation with his or her party peers and the party leadership. All this amplifies party cohesion even beyond that which the extent of constituency-based ideologically homogeneity would dictate. It is important to remember, however, that House members want an active party and a strong leadership because these are prerequisites for members to advance their goals in the current political environment of narrow margins and great ideological distance between the parties.

What does this mean for legislative productivity? One would expect that a strongly led and cohesive majority party in a majority-rule chamber would be productive. From the 1950s through the 1970s, the Democratic majority often had to contend with conservative southern committee chairs who blocked legislation that mainstream Democrats favored and with a majority that splintered along ideological lines on the floor. That does not happen to either party today. Committee chairs do not hold up legislation their party colleagues want; they might well lose their chairship were they

---

16. Barbara Sinclair, *Legislators, Leaders and Lawmaking* (Baltimore, MD: Johns Hopkins University Press, 1995), p.108.

to do that. The majority party seldom loses an important vote on the floor, even though its majorities are narrow.

Overall, little majority party-supported legislation dies in the House. Of the major measures that failed in the selected congresses from the 103rd through the 107th (1993–2002), less than four percent passed the Senate but did not pass the House; and quite likely those were bills the House majority party did not want passed. Thus, in the 104th Congress (1995–1996), the newly Republican House passed all but one of the items in the Contract with America, the ambitious agenda House Republicans had run for office on in 1994. The only exception was congressional term limits, which, as a constitutional amendment, required a two-thirds vote.

If the president's party controls the House, it now serves as an extremely valuable ally. The president can expect the majority party leadership to work with (and, if necessary, lean on) the committees to report out his program in a form acceptable to him and in a timely fashion; to deploy the extensive whip system to rally the votes needed to pass the legislation; to bring the bills to the floor at the most favorable time and under floor procedures that give them the best possible chance for success; and, if necessary, to use the powers of the presiding officer to advantage the legislation.[17] Congressional party leaders are elected by and thus are agents of their members and furthering their members' policy and reelection goals is their first priority, but, in a time of high partisan polarization, that usually means passing the president's program. Members of Congress are likely to have similar policy goals to those of a president of their party—not infrequently his program includes policy proposals that originated with them. Furthermore, members are aware that the president's success or failure will shape the party's reputation and so affect their own electoral fates.

Even though the House Democrats were never as ideologically homogeneous a majority party as the current House Republican party is, House Democrats in the 103rd Congress (1993–1994) nevertheless passed all but two of the bills that carried Clinton's program and all those in a form Clinton supported. By far the most important failure was the House's inability to pass the Clinton health care program, reminding us that, even among a president's program, some bills are much more important than others. That failure did not result from a lack of effort on the Democratic leadership's part. House Majority Leader Dick Gephardt himself managed the process of negotiation. When opponents, through a massive media and grassroots campaign, persuaded a majority of the public that major reform was too risky, it became

---

17. See Sinclair, "Trying to Govern Positively in a Negative Era" and "Context, Strategy and Chance: George W. Bush and the 107th Congress," in Colin Campbell and Bert Rockman, eds., *The George W. Bush Presidency: An Early Appraisal* (Chatham, NJ: Chatham House Publishers, forthcoming 2003).

impossible for the leaders to put together a bill that would pass. Democrats feared that their constituents would punish them for not delivering on the promised health care reform, but they feared the electoral consequences of passing an unpopular bill even more. Still, the leadership and House Democrats did succeed on a number of tough issues, most importantly the economic package that included a tax increase on the well-off but paved the way for the budget surpluses that characterized the late 1990s.

The House Republicans and their leadership in the 107th Congress (2001–2002) had a still more impressive record, especially given the narrow margin in the chamber. In the 103rd Congress, there were 258 Democrats, well above the 218 that make up a simple majority; in the 107th, there were only 221 Republicans. Yet the House passed every one of the bills that carried Bush's agenda and all but two of these in a form Bush clearly supported.[18] A number of these bills confronted some Republicans with tough votes. For example, the energy bill and the faith-based initiative were politically touchy for northeastern moderates; trade promotion authority was very unpopular in southeastern textile-producing districts; and the Democratic version of the patient's bill of rights was popular across the country, and so voting for the Republican version raised difficulties for many members.

Realizing that the Senate would be a problem for the type of strongly conservative bills that Bush and the bulk of their membership favored, the House Republican leaders undertook to pass extremely conservative bills in the House. Under this strategy a compromise between the House bill and a more moderate Senate bill would still be quite far to the right. House leaders used the argument that the House bill would not be the final bill when pressing moderates for their votes. For moderates it nevertheless meant taking some tough votes that would be hard to explain to their constituents. It is under these circumstances that the incentives to be team players stemming from internal arrangements—from the influence of the party over advancement in the institution—become important.

Speaker Hastert also undertook to block legislation Bush opposed from getting to the president's desk and so forcing Bush to veto. Bush's having to veto a bill passed by a Republican-controlled House would make both the president and congressional Republicans look weak and in disarray, he believed. Again, Hastert knew that it would have to be the House that acted as the bulwark against such legislation. "[Hastert] made it clear that they would not allow bills that would be vetoed to reach the president's desk," according to Nick Calio, former head of White House liaison for Bush.[19] Thus, Hastert made sure that the version of the Patient's Bill of Rights

---

18. On the other two, Bush supported some of the provisions and opposed others, a midpoint in my coding.

19. *Roll Call,* December 15, 2003.

legislation that the House sent to conference was sufficiently different from the Senate version the president strongly opposed that the bill was likely to die in conference, as it in fact did. Bush did not veto a single bill during his first term in office.

The lack of vetoes largely, though not completely, signifies the success of Hastert's strategy. Hastert's one big failure reveals a good deal about the limits of even a highly cohesive party's ability to always prevail on policy issues. Hastert could not prevent campaign finance reform from getting to the House floor and passing in a form most Republicans detested. Proponents used seldom-successful procedures for circumventing the majority party leadership's grip on the floor schedule.[20] They were able to do so and then win on the floor because of intense media attention and public pressure. Many Republicans feared constituent punishment for voting against the popular bill and so voted for a bill they disliked. When the legislation got to Bush, he signed it, though without the usual signing ceremony. Considering the media spotlight on the issue and the strong public support for campaign finance reform, Bush was unwilling to pay the price that a veto would have entailed.

A strongly led and cohesive House majority party, if of the opposition party, is a formidable competitor to the president. Not only are the president's priorities likely to get less consideration but the party can force its own agenda onto center stage and compel the president to react to it. Opposition control of congress was less of a problem for presidents when the parties were less cohesive and less ideologically distinct. Thus, in 1969–1970, Nixon's first two years as president, 76 percent of the president's sizeable agenda was enacted. Although he certainly did not do as well overall and on his agenda as presidents of the same era who had congresses controlled by their own party, Nixon nevertheless won more often than he lost in committee and on the floor.[21] That is decidedly no longer the case.

In the 100th Congress (1987–1988), President Reagan's last and a convenient point at which to date the beginning of the period of high cohesion, the rate of enactment of major legislation was high, in fact at 84 percent unusually high for the post-1960s period. However, this signals not presidential success but the opposite. Much of the legislation enacted was imposed on Reagan by a Democratic Congress, led by Speaker Jim Wright. Wright proposed an agenda for House Democrats and saw it all through to enactment, much of it over Reagan's opposition.[22] Democrats overrode

---

20. Proponents used a discharge petition. See Walter Oleszek, *Congressional Procedures and the Policy Process,* 6th ed. (Washington: Congressional Quarterly Press, 2004), 141-143.

21. See Sinclair, "Leading and Competing," Table 3.

22. Sinclair, *Legislators, Leaders and Lawmaking,* pp. 271–74.

Reagan's veto on a massive transportation bill, a large clean water bill, and the Civil Rights Restoration Act; they forced a very reluctant Reagan to accept plant-closing notification legislation; and they passed a number of other items, such as aid to the homeless, that Reagan was not enthusiastic about. The Democrats even forced him to accept a tax increase to stem the growing deficit.

George H. W. Bush's experience with an opposition party–controlled congress in 1989–1990 has already been discussed. Although he had, at best, a mediocre record in terms of winning legislation in the form he desired, Democrats did consider his agenda, and the overall rate of enactment was about the same as for Clinton and George W. Bush in their first congresses. There was still enough area of agreement between the Republican president and the congressional Democrats to make compromise and thus some productivity possible. After 1994, when Republicans won majorities in the House and Senate, the rate of enactment plummeted. With a very conservative Republican party controlling the House and confronting a mainstream Democrat in the White House, the realm of possible compromise shrank. To be sure, when political necessity dictated that legislation be enacted, it was. Thus, welfare reform and an increase in the minimum wage were enacted in the run-up to the 1996 elections; public pressure and the fear of electoral consequences forced Clinton to make concessions that went well beyond what his core constituencies approved on welfare reform, and the same happened to the Republicans on the minimum wage. In 1997, Clinton and the Republican Congress came to an agreement on a balanced budget deal that also set up a new program for children's health care for the near-poor. Even in a period of high partisan polarization and considerable partisan hostility, some legislative productivity is possible. Still, the overall rate of enactment was low. The next president who confronts a Congress controlled by the opposition party is likely to have a very hard time.

The 60-Vote Senate

If Clinton and George W. Bush did so well in the House, getting most of their program passed and in a form they liked, why are their overall records not more impressive? The most obvious part of the answer is that Congress has two chambers and legislation must pass both. The second and less obvious part is that the second chamber—the Senate—works under very different rules than the House.

The Senate operates under the most permissive floor rules of any legislature in the world. Senators can offer as many amendments as they like to any bill and, in most cases, the amendments need not even be germane. A senator can hold the floor as long as she wants, and a supermajority—now

60 votes—is required to shut off debate. Thus, Senate rules vest enormous power in each individual senator.

Yet senators have not always exploited the possibilities inherent in the rules to the same extent. In the 1950s and early 1960s, senators were quite restrained, but then the incentives for senators began to change.[23] With an explosion of issues and of interest groups needing champions and spokespeople, and the media, which had become increasingly important, needing credible sources to represent issue positions and for commentary, senators could expand their influence well beyond the chamber. Doing so required senators to become much more active on the Senate floor, offering more amendments to a wider range of bills; to exploit extended debate to a much greater extent; and to use the media as a forum for influencing the legislative process.

Senators began to use their prerogatives under Senate rules, including extended debate, much more aggressively. In the 1950s, filibusters were rare; the average was one per congress. They increased during the 1960s to an average of 4.6 per congress. They shot up to 11.2 per congress during the 1970s and to 16.7 during the period of 1981–86. By the late 1980s, filibusters had become routine; they averaged 29 per congress from 1987 through 2002.[24]

Senate debate rules make it possible for any senator to disrupt the chamber's business. Specifically, the motion to proceed to consider a bill, which is one of two procedural motions the Senate majority leader uses to bring legislation to the floor, can be filibustered; when that happens, the majority leader's legislative schedule is shot. Since the majority leader and other senators want the Senate's time used efficiently, most legislation is brought to the floor under a unanimous consent agreement (UCA). Getting unanimous consent requires an elaborate process in which the majority leader effectively consults every other senator in the chamber to get his or her assent and consequently gives each senator a veto over what is brought to the floor.[25]

If the legislation at issue is very important—a must-pass appropriations bill or a central element of the president's agenda, for example—the majority leader cannot allow its floor consideration to be blocked so easily. If negotiations with opponents fail to yield a UCA, the majority leader may

---

23. The classic work on the Senate of the 1950s is Donald E Matthews, *U.S. Senators and Their World* (Vintage Books, 1960). For an analysis of how the Senate changed, see Barbara Sinclair, *The Transformation of the U.S. Senate* (Johns Hopkins University Press, 1989).

24. Barbara Sinclair, "The New World of U.S. Senators," in Lawrence C. Dodd and Bruce I. Oppenheimer, eds., *Congress Reconsidered,* 8th ed. (Washington, DC: CQ Press, 2005).

25. Ibid.

attempt to bring the legislation up under a motion to proceed to consider. But if opponents decide to filibuster that motion, the majority leader will need 60 votes to impose cloture, that is, close debate, and, if that succeeds, opponents can then filibuster the bill itself. If the bill passes, they can filibuster the motion to go to conference and, if a conference agreement is reached, they can filibuster the conference report. Passing legislation or approving nominations in the Senate over the opposition of a determined minority is a time-consuming enterprise. If the minority is large—41 or greater—it can be impossible.

Driven by the same exogenous political forces that accounted for a similar change in the House parties, the Senate parties became more internally ideologically homogeneous and more polarized in the late 1980s and the 1990s. The minorities exploiting Senate rules increasingly became partisan ones. By examining the legislative history of each major measure, it is possible to determine if the bill ran into an extended-debate problem (an actual or threatened filibuster) in the Senate. During the 1990s and early 2000s, about half of major measures experienced such a problem in each congress for which data are available. Compare that with the mean for earlier congresses from the late 1960s through 1990 of about 20 percent.[26]

From the 1990s forward, because the minority party, not an individual or small group of senators, was most often the source of the filibuster problem, the impact on legislative outcomes has been considerable. The minority party is not just bigger; it has preexisting organization. Both characteristics make its use of extended debate more likely to be devastating. In the 103rd Congress (1993–1994), the first in which extended debate was employed as a comprehensive strategy by a party, the minority Republicans used actual and threatened filibusters to deprive Clinton and the majority Democrats of numerous policy successes; Clinton's economic stimulus package, campaign finance and lobbying reform bills, bills revamping the superfund program, a revision of clean drinking water regulations, an overhaul of outdated telecommunications law, and applying federal labor laws to Congress were among the casualties. In the 104th and 105th Congresses, the Democrats, now in the minority, used extended debate to kill a number of Republican priorities, including ambitious regulatory overhaul legislation and a far-reaching property rights bill.

In the 108th Congress (2003–2004), several versions of medical malpractice legislation, the asbestos claims compensation bill, and class-action lawsuit overhaul legislation were stopped when minority Democrats filibustered the motion to proceed to consider the legislation and Republicans

---

26. 103rd–105th, 107th for the later period; 91st, 95th, 97th, 101st for the
    earlier period. Percentages are of legislation subject to a filibuster.

could not invoke cloture. Majority Leader Bill Frist (R–Tenn.) pulled the welfare reform authorization from the floor when Republicans failed in their attempts to invoke cloture; he never brought the ban on human cloning to the floor because he lacked the 60 votes to shut off debate. The big energy bill died when cloture failed on the conference report. "The status in the Senate right now is total gridlock," Majority Whip Mitch McConnell (R–Ky.) complained in the spring of 2004.[27]

The Senate majority's most powerful weapon is the budget process. The Budget Act protects both budget resolutions and reconciliation bills that implement the budget resolution from filibusters in the Senate, so passing them only requires a simple majority—not 60 votes. The Budget Act also makes amending the budget resolution and the reconciliation bill more difficult than usual Senate procedure; amendments must be germane and deficit neutral, and waiving these Budget Act requirements requires 60 votes.[28] All of the ambitious economic plans since Ronald Reagan's in 1981 have been considered under this special procedure—the budget deal between George W. H. Bush and Congress in 1990, Clinton's economic program in 1993, the Gingrich balanced budget in 1995, and George W. Bush's tax cuts in 2001 and 2003 to mention only the most prominent. Most of these would have had little chance of passing in the Senate without that special protection from filibusters. Because of the protection from filibusters, the majority party has an enormous incentive to do as much legislating as it can get away with in the reconciliation bill. Senate rules, however, limit what can be included in such bills.

Nominations as well as bills can be filibustered, and some of the most intense partisan battles in recent years have focused on judicial nominations. The Senate Republican majority after 1995 blocked a number of President Clinton's judicial nominees in the Judiciary Committee. Altogether the Republican Senate failed to confirm 36 of Clinton's 79 appellate court nominees—46 percent.[29] When Bush became president in 2001, Democrats were unwilling to give him great deference and warned him not to nominate highly conservative "outside-the-mainstream" judges. By the time Bush sent up his first nominees, the Senate was under Democratic control. The Judiciary Committee promptly held hearings on and voted out uncontroversial nominees, even some that were quite conservative. Those appellate court nominees that Democrats perceived as ideologues, however, fared less well; confirmation hearings

---

27. *Roll Call,* April 6, 2004.

28. Oleszek, *Congressional Procedures and the Policy Process,* chap. 2.

29. Sheldon Goldman, "The Senate and Judicial Nominations," *Extensions: A Journal of the Carl Albert Congressional Research and Studies Center* (Spring 2004): 8–9.

were delayed, and two were voted down in committee on straight party-line votes.

When Republicans took back control of the Senate after the 2002 election, they were able to report the controversial nominees out of committee. But if Democrats were willing to filibuster the nominations and were able to stick together, Republicans could not muster the 60 votes necessary to cut off debate and bring the nominations to a vote. With Democrats refusing to agree to an up-or-down vote on a number of nominees, Majority Leader Frist decided to bring the appellate court nomination of Miguel Estrada to the floor in early 2003. Republicans were testing whether Democrats would be willing to block a Hispanic nominee in a highly public forum. The nomination was debated for almost 100 hours over the course of a month before the Majority Leader filed a cloture petition, and during that period the Senate did little else.[30] Democrats beat back cloture by a vote of 55 to 45 and, over the course of several months, won six more cloture votes on Estrada. After the seventh failure, Estrada withdrew his name from consideration. Democrats blocked 9 other controversial appellate nominees during the 108th Congress, winning 13 cloture votes.[31]

The Senate's non-majoritarian rules exert pressure on senators to compromise across party lines if they want to get anything done. Floor voting is about as partisan in the Senate as in the House when gauged by the usual voting measures, but the Senate is less partisan than the House at the committee level. However, when agreement across party lines is not possible, as is often the case in this period of high partisan polarization, the result is likely to be a stalemate. Passing anything controversial in the Senate now requires 60 votes. Major measures are much more likely to fail in the Senate than in the House; in recent congresses for which data are available, 10 times as many major bills passed the House and not the Senate as vice versa.[32]

WHAT'S THE BOTTOM LINE?

Although I still cannot give a clear-cut answer to the question the title asks, my examination of the factors that contribute to gridlock and those that facilitate legislative productivity does provide the basis for some conclusions. Partisan polarization and the attendant stronger party leadership has made the House of Representatives a more efficient bill-producing factory. Gridlock is

---

30. *Congressional Record,* March 6, 2003, S3216.

31. *Congressional Quarterly Weekly,* July 24, 2004, p. 1785.

32. Sinclair, "The New World of U.S. Senators," p. 17.

seldom a problem *within* the House. In contrast, partisan polarization has exacerbated the problems the Senate has in making decisions. Supermajority requirements always increase the status quo bias of decision-making processes; that is, they make gridlock more likely. Combine supermajority requirements with parties that are highly polarized and fairly equal in size—as is the case in the Senate today—and the potential for gridlock goes up exponentially.

Considering the barriers to legislative productivity, perhaps one should ask "Why not more gridlock?" A part of the answer is that members of Congress do pay attention to strongly expressed public sentiment, and when that dictates legislative action, they will respond. In the aftermath of the September 11 attacks, for example, Congress acted with speed and near unanimity to pass a number of the measures the president deemed necessary. Nor need the catalyst be something so drastic. When a federal court ruled that the Federal Trade Commission had gone beyond the scope of existing law in setting up a do-not-call list, Congress fixed the law within two days. Congress had no intention of disappointing the 50 million potential voters who had signed up for the list. In 1995, the new Republican Congress tried to force President Clinton to accept their budget-balancing plan by refusing to pass appropriations bills. When, as a result, the government shut down and the public blamed the Republicans, congressional Republicans learned that this was not a viable strategy for extracting concessions from a president of the other party. Ever since, Congress has passed the necessary appropriations legislation. The minority party in the Senate is only willing and able to use its prerogatives under Senate rules to block so long as its members believe they will pay little political price for doing so. Thus, Senate Democrats did not filibuster the final version of the Medicare prescription drug bill even though many strongly opposed it. They feared being blamed by seniors eager for a drug benefit.

Much of the seeming gridlock of recent years, I would argue, is a reflection of a divided country. And when the citizenry is narrowly divided on the appropriate direction that policy should take, a lack of action may not be altogether a bad thing. Do we want truly major legislation, legislation that represents a nonincremental departure from past policy, enacted by bare congressional majorities and without broad support in the public?

Even if we agree that a certain amount of gridlock is not that awful, how Congress goes about doing its essential work is a cause for concern. To fund the myriad programs and activities of the national government, Congress is supposed to pass 13 appropriations bills each year. The process of putting together these bills in committee and debating them on the floor gives the members of Congress an opportunity to examine programs and weigh in on their comparative importance. The policy choices made in appropriations bills are all the more important as Congress has not passed reauthorization legislation for many of the programs.[33] Yet, of late, Congress has failed to pass and, in many cases, even debate 13 freestanding bills on the floor. In 2004, for example, the Senate never considered 7 of 13 appropriations bills. Instead, the party leadership has superintended a process in which all the appropriations are rolled into one huge omnibus bill in conference that members are then forced to vote on as a single package. Members are presented with these multi-thousand page bills with little time to examine the contents before they must vote. In late 2004, after the third year in a row of such omnibus bills, Brian Baird (D-Wash.), in an op-ed piece entitled "We Need to Read the Bills," complained of having "only a few hours to read bills that are thousands of pages in length and spend hundreds of billions of the people's dollars."[34] This process excludes most members from the decision making, it makes a mockery of deliberation, and it invites stealth lawmaking.[35] Not only does the leadership routinely drop provisions that have been approved by majority vote in one or both chambers but it also adds provisions that lack majority support.[36] In late 2004, the process made news because someone discovered a provision in the megabill that gave the Appropriations Committee chairs and their staff unrestricted access to the income-tax returns of ordinary Americans with no penalties for public disclosure. After a public outcry, that provision was removed; but an antiabortion provision that would never have passed the Senate as freestanding legislation received much less media attention and became law without debate or a separate vote.

The congressional majority party and its leaders argue that their approach to legislating—not just employing omnibus bills but routinely using the full clout of the majority and its leadership to enact legislation in a form the president and the majority party prefers—is necessary for Congress to function under current conditions of partisan polarization and narrow margins. Their duty, especially when Congress and the presidency are controlled by the same party, is to govern. There are costs as well, however. Whether the benefits outweigh the costs is for the citizenry to decide.

---

33. Alex Wayne and Bill Swindell, "2004 Legislative Summary: Capitol Hill Gridlock Leaves Programs in Limbo."

34. *Washington Post,* November 27, 2004.

35. Scott Lilly, "When Congress Acts in the Dark of Night, Everyone Loses," *Roll Call,* Dec. 6, 2004.

36. Andrew Taylor and John Cranford, "Omnibus Wielding Majority Finds Power in the Package," *Congressional Quarterly Weekly* (November 20, 2004): 2724–28.

12

Why Not the Best?

The Loyalty–Competence Trade-Off in Presidential Appointments

GEORGE C. EDWARDS III
Texas A&M University

Every new administration promises to nominate highly talented, well-qualified people to fill appointed positions in the executive branch of the federal government.[1] Yet every president nominates to positions of responsibility more than a few people who do not satisfy the National Academy of Public Management's call for "able, creative, and experienced people," who will serve as "the most important ingredient in the recipe for good government."[2]

1. There are 3000 political appointees. These appointments fall into three categories. First, there are the Executive Schedule appointees, including the secretaries of cabinet departments; the heads of independent agencies and their deputies; and the heads of major departmental or agency bureaus or divisions, such as assistant secretaries. These appointees are nominated by the president and confirmed by the Senate. There are nearly 600 appointees in the Executive Schedule.

   A second category of political appointees is comprised of noncareer senior executives. These officials include senior staff in the immediate offices of cabinet secretaries, deputy secretaries, agency heads, and deputy assistant secretaries. There are currently more than 700 noncareer senior executives, who are not subject to Senate confirmation.

   The more than 1,700 Schedule C employees constitute the largest category of political appointees. Most hold titles such as "executive assistant" or "special assistant" and provide confidential support services to those in the Executive Schedule or to noncareer senior executives. A few hold management positions in special staff offices or small field offices. These officials are also not subject to Senate confirmation.

2. John W. Macy, Bruce Adams, and J. Jackson Walter, *America's Unelected Government* (Cambridge, MA: Ballinger, 1983), p. 100.

Table 12–1 Appointees' Evaluation of Senate-Confirmed Appointees

They represent the best and brightest America has to offer.	11%
They are a mixed lot: Some are highly talented while others do not have the skills and experience their positions require.	79
They are not the most talented Americans, but they are adequate to perform the tasks assigned to them.	8
Overall, their talents are not adequate to the demands of their positions.	1

SOURCE: Paul C. Light and Virginia L. Thomas, *The Merit and Reputation of an Administration; Presidential Appointees on the Appointments Process* (Washington, DC: Brookings Institution and Heritage Foundation, 2000), p. 33.

Although there may be disagreement on just who qualifies as a "quality" appointment, almost everyone also agrees that overall, the quality of appointees could—and should—be higher. A survey conducted for the Brookings Institution's Presidential Appointee Initiative queried 435 senior-level appointees who served in the second Reagan, Bush, and Clinton administrations. Table 12–1 shows that when asked to rate their fellow appointees, they gave mixed reviews. Clearly, there is room for improvement.

Given the good intentions of all administrations to nominate "good" people, why do they so often fail to do so? Equally important, what can a new administration do to avoid making the same mistake? To answer these questions, this chapter focuses on the competing criteria by which the White House evaluates potential appointees, delineates the reasons why presidents feel they need to emphasize loyalty in making their appointments, and then challenges both the necessity and the utility of weighing loyalty over competence.

THE DIMENSIONS OF "QUALITY"

Although there is widespread agreement that presidents should make high-quality appointments to run the bureaucracy, this consensus may quickly dissolve when we begin to define terms. Just what is a "quality" appointment?

Quality, like beauty, is in the eye of the beholder. Evaluations of quality depend heavily on what the evaluator wants from the bureaucracy. At a minimum, everyone wishes to avoid corruption and scandal. Most of those who urge higher-quality appointments explicitly or implicitly refer to job-related characteristics of appointees, such as analytical intelligence, substantive expertise, and managerial skills. Their primary goal is that policies be implemented in an efficient and effective manner. Conversely, the White House places a premium on reliability and trust over such impersonal qualities because the president's highest priority is the responsiveness of the executive branch to his policies. In addition, the president faces a need to reward individuals, constituencies, and contributors who helped him win office and to meet the demands of high-level appointees to name some of their subordinates.

Integrity

Most everyone agrees that integrity is the *sine qua non* appointment criterion. Officials lacking in integrity are unlikely to provide good advice and competent administration. Equally important, lapses in integrity can cause the president irreparable harm. Integrity is essential, but it is a filter with a wide mesh that will screen out only a few potential nominees. Thus, although integrity is an essential dimension of a quality nominee, it is not a sufficient criterion for choosing among potential officeholders. If quality is related to performance, it must represent more than the absence of ethical problems.

Loyalty to the President

Presidential recruiters agree that one important criterion for a quality presidential appointment is loyalty to the president as a person. According to George H. W. Bush's White House personnel director Chase Untermeyer, this type of loyalty holds up when the going gets tough—as it inevitably will.[3] Although there are many exceptions, the loyalty credential is most typically established by working on the presidential campaign. The campaign is a trial by fire in which devoted followers choose among rivals for the nomination and sacrifice for the candidate, battling their adversaries within and outside the party during a protracted struggle. It is only natural that this process creates strong bonds between the candidate and his supporters, and that this bond continues into the presidency.

The question, of course, is whether those who are skilled at helping the president obtain the White House are also those best-suited for governing once the election is over. There are significant differences between campaigning and governing. Implementing government programs is largely an anonymous, long-term, service-delivery activity where success is measured in terms of productivity, operational efficiency, cost effectiveness, and client benefit. A political campaign, on the other hand, is a relatively short-term enterprise that markets a particular person and whose object is to demonstrate why one choice is good and the other is bad. Campaigns lend themselves to superficial treatment of complicated issues through short commercials or news sound

---

3. White House Interview Program, Interview with Chase Untermeyer by Martha Joynt Kumar, July 6, 1999, Houston, Texas.

bites. Success is measured in terms of votes cast.[4] Although the skills required for governing and campaigning overlap, effective governing, which is primarily the implementation of public policy, requires more than expertise in running political campaigns.

Commitment to the President's Program

Related to loyalty to the president is adherence to his political philosophy and commitment to his program. The Reagan administration placed an especially high priority on ideological screening. As White House personnel director Pendleton James put it, "You have to keep thinking, What does the President want?" From this perspective, being a good manager or a policy expert is not enough. When the going gets tough, the issues that become politicized are usually value issues, not technical questions. Appointees committed to the president's program are more likely to display the toughness, courage, and stamina necessary to implement his policies in the face of resistance from many quarters of the political system.[5] People who disagree with the president's policies are unlikely to implement his directives with the same vigor as those who agree with the policies. In addition, those who are committed to the president's program are more likely to mobilize the resources of their agencies to think creatively about advice they offer the president to further the accomplishment of his goals.

It is for these reasons that Donald Devine and Jim Burnley argue that the most important criteria for selecting political appointees are (1) their character, toughness, and reliability; and (2) their loyalty to the president and his program. Only then, they say, should an evaluation of a potential appointee's skills come into play.[6] The danger in such a formulation is that loyalty trumps skill, and the president ends up with committed appointees who are ineffective in achieving their collective goals.

Ability

What most people mean when they discuss the quality of an appointment is a person's *ability*. There are many dimensions to ability, however.

Intellectual Ability. One important component of ability is a person's intellectual skills. These include both analytical skills and substantive expertise.

---

4. On this point, see David M. Cohen, "Amateur Government," *Journal of Public Administration Research and Theory* 8 (October 1998), pp. 488–89.

5. White House Interview Program, Interview with Pendleton James by Martha Joynt Kumar, November 8, 1999, Washington, DC.

6. Donald J. Devine and Jim Burnley, "The Role of the Agency Head," in Charles L. Heatherly and Burton Yale Pines, eds., *Mandate for Leadership III* (Washington, DC: Heritage Foundation, 1989), p. 806.

Few would argue against naming intelligent and knowledgeable people to positions of responsibility, but there are mixed opinions about the priority to assign brainpower in evaluating job candidates. For example, Pendleton James argues that appointees do not have to be brilliant. Instead, they need only "a minimum of competence."[7] Others argue that often a person who has gained program knowledge by working in an area with which his or her agency has a close relationship is the "worst" appointee because that person may find it difficult to be loyal to the administration rather than the interest with which he or she has been associated.[8]

Richard Nixon preferred loyalty to ability. While at Camp David preparing for his second term, he told his top aides that when it came to evaluating appointees, "we want loyalty" and "not brains." He also wanted to base foreign service appointments "first on loyalty, then competence." As a result of his criteria, he preferred to "get good hacks" as secretaries in the various departments.[9]

Political Skills. Both the White House and more detached observers agree that an ideal appointee would be savvy in the ways of Washington and possess significant political skills. These skills include prowess at the critical tasks of dealing with the press, Capitol Hill, the courts, state and local officials, and interest groups. Proficiency at negotiating and public speaking may also be important to an appointee's success.

There are many examples of failure to meet these standards. Bill Clinton's first Surgeon General, Jocelyn Elders, had to resign because of her insensitivity to the political implications of her public remarks. In the Reagan administration, Secretary of the Interior James Watt and Director of the Environmental Protection Agency Anne Gorsuch Burford displayed a similar insensitivity, as well as a heavy-handed approach in implementing policies. The resulting popular outcry and the mobilization of opposition groups led the Reagan administration to remove them from office and to retreat from its own policy goals in the area of environmental protection.

Managerial Skills. Most high-level appointees have responsibility for *managing* a part of the federal bureaucracy. It makes sense that these appointees be skilled at working within a bureaucracy. Managerial skills are varied, ranging from planning, organizing, and motivating employees to creating open communication with subordinates and good working conditions for employees. Equally important, managers must develop administrative strategies for accomplishing the president's goals. A poor design can be detrimental to bringing about change.

---

7. White House Interview Program, Interview with Pendleton James.

8. Devine and Burnley, "The Role of the Agency Head," p. 806.

9. Quoted in Richard Reeves, *President Nixon: Alone in the White House* (New York: Simon and Schuster, 2001), p. 547.

Personal Characteristics. A final component of ability is the personality of the appointee. For our purposes, personality includes job-related characteristics such as interpersonal skills,[10] personal stability, sense of self-esteem, flexibility, tolerance for conflict, ability to accept criticism, and a sense of duty. People lacking in these characteristics are less likely to be effective leaders within their agencies.

Presidents also value appointees who are team players. They want appointees who can work with both the White House and other administration officials. The president is unlikely to nominate people who he views as likely to be uncooperative or who will engage in visible self-promotion.

WHY DOES THE WHITE HOUSE DISTRUST THE BUREAUCRACY?

There is tension between the White House's need for loyal and committed appointees and the country's more abstract requirement for men and women of exceptional integrity and ability to run the executive branch. Why do different observers and participants weigh dimensions of quality differently? The essence of the explanation is that the White House feels it needs to use appointees to lead career bureaucrats, whose responsiveness to the president it distrusts.

Agency Discretion

Laws often permit agency heads wide latitude in making public policy. They may influence the rules, procedures, design, and substance of agency action.[11] This latitude provides implementers with the leeway to give new meaning to policies, which sometimes inhibits intended change or brings about unintended consequences.

The leeway in policy implementation can be attributed to several factors. Perhaps the most important is the sheer complexity of policy making. When they establish policy, neither presidents nor members of Congress have the time or expertise to develop and apply all the requisite details for how it will be carried out. They have to leave most (and sometimes all) of the details to subordinates (usually in the executive branch). Thus, although

---

10. For the importance of interpersonal skills, see Paul C. Light, "When Worlds Collide: The Political-Career Nexus," in G. Calvin Mackenzie, ed., *The In-and-Outers: Presidential Appointees and Transient Government in Washington* (Baltimore, MD: Johns Hopkins University Press, 1987), pp. 165, 171.

11. On administrative discretion, see Gary S. Bryner, *Bureaucratic Discretion* (New York: Pergamon Press, 1987).

it is the president's responsibility to implement the policies of the national government no matter who initiates them, much of this responsibility must be delegated to others.

The difficulty in reaching consensus on policy goals also inhibits clarity in implementation directives. In the United States, we share wide agreement on the goals of avoidance of war, equal opportunity, and efficiency in government, but this consensus often dissolves when specific policy alternatives are under consideration. As Lyndon Johnson once said, "If the full implications of any bill were known before its enactment, it would never get passed."[12]

Imprecise decisions make it easier for presidents to develop and maintain winning coalitions. Different people or groups can support the same policy for different reasons, as each may hold its own conception of the goal or goals the program is designed to achieve. Ambiguous goals also may make it less threatening for groups to be on the losing side of a policy conflict, which may reduce the intensity of their opposition.

The problems of starting up a new program may also produce confusion in the implementation instructions. Often, the passage of a new policy is followed by a period of administrative uncertainty in which a considerable time lag occurs before any information on the program is disseminated. This period is followed by a second phase in which rules are made but are then changed quickly as high-level officials attempt to deal with unforeseen problems of implementing the policy and of their own earlier directives.

A cynical, yet realistic, explanation for the lack of clarity in federal statutes is that Congress does not want them to be detailed. Some members of the legislature would rather let the executive branch agencies (and sometimes the courts) provide the specifics, not because of the latter's expertise but because the agencies and judges can later be assigned the blame for the rules that turn out to be unworkable or unpopular. Such broad language allows Congress to sidestep many touchy questions and leave their resolution to the president and his appointees. Moreover, individual members of Congress can gain credit with their constituents by intervening on their behalf regarding the application of regulations. In addition, if the goals are not precise, Congress cannot be held accountable for the failure of its policies to achieve them.

Inconsistency as well as vagueness in guidance from the president and Congress may provide operating agencies with substantial discretion in the interpretation and implementation of policy. For example, the Immigration and Naturalization Service was often confronted with inconsistencies: The

---

12. Quoted in Doris Kearns, *Lyndon Johnson and the American Dream* (New York: Harper and Row, 1976), p. 137.

agency was supposed to keep out illegal immigrants but allow necessary agricultural workers to enter the country; it had to carefully screen foreigners seeking to enter the country but facilitate the entry of foreign tourists; and it had to find and expel illegal aliens yet not break up families, impose hardships, violate civil rights, or deprive employers of low-paid workers. As James Q. Wilson points out, "No organization can accomplish all of these goals well, especially when advocates of each have the power to mount newspaper and congressional investigations of the agency's failures."[13] Similarly, the Forest Service is supposed to both help timber companies exploit the lumber potential in the national forests *and* preserve the natural environment.

Many of the factors that produce unclear communications are also responsible for inconsistent directives. The complexity of public policies, the difficulties in starting up new programs, and the multiple objectives of many policies all contribute to inconsistency in policy communications. Another reason why decisions are often inconsistent is that the president and top officials constantly attempt to satisfy a diverse set of interests that may represent views on both sides of an issue. Consequently, policies that are not of high priority to the president may simply be left to founder in a sea of competing demands.

Because implementation instructions are rarely specific, personnel at each rung in the bureaucratic ladder must use their judgment to expand and develop them. Obviously, this process creates the potential for distorting the president's wishes. Moreover, the further down in the bureaucracy presidential implementation directives go, the greater is the potential for distortion. Bureaucrats may use their discretion to further their personal interests and those of their agencies. Interest groups take advantage of the discretion granted to bureaucrats by pushing for their own demands at intermediate and low decision-making levels. It is for these reasons that observers of the federal bureaucracy often recommend that presidents and other high officials make every attempt to commit their directives to writing (in detail where possible), use personalized communications where appropriate, and show persistence in attempting to accurately convey their orders to those who actually implement the policies.

Agency Parochialism

Government agencies have a tendency toward inbreeding, as the selective recruitment of new staff serves to develop homogeneous attitudes. People who are attracted to work for government agencies are likely to support the

---

13. James Q. Wilson, *Bureaucracy: What Government Agencies Do and Why They Do It* (New York: Basic Books, 1989), p. 158.

policies carried out by those agencies, whether they are in the fields of social welfare, agriculture, or national defense. Naturally, agencies prefer hiring like-minded people. Within each agency, the distribution of rewards creates further pressure to view things from the perspective of the status quo. Personnel who do not support established organizational goals and approaches to meeting them are unlikely to be promoted to important positions. Moreover, all but a few high-level members of the civil service spend their careers within a single agency or department. Even with the introduction of the Senior Executive Service (SES) in 1978, few career SES officials have moved across agency lines.[14] Because people want to believe in what they do for a living, this long association strongly influences the attitudes of bureaucrats.

Related to longtime service in an agency is the relatively narrow range of each agency's responsibilities. Officials in the Department of Education, for example, do not deal with the budget for the entire national government but only with the part that pertains to their programs. It is up to others to recommend to the president what is best allocated to education and what should go to national defense, health, or housing. With each bureaucratic unit focusing on its own programs, few people are in a position to view these programs from a wider national perspective.

Influences from outside an agency also encourage parochial views among bureaucrats. When interest groups and congressional committees support an agency, they expect continued bureaucratic support in return. Since these outsiders generally favor the policies the bureaucracy has been carrying out all along and which they probably helped initiate, what they really want is to perpetuate the status quo.

The combination of these factors results in a relatively uniform environment for policy making. Intraorganizational communications pass mainly among people who share similar frames of reference and reinforce bureaucratic parochialism by their continued association.

The influence of parochialism is strong enough that some presidential appointees, who are in office for only short periods of time, are "captured" and adopt the narrow views of their bureaucratic units. The dependence of such officials on their subordinates for information and advice, the need to maintain organizational morale by supporting established viewpoints, and pressures from their agencies' clienteles combine to discourage high-ranking officials from pursuing changes in policies.

President Nixon observed that "it is inevitable when an individual has been in a Cabinet position or, for that matter, holds any position in Government,

---

14. See Mark W. Huddleston and William W. Boyer, *The Higher Civil Service in the United States: Quest for Reform* (Pittsburgh, PA: University of Pittsburgh Press, 1996).

[that] after a certain length of time he becomes an advocate of the status quo; rather than running the bureaucracy, the bureaucracy runs him."[15] Thus, parochialism can lead officials to see different faces on the same issue.

President Reagan had the same concerns about bureaucratic parochialism as Nixon did. It was for this reason that his administration went to considerable lengths to insulate new cabinet appointees from the traditional agency arguments in defense of programs that the White House had slated for cuts. The appointees received their initial briefings from the president, the director of the Office of Management and Budget, and citizens groups rather than from the bureaucracy; they were often assigned deputies with close personal and ideological ties to the White House; and as a condition of appointment, they were given little time to react to the president's proposals before having to agree to support them.

White House Distrust

The facts that bureaucrats hold particular policy views and have discretion in the implementation of policy do not in themselves pose problems for presidents. If implementers are well disposed toward a particular policy, they are likely to carry it out as the president intended. Other policies fall within a "zone of indifference." Lacking strong feelings about these policies, bureaucrats should implement them faithfully.

The core of the tension over standards of quality is the view that recent administrations have brought to Washington that the bureaucracy is not a neutral instrument. As the author of one prominent study put it,

> It is a rare political appointee . . . who does not take up his or her office convinced that senior career officials are . . . recalcitrant adversaries, saboteurs-in-waiting, obstinately committed to existing programs, and resistant to new policy initiatives.[16]

The new president and his staff believe that officials and the agencies they represent have interests of their own to advance and protect and may not necessarily view issues from the president's perspective.[17] If policies are in direct conflict with the policy views or personal or organizational interests of the implementers, they may exercise their discretion, sometimes in subtle

---

15. Richard M. Nixon, *Public Papers of the Presidents: Richard Nixon, 1972* (Washington, DC: Government Printing Office, 1974), p. 1150.

16. Mark W. Huddleston, *The Government's Managers* (New York: Priority Press, 1987), p. 61.

17. See, for example, Rosemary O'Leary, "The Bureaucratic Politics Paradox: The Case of Wetlands Legislation in Nevada," *Journal of Public Administration Research and Theory* 4 (No. 4, 1994): 443–67.

ways, to hinder implementation. Moreover, bureaucrats "have resources of organization, time, and information that enable them to pursue those interests with vigor and persistence."[18]

The White House emphasizes political appointees because it distrusts the career bureaucracy.[19] A principal responsibility of political appointees is to elicit responsiveness of career officials to their directions. Many White House officials view this task as posing a challenge to even the most committed, adroit, and persistent appointees. As the size and scope of the federal government have grown since the 1960s, so has distrust toward it, especially among Republican presidents and the general public. Richard Nixon told his cabinet, "We can't depend on people who believe in another philosophy of government to give us their undivided loyalty or their best work."[20] Similarly, Gerald Ford observed,

> There are bureaucratic fiefdoms out in the states or in various regions, and the people who occupy those pockets of power want to do things in their own way. They are pros at it. They have been disregarding Presidents for years, both Democratic and Republican.[21]

As a result, presidents are more likely to focus on increasing their control of the bureaucracy than they are on improving the quality of the management of it.[22] According to Terry Moe,

> Whatever his particular policy objectives, whatever his personality and style, the modern president is driven . . . to seek control over the structures and processes of government. . . . He is not interested in efficiency or effectiveness or coordination per se, and he does not give preeminence to the "neutral competence" these properties may seem to require.[23]

---

18. David Lowery, "The Presidency, the Bureaucracy, and Reinvention: A Gentle Plea for Chaos," *Presidential Studies Quarterly* 30 (March 2000), p. 93.

19. See Lawrence R. Jacobs and Robert Y. Shapiro, *Politicians Don't Pander* (Chicago: University of Chicago Press, 2000), pp. 88–89, on how the Clinton administration distrusted civil servants in developing their health care reform plan in 1993.

20. Quoted in Carl M. Brauer, *Presidential Transitions: Eisenhower through Reagan* (New York: Oxford University Press, 1986), p. 150.

21. Gerald R. Ford, "Imperiled, Not Imperial," *Time* (November 10, 1980): 30.

22. Richard P. Nathan, *The Administrative Presidency* (New York: John Wiley and Sons, 1983).

23. Terry M. Moe, "The Politicized Presidency," in James P. Pfiffner, ed., *The Managerial Presidency,* 2nd ed. (College Station, TX: Texas A&M University Press, 1999), p. 147.

The White House has acted to constrain the exercise of bureaucratic discretion by requiring clearance of regulations and congressional testimony, limiting agency budgets, and establishing process restrictions on procurement and other spending.[24] Perhaps most importantly, the White House has sought to more centrally control personnel decisions and has deepened the penetration of political appointees into departments and agencies. The number of political appointees at the top of the executive bureaucracy has increased substantially, as has the number of political appointees at lower ranks.[25] Employing a related technique, presidents have also made efforts just before leaving office to place political appointees in career positions. In addition, presidents and their appointees have used provisions of the Civil Service Reform Act of 1978, which allows them to reassign top-level civil servants.

In short, presidents and their advisors have taken to heart the findings of scholars of public administration, who more than a half century ago discredited the notion of a dichotomy between administration and politics.[26] Instead, the White House sees administration pervaded by politics, and it fears that this politics will not serve its interests.

What evidence is there to support the expectation that the bureaucracy will not be responsive to the president? Executive departments and independent agencies have agendas set by laws that predate the president's arrival in office and that serve as a force for continuity rather than change. In addition, it does not stretch the imagination to consider that how officials exercise their discretion depends to some degree on their dispositions about the policies and rules they administer.[27]

There is plenty of evidence that at times the ideologies of the White House and senior members of the civil service have clashed, although this

---

24. William T. Gormley, *Taming the Bureaucracy: Muscles, Prayers, and Other Strategies* (Princeton, NJ: Princeton University Press, 1989); Paul C. Light, *The Tides of Reform: Making Government Work, 1945–1995* (New Haven, CT: Yale University Press, 1997); Peri Arnold, *Making the Managerial Presidency: Comprehensive Reorganization Planning, 1905–1996* (Lawrence: University Press of Kansas, 1998); William F. West, *Controlling the Bureaucracy* (Armonk, NY: M. E. Sharpe, 1995).

25. See Paul C. Light, *Thickening Government* (Washington, DC: Brookings Institution, 1995).

26. Herbert A. Simon, *Administrative Behavior* (New York: Macmillan, 1947); Dwight Waldo, *The Administrative State* (New York: Ronald Press, 1949); Paul H. Appleby, *Policy and Administration* (University, Alabama: University of Alabama Press, 1949).

27. John Brehm and Scott Gates, *Working, Shirking, and Sabotage: Bureaucratic Responses to a Democratic Republic* (Ann Arbor: University of Michigan Press, 1997), p. 73, chap. 5.

potential for resistance to presidential initiatives has varied across agencies.[28] Verifying that the policy predispositions of civil servants are critical to their compliance with their political principals is more difficult.

In his study of political appointees, Hugh Heclo concluded that bureaucratic sabotage of political appointees was common, but he did not provide systematic evidence in support of this conclusion.[29] He also maintains that most sabotage is not proactive but rather takes the form of passive acceptance of orders and failure to share information with appointees that would help them accomplish their goals. In a more rigorous study, B. Dan Wood and Richard Waterman found that the Environmental Protection Agency maintained and even increased its inspections and citations of violations of environmental regulations in the face of strong efforts by the Reagan administration to constrain the enforcement of environmental protection laws.[30] Marissa Golden[31] and Karen Holt[32] found some resistance to Reagan initiatives in the Civil Rights Division of the Justice Department.

28. See, for example, Joel D. Aberbach and Bert A. Rockman, "Clashing Beliefs within the Executive Branch: The Nixon Administration Bureaucracy," *American Political Science Review* 70 (June 1976): 456–68; Richard L. Cole and David A. Caputo, "Presidential Control of the Senior Civil Service: Assessing the Strategies of the Nixon Years," *American Political Science Review* 73 (June 1979): 399–413; Robert Maranto, "Still Clashing after All These Years: Ideological Conflict in the Reagan Executive," *American Journal of Political Science* 37 (August 1993): 681–98; Marissa Martino Golden, "Exit, Voice, Loyalty, and Neglect: Bureaucratic Responses to Presidential Control during the Reagan Administration," *Journal of Public Administration Research and Theory* 2 (January 1992): 29–62; Robert A. Maranto, *Politics and Bureaucracy in the Modern Presidency; Careerists and Appointees in the Reagan Administration* (Westport, CT: Greenwood Press, 1993); Judith E. Michaels, *The President's Call: Executive Leadership from FDR to George Bush* (Pittsburgh: University of Pittsburgh Press, 1997).

29. Hugh Heclo, *A Government of Strangers* (Washington, DC: Brookings Institution, 1977), pp. 171–72, 224–32.

30. B. Dan Wood, "Principals, Bureaucrats, and Responsiveness in Clean Air Enforcements," *American Political Science Review* 82 (March 1988): 213–34; B. Dan Wood and Richard W. Waterman, "The Dynamics of Political-Bureaucratic Adaptation," *American Journal of Political Science* 37 (May 1993): 497–528; B. Dan Wood and Richard W. Waterman, *Bureaucratic Dynamics* (Boulder, CO: Westview, 1994). See also Marissa Martino Golden, *What Motivates Bureaucrats: Politics and Administration during the Reagan Years* (New York: Columbia University Press, 2000), chap. 6.

31. Golden, "Exit, Voice, Loyalty, and Neglect;" *What Motivates Bureaucrats,* chap. 5.

32. Karen E. Holt, *When Officials Clash: Implementation of the Civil Rights of Institutionalized Persons Act* (Westport, CT: Praeger, 1998).

ARE CAREERISTS RESPONSIVE
TO THE PRESIDENT?

Despite some evidence of bureaucratic resistance to presidential initiatives, there is good reason to expect the bureaucracy to cooperate with the president's wishes. The professional norms of career civil servants offer political appointees considerable flexibility in directing agencies.[33] Francis Rourke argues that cases of bureaucratic challenge to presidential authority have been "a rare occurrence" and that senior bureaucrats follow the election returns and defer to the president.[34] "What is surprising," agrees James Q. Wilson, "is not that bureaucrats sometimes can defy the president but that they support his programs as much as they do. The reason is simple: . . . bureaucrats want to do the right thing."[35]

If necessary, which it rarely is, political appointees have a range of management tools to prevent or discourage resistance to their policies. Civil servants typically wish to avoid demotions, transfers, or dismissals. Appointees may bypass civil servants; exclude them from critical meetings; and demote, transfer, or dismiss them.[36]

Richard Waterman and Kenneth Meier concluded, "All political–bureaucratic relationships are not a caldron of conflict."[37] Steven Stehr found that during the Reagan administration, high-level bureaucrats thought the president's political appointees were very influential in their agencies and wanted even more influence to be exercised by key political executives as opposed to other influences on policy implementation.[38] Patricia Ingraham interviewed

---

33. Robert Maranto and B. Douglas Skelley, "Neutrality: An Enduring Principle of the Civil Service," *American Review of Public Administration* 22 (September 1992): 173–88; Golden, *What Motivates Bureaucrats,* pp. 155–56.

34. Francis Rourke, "Bureaucracy in the American Constitutional Order," *Political Science Quarterly* 102 (Summer 1987), p. 219; Francis E. Rourke, "Grappling with the Bureaucracy," in Arnold J. Meltsner, ed., *Politics and the Oval Office: Towards Presidential Governance* (San Francisco, CA: Institute for Contemporary Studies, 1981), p. 137.

35. James Q. Wilson, *Bureaucracy: What Government Agencies Do and Why they Do It,* p. 275. See also Colin Campbell and Donald Naulls, "The Limits of the Budget-Maximizing Theory: Some Evidence from Officials' Views of Their Roles and Careers," in Andre Blais and Stephane Dion, eds., *The Budget-Maximizing Bureaucrat: Appraisals and Evidence* (Pittsburgh, PA: University of Pittsburgh Press, 1991), pp. 85–118.

36. See Golden, *What Motivates Bureaucrats,* pp. 156–60.

37. Richard W. Waterman and Kenneth J. Meier, "Principal-Agent Models: An Expansion?" *Journal of Public Administration Research and Theory* 8 (April 1998): 173–202, 197.

38. Steven D. Stehr, "Top Bureaucrats and the Distribution of Influence in Reagan's Executive Branch," *Public Administration Review* 57 (January/February 1997): 75–82.

officials in health, housing, and transportation. On the whole, she found, key career participants did *not* oppose change.[39]

Other scholars, including Terry Moe, B. Dan Wood, James Anderson, Richard Waterman, Marissa Golden, and Evan Ringquist, have found substantial evidence of bureaucracies changing their implementation of policy in line with the president's wishes, even in areas of political controversy.[40] These agencies include the Equal Opportunity Employment Commission, the Federal Trade Commission, the Food and Drug Administration, the Office of Surface Mining and Reclamation, the Securities and Exchange Commission, the Nuclear Regulatory Commission, the National Highway Traffic Safety Administration, the Food and Nutrition Service, the Environmental Protection Agency, the National Labor Relations Board, the Justice Department's Antitrust Division, and the Interstate Commerce Commission.

James Pfiffner argues that despite their initial suspicion and hostility, political appointees usually develop trust in the career executives who work for them. He and others have found that the relationship between political appointees and career executives is characterized by a "cycle of accommodation." This cycle occurs among most presidential appointees in all recent presidential administrations. Table 12–2 shows the results of surveys of appointees in the Johnson through first-term Reagan administrations. *Regardless of party, ideology, or administration, the overwhelming majority of political appointees find that career executives are both competent and responsive.*[41] As Paul

---

39. Patricia W. Ingraham, "Political Direction and Policy Change in Three Federal Departments," in James P. Pfiffner, ed., *The Managerial Presidency,* 2nd ed. (College Station TX: Texas A&M University Press, 1999), pp. 209–11.

40. Terry M. Moe, "Regulatory Performance and Presidential Administration," *American Journal of Political Science* 26 (February 1982): 197–224; Terry M. Moe, "Control and Feedback in Economic Regulation: The Case of the NLRB," *The American Political Science Review* 79 (December 1985): 1094–1116; Wood, "Principals, Bureaucrats, and Responsiveness in Clean Air Enforcements"; B. Dan Wood and James E. Anderson, "The Politics of U.S. Antitrust Regulation," *American Journal of Political Science* 37 (February 1993): 1–39; B. Dan Wood and Richard W. Waterman, "The Dynamics of Political Control of the Bureaucracy," *American Political Science Review* 85 (September 1991): 801–28; B. Dan Wood and Richard W. Waterman, "The Dynamics of Political-Bureaucratic Adaptation," *American Journal of Political Science* 37 (May 1993): 497–528; Wood and Waterman, *Bureaucratic Dynamics;* Evan J. Ringquist, "Political Control and Policy Impact in EPA's Office of Water Quality," *American Journal of Political Science* 39 (May 1995): 336–63; Golden, *What Motivates Bureaucrats.*

41. James P. Pfiffner, *The Strategic Presidency,* 2nd ed. (Lawrence: University Press of Kansas, 1996), pp. 78–81; James P. Pfiffner, "Political Appointees and Career Executives: The Democracy-Bureaucracy Nexus in the Third Century," *Public Administration Review* 47 (January/February 1987): 57–65. See also Light, "When Worlds Collide"; Robert Maranto, "Does Familiarity Breed Acceptance? Trends in Career–Noncareer Relations in the Reagan Administration," *Administration and Society* 23 (August 1991): 247–66.

Table 12–2 Johnson–Reagan Appointees' Perception of Career Civil Servants

	Percentage Who Rated Careerists As Competent	Percentage Who Rated Careerists As Responsive
Party		
Democratic	92%	86%
Independent	85	87
Republican	83	78
Ideology		
Liberal	78	84
Moderate	90	85
Conservative	82	80
Administration		
Johnson	92	89
Nixon	88	84
Ford	80	82
Carter	81	86
Reagan*	77	78

*1981–1984

SOURCE: National Academy of Public Administration, Presidential Appointee Project, *Leadership in Jeopardy: The Fraying of the Presidential Appointments System* (Washington, DC: National Academy of Public Administration, 1985). This table is adapted from Paul C. Light, "When Worlds Collide: The Political-Career Nexus," in G. Calvin Mackenzie, ed., *The In-and-Outers: Presidential Appointees and Transient Government in Washington* (Baltimore, MD: Johns Hopkins University Press, 1987), p. 158.

Light put it, "In interview after interview, presidential appointees celebrate the dedication of their bureaucrats."[42]

Similarly, a survey of Bush political appointees found that they relied heavily on careerists for all aspects of their jobs, from formulating policy to implementing it. The political appointees also reported that they found career civil servants helpful in everything from mastering substantive policy details and anticipating policy implementation problems to liaisons with Congress and other components of the bureaucracy.[43] In Table 12–3 we can see the results from another survey of Bush political appointees. Most found that civil servants brought valuable experience to the job and had good leadership qualities and management skills. Equally important, these political appointees saw senior civil servants as working hard to carry out administration policies. Indeed, they perceived of themselves as less likely to have

---

42. Light, "When Worlds Collide," p. 166.

43. Michaels, *The President's Call*, pp. 234–35.

Table 12–3 Bush Appointees' Perception of Career Civil Servants and Political Appointees

	Percentage Agreement of Political Appointees About Civil Servants	Percentage Agreement of Political Appointees About Political Appointees
Bring valuable experience to the job	98%	82%
Have good leadership qualities	59	64
Have good management skills	61	55
Work hard to carry out administration initiatives and priorities	71	100

SOURCE: Adapted from Joel D. Aberbach and Bert A. Rockman, *In the Web of Politics: Three Decades of the U.S. Federal Executive* (Washington, DC: Brookings Institution, 2000), p. 123.

valuable experience and be good managers than the civil servants who worked for them.

The most recent data on the views of political appointees regarding career officials comes from the Brookings Institution's Presidential Appointee Initiative. Table 12–4 shows that once again, political appointees under the past three presidents find the career officials with whom they have worked to be both responsive and competent. In addition to the percentages given in the table, another 11 percent of the appointees found careerists to have medium responsiveness, and another 13 percent found them to display medium competence. It is especially interesting that it was Reagan administration officials, ostensibly the most anti-bureaucracy appointees, who were most likely to find career officials to be the competent and responsive.

When asked about the difficulty of the various elements of their jobs, only 25 percent of appointees found it difficult to direct career employees (shown in Table 12–5). To put this finding in perspective, political appointees were more likely to find *every* other task on the list to be difficult. A significantly higher proportion of appointees—36 percent—found dealing successfully with the White House to be difficult.

It is also the case that the clashing of beliefs between career managers and political appointees has receded over time as the political views of the permanent bureaucracy shifted to the right and the senior civil service became more centrist. An increasing number of Republicans and Independents have moved

Table 12–4 Reagan, Bush, and Clinton Appointees' Perception of Career Civil Servants

Appointees	Percentage Who Rated Careerists As Competent	Percentage Who Rated Careerists As Responsive
All	83%	81%
Reagan	86	87
Bush	85	83
Clinton	82	78

SOURCE: Paul C. Light and Virginia L. Thomas, *The Merit and Reputation of an Administration: Presidential Appointees on the Appointments Process* (Washington, DC: Brookings Institution and Heritage Foundation, 2000), pp. 9, 31, 32.

into career managerial positions.[44] Moreover, the Civil Service Reform Act of 1978 has given the White House the opportunity to place senior civil servants of its choosing in key positions. There is little need to make a trade-off between ability and loyalty in order to "control" the civil service.

In sum, the bulk of the evidence supports a view that federal bureaucrats are "principled agents."[45] As Joel Aberbach and Bert Rockman point out, there is little evidence to support assertions of recalcitrant career civil servants in the presence of effective administrative leadership, including open channels of communication, willingness to listen to advice, clear articulation of goals, and mutual respect. Good management is not incompatible with good politics.[46]

---

44. Joel D. Aberbach and Bert A. Rockman, with Robert M. Copeland, "From Nixon's Problem to Reagan's Achievement: The Federal Executive Reexamined," in Larry Berman, ed., *Looking Back on the Reagan Presidency* (Baltimore, MD: Johns Hopkins University Press, 1990); Joel D. Aberbach and Bert A. Rockman, "The Political Views of U.S. Senior Federal Executives, 1970–1992," *Journal of Politics* 57 (August 1995): 838–52; Joel D. Aberbach, "The Federal Executive under Clinton," in Colin Campbell and Bert A. Rockman, eds., *The Clinton Presidency: First Appraisals* (Chatham, NJ: Chatham House Publishers, 1996); Joel D. Aberbach, "The President and the Executive Branch," in Colin Campbell and Bert A. Rockman, eds., *The Bush Presidency: First Appraisals* (Chatham, NJ: Chatham House Publishers, 1991); Robert Maranto and Karen Marie Hult, "RIGHT TURN? Political Ideology in the Higher Civil Service, 1987–1994," *American Review of Public Administration* 14 (June 2004): 199–222.

45. Brehm and Gates, *Working, Shirking, and Sabotage*, p. 202. They also found that federal employees do not shirk and are hard workers, see chapter 5.

46. Joel D. Aberbach and Bert A. Rockman, "Mandates or Mandarins?" in James P. Pfiffner, ed., *The Managerial Presidency* (College Station, TX: Texas A&M University Press, 1999), p. 168.

Table 12–5 Reagan, Bush, and Clinton Appointees' Perceptions of the Difficulty of Job Tasks

In your (current/most recent) . . . job, how difficult (do/did) you find it to master . . . ?

Task	Very Difficult	Somewhat Difficult	Not Too Difficult	Not Difficult at All	Don't Know/ Refused to Answer
The substantive details of the policies you (deal/dealt) with	5%	26%	39%	28%	2%
The decision-making procedures of your department or agency	9	31	35	24	7
The informal political networks that affect(ed) the work of your agency or department	11	31	36	20	3
The federal budget process	19	32	24	20	3
Directing career employees	5	20	37	36	3
Dealing successfully with Congress	11	38	32	16	3
Dealing successfully with the White House	8	28	32	25	7
Managing a large government organization or program	9	34	32	23	3

SOURCE: Paul C. Light and Virginia L. Thomas, *The Merit and Reputation of an Administration: Presidential Appointees on the Appointments Process* (Washington, DC: Brookings Institution and Heritage Foundation, 2000), p. 31.

Why do new administrations persist in the expectation of facing bureaucratic resistance in the face of strong evidence of bureaucratic responsiveness? The answer seems to be that most political appointees have viewed their experience with careerists as somehow unique, believing the careerists with whom they served were different from others.[47] The recalcitrance of bureaucracy is such a strong element of the conventional wisdom about how government works that it perseveres in the face of widespread contradictory experience.

One of the greatest obstacles to presidential direction of the bureaucracy is the fact that bureaucracies have multiple principals. Congress passes the laws that establish and fund the programs that bureaucrats administer, and with increasing frequency, courts issue orders regarding implementing policies. In addition, agencies have extensive ties with external groups and congressional committees.[48] From one perspective, then, career civil servants have a strong political base from which to resist White House direction, including playing other political actors off against each other to diminish presidential influence.[49]

Nevertheless, many would agree with James Pfiffner that the "frustration of presidential desires is more often due to opposition from interest groups, Congress, and the president's own appointees than from the career bureaucracy." As likely as not, the cleavages may run between agencies and programs with appointees and careerists on the same side. The primary instigators for resistance to presidential policies are likely to be members of Congress, interest groups, and executive agencies rather than career officials.[50]

At other times, the president's efforts to change the course of policy mobilizes opponents, as when Reagan's efforts to reduce enforcement activity in the EPA's Office of Water Quality encouraged citizen suits that had the effect

---

47. Light, "When Worlds Collide," p. 160.

48. Scott R. Furlong, "Political Influence on the Bureaucracy: The Bureaucracy Speaks," *Journal of Public Administration Research and Theory* 8 (January 1998): 39–65.

49. Moe, "Control and Feedback in Economic Regulation"; Shep Melnick, *Regulation and the Courts: The Case of the Clean Air Act* (Washington, DC: Brookings Institution, 1983); George A. Krause, "Federal Reserve Policy Decision Making: Political and Bureaucratic Influences," *American Journal of Political Science* 38 (February 1994): 124–44; Richard W. Waterman, Amelia Rouse, and Robert Wright, "The Venues of Influence: A New Theory of Political Control of the Bureaucracy," *Journal of Public Administration Research and Theory* 8 (January 1998): 13–38; Richard W. Waterman and Kenneth J. Meier, "Principal-Agent Models: An Expansion?" *Journal of Public Administration Research and Theory* 8 (April 1998): 173–202; Jeff Worsham, Marc Allen Eisner, and Evan J. Ringquist, "Assessing Assumptions: A Critical Analysis of Agency Theory," *Administration and Society* 28 (February 1997): 419–40.

50. Pfiffner, *The Strategic Presidency*, pp. 73, 84–85.

of producing *lower* levels of political control in long run.[51] More broadly, the Reagan efforts to reduce the rigor of EPA regulation reinvigorated a flagging environmental movement and infuriated EPA's patrons in Congress, who resented what they saw as a blatant attempt to circumvent legislative intent by administrative action.[52]

In sum, a trade-off between ability and loyalty may not be necessary. Unless the president is aiming at altering the core mission of an agency, the White House is unlikely to meet stiff resistance from the bureaucracy. If the president does wish to change the fundamental role of an agency, he would be wise to concentrate on obstacles to change that lie outside the executive branch. In either case, he will need able managers to successfully implement policy.

ARE THERE COSTS TO EMPHASIZING LOYALTY ABOVE ABILITY?

We have seen that an emphasis on ideological and personal loyalty may not be necessary to achieve the president's administrative goals. Whether necessary or not, does such an emphasis contribute to improving policy implementation?

A president-elect's transition team will be inundated with studies regarding the nomination and confirmation processes, the retention of appointees, and the many ethics requirements for appointed officials. In addition, there are hundreds, indeed thousands, of studies of the impact of organizations, procedures, budgets, personnel resources, organizational cultures, decision rules, and related matters on the implementation of public policy. What is striking is that almost nothing is known about the impact of individual appointees on the quality of performance of the federal executive branch. Indeed, not a single study focuses systematically on this critical question. Thus, we know much more about the process of placing appointees in their positions than we do about the difference they make once they are in place.

Despite the absence of systematic data on the performance of appointees, there is no shortage of commentary on it. For example, David Cohen, a former career senior executive, has forcefully argued that no matter what the selection criteria, appointees are often not responsive to the White House because they come with personal agendas, have multiple loyalties, and are layered upon each other.[53] Patricia Ingraham adds that there are frequently unclear and tenuous

---

51. See, for example, Ringquist, "Political Control and Policy Impact in EPA's Office of Water Quality."

52. Richard A. Harris and Disney M. Milkis, *The Politics of Regulatory Change: A Tale of Two Agencies* (New York: Oxford University Press, 1989), p. 276.

53. Cohen, "Amateur Government," pp. 450–97.

links between White House and political appointees, providing everyone more discretion.[54]

Even where they are responsive to presidential agendas, Cohen says, appointees tend to lack the managerial skills necessary to enact those agendas successfully. No matter how loyal to the president the appointees are, they need to know what to do and how to do it once they obtain their positions. Most appointees are lawyers, legislators, congressional staffers, academics, lobbyists, presidential campaign workers, and trusted aides to senior appointees. Some of these officials may have substantial policy expertise, but almost all of them are essentially individual entrepreneurs, are not team players, and have little managerial experience. Many of them are quite young.[55]

In addition, Cohen argues, noncareer Senior Executive Service appointments are often ideologues, possessing only political credentials. Policy or technical expertise is rarely a criterion for Schedule C appointments. Instead, past working relationships and loyalty to relevant political executives may be key, or these appointees may have been outplaced by the White House or may be connected to members of Congress or influential groups. Some have policy expertise, others do not; some are experienced, others are not. The point is that the White House and department or agency officials essentially ignore managerial experience or competence in filling these positions.[56]

Thus, Cohen maintains, when it comes to selecting the top leadership of the executive branch of government, the White House largely abandons professional standards. When professional standards are employed, they are limited to technical and program expertise. The ability to manage, design, and effectively carry out new programs, implement key legislation, or deliver services are not prominent criterion for evaluating potential appointees. Would any large corporation, Cohen asks, place at the head of a major operating division a person with no experience at managing funds or supervising people? What enterprise would fill every senior management position with persons with little or no inside experience? Who would accept the "mindless notion that any bright and public-spirited dilettante can run a government agency"?[57] It is not surprising, then, that John Gilmour and David Lewis found that programs administered by senior civil service executives are better managed than those administered by political appointees requiring Senate confirmation.[58]

54. Patricia W. Ingraham, "Political Direction and Policy Change in Three Federal Departments," in James P. Pfiffner, ed., *The Managerial Presidency*, 2nd ed. (College Station, Texas: Texas A&M University Press, 1999), p. 211.

55. Cohen, "Amateur Government."

56. Cohen, "Amateur Government," p. 463.

57. Cohen, "Amateur Government," pp. 450–52.

58. John B. Gilmour and David E. Lewis, "Political Appointees and the Competence of Federal Program Management" (paper presented at the Annual Meeting of the Midwest Political Science Association, 2004).

Paul Light provides evidence to support Cohen. He found that preparation for the job, whether defined in terms of management experience, negotiating skills, congressional relations, or personal style, makes a difference. Most importantly, appointees' preparation for office directly affects their ability to use the career service to an administration's advantage. The better prepared political appointees were for office, the more they saw the careerists with whom they worked as responsive and competent. Good preparation for their job helps political appointees to mobilize the resources of the career bureaucracy. Those appointees who knew what they wanted and how to get it were most inclined to view the career service as helpful in all areas, including management, substantive policy, technical analysis, and congressional relations. Good preparation also helps appointees evaluate the strengths and weaknesses of careerists, and which questions to ask. Thus, "skills are the crucial link between appointees and careerists."[59]

Political appointees face many challenges. One of the greatest is simply learning their new jobs. The short tenure in the same job of typical political appointees diminishes their ability to implement policy effectively, undermining the president's administrative strategy.[60] As administrative positions become more and more complex, both politically and substantively, it takes appointees more time to learn their jobs and forge the relationships that make effective implementation possible. Moreover, the more layers there are in a bureaucracy, the more complex the management job becomes. Carolyn Ban and Patricia Ingraham found that the greatest tension between appointees and careerists was where the tenures of political appointees were the shortest and where they were trying to implement sharp change from past policies.[61] It is reasonable to conclude that a well-qualified, and thus well-prepared, appointee has the greatest probability of mastering the demands of his or her position and effectively implementing policy before the inevitable turnover in personnel starts the process anew.

The administrative strategies of recent presidents in which they have sought to take control of the bureaucracy have been premised on influencing the behavior of bureaucrats in agencies as they exercised discretion over the

---

59. Paul C. Light, "When Worlds Collide." See also, Paul C. Light and Virginia L. Thomas, *The Merit and Reputation of an Administration; Presidential Appointees on the Appointments Process* (Washington, DC: Brookings Institution and Heritage Foundation, 2000), p. 19.

60. See, for example, Ingraham, "Political Direction and Policy Change in Three Federal Departments," pp. 212–13; On short tenure, see Heclo, *A Government of Strangers*; Carolyn Ban and Patricia Ingraham, "Short-Timers: Political Appointee Mobility and Its Impact on Political-Career Relations in the Reagan Administration," *Administration and Society* 22 (May 1990): 106–24; Maranto, *Politics and Bureaucracy in the Modern Presidency*; Michaels, *The President's Call*.

61. Ban and Ingraham, "Short-Timers," p. 114.

policies and programs for which they were responsible.[62] But success in many policy areas often requires less bureaucratic rigidity, not more. Patrick Wolf's analysis of 170 case studies of administrative performance in 104 federal agencies found that the best predictor of effective bureaucratic performance was autonomy from direct political control.[63]

In addition, hierarchical control designed to limit bureaucratic discretion seems inappropriate for new approaches to public administration. Rather than being direct service providers or regulators, large elements of the federal service are becoming arrangers and monitors of proxy or third-party government. Thus, the success of policy implementation now frequently depends on how adroitly federal agencies operate in nonhierarchical, loosely coupled networks of organizations that cut across the public, private, and nonprofit sectors, and where discretion is either shared or shifts entirely to bureaucrats in the private and nonprofit sector. In any case, control is beyond the range of a single federal agency.[64]

Even when implementation follows a more traditional mode, the design of a policy must be appropriate to the president's goals. Robert Durant challenges the assumption that presidents and their emissaries know what they are doing when they apply the tools of the administrative presidency. For example, the Reagan administration decreased staff in areas such as antitrust, civil rights, and environmental protection in an effort to reduce enforcement activities to which it was opposed.[65] Such a strategy may be useful for stopping an activity, such as regulatory behavior, but, as Durant points out, it undermines efforts to take the positive actions that the administration may desire.[66]

Laurence Lynn is one of the few scholars to focus on the impact of the quality of appointees on policy implementation.[67] He found that the Reagan

---

62. See Lowery, "The Presidency, the Bureaucracy, and Reinvention: A Gentle Plea for Chaos."

63. Patrick J. Wolf, "Why Must We Reinvent the Federal Government? Putting Historical Developmental Claims to the Test," *Journal of Public Administration Research and Theory* 7 (July 1997): 353–88.

64. See Donald F. Kettl, *Sharing Power: Public Governance and Private Markets* (Washington, DC: Brookings Institution, 1993); Thad E. Hall and Laurence J. O'Toole, "Structures for Policy Implementation: An Analysis of National Legislation, 1965–1966 and 1993–1994," *Administration and Society* 31 (January 2000): 667–86.

65. See, for example, Wood and Anderson, "The Politics of U.S. Antitrust Regulation"; Wood and Waterman, *Bureaucratic Dynamics,* chap. 4; and Ringquist, "Political Control and Policy Impact in EPA's Office of Water Quality."

66. Robert F. Durant, *The Administrative Presidency Revisited* (Albany: State University of New York Press, 1992).

67. Laurence E. Lynn, Jr., "The Reagan Administration and the Renitent Bureaucracy," in Lester M. Salamon and Michael S. Lund, eds., *The Reagan Presidency and the Governing of America* (Washington, DC: Urban Institute, 1985).

administration embraced the view that faithful supporters in key executive positions could be a potent tool of administrative leadership, serving as agent provocateurs, enforcers, and proconsuls in the agencies. The primary qualification for appointment, overshadowing managerial competence and experience or familiarity with issues, appeared to be the extent to which the appointee shared the president's values and could be expected to be reliable and persistent both in transfusing these values into agency practices and in executing central directives that were unpopular in the agency.

Lynn examined five agencies for evidence of lasting changes in the character of their core activity that were consistent with Ronald Reagan's policy preferences. He found that rather than being dependent on an appointee's loyalty to the president and commitment to his policies, the effectiveness of appointees in changing the behavior of an agency was related to four factors: the opportunities in the environment to accomplish change, managerial skills and experience, the appointee's personality, and the appointee's design for achieving his or her goals. Although the environment of an agency is not subject to the discretion of the president, appointing skilled and experienced managers with appropriate personalities and designs for achieving goals is an option for the president, and one he should choose to exploit.

CONCLUSION

Every president is dependent on the bureaucracy to achieve many of his goals. With divided government the norm over the past three decades, presidents more than ever turn to the bureaucracy to accomplish changes in policy.[68] The president's greatest leverage with the bureaucracy comes from the appointments he makes to positions within it. The challenge for all presidents is how to use their appointments to make the bureaucracy most responsive to their policies.

Conventional wisdom urges the president-elect to stress personal loyalty and commitment to his program in evaluating candidates for positions in the bureaucracy. Accepting this view, recent administrations have rarely assessed a candidate's intellectual ability, political and managerial skills, personality, and related factors in relationship to the demands of an appointee's job. Yet the best evidence is that bureaucratic resistance to change does not pose a substantial obstacle to the president achieving his goals.

In addition, loyalty to the president and commitment to his program are not sufficient for effective policy implementation. Skills and personal characteristics play an important role. Moreover, the greater the administrative

---

68. See, for example, Nathan, *The Administrative Presidency;* and Moe, "The Politicized Presidency, pp. 144–61.

challenge and thus the more sophisticated the design needed to exploit it, the greater the premium on analytical ability, managerial and political skills, and personality. And different skills are appropriate for different situations. Expansion makes different demands on appointees than does contraction; controversial policies require more emphasis on coalition building, negotiation, and bargaining than on more traditional management skills.

No president is going to appoint political opponents to positions in the executive branch. The issue is not either/or but rather one of relative emphases. Quality matters. A president-elect who can see beyond the conventional wisdom and focus on the ability of potential appointees as the first (but not the sole) criterion of selection will increase the likelihood that his administration will effectively administer public policy.

13

⚜

Is There a Crisis
in Judicial Selection?

SHELDON GOLDMAN
University of Massachusetts–Amherst

The appointment of federal judges in recent years has become one of the most controversial areas of American politics. I will explore the reasons for this, but at the outset we can note the bottom line: American presidents have sought to promote their policy agendas by way of naming to the federal courts those who can be expected to further those agendas. Senators opposed to the president's agenda have sought to block the confirmation of those who appear to be the most zealous supporters of the president's policy views. This was evident to the public during the congressional campaign of 2002 when President George W. Bush, incensed that Senate Democrats in control of the Senate were obstructing or delaying the confirmation of his judicial nominees, campaigned for Republican senate candidates, urging their election to help him win confirmation of his embattled nominees.[1]

After the Republicans narrowly regained control of the Senate, the Democrats, much to the surprise of the Republicans and many observers, successfully resorted to the use of the filibuster to prevent the Senate from voting on several of President Bush's nominees to the courts of appeals. The battle over the most controversial nominees continued into the years 2003 and 2004, becoming an issue in the 2004 presidential election. That battle has continued into Bush's second term and also is expected to include Supreme Court nominees.

No one following the news can have any doubt that it takes a presidential nomination and senatorial confirmation to win a place on the federal bench. And no one can have any doubt that presidential agendas play a crucial role in the selection and confirmation processes. In the case of President

---

1. Neil A. Lewis, "Bush Places Senate's Delays on his Judicial Appointees at the Core of Campaigning," *New York Times,* October 16, 2002, p. A20.

George W. Bush, his policy agenda with regard to the judiciary is to name highly conservative individuals who share his political and judicial philosophy. This has placed him on a collision course with Senate Democrats that some see as constituting a crisis. This chapter will explore the extent to which there is indeed a crisis and how presidential policy agendas are related to judicial selection and confirmation processes.

PRESIDENTIAL POLICY AGENDAS AT THE NOMINATION STAGE

Throughout American history, nominations to fill vacancies on the Supreme Court and the lower federal courts have typically gone to respected lawyers and judges of the president's party who share the president's ideological, philosophical, policy, and/or partisan orientation.[2] More than 9 out of 10 appointees have been members of the president's party.

Appointments to the federal courts involve numerous participants at the nomination stage, and they include (1) the president and his advisors, who are primarily located in the office of the White House Counsel; (2) officials in the Justice Department; (3) for the lower federal courts, the senators of the president's party from the state where there is a vacancy; (4) the chair of the Senate Judiciary Committee, who in recent years has been consulted or informed before nominations are made; (5) for the lower federal courts, when there are no senators from the president's party, members of the House of Representatives from the president's party as well as other party leaders from the president's party, including governors and/or mayors of large cities from the state where the judicial vacancy is to be filled; (6) advocacy or interest groups associated with the president's core constituency; (7) the American Bar Association's Standing Committee on Federal Judiciary (this was true from the presidency of President Dwight D. Eisenhower until the presidency of George W. Bush, who discontinued the role of the ABA Committee in the nomination process); and (8) for lower court judgeships, those who aspire to federal judgeships (and their supporters among the bar and bench) who campaign for a position by contacting the president, their home-state senators, and other state party leaders.

---

2. In general, see Henry J. Abraham, *Justices, Presidents, and Senators: A History of the U.S. Supreme Court Appointments from Washington to Clinton,* rev. ed. (Lanham, MD: Rowman and Littlefield, 1999); and Sheldon Goldman, *Picking Federal Judges: Lower Court Selection from Roosevelt through Reagan* (New Haven, CT: Yale University Press, 1997).

The nomination of any one judge is the culmination of a unique series of interrelated events that propel one person and not another toward the nomination. Understanding any one particular nomination requires access to a myriad of confidential sources. No one appointment can be adequately understood without study of the unique transactions involved.[3]

A candidate for a lower court judgeship who has strong home-state senatorial backing and the support (or at least no opposition) from state party leaders will typically have the inside track for the nomination. Before George W. Bush's presidency, the ABA Committee rated the leading contender or contenders for the nomination (Justice officials provided the names). Usually (but not always) when the Committee indicated that the candidate was not professionally qualified, the prospective nomination was doomed. Although George W. Bush eliminated the ABA from the prenomination process, the Committee has continued to rate each nominee after the White House has announced the nomination and sent it to the Senate. The administration, like others before it, evaluates potential nominees in terms of its standards of competency and judicial philosophy. When there is no consensus as to the nominee for a particular judgeship, Justice and White House officials must engage in negotiations with home-state senators and/or party leaders of the president's party.

When a president sees federal court decisions as important for his policy agenda, ideology will be a major variable in the selection process. President Franklin D. Roosevelt named to the federal courts supporters of his New Deal program, particularly during his second term. These nominations were especially important at that time because the federal courts were generally hostile to the president's programs. Once New Deal legislation met with success in the courts, however, the administration essentially reverted to more traditional patronage considerations in the selection process.

It was early in the administration of Richard M. Nixon, in 1969, that the idea emerged to systematically screen lower court candidates for their ideological and philosophical compatibility with the president. A young White House aide, Tom Charles Huston, just two months into the Nixon presidency wrote a detailed memo to the president that read in part:

> Through his judicial appointments, a President has the opportunity to influence the course of national affairs for a quarter of a century after he leaves office. . . . *In approaching the bench, it is necessary to remember that the decision as to who will make the decisions affects what decisions will be made.*

---

3. See David J. Danelski, *A Supreme Court Justice Is Appointed* (New York: Random House, 1964).

Huston concluded by observing that if the president "establishes *his* criteria and establishes *his* machinery for insuring that the criteria are met, the appointments he makes will be *his,* in fact, as in theory." Nixon not only read the memo carefully, but he directed it to Deputy Attorney General Richard Kleindienst with a handwritten notation: "RN *agrees*—Have this analysis in mind in making judicial nominations."[4]

But there was no follow-through. There was no bureaucratic apparatus established to ideologically screen candidates for judgeships—that was to await the presidency of Ronald Reagan. To be sure, most appointees of Richard Nixon were conservative Republicans—but he appointed some moderates because they were sponsored by the several moderate-to-liberal Republican senators then in the Senate.

In the 1970s and 1980s, the federal courts' policymaking activity in civil liberties and civil rights led the courts themselves to become a political issue. Court rulings defined the so-called social issues of abortion, prayer in the public schools, busing for the purpose of school desegregation, affirmative action in public higher education and at the workplace, and the rights of criminal defendants.

Beginning with the Carter administration, the White House became actively immersed in judicial selection through the Office of the White House Counsel.[5] That office became increasingly involved with negotiations with senators which meant, by the Clinton administration, that the White House Counsel's office was a major player.

When Ronald Reagan took office, his administration perceived the federal courts as being so activist as to have created an imbalance in the federal system that threatened state powers and that also had expanded federal judicial policymaking beyond the competence and capacity of the courts. The Reagan administration saw judicial appointments as intimately linked to the success of the president's domestic affairs policy agenda and consequently sought to appoint judges who shared his judicial and political philosophy.

With the presidency of Ronald Reagan, an institutional apparatus was created to assure that Reagan judicial nominees shared the philosophical and policy orientation of the president. That institutional apparatus was the President's Committee on Judicial Selection, a joint White House Justice

---

4. All quotes from the Huston memo can be found in "Memorandum for the President," March 25, 1969, Ex FG 50 The Judicial Branch [1969–70], WHCF, Nixon Materials Project. Nixon's notation with emphasis in original can be found on the cover memo from Ehrlichman to the Staff Secretary, March 27, 1969, *News Summaries* (March 1969), Box 30, President's Office Files, Nixon Materials Project. This chapter draws from material presented in Sheldon Goldman, "Judicial Confirmation Wars: Ideology and the Battle for the Federal Courts," *University of Richmond Law Review* 39 (2005): 871–908.

5. See Goldman, *Picking Federal Judges,* chap. 7.

Department committee chaired by the White House Counsel. By designating the White House Counsel as chair of the Judicial Selection Committee, the Reagan administration signaled that the White House would be more systematically involved in judicial selection. Reagan, George H. W. Bush, Clinton, and George W. Bush have all utilized the committee, and it appears to be a permanent judicial selection institution. Membership on that committee includes key White House staffers as well as the attorney general, deputy attorney general, and the assistant attorney general heading the office the Reagan administration created to oversee judicial selection (the office was appropriately called the Office of Legal Policy).

The new Office of Legal policy and an expanded White House Counsel's office undertook the task of ideologically vetting candidates for judicial office. And the Judicial Selection Committee coordinated the selection process and made the final decision as to whom to recommend to the president. Indeed, the evidence is compelling that the Reagan administration thoroughly vetted the judicial philosophy of potential nominees. Some examples from the Reagan presidential papers underscore this point.

For example, a memorandum sent by Reagan's White House Counsel Fred F. Fielding to the members of the joint White House–Justice Department Judicial Selection Committee provided an analysis and recommendation for filling a vacancy on the district court bench of Montana, which at the time had two Democratic senators.[6] The memo discussed three candidates for the nomination: Charles C. Lovell, Jack D. Shanstrom, and Sam E. Haddon.

Charles C. Lovell was seen as a highly qualified lawyer who "has always been an active member of the Republican Party and has served since 1976 on the Montanans for Marlenee Committee; he has been strongly endorsed for this position by [U.S.] Rep. Ron Marlenee. . . . His views on crime issues and social policy appear consistent with those of this Administration."

The second candidate, Jack D. Shanstrom, had previously been elected county attorney running on the Republican ticket. Shanstrom had received an interim appointment by Republican Governor Jim Babcock to a state judgeship at the age of 32. He was defeated for reelection some 18 years later and was subsequently appointed the first full-time United States Magistrate for the District of Montana. The memo noted:

> As a trial judge, Jack Shanstrom had a consistent reputation for being strong on law enforcement—he has upheld the death penalty, lobbied actively for a "good faith" amendment to the exclusionary rule, and was rated one of the state's toughest judges in sentencing criminals.

---

6. Judicial Selection Materials, Dec. 1984 [of 5] CF 514, Fielding Files, Ronald Reagan Library, Simi Valley, CA.

Though not regarded as a scholar, his service and experience on the bench are highly regarded by both the judiciary and the bar throughout Montana. . . . Although all three leading candidates are clearly conservative, [the Department of] Justice notes that Judge Shanstrom's long track record on the bench makes him the "safest" nomination in terms of the consistency of his judicial philosophy with that of this Administration.

The third candidate was Sam E. Haddon. The memo pointed out that he graduated first in his law school class at the University of Montana and was "the most scholarly and articulate of the judicial candidates considered here. . . . [He is] one of the smartest and finest trial lawyers in the state. Haddon has been active in supporting Republican candidates, a very pro-law enforcement NRA member; and he is regarded by his colleagues as conservative."

Although the Reagan Justice Department recommended selecting Shanstrom, the Judicial Selection Committee recommended the candidate with the strongest political backing, Lovell, who was nominated and confirmed in 1985. President George H. W. Bush nominated Shanstrom to fill another vacancy on the federal district bench in early 1990, and the Senate confirmed him later that year. President George W. Bush named Haddon to the seat made vacant when Lovell assumed senior status at the end of the Clinton administration. The Senate confirmed Haddon in 2001.

An example of ideological vetting by the Reagan administration for the courts of appeals occurred with the scrutinizing of candidates for a position on the Tenth Circuit, which was to be filled by a citizen of Colorado. White House Counsel Fred Fielding reported in a memo[7] that Colorado Republican Senator Armstrong recommended elevating Federal District Judge John P. Moore. The memo further stated that four members of the House recommended the elevation of Chief U.S. District Judge in Colorado Sherman G. Finesilver. In discussing Moore, the memo reported "[The] Justice [Department] states that a preliminary review of Judge Moore's reported decisions indicate his judicial philosophy is compatible with the President's." Not so with Judge Finesilver, who originally had been appointed to the federal district bench by Richard Nixon. The memo stated:

> Justice's review of Judge Finesilver's articles and reported decisions showed that he is a "hardliner" on crime, but that he is relatively moderate on civil rights issues. . . . Justice has expressed particular concerns over Judge Finesilver's analysis of constitutional rights in *Foe v. Vanderhoof,* 389

---

7. Judicial Selection Materials, Aug. 1984 [of 3] CF 514, Fielding Files, Ronald Reagan Library, Simi Valley, CA.

F. Supp. 947 (D. Colo. 1975). In *Foe*, Judge Finesilver declared unconstitutional a Colorado statute which required parental consent before an unmarried minor could obtain an abortion, and stated that "the right to privacy as expounded in Roe and Doe to include a decision to terminate a pregnancy extends to minors." 389 F. Supp. at 953. Additionally, the judge referred to parents in Foe as "third parties" who should not have "exclusive control over the activities of minors in this area," 389 F. Supp. at 956. Based on an analysis of Judge Finesilver's writings, Justice has concluded that he is not a suitable candidate for the Tenth Circuit.

And that was the end of Finesilver's candidacy.

President Reagan's immediate successor, George H. W. Bush, also sought to appoint like-minded judges. The evidence is compelling that the first Bush administration scrutinized potential judicial nominees in terms of their ideology and judicial philosophy. Although the president's papers have yet to be fully opened, examples from the already-released papers point to the vetting process. An example is the evaluation of then-Federal District Court Judge Jose A. Cabranes' record as a potential Second Circuit nominee.[8] The memo on Cabranes conceded that his "judicial writings are scholarly, reflecting a lucid style and careful attention to detail. He is seldom reversed. . . ." Nevertheless, the memo asserted, "In general . . . Judge Cabranes' academic writings and judicial opinions mark him as a judicial activist with deeply held views regarding the power of the courts to bring about social change." The evidence provided in the memo was a speech Cabranes made in a 1982 symposium, in which he defended the federal courts as a forum for protecting individual rights, particularly when state courts do not do the job. In addition, the memo opined, "Some of Judge Cabranes' criminal law decisions reflect a greater solicitude for the rights of criminal defendants than is found among conservative jurists." Finally, the memo concluded that "in construing the Constitution, Judge Cabranes is willing to look beyond the text and the intent of its Framers." Needless to say, the Bush administration did not promote Jose Cabranes. President Bill Clinton, however, did elevate Judge Cabranes to the Second Circuit in 1994.

Another example of ideological vetting by the George H. W. Bush administration for a circuit court post concerned the evaluation of an Idaho state judge, Duff McKee, who was one of four men recommended by Idaho Republican Senator McClure.[9] The memo noted that the Justice Department

---

8. Lee Liberman Subject Name Files, Box 40964, Cabranes, Jose A. [OA/ID 02081], George Bush Library, College Station, TX.

9. Counsel's Office, White House OF 56, Liberman, Lee S., Circuit/Supreme Court Files, Box 40950, Ninth Circuit Court of Appeals [20356] George Bush Library, College Station, TX.

had asked Judge McKee to submit "his ten favorite opinions." But the memo also noted "Three of these are quite problematic." One opinion concerned the counting of time spent on parole in favor of the convicted criminal. Another involved Judge McKee's refusal to apply a "good-faith" exception to the exclusionary rule. The third was a finding that allowed a plaintiff to sue in a civil suit. The memo concluded: "These three opinions would likely be sufficient cause for rejecting Judge McKee even if they were part of a random sample of his work. That he selected them from his corpus as three of his favorites seems dispositive." McKee was not nominated.

While campaigning for the presidency in 2000, President George W. Bush committed himself to naming judges like Justices Antonin Scalia and Clarence Thomas, two of the most conservative justices on the U.S. Supreme Court. As president, he has stated bluntly that he is looking to appoint conservatives to the courts.[10] His administration followed through, and almost all of the over 225 nominees to the lower federal courts during Bush's first term can fairly be characterized as conservatives who share the president's judicial philosophy. To an even greater extent than during the Reagan and first Bush administrations, the White House Counsel's Office has taken responsibility for philosophically screening potential candidates, including conducting interviews. The overall success of President Bush in selecting judicial nominees consistent with his presidential policy agenda undoubtedly increases his appeal to his conservative base.

PRESIDENTIAL POLICY AGENDAS AT THE CONFIRMATION STAGE

With this backdrop of policy agenda/ideological concerns as part of the presidential nomination process, what happens at the senatorial confirmation stage is better understood. We first look at the confirmation of Supreme Court nominees and then nominees for the lower federal courts.

Supreme Court Confirmations

Historically, a significant proportion of Supreme Court nominees have been challenged in the Senate, usually for ideological or partisan reasons.[11] In the 19th century, close to one out of three nominees were not confirmed by the

---

10. Elisabeth Bumiller, "Bush Vows to Seek Conservative Judges," *New York Times,* March 29, 2002, p. A24.

11. See Abraham, *Justices, Presidents, and Senators;* and Michael J. Gerhardt, *The Federal Appointments Process: A Constitutional and Historical Analysis* (Durham, NC: Duke University Press, 2000).

Senate. In the first two-thirds of the 20th century, only one Supreme Court nominee was rejected (President Herbert Hoover's nomination of Fourth Circuit Judge John J. Parker). But since 1968 there have been four Senate rejections, with three of the four occurring between 1968 and 1970.[12]

Typically a president will sound out members of the Senate Judiciary Committee or the leadership of both parties of the Senate to gauge probable senatorial reaction to a Supreme Court nomination. In fact, this is what President Lyndon Johnson had done before nominating Justice Abe Fortas for the chief justiceship in 1968. The Republican Senate Minority Leader, Everett Dirksen, offered no objection, and Johnson went ahead. But junior Republican senators and conservative southern Democrats were unhappy with Fortas, whom they saw as a liberal activist, and they waged a filibuster that withstood a cloture vote (this would provide a precedent for Democrats some 35 years later when opposing several George W. Bush nominees to the appeals courts). Fortas then withdrew himself from consideration.[13]

The following year, newly-elected Richard Nixon exploited a media attack on an ethical lapse by Justice Fortas and succeeded in pressuring him to resign, thus creating a vacancy for him to fill.[14] The chair of the Senate Judiciary Committee was a conservative southern Democrat, James O. Eastland from Mississippi, who supported Nixon's choice of Fourth Circuit Judge Clement Haynsworth to replace Fortas. But most Democrats were unhappy with Haynsworth's conservatism. When seemingly ethical lapses concerning Haynsworth were discovered, he was ultimately defeated on the floor of the Senate. So, too, was G. Harrold Carswell, an undistinguished Fifth Circuit appeals court judge with a history of racism whose nomination was seen by some Democrats as an affront to the Senate. The third attempt to fill the vacancy was successful, with Harry Blackmun winning overwhelming support.

---

12. In general, see John Massaro, *Supremely Political: The Role of Ideology and Presidential Management in Unsuccessful Supreme Court Nominations* (Albany: State University of New York Press, 1990); Mark Silverstein, *Judicious Choices: The New Politics of Supreme Court Confirmations* (New York: W. W. Norton, 1994); George L. Watson and John A. Stookey, *Shaping America: The Politics of Supreme Court Appointments* (New York: HarperCollins, 1995); John Anthony Maltese, *The Selling of Supreme Court Nominees* (Baltimore, MD: Johns Hopkins University Press, 1995); David A. Yalof, *Pursuit of Justices: Presidential Politics and the Selection of Supreme Court Nominees* (Chicago: University of Chicago Press, 1999); and Michael Comiskey, *Seeking Justices: The Judging of Supreme Court Nominees* (Lawrence: University Press of Kansas, 2004).

13. For details of the complex story, see Bruce Allen Murphy, *Fortas: The Rise and Ruin of a Supreme Court Justice* (New York: William Morrow and Company, 1988), chaps. 11–23.

14. Murphy, *Fortas*, chap. 24.

There is no evidence that Ronald Reagan consulted with the Demo-cratic leadership of the Senate in 1987 prior to the nomination of District of Columbia appeals court Judge Robert Bork to fill the vacancy caused by the retirement of Lewis Powell. Reagan administration officials undoubtedly expected that Bork would be confirmed for a seat on the Supreme Court, since he had been confirmed for his position on the Court of Appeals only several years earlier. But Bork was defeated in the Senate because liberal and moderate senators saw him as a right-wing extremist who refused to recog-nize a constitutional right to privacy, including the right of a woman to have an abortion during the first two trimesters when the fetus cannot live inde-pendently of the mother.

The fight over Bork was particularly contentious, and the Republican minority in the Senate was extremely bitter about the tactics of their Democratic colleagues and their interest group allies.[15] The very public involvement of interest groups in the Bork fight was a turning point in con-temporary confirmation politics. Although, on occasion, interest or advo-cacy groups had been involved before in a relative handful of nominations, after Bork these groups became more systematically involved in the process for appointments at all levels of the judiciary, inserting themselves into the nomination and confirmation processes by lobbying and rallying supporters for and against certain nominees.[16]

After Bork's defeat by a vote of only 42 votes for and 58 votes against confirmation, President Reagan announced that he would nominate another appellate judge from the District of Columbia circuit, Douglas Ginsburg. But this would-be nomination was scuttled before being sent to the Senate after the press ran stories that Ginsburg had smoked marijuana. The president then turned to a more moderate conservative, Ninth Circuit Appeals Court Judge Anthony Kennedy, who was easily confirmed.

The first President Bush worked with a Democratic Congress, as did President Reagan in his last two years in office, and aimed to place on the bench at all levels the most conservative judges who were confirmable. President Bush correctly saw David Souter as easily confirmable but

---

15. In general, see Mark Gitenstein, *Matters of Principle: An Insider's Account of America's Rejection of Robert Bork's Nomination to the Supreme Court* (New York: Simon & Schuster, 1992).

16. See Paul Simon, *Advice and Consent: Clarence Thomas, Robert Bork and the Intriguing History of the Supreme Court's Nomination Battles* (Washington, DC: National Press Books, 1992); Gerhardt, *Federal Appointments Process;* Lauren Cohen Bell, *Warring Factions: Interest Groups, Money, and the New Politics of Senate Confirmation* (Columbus: Ohio State University Press, 2002); Comiskey, *Seeking Justices;* and Nancy Scherer, *Scoring Points: Politicians, Activists and the Lower Federal Court Appointment Process* (Palo Alto, CA: Stanford University Press, 2005).

incorrectly assumed that Souter's conservative background as a New Hampshire Supreme Court justice and briefly as a judge on the federal First Circuit court of appeals would assure his joining the Rehnquist–Scalia wing of the Court. Bush's nomination of the second African American named to the Court to replace the first also seemed to be designed to win confirmation. Although the White House expected Clarence Thomas's conservatism to raise some controversy, no one in the administration had any inkling that sexual harassment charges would surface and turn an already-contentious confirmation battle into a melee.[17] Eventually, however, Thomas was confirmed by a bare majority of 52 votes.

President Bill Clinton took great pains when filling vacancies created by the retirements of Byron White and Harry Blackmun to select noncontroversial candidates who would be easily confirmed. He scrupulously consulted key Republican leaders.[18] His strategy was successful, and his nominees, Ruth Bader Ginsburg in 1993 and Stephen Breyer in 1994, were confirmed by overwhelming majorities. Furthermore, during its last six years, the Clinton administration routinely checked with the chair of the Senate Judiciary Committee, Orrin Hatch, before nominating lower court judges. The administration avoided nominating anyone who appeared to be controversial. Even so, a number of Clinton's lower court nominees ran into trouble with the Republican Senate.[19]

As of February 2005, President George W. Bush has not had an opportunity to name a justice of the Supreme Court. There has been ongoing speculation as to whom he might nominate to replace the ailing Chief Justice, William Rehnquist, and the possible difficulty of the confirmation process, assuming that the nominee would be seen as a conservative activist meant to further the president's policy agenda. If that nominee for Chief Justice or for an associate justiceship were also Hispanic, senators from states with large Hispanic populations would no doubt be under pressure to vote to confirm. The presidential election of 2004 may well go down in history

---

17. Comiskey, *Seeking Justices,* chap. 5; Jane Mayer and Jill Abramson, *Strange Justice: The Selling of Clarence Thomas* (Boston: Houghton Mifflin, 1994); Timothy Phelps and Helen Winternitz, *Capitol Games: The Inside Story of Clarence Thomas, Anita Hill, and a Supreme Court Nomination* (New York: Hyperion, 1992); and Simon, *Advice and Consent.*

18. Orrin Hatch, *Square Peg: Confessions of a Citizen Senator* (New York: Basic Books, 2002), p. 180.

19. In general, see Sheldon Goldman and Elliot Slotnick, "Clinton's First Term Judiciary: Many Bridges to Cross," *Judicature* 80 (1997): 254–73; Sheldon Goldman and Elliot Slotnick, "Clinton's Second Term Judiciary: Picking Judges Under Fire," *Judicature* 82 (1999): 264–84; Sheldon Goldman, Elliot Slotnick, Gerard Gryski, and Gary Zuk, "Clinton's Judges: Summing up the Legacy," *Judicature* 84 (2001): 228–54.

as one of the most important for determining the direction of the Supreme Court and the fate of a number of civil liberties precedents that conflict with George W. Bush's policy agenda.

The Lower Federal Courts

Once a nomination is sent to the Senate, it is referred to the Senate Judiciary Committee. Then, as a matter of routine, the chair of the Committee sends "blue slips" to the senators from the nominee's state. The "blue slip" is a form that officially notifies the senators that the nomination has been received. The form has a space for the senator's reply. It also contains a caveat: "Under a rule of the Committee, unless a reply is received from you within a week from this date, it will be assumed that you have no objection to the nomination." In practice, before 1979, a senator who opposed the nominee from his or her state would quietly inform the chair and withhold the blue slip. The nomination would not be acted on by the Committee and would be, in effect, killed.[20] When Senator Edward Kennedy became chair in 1979, he announced that no longer would a nomination die by failure to return the blue slip. Instead, Kennedy declared that all nominations would be discussed by the full committee, who would determine whether or not to hold hearings and proceed with the nomination. The Kennedy policy was ignored by subsequent committee chairs. But after the 2002 election, Republican Senate Judiciary Committee Chair Orrin Hatch announced, over the objections of Democrats on the committee, that he would return to the Kennedy policy.

When Senator Kennedy became chair of the Senate Judiciary Committee in 1979, he established an investigatory staff for the committee to examine the backgrounds and professional records of the nominees so that the committee would not have to rely on the Justice Department. Kennedy's successor as chair, Senator Thurmond, continued the practice, and to this day there are Democratic and Republican investigatory staffs. These staffs may work with advocacy groups and may target certain nominees. This appears to have happened in the 1990s, with conservative groups opposing some Clinton nominees and more recently with liberal groups opposing some George W. Bush nominees.[21]

In terms of the confirmation process historically, and in general even today, when senators of the president's party from whose state the nominee comes approve the nomination and neither the majority nor minority investigative

---

20. Brannon P. Denning, "The Judicial Confirmation Process and the Blue Slip," *Judicature* 85 (2002): 218–26.

21. See Sheldon Goldman, "Unpicking Pickering in 2002: Some Thoughts on the Politics of Lower Federal Court Selection and Confirmation," *U.C. Davis Law Review* 36 (2003): 717–18; "Senate Wraps up Judiciary Memo Probe." *Associated Press,* March 3, 2004.

staffs come up with negative findings, the Judiciary Committee typically votes to recommend confirmation and sends the nomination to the floor of the Senate. Occasionally one or more senators may voice opposition to such a nomination on the Senate floor, but typically the Senate votes to confirm a nominee recommended by the Committee. Once the nomination is confirmed, the president signs the appointment documents, and the individual is sworn into office and begins serving on the federal bench.

Yet the confirmation process has been much in the news for close to a decade, with Democrats and Republicans accusing each other of obstruction and delay of judicial nominees. The well-publicized filibusters by Democratic senators in 2003 and 2004 of Bush nominees to the appeals courts suggest that the confirmation process may not be working well and that George W. Bush's insistence on naming prominent supporters of his policy agenda may have been counterproductive, fomenting a crisis. We turn our attention to this very issue.

OBSTRUCTION AND DELAY
IN THE CONFIRMATION PROCESS

The confirmation process has become more contentious because the trend in judicial selection has been to move away from primarily patronage concerns to concerns about furthering the president's policy agenda through judicial appointments.[22] Since the 1980s, senators have felt free to oppose judicial nominees on policy and judicial philosophical grounds. If the president uses ideological criteria to make policy agenda nominations, then senators seem to think they are entitled to do the same when considering confirmation of those nominees. Most opposition to presidential nominations, when it has occurred, has centered around nominees to the courts of appeals. This was true during the last six years of the Clinton presidency when some Republican senators opposed and either delayed or killed some nominations. And it has been true with Democratic senators during the presidency of George W. Bush.

For the courts of appeals during the last six years of the Clinton presidency, with a Democrat in the White House and Republicans in control of the Senate:[23]

- Eight nominees waited more than one year from their initial nomination to confirmation.

---

22. See Goldman, *Picking Federal Judges.*

23. These figures, like all of the figures in this section, are for lifetime appointments to courts of general jurisdiction. This section draws from Goldman, "Judicial Confirmation Wars," pp. 889–908.

- Another 23 nominees went unconfirmed, 20 of whom did not even receive hearings.

- A total of 43 nominees were confirmed, for a confirmation rate of 65.2 percent.

For the courts of appeals during the first four years of George W. Bush's presidency and with Democrats narrowly controlling the Senate for the first two years and Republicans narrowing controlling the Senate for the last two:

- Eight nominees waited more than one year from their initial nomination to confirmation.

- Another 17 nominees went unconfirmed, 2 of whom had no hearings.

- A total of 34 nominees were confirmed, for a confirmation rate of 66.7 percent.

For the district courts during the last six years of the Clinton presidency:

- Fourteen nominees waited over one year from nomination to confirmation.

- Another 40 never made it through confirmation, 34 of whom had no hearings.

- A total of 198 were confirmed, for a confirmation rate of 83.2 percent.

For the district courts during the first four years of George W. Bush's presidency:

- Five nominees waited over one year from nomination to confirmation.

- Another 9 remained unconfirmed, 7 of whom had no hearings.

- A total of 168 were confirmed, for a confirmation rate of 94.9 percent.

These figures suggest that it is the courts of appeals where there is an approaching judicial appointment crisis.

In opposing the Bush nominees, Democratic senators have suggested that their concern is that George W. Bush, like his father and Ronald Reagan before him, is trying to pack the courts with conservative activists in accord with the president's policy agenda. Democrats are concerned, among other things, that such judges would undermine the rights of women in consultation with their physicians to make medical decisions concerning unwanted pregnancies, weaken the separation of church and state, dilute the rights guaranteed in the Bill of Rights to those accused of crimes, be unsympathetic to the rights of workers and organized labor, weaken the laws and regulations meant to protect the environment, and compromise gender and racial equality.[24]

Republicans counter that it is neither the business of judges to create rights nor to go beyond the intent of the framers of the Constitution. They contend that liberal judicial activists overlook compelling competing values such as states rights and federalism, the right of a fetus to life, the guarantee of the free exercise of religion, the rights of victims of crimes, the rights of those who own property, and the right to be treated fairly and not be discriminated against by ethnic and gender preference programs.[25]

Ideological warfare between liberal and conservative senators, fueled by advocacy groups since the late 1980s, was especially severe when there was divided government, with the White House controlled by one party and the Senate by the other. Democrats were particularly resentful of the way President Clinton's nominees were treated during the last six years of his presidency, when Republicans controlled the Senate. Republicans, in turn, were angry when Democrats controlled the Senate during the 107th Congress and were furious during the 108th Congress when even with Republican control of the Senate, the Democrats successfully filibustered or otherwise held up the appeals court nominations of 16 nominees, including Miguel Estrada (who subsequently withdrew his candidacy), Charles Pickering (who was subsequently given a recess appointment by President Bush on January 16, 2004), Priscilla Owen, William Pryor (subsequently given a recess appointment on February 20, 2004), Janice R. Brown, Carolyn Kuhl, and four nominees from Michigan to the Sixth Circuit.

The portrait of the confirmation process thus far suggests that it has deteriorated in recent years and that the return to unified government has not dramatically improved the situation. Table 13-1 presents an objective summary statistic of obstruction and delay for the district and appeals courts from the 95th Congress through the 108th Congress, the Index of Obstruction and Delay.[26]

"Obstruction" occurs when no action is taken on a nomination. "Delay" occurs when it takes more than 180 days from nomination to confirmation. I calculate the Index by adding the number of nominees who remained unconfirmed at the end of the Congress to the number for whom the confirmation process took more than 180 days, which I then divide by the total number of nominees for that Congress. When the Senate remained in control of the same party in the subsequent Congress, I count the original date

---

24. Goldman, "Unpicking Pickering," p. 704.

25. Ibid., p. 705.

26. See Sheldon Goldman, "Assessing the Senate Judicial Confirmation Process: The Index of Obstruction and Delay." *Judicature* 86 (2003): 251–57.

Table 13–1 Index of Obstruction and Delay

Congress	District Court Index	Appeals Court Index
95th (1977–1978)	0.0000	0.0000
96th (1979–1980)	0.0750	0.0682
97th (1981–1982)	0.0000	0.0000
98th (1983–1984)	0.0545	0.1429
99th (1985–1986)	0.1364	0.0690
100th (1987–1988)	0.2800	0.4762
101st (1989–1990)	0.0488	0.0625
102nd (1991–1992)	0.3465	0.5000
103rd (1993–1994)	0.0375	0.0625
104th (1995–1996)	0.3780	0.5263
105th (1997–1998)	0.5000	0.6932
106th (1999–2000)	0.4722	0.7931
107th (2001–2002)	0.2432	0.8387
108th (2003–2004)	0.3258	0.6471

of the nomination of a renominated individual in the calculation of delay. Also, I do not include nominations made after July 1 of the second session of each Congress in the calculations so as not to inflate the Index artificially by end-of-second-session nominations that realistically would not ordinarily be able to move through the process under an approximately 180-day time frame. I calculate the Index to four places to the right of the decimal point, and thus it ranges from 0.0000, which indicates an absence of obstruction and delay, to 1.0000 which indicates the maximum level.

As suggested in Table 13–1, there were low levels of obstruction and delay for the district courts until the 100th Congress, and that was followed by a further increase in the 102nd Congress. The same was true for the appeals courts during the 100th and 102nd Congresses, whose indexes were even higher than those for the district courts. Since the Senate of these Congresses was controlled by the Democrats with a Republican in the White House, the Republicans' charge that the Democrats were responsible for initiating the obstruction and delay phenomenon is supported by the objective evidence. But with the situation reversed with a Democrat in the White House and the Republicans in control of the Senate, the evidence clearly shows that the Republicans ratcheted up obstruction and delay with all-time records for the district and appeals courts, including the then-unprecedented index of 0.7931 for appeals court nominees by the 106th Congress. Also, it should be noted that in every even-numbered Congress (with the exception of the district courts for the 106th

Congress and the appeals courts for the 108th), which always overlaps a presidential election year, the Index was higher than for the previous non-presidential-year Congress.

The Democrats assumed control of the Senate after the first five months of the 107th Congress, with a Republican now in the White House, and the Index for the appeals courts reached its highest point for the period analyzed—0.8387. However, the Index for the district courts dropped significantly from the 104th–106th Congresses and was even lower than that for the 102nd Congress. This relatively low level of obstruction and delay appeared to reflect a decision of the Democrats to focus their attention on the appeals courts and to readily expedite almost all of Bush's district court nominees.

With the Republicans once again in control of the Senate in 2003 and with a Republican still in the White House, we might have expected sharp drops in the Index. For the 108th Congress, the Index for the appeals court nominees did indeed fall—from 0.8387 to 0.6471, but the Index nevertheless was the highest ever for unified government (at least from the 95th Congress to the present). This level undoubtedly reflected the efforts by the Democrats to use whatever means at their disposal, including filibusters, to obstruct and delay the confirmation process of primarily nominees whom they found objectionable. On the other hand, the Index for district court nominees, although lower than that for the appeals court nominees, was nevertheless 0.3258, also the highest ever for unified government (from the 95th Congress to the present). Part of the problem for the district court nominees seems to be related to the elimination of the American Bar Association from the prenomination process, resulting in the nomination of a few unqualified or barely qualified (by ABA standards) nominees.

Additionally, contributing to the delay, was the Democrats' shutdown of the confirmation process for several months in early 2004 in protest of President Bush's use of recess appointments to place Pickering and Pryor on the bench. Only when the White House gave assurances that it would not name any other judge by way of a recess appointment did the Democrats agree to stop their obstruction—but even then part of the deal was to allow votes on just 25 nominees.

It does not bode well for the confirmation process that the indexes for the 108th Congress were so relatively high. Previously it was just divided government that had been associated with high indexes. It appears that obstruction and delay are becoming more common under unified government and that what once was a relatively civilized and functional process has increasingly become an unpleasant, prolonged, and, in the eyes of many, dysfunctional process.

CONCLUSION

We have seen how modern presidents whose domestic policy agendas are shaped by opposition to federal court policies have sought to use judicial appointments as a way to further their agendas. As a consequence, these efforts have turned the confirmation process into a battle over policy and ideology. This in turn has set the stage for an emerging crisis, particularly at the appeals court level and potentially at the Supreme Court level as well. Is there anything that can be done?

An obvious solution is for the president to exercise restraint and mute the use of judicial appointments to further his policy agenda. More moderate, less ideological nominees would undoubtedly help resolve the crisis, such as it exists. Another solution would be for the country to elect enough senators of the president's party to prevent the use of the filibuster and other techniques to obstruct and delay judicial nominations. But if judicial appointees are seen as other than fair and impartial arbiters of the law, this latter "solution" runs the risk of fundamentally undermining the legitimacy of the judicial branch of government and Americans' belief in the rule of law.

Another take on the "crisis" is that what is going on is essentially American politics, not at its worst but at its best. Republicans and Democrats are arguing about public policy and the role of the judiciary. This robust, albeit contentious, debate is the hallmark of a vibrant democracy. And at the end of the day, substantial numbers of judicial nominees are indeed being confirmed and the courts are being staffed. It is likely that the use of judicial appointments to further a president's policy agenda will continue to occur as long as the courts are vehicles for the articulation of public policy. From the Supreme Court down, there is little indication that federal courts are refraining from using their power to interpret the federal Constitution. Whenever we have a president and senators whose policy agendas are in conflict with the courts, we can expect the judicial appointment process to be contentious.

Index